D1213051

Only Victims

To A. L. Lowenstein whose relentless struggle for justice and human dignity inspired so many of us so often

Only Victims

A Study of
Show Business Blacklisting

by Robert Vaughn

With a Foreword by
Senator George McGovern

G. P. Putnam's Sons
New York

Contents

Foreword   11

Preface and Acknowledgments   15

Introduction   21

  I. Only Victims   31

  II. Martin Dies' 1938 Investigation
of the Federal Theatre Project   48

  III. J. Parnell Thomas' 1947 Investigation of Communist
Infiltration in the Motion Picture Industry   75

  IV. John S. Wood's Marathon Ten-Part 1951-1952
Investigation of Communism in the Entertainment Field   118

  V. Harold H. Velde and Francis S. Walter's 1953-54-55
Entertainment Hearings and the Committee's 1956
Investigation of the Fund for the Republic's Report
on Blacklisting   180

  VI. The Paul Robeson-Arthur Miller Passport Investigations,
1956, and the Most Recent 1957-58
Show Business Hearings   216

  VII. The 1969-70 New Primary Data Gathered from
Correspondence, Questionnaires, and Personal
Taped Interviews   240

VIII. Conclusions and Implications   267

Appendix I   The Friendly Witnesses and the Persons They
Identified as Communists   275

Appendix II   The Committee's Evidence of Communist Party
Membership of Two of the Unfriendly Ten   293

Appendix III   The Briefs of the Hollywood Ten   315

Appendix IV   Cover Letter and Questionnaire Used in Securing
New Primary Data   335

Bibliography   340

Index   349

Foreword

by Senator George McGovern

ONLY VICTIMS is a sobering book indeed in today's context. It is a work of history, recounting and interpreting ugly events in our recent past. It provides timely lessons and tells much about what is happening, and what can happen, in the America of the 1970's.

The following pages document past decades of shameful attack by the House Un-American Activities Committee against some of this country's most creative writers and artists. The Committee—in its resort to trial by accusation, publicity, and presumption of guilt, in its reliance upon innuendo, in its smug trust that one under attack will turn against a friend to save himself, in its wanton use and abuse of the contempt power—symbolized an issue which perpetually confronts a society professing intellectual and political freedom.

We must expect that a diverse society will always have extreme elements, willing to blame the nation's troubles on foreign subversion or alien ideologies and to adopt totalitarian strategies to rid us of the threat they alone perceive—to set their own standards for what is and is not good American thought and to pursue that deemed improper with almost total abandon.

Such groups are sad in themselves. But HUAC was something more. It brought the unparalleled power and respectability of the national government to the assault. It was able to stimulate

11

the destruction of numerous careers, to crush individual expression and creativity to a much greater extent, and to kill many more new concepts than any collection of private extremists could possibly accomplish. Beyond its own direct actions, it lent at least some credence to any private charge of subversion against any individual or group or any novel idea. It helped damage the tone of our national politics for years. We can still feel its influence.

Were Mr. Vaughn's work no more than an account of past events we could simply rejoice that they are over and appreciate the depth of comprehension the author supplies. But many of the same conditions that nourished HUAC from the 1930's through the 1950's—economic unrest, rapid social change, disappointments abroad, and others—pose an equal challenge today. They lend inevitable pressure toward finding scapegoats and toward blindly defending established symbols without regard for truth or justice.

In recent years we have seen carefully orchestrated attempts to discredit those who have protested American involvement in Vietnam and to discourage participation in protests through threats of violence. We have seen assaults on the integrity of the press because it has reported the bad about national political leaders along with the good. We have learned of government dossiers on millions of citizens. We have seen the one constant guardian of our civil liberties, the Supreme Court, first blamed for some of our deepest ills, then treated as a device for political expedience. We have seen the government's right of self-preservation distorted into a right of political leaders to undermine constitutional safeguards for the sake of their own survival in office.

The human damage HUAC and its contemporary agencies and societies have done is cause enough for vigilance against a more modern repetition. But we can find still more reason, and also find the proper response, through a broader understanding of why it was wrong.

We give most attention to the protection of individual speech and thought afforded by the First Amendment of the Constitution. But the operation of the amendment protects the whole of society as well. It prohibits any small group from deciding, on behalf of the whole, what ideas should be allowed free expression and consideration as we seek solutions to pressing national problems.

In a society which bases its decisions on democratic process, full expression is not only desirable, it is essential. The very root of our political system is the premise that an informed people can govern themselves better than even a benevolent elite claiming the right to know and think for them.

Thus Supreme Court Justice Benjamin Cardozo wrote in 1937 that freedom of speech is "the matrix, the indispensable condition, of nearly every other form of freedom." Further, according to Justice William O. Douglas in 1949, one function of free speech ". . . is to invite dispute. It may indeed best serve its high purpose when it induces a condition of unrest, creates dissatisfaction with conditions as they are, or even stirs people to anger."

It can be said fairly that the creation and operation of an agency to chill the expression of unpopular views is itself dangerously un-American. Free speech and thought are eminently American, not because all words and ideas are correct or even deserving of much attention, but because a democratic system cannot operate otherwise. HUAC's behavior was an exercise in stifling the very essence of democracy.

The answer is not to find scapegoats for national problems but to undertake a serious search for their solution, drawing on all of the intellectual power and energy we can find. The answer is not restrictions on the right for its damage to others, but leadership which encourages the expression of all points of view.

In sum, the priority aim of government should be to invite more freedom of speech, not less, and to instill widely the understanding that those who espouse the unusual are not only exercising legitimate rights but performing a patriotic obligation to share the truth as they see it.

When you who are in your forties or younger look back with curiosity on that dark time, as I think occasionally you should, it will do no good to search for villains or heroes or saints or devils because there were none; there were only victims.

DALTON TRUMBO

Preface and Acknowledgments

ON May 26, 1938, the United States House of Representatives authorized the formation of the Special House Committee on Un-American Activities.* The purposes of this committee were stated as follows:

> Resolved, that the Speaker of the House of Representatives be, and he is hereby, authorized to appoint a special committee to be composed of seven members for the purpose of conducting an investigation of (1)the extent, character, and object of un-American propaganda activities in the United States, (2)the diffusion within the United States of subversive and un-American propaganda that is instigated from foreign countries or of a domestic origin and attacks the principle of the form of government as guaranteed by the Constitution, and (3)all other questions in relations thereto that would aid Congress in any necessary remedial legislation.**

During the first twenty years of its existence, the committee investigated many individuals (*e.g.*, Alger Hiss), organizations (*e.g.*, the Communist Party), and cultural groups (*e.g.*, the American theater).

* Subsequently often abbreviated to "the committee."
** Walter Goodman, *The Committee; the Extraordinary Career of the House Committee on Un-American Activities* (New York, Farrar, Straus & Giroux, 1968), p. 16.

This book focuses on five important but erratically publicized series of hearings that affected American theater and closely related activities:

1. Martin Dies' 1938 investigation of the Works Progress Administration's Federal Theater Project.

2. J. Parnell Thomas' 1947 hearings regarding Communist infiltration of the motion picture industry.

3. John Wood's marathon ten-part 1951-52 entertainment hearings.

4. Harold H. Velde and Francis Walters' 1953 — 55 entertainment hearings and the committee's investigation of the Fund for the Republic report.

5. The Arthur Miller-Paul Robeson passport investigations and the last show business hearings in 1958.

My purpose in this book was to examine the influence of the House Committee on Un-American Activities on the American theater, 1938-58. This problem was divided into the following constituent questions:

I. What were the *actual* effects of the committee hearings on the American theater?
   A. What theaters closed?
   B. What theater people lost work?
II. What were the *probable* effects?
   A. Was there a moral dilemma faced by the witnesses?
   B. Were there personal enmities created by the hearings?
   C. Did the committee's procedures influence the nature and results of its findings?
III. What were the *possible* effects?
   A. Was the evolution of the American theater modified?
   B. Was there a constructive influence?
   C. Are there effects that cannot yet be evaluated?

I attempted to answer these three major questions primarily by a complete review of all the dialogue given in the public hearings; secondly, by correspondence and interviews with individuals who offered new primary data; thirdly, by studying

written observations published about the time periods surrounding each of the five hearings; and lastly, by assessing the
committee's annual reports. Furthermore, I appraised the
significance of these questions in the light of their effect on the
overall development of the American theater.

There is a current and growing interest in America concerning
the right of the individual to hold political beliefs that are
unpopular with a majority of the electorate. To the extent that
these beliefs are labeled un-American because they do not
conform with generally accepted standards of patriotic orthodoxy is a matter of continuing controversy in this democracy.

Therefore, of primary significance in this book was the role
played by the House Committee on Un-American Activities in
creating an atmosphere where the very process of its investigation of the political beliefs of individual theater artists
produced subsequent un-American labeling and how that
labeling affected the American theater.

Secondly, I thought this book significant because of the
probability of securing important new primary data. I believed
that my position as a working professional in the entertainment
industry would provide direct access to and personal testimony
from some of the artists who had been seriously involved in the
committee's investigations and that my professional reputation
would encourage the artists to speak more freely and frankly
than previously.

Although most of the committee's post-World War II
investigations of the entertainment field dealt with Hollywood
studios, producers, directors, writers, and actors, I limited my
final attention and conclusions to those individuals whose work
in the living theater was affected by these examinations.

There was no attempt made to study the effect of such
anti-Communist publications as *Counterattack, Red Channels,*
or groups like AWARE, Inc., on the American theater or
individual artists. This book was limited to the committee's
effect on the artist and the theater.

I am aware that the singling out of specific passages from the
testimony of various witnesses makes it possible to build a case
for or against the committee and the witnesses. A totally

accurate impression of the hearings can be gained only by reading all the testimony made available to the public. This I did and then excerpted from the hearings the words that, in my judgment, best reflected the caliber of the dialogue of each witness.

Because I promised anonymity to those correspondents and interviewees supplying new primary data, Chapter VII, containing these data, is organized in the following manner. The names of the persons supplying the new information are listed. However, their pertinent answers to the correspondence, questionnaires, and personal interviews are not aligned with their names. This approach thus satisfies my promise of privileged communication in return for their cooperation in this book.

Though Chapters III and IV deal almost exclusively with the committee's investigations of Communism in the motion picture industry, the new primary data offered in Chapter VII will define how the cinema probes influenced individual artists who also earned a portion of their living from the stage and how the investigations affected the theater in general.

Several terms underlie an understanding of this book and the committee's influence on the American theater and are important to this study. They are "living theater" or "the theater," "friendly witness," "unfriendly witness," and "blacklisting."

Living theater or the theater—These two terms are offered as having the same meaning and are also used interchangeably throughout this study. Contrary to the generic use of "theater" as an all-encompassing term meaning show business or the entertainment industry, the denotation here relates to the activities of the American stage. Thus when I refer to "theater" or "living theater," I am applying those words to people and their productions that occur live and in front of an audience.

Further, the word "theater" in this book does not mean motion pictures, television, radio, burlesque, or any allied forms of show business or the entertainment fields. "Living theater" in this study deals specifically with plays or their variations (*e.g.*, "living newspaper") and those people associated with their creation and production.

Friendly witness—In their appearances before the committee, certain witnesses were considered friendly if they responded to the questioning of their interrogators by naming persons they believed were or had been Communists. These witnesses generally indicated they also had been Communists in the past and were no longer affiliated in any way with the Communist Party, U.S.A. Their ability to name former or current Communists was usually based on their previous involvement with groups that had been identified publicly by government agencies as Communist-inspired, -controlled, or -oriented.

Unfriendly witness—A person was categorized as an unfriendly witness if he appeared before the committee and failed to answer questions involving his current or prior association with the Communist Party.

In nearly every case where a witness before the committee refused to answer questions pertaining to his political beliefs, past or present, he did so based on his immunity to such interrogation under the First or Fifth Amendment to the Bill of Rights.

Blacklisting—In this study the word "blacklisting" refers to the unwritten understanding among persons in a position to employ theater artists that they would not hire these artists if (1) they had been named as current or former Communists during the committee hearings, or (2) if when testifying before the committee, the artist refused to answer questions by claiming constitutional immunity.

The exception to this unwritten understanding occurred when a friendly witness confessed that he had been a Communist in the past, that he no longer was a Communist, and offered the committee the names of persons he suspected had been or were currently Communists.

The guidance of this book, in its original form as my doctoral dissertation, was in the able hands of Drs. James Butler, Herbert Stahl, and Howard Miller and Mr. Arthur Knight of the University of Southern California. Dr. Milton Dickens, cochairman with Dr. Butler on my dissertation committee, was of enormous help in every area of its academic creation from structure to detail, from organization to psychological encouragement. I owe Dr. Dickens my most respectful and profound

thanks. John Randell, a psychiatric social worker and my friend
of so many years, assisted greatly in the preparation of the
cover letter and questionnaire used in securing the new data.

USC's Dr. Joseph Nyomarkay's assistance and contribution
to the introductory remarks about radical extremism in
contemporary America were invaluable as a background to this
work.

Juanita Sayer, my consummate researcher, saved me hundreds of hours of legwork—work that would have been doubly
difficult for me because of my public visage. She also was a
never-ending source of good humor, inspiration, and light on
those darkest of empty legal pad days.

William Targ, my Putnam's editor, was a patient and gentle
provocator when I needed those qualities most.

Finally, to my secretary, Sharon Miller, my enduring affection and appreciation for all those hours of transcribing my
near-indecipherable printing to the typewritten pages of so
many drafts over so many years.

                                                    R.F.V.

Introduction

IN the nineteenth century Karl Marx and Friedrich Engels observed that Communism was as a specter haunting Europe. The use of the metaphor was accurate, for during that period the Communist movement was hardly more than an illusion: It had no strong political base. It was rather a concept of social order with a small group of energetic devotees. It was indeed a disembodied phantom.

Today, Communism is no longer a bodiless specter. It has discovered political power, created a working bureaucracy, and destroyed antithetical systems in myriad areas of the globe. No longer is Communism an aberration. It has become a functioning form of authoritarian government. In areas under its domination, it is not an illusion but a political apparatus handling the pragmatics of power and impelled by legitimate political goals much like other orthodox systems of ruling peoples.

Due to this evolvement, Communism is no longer an enigma among the intelligent and sophisticated. Definitive political, sociological, economic, and historical examinations have shown how Communist systems work and why Communist revolutions succeed or fail. We are aware to a great extent of the nature of its attraction, the social makeup of its adherents, the framework and methodology of its political apparatus, and the theories supporting its philosophy.

In the past, Communism, as well as Fascism, Nazism, and anarchism, has wandered the fringes of American politics. The American public has, with justification, viewed these philosophies as alien to our democratic traditions.

The rise of the radical right in the 1950's and '60's and the radical left in the last part of the '60's and presently is astonishing in the light of economic prosperity, ascending quality of life, and a slow amelioration of social injustices extant in this land. Extremism has generally been connected with unemployment and economic deprivation, extensive political and social inequities, and national timidity. Yet this time of the radical left and right in the land has come at the point in our history when we enjoy our largest internal economic solvency and domestic prosperity and incredible international strength and prestige. Thus, the ascent of the radical right and left has not been clear either in relation to our historical development or relative to our current socioeconomic position. Because of this lack of clarity, many persons consider the challenge on the right and left as a temporary aberration encouraged by a few lunatics on society's periphery. Public cognizance and worry have fallen dramatically behind the true vitality and menace of the political extremes on the left and right.

Thus, briefly I should like to address myself to two questions that are pertinent to this book and will serve to throw further light on the nature and challenge of the right and left as they relate to extremism. The first question deals with the problem of the definition of "extremism" or "radicalism," the second with its sociological and psychological foundations.

A major difficulty in dealing with the subject of left- and right-wing extremism is distinguishing legitimate conservatism and liberalism from their extremist variants. On what basis can we classify a group as extremist or denounce it as radical? I propose that this difference cannot be made solely on the core of the issues but rather strictly on the reasons behind their motivations and the methods they use. To ask for an end to the income tax is rationally legitimate within our democratic system which makes all political matters open to opinion, hence also open to debate. The same can be said of the argument that we should abandon the United Nations. There is nothing wrong with asking for the impeachment of the Chief Justice of the Supreme Court or, for that matter, of the President of the United States or for the abdication of FBI head J. Edgar Hoover. Our constitutional system is based on the concept that there is nothing divine about political issues or political leaders. Indeed, arguments on all matters political is a prerequisite of our open society based on the principle of conflict within consensus.

Thus, in the liberal-democratic tradition, all political issues, all governmental policies are by definition controversial and hence open to debate. Supreme Court decisions, Presidential decisions, Congressional actions are not divine revelation but thinking developed by fallible men on the basis of incomplete information and personal value judgments. To oppose or favor the Social Security System, fluoridation of water, the Vietnamese War, federal aid to education, foreign aid, reapportionment, or integration is legitimate, and conservatives and liberals may oppose or advocate these situations for some relevant reasons.

What makes the attacks of the extreme right and the extreme left illegitimate is that they oppose these measures not so much because they may be bad in themselves but because they represent aspects of a Communist or Fascist conspiracy. The right and the left may oppose the United Nations, the federal government, the income tax, and hundreds of other aspects of our politics not for some sane reason but for essentially paranoiac reasons. The right opposes fluoridation because fluoridated water may be used by members of the Communist conspiracy to poison the American population. The right opposes welfare measures because they are "Socialistic" and therefore represent the first steps toward Communism. The radical left opposes the system as a whole for essentially the same paranoiac reasons—that the United States government is actually functioning Fascism.

To oppose policies not because they are bad in themselves but because they represent aspects of an international or domestic conspiracy is essentially inimical to democratic politics, first, because it voids compromise and, second, because it indicates not so much an opposition to specific problems but to the system itself. In the minds of the radical left, isolated efforts at bettering society's ills are only manifestations of corrupt systems and treasonous officials. Their essential aim is to get rid of what they consider the *source of evil*—that is, the *system* and its *representatives*, not the *manifestations* of the system. Thus the conflict they represent is not within the bounds of consensus. The conflicts they generate by their propaganda are not conflicts from which new consensus may arise through democratic debate and procedures. What they challenge is the consensus itself, which they would like to subvert in order to establish their ideological closed society.

Hence I am suggesting that it is not their attacks of particular policies that makes certain right-wing and left-wing groups extremists but the *nature* of their attacks, which are designed to shake the faith of the people in the established institutions and their servants. What makes these groups radical is that they detest the pragmatic politics of compromise, that they refuse to see that bad policies may be the result of shortsightedness, foolishness, or simple self-interest rather than conspiracy, treachery, and bad faith. What makes them radical is that they challenge the *system*, not simply the particular policies that are made under it. What makes them extremist is their willingness to sacrifice the means for the ends, procedures and institutions for political goals.

This distinction between the substance and the nature of political conflict is basic to the understanding of extremism. The inadequate realization of this distinction not only has confused many legitimate conservative and liberal organizations with right- and left-wing extremism but also has helped disguise the real danger of extremism. Extremist groups have appeared to be pursuing legitimate politics by attacking such perennial problems of modern societies as bureaucratization, centralization, and increasing governmental controls over more and more aspects of our lives. But only few have come to realize that their attacks on these problems are merely smoke screens for their essential objective of subversion. When Adolf Hitler attacked the deadlocked party system of the Weimar Republic, he made sense to a great many people. When he talked about the Communist menace, the imminent collapse of the economic system, the growing crime rate, the decline of traditional morality, he spoke the language of people who had been vaguely aware of these real problems of postwar German democracy. But what the great majority never realized, or realized only too late, was that these problems were only instruments in Hitler's hands. They opened doors for him, they gave a sham substance to his essential aim of establishing his dictatorship over the country.

Exploitation of real problems for ideological purposes has been a characteristic of all totalitarian movements. The Communists have exploited the issues of social justice, independence of colonial people, and the quest for social and economic equality and freedom. Fascists have exploited the quest for nationalism, order, and destiny. The radical right in the United States exploits the problems facing us in the twentieth century from bureaucratization to crime and the international Communist challenge. The radical left's view of the national condition is equally myopic, dangerous, and without basis in fact.

The last question I should like to raise and reflect upon is the sociological and psychological foundations of extremist movements. Wherein lies the success of their appeals? What makes for their rise? What people do they tend to attract? What explains their relative success in the United States in the 1950's, '60's, and '70's?

These are questions of such magnitude that only tentative answers can be given, despite the existence of impressive scholarly material on the subject. Hannah Arendt, Eric Fromm, Daniel Bell, David Riesmann, Eric Hoffer, and many others have led me to certain conclusions which I would like to summarize here briefly. The insights I have gained from these writers I have seen confirmed time and time again in the course of my not infrequent contacts with representatives of the extreme right and left.

To my mind, the predominant cause of extremism and the invariable characteristic of adherents of extremist groups is confusion. Confusion and bewilderment have become part of man in the twentieth century. People do not understand why our centuries-old security from outside attack has suddenly disappeared and why we have become vulnerable in the nuclear age. They do not understand why the most powerful nation in the world has to tolerate a hostile regime only ninety miles from its shores. They do not understand why we couldn't win the traditional victory in Korea and why we are leaving Vietnam in a fashion not consonant with our military history—victory. They do not understand why they have to pay so much income tax, why prayers may no longer be said in schools, why we trade with the USSR, which we also say is our greatest enemy, and why Richard Nixon is extending the olive branch to our purported second greatest enemy, the People's Republic of China. The man in the street does not understand many things, and what is worse, he gets no clear answers. He has to rely on secondary authorities on all important questions affecting his life, and such reliance is never conducive to the feeling of security. Moreover, most of the time he receives contradictory information, yet he has no basis to make an intelligent, rational judgment. Thus, how can an ordinary man decide whether nuclear testing contaminates the atmosphere to the extent of endangering future life, when the most reputable experts in the field disagree? With whom should he side, Pauling or Teller? Or, perhaps, with his favorite TV commentator? Or, perhaps, with that commentator's nemesis, Spiro Agnew? Modern man has become the object of forces that he not only cannot control but cannot even understand.

The radicals offer an escape from this resulting confusion by their monistic explanation of reality. They suggest that it is not necessary to examine each problem individually, since they all are part of a universal conspiracy or a universal truth (whichever best suits needs or goals). To accept their ideology is to find answers to all the questions instantaneously and without the exertion of too much time or mental energy. The appeal of this form of escape from freedom appears to be irresistible to some of the confused. Thus the cessation of nuclear testing is wrong because the Communists are for it, and so is the Supreme Court decision concerning school prayers because the Communists are atheists, hence it is in their interest not to have children pray. And so on.

The appeal of radicalism is that it promises hope to the culturally, politically, and psychologically dispossessed. The tremendous changes brought about by industrialization and automation have been beneficial to some segments of society but have adversely affected others. These changes have eroded many traditions and altered social and political relationships. The managerial, technically trained class has taken over industries, dispossessing individual entrepreneurs; this managerial class is in the process of taking over the Defense Department, dispossessing the traditional military man. The rise of the blacks in our society has altered social and political relationships in many communities, dispossessing old elites and eroding traditional privileges. Chain stores and large industrial combines are dispossessing small shops and powerful trade unions are making inroads on managerial independence.

Many people dispossessed by changes of the twentieth century would like to reverse the trend of events. For these people history has ceased to be a history of progress. They have little to expect from the established system which appears to be continuing the prevailing trends. They want to get off and the radical groups extend to them the promise of extreme change. People who are dissatisfied with the present and have no confidence in the future are prone to grab at the promise of radical change even if they are not entirely certain about the nature of that change. They eagerly join in the condemnation of the system and are prone to believe in a conspiracy of some sort rather than to realize the changing nature of society. It is more comforting to assume that some individuals or groups have been responsible for these changes than to deal with the complexities of modern existence. For these reasons the radical appeal and the scapegoat theory of the extremists tends to be attractive to the dispossessed.

Lastly, I want to mention those who attempt to escape the failures of their individual lives by giving themselves to movements promising universal salvation. In this sense radical movements offer an escape from individual responsibility by substituting for it a collective, all-encompassing purpose. The large numbers of misfits and social outcasts in radical movements hardly need repetition.

Eric Hoffer has pointed out that "The chief preoccupation of an active mass movement is to instill in its followers a facility for united action and self-sacrifice" and that it achieves this facility "by stripping each human entity of its distinctness and autonomy and turning it into an anonymous particle with no will and no judgment of its own." The precondition for conversion is always an estrangement from self and almost always is fused in an atmosphere of intense passion. The man who has achieved inner balance is not a candidate for the fanatical movement. So the fanatic, seeking followers, must first attempt to throw off any inner balance in his potential followers. Such fanatical leaders do this through those precise methods that enflame the passions. And where fanatical passion rules, reason is a stranger.

So we find that this fanatic who has lost his reason is beyond being susceptible to rational conversion through reasoning. However, he can switch to another cause, even an opposing cause, if that cause is led by passion and not reason. Thus we find the hard-core Nazi more easily converted to hard-core Communism and vice versa than to liberal democracy.

In conclusion, the rise of radicalism in the United States in the 1950's, '60's, and '70's is rooted in the basic causes of confusion, dislocation, and rapid change. The breakdown of many traditional values, the erosion of traditional morality and customs, the rise of new status groups are often noted phenomena of our times. We are in the process of making a new society, not by any grand design but piecemeal, not as a result of any blueprint but as a result of the complex structural changes that need accommodation. This new society has many promises, but it has also many strains and stresses which radical groups seek to exploit by their demogoguery, their simple answers to complex problems, their scapegoats.

The interpretation of Communism as the chief scapegoat and synonym for evil in our society has long been a vision the

radical right has fostered in our national mythology. Shortly
after World War I the first of many Red scares swept the nation.
America had won the Great War and the Bolsheviks led by
Vladimir Lenin had seized power in Russia from the weak
Aleksandr Kerensky regime and the world's first Communist
state was a reality. International in its revolutionary intentions,
the Soviet leaders set out by word and deed to export the
Communist system to all the capitalist world that surrounded
them. America was the largest and most rapidly expanding free
market economy in this postwar period, and the Kremlin
wanted hegemony over this most Western of *laissez-faire*
nations. Myriad Socialist-oriented organizations that had
formed in the late nineteenth and early twentieth centuries in
America now found a standard-bearer in the New World
Communist movement. American politicians also found in the
Red menace not only an issue of great emotional value but also
a magnificent opportunity for asserting their patriotism as well.
All radicals of the left were called Reds and depicted in the
cartoons of the day as bearded bomb-throwers—a characteriza-
tion still much in favor and probably more accurate today. The
twenties saw much open militancy between the radical left and
right, but not until the end of the twenties and the Depression
did the Communist Party, U.S.A., see some light at the end of
the capitalist corridor. With the advent of the Roosevelt New
Deal and that administration's diplomatic recognition of the
USSR, the CP-U.S.A. pulled out all stops in an effort to move
FDR's social welfare state farther to the left. By the mid-1930's
a committee of Congress was established for the expressed
purpose of ferreting out radicals, anti-Americans, and specifically Communists. Its title was the House Committee on
Un-American Activities, and how they affected a specific
American art form is the subject of this book.

Chapter I

Only Victims

NOW there was and is a curious madness in America. It is called "fear of Communism." Not the rational fear of humans who have personally experienced that most heinous of ideologies, but rather the irrational fear of those true believers who find solace in a scapegoat interpretation of the evils in the world about them.

To those individuals who see the omnipresence of the Red "goat" in all revolt against the established order in America, the Communist problem in this country is specifically synonymous with radical liberals, bleeding-heart leftism, New Deal-Fair Deal-New Frontier programs, and Democratic politics in general. The failure of this terrified and growing minority to attempt any intellectual comprehension of how Communism has come to power through violent revolution in the twentieth century and therefore why that same kind of revolution cannot occur in America is a mystery to the educated anti-Communist American left.

Equally as incomprehensible is the failure of the pro-Marxist-Maoist violence-oriented radical left to understand that its revolution cannot happen here. In this sense the radical paranoiacs of the left and right and the silent center share a common misinterpretation of twentieth-century revolution and for essentially the same reasons: a failure to examine the realities of the times while pursuing and listening only to rhetoric complementary to their paranoia. The left radical and right reactionary, and an enormous number of the gradually less silent majority, all see a slowly evolving violent revolution that will conclude, unless militantly repressed, with a Weathermen *coup d'état* and a Black Panther in the Oval Office. They are wrong.

Communist revolution, of an internal violent nature, has occurred successfully three times in this century—in Russia, China, and Cuba. In each instance an oppressive minuscule ruling elite has held power over an enormous peasant majority. The imaginations of vast numbers of that majority were galvanized by the Communist revolutionaries and eventually right ruling elites were replaced violently by an equally repressive ruling elite of the left. No such circumstances have ever existed in America, and least of all today is the affluent middle-class American that elected Richard Nixon President vaguely vulnerable to internal revolution from the left. As was discussed in the Introduction of this book, the case to be made today against the possibility of a right revolution in the form of an alliance of militarist and paranoiac politicos is not so easily made. It is my intention to touch briefly in this chapter on the role of the American right in the thirties, as personified by the House Committee on Un-American Activities rather than on anything so grandiose as a military-political cabal in the seventies.

"There is nothing un-American about the Un-American Activities Committee . . . this is not the land exclusively of Lincoln and Jefferson."[1]

This is the land of the Ku Klux Klan and the White Citizens Council. It is the land of Bull Connor and Sheriff Jim Clark. And it is also the land of Franklin Roosevelt and Samuel Dickstein.

Dickstein was a New York City Congressman for twenty-two years, from 1923 to 1944, and served a district inhabited by immigrants from Eastern Europe, many of whom had fled the first rumblings of the Third Reich for the comparative calm of Franklin Roosevelt's New Deal.

Roosevelt was President of the United States for twelve years, from 1933 to 1945, and endeavored, through his New Deal, to involve the federal government in the economic welfare of the American people to an extent undreamed of by some of the most progressive minds of the period.[2] To those minds the New Deal appeared radical and revolutionary in its liberal extremism, when in essence it was a model of moderation.

Actually Roosevelt's revolution was profoundly conservative—conservative in the democratic tradition of Thomas Jefferson and Woodrow Wilson. Its main thrust was to deter violence from the left or right and to conserve and preserve resources, constitutional interests, and security and liberty as guaranteed by the founding fathers.

The philosophy of the New Deal was also evolutionary in its democratic methodology. Conservation policies, railroad and trust laws, banking and currency reforms, farm relief programs, labor legislation, reformation of the judiciary, and even the international relations policy of championing democracy in the Western world had their precedents in the earlier America of Wilson, Theodore Roosevelt, and Abraham Lincoln.[3]

One New Deal champion of democracy in the Western world and in particular eastern New York City was indeed Sam Dickstein. With his parents, he arrived at the age of three in the East Side ghetto on Manhattan Island.

The Dickstein family was one of thousands that fled Eastern Europe and the pogroms of the Old World only to find the New World almost as denigrating to their spirit as Europe.

Between the time Dickstein commenced his career as a special deputy attorney general in New York State and the conclusion of that career as a State Supreme Court Justice, he managed to earn the dubious designation "father of the committee."[4]

The political and economic setting of New York City and State in the early and mid-1930's was a microcosm of the United States. Politicians were searching for a scapegoat to bear the burden for the economic depression that had begun in the previous decade.

One such politician, Representative Hamilton Fish of New

York, was certain that once the country was rid of the Communists one could "give jobs to honest, loyal American citizens who are unemployed."[5] If Dickstein was the father of the committee, Fish could probably be called the grandfather. He chaired Congressional hearings from July to December, 1930, and produced a report indicating that there were about 12,000 dues-paying members of the Communist Party in the United States. Fish recommended that the party be declared illegal, alien Communists deported, and federal laws enacted to prevent Communists from spreading false rumors that might cause runs on banks. He demanded an embargo on all articles imported from Russia.[6]

The less-than-sanguine view of America that prevails on the political left today was also characteristic of much of the radical thought of the thirties. Responsibility in that decade for the country's inability to solve its internal problems, according to some of the radical left, lay in the system itself.

In 1931, 9,000,000 men and women were jobless, the cities were miserable, and the rural life was bankrupt; industry was in a state comparable to the period in England before the Factory Acts of a century earlier. Banks were failing and unions in the South were renewing their struggle for recognition. In Europe and South America economic inequities were also the order of the day and the observation was made that "not simply the machinery of representative government but the capitalist system itself" had broken down.[7]

However, the difference between the radical left then and now is that the Marxist-Leninist experiment in revolution, as distorted by Stalin, was thought by many naïve Americans in the thirties to be the panacea of governments. Today, as that experiment has further evolved and been distorted, it is considered obsolete by the extreme left.[8]

In the sixties and seventies that obsolescence was consistently voiced on American and foreign university campuses as well as in the streets. More recent leftist leaders, such as Mark Rudd and Tom Hayden, certainly do not share Dickstein or Fish's vision of Americanism; but for vastly different reasons, the quartet definitely would be in concert in the area of being anti-Soviet Communism.

In 1932, Dickstein brought Martin Dies' anti-Communist bill
to the floor of the house. In 1933, he championed a movement
for Congressional investigation of anarchists. However, it was
the rise of Adolf Hitler that put Dickstein in the forefront of
investigating un-American activities. The "Dickstein Committee," under its first chairman, John McCormack, began its
anti-Nazi hearings in the summer of 1934.

By the next year it was entirely possible for men of reason
and intellect to peruse the Washington investigations of Communists and Nazis, and their attendant support from the Hearst
press on the right and those sympathetic to the Soviet
experiment on the left, and concur with Arthur M. Schlesinger,
Jr.: "For a moment in 1935, intelligent observers could almost
believe that the traditional structure of American politics was
on the verge of dissolution."[9]

In 1936, the Hearst papers supported Alfred M. Landon,
governor of Kansas, against Roosevelt and indulged in a bit of
poetry:

> The Red New Deal with a Soviet seal
> Endorsed by a Moscow hand,
> The strange result of an alien cult
> In a liberty-loving land.

Hearst's meter was of scant help to Landon, and Roosevelt
was reelected for a second term by an overwhelming popular
mandate, the largest plurality in American history—27,480,000
to Landon's 16,675,000. Roosevelt also swept the electoral
college with 528 votes to Landon's 8.[10]

The enormous victory of the 1936 New Deal gave even
greater confidence to its early supporters, and as a result it
created an atmosphere in Washington that was particularly
conducive to an amalgam of progressives, liberals, New Dealers,
Socialists, and some Communists.

It is in this environment that the purported subverting of the
American government by Communists must be appraised. The
curiosity is not that there were undoubtedly many Reds that
made government their vocation but rather that the entire
Communist Party was not on the federal payroll.[11]

If "Members of the Communist Party did indeed enter the

government in the early months of the New Deal, but the entry seems to have occurred without plan, and it is even possible that the party bureaucracy at first looked at it askance,"[12] by 1938 Messrs. Dickstein and Dies were not quite as myopic as their Communist peers.

The two joined in supporting a resolution that stated some curiously indefinable purposes. Among them were investigating un-American activities in the United States and un-American and subversive propaganda initiated abroad or at home. They concluded their statement of resolve with a catchall phrase that read, ". . . all other questions in relations thereto that would aid Congress in any necessary remedial legislation."[13]

In the Congressional debate that preceded the passage of this resolution, a phrase that was to be much bandied about during the McCarthy investigations of the 1950's was first uttered by Dies when he said, "I am not inclined to look under every bed for a Communist."[14]

The Dies resolution, after much heated dialogue, passed the House, 191 to 41.

When the triumphant Dickstein stood and asked to speak he was denied the privilege, and a week and a half later the chairman of the new committee, Dies, failed to appoint to the fledgling body the man "who had labored with all his heart," Sam Dickstein.[15]

Dies was classified as the Democratic equal of Hamilton Fish, "physically a giant, very young, ambitious, and cocksure." And, concluded the *New Republic*, "If the powerful energies of Mr. Dies are not given over to hounding Communists, it will be a miracle."[16]

Dies, as would virtually all future chairmen of the committee, sensed an immediate need for publicity for his new special committee. He announced that representatives of public organizations were to be asked to offer relevant information[17] and reported that many Nazis and Communists were leaving the United States because of his pending interrogations.[18]

But it was the New Deal's Works Progress Administration that was to give Chairman Dies his first and most spectacular publicity coup.

Dies elucidated his cognizance of the threat the project presented to America when he wrote:

> W.P.A. was the greatest financial boon which ever came to the Communists in the United States. Stalin could not have done better by his American friends and agents. Relief projects swarmed with Communists—Communists who were not only recipients of needed relief but who were entrusted by New Deal officials with high administrative positions in the projects. In one Federal Writers' Project in New York, one third of the writers were members of the Communist Party. This was proven by their own signatures. Many witnesses have testified that it was necessary for W.P.A. workers to join the Workers Alliance—high-pressure lobby run by the Communist Party—in order to get or retain their jobs. . . .
>
> Several hundred Communists held advisory or administrative positions in the W.P.A. projects. . . .[19]

Although Dies had access to records and researchers for his book *The Trojan Horse in America*, it is almost totally devoid of citations and contains no index or bibliography, and therefore his vivid analysis above could have been rendered entirely from his imagination.

However, imagination was by no means the special blessing of ambitious politicians in the thirties. Probably in no other decade in this century has the cultural environment of the nation been so fraught with imaginative social commitment from writers of the drama, both stage and screen.

Indeed, if it is true that "if all art is a gesture against death . . . it must commit itself," as Kenneth Tynan argues,[20] then it can fairly be said that the thirties saw more cultural gesturing against the "grim reaper," with concomitant commitment, than any time in the nation's theater history.

John Howard Lawson had a commitment to American radicalism, as to a lesser extent did Clifford Odets. Both endeavored to arouse in their audiences a passion that could be translated into a program that would modify at least, and nullify at best, the social ills that prevailed in the Depression-ridden nation of the 1930's.

The new art, "the talkies," then still awaiting final judgment

as a contributor to culture, produced such motion pictures as
Mr. Deeds Goes to Town and *Mr. Smith Goes to Washington*
and showed the common man in the audience how, if he really
tried, he could influence his government to offer him redress for
his grievances.

The films of Cary Grant, William Powell, and Robert
Montgomery, like the plays of S. N. Behrman, offered the
unemployed viewer a dream of what high society was and could
be like—if he really tried.

Another playwright, Elmer Rice, made his most serious
commitment to the drama of protest in the early thirties, at the
height of the Depression, when he, "like many liberals, allied
himself with the radicals as a gesture of protest against the
social chaos"[21] and condemned the Broadway theater in a
manner that Martin Dies would have probably considered a
Marxian dialectic.

According to Rice, the theater was in the hands of
businessmen, real-estate operators, and capitalists, where primary artistic interest dealt with the dollar sign. In his purview,
the drama and commerce were as one and the artist and his
audience were estranged by crass commercialism. Rice viewed
America as a profit system that "stifles the creative impulse and
dams the free flow of vitality."[22]

Whatever Rice's political leanings were at the time of this
comment, it must be said that the "profit system" was doing a
most inadequate job of stifling the "creative impulse" and
damming the "free flow of vitality" along the Great White Way.

The Theatre Union directed its plays at what it hoped would
result in an egalitarian audience. It announced that it would
produce plays that dealt audaciously with the social, cultural,
economic, and psychological problems of the period. It wanted
its plays to address themselves to the people who shared the
problems, the majority of alienated Americans. Moreover, the
union wanted its theater to create a new professional theater
"based on the hopes of the great mass of the working
people."[23]

The Theatre Union "represented Marxism's most ambitious

excursion into the mainstream of the American theater,"[24] but it was by no means alone in its efforts to create a professional theater that would glean its support from the proletariat.

Of the many worker-oriented theaters that paralleled and followed Theatre Union, two stand out because of their significance today. The Group Theatre managed to make its "method" approach to plays so stimulating that now, more than a quarter of a century since the company's dissolution, the method still remains the basic acting style for the aspiring theater artist.

Additionally, it produced the tyro efforts of Sidney Kingsley and William Saroyan, as well as works by John Howard Lawson, Paul Green, and Maxwell Anderson. And "its playwriting contest awarded public recognition for the first time to a young writer named Tennessee Williams."[25] Harold Clurman, Stella Adler, Bobby Lewis, Cheryl Crawford, Elia Kazan, and Lee Strasberg are but a few of the Group Theatre's membership who went on to teach and direct in the style advocated by Konstantin Stanislavski.

And the most theatrically articulate voice of the thirties, the personality most identified with the drama of the Depression, was the Group Theatre's leading playwright, Clifford Odets.

It is fair to say that "In sum, the record of American dramatic accomplishment in the thirties is very largely the dramatic contribution of the Group Theatre."[26]

The second theater that still remains unique in the twentieth century was the nation's first and only nationally subsidized Federal Theatre. For four years, from 1935 to 1939, under its director, Hallie Flanagan, it produced more plays seen by more people than in any similar period in the nation's history. Why such an enormously exciting, diversified, and voluminous enterprise should have come to such an abrupt end—it was killed by Congress in one day—is explored in the following chapter.

It may safely be said that "the project's main contribution was theatrical, not dramatic—in the principle rather than in the results of government-sponsored drama," and further that "the

Federal Theatre was unable to reconcile its commitment to the principle of economic relief with its commitment to a viable, socially-conscious theatre."[27]

Many believed the two obligations canceled each other out, but it is likely that had the theater been allowed the opportunity to continue, it might well have produced as many significant theatrical figures as its precedent, the Group Theatre.

With the exception of the cinema, the cultural atmosphere of the thirties may indeed have been influenced most by the Federal Theatre in the sense that more people saw plays than any other form of live entertainment. And this was quite simply because there were more plays to be seen, as the direct result of the often free Federal Theatre.

But before we investigate in greater depth the living theater's role in the environment of the period, let us turn briefly again to the nonlive but loud phenomenon that began with the Depression decade, "the talkies," and then, last, to the dance.

"Sound is not merely a mechanical device where-by a director can make the image appear more natural. . . . I am sure that the sound film is potentially the art of the future,"[28] wrote V. I. Pudovkin in the early thirties. More importantly, the Russian film maker saw sound as an embellishment to Lenin's great confidence in the film as a political weapon.

He saw film neither as an orchestral creation centering on music nor as the stage where man pervades; neither did he see it as akin to opera but rather as a synthesis of all theatrical components—oral, visual, and philosophical. Pudovkin saw the cinema as a new art that had succeeded and would supersede all the older art; the "supreme medium" for expressing today and tomorrow. [29]

When Al Jolson first went down on one knee to express his singing affection for his "mammy" in Warner Brothers' *The Jazz Singer*, it is doubtful that he was aware of anything quite so profound as philosophizing in the "supreme medium."

However, the revolutionary artist writing for the cinema was a potential reality, probably to a somewhat greater extent in the thirties than in the forties, when the committee was busy getting headlines from its 1947 Hollywood investigations.

The responsibility of the radical screenwriter was propaganda. He must be able to force a disinterested audience to listen despite its inclinations and when through to agree with him and move to action. To do this, the revolutionary scenarist must get the attention of the audiences, middle and working class, by using familiar sounds. Since Hollywood owned and fed movie audiences, it was the logical goal of all radical writers endeavoring to undermine the ideological structure of the middle class and consolidate the working class to "consider seriously the question of working through Hollywood."[30]

A few of the radical theater writers of the thirties did try the new medium, but generally speaking they were far more interested in the fast buck that Hollywood offered than anything politically profound. Lawson and Odets took brief turns in the new medium but retreated hastily to the familiar and more flexible environs of the New York theater.

The Hollywood writer was considered in those early days of the talkies as "the well-fed prisoner of a medium which he felt beneath his capacities."[31]

The most accurate and fair assessment of the film maker's or producer's predilection toward revolutionary conspiring, whether it be in the thirties or contemporary times, was proffered by Richard Watts, Jr., when he observed:

> It is, I think, a great mistake to believe that the California film-makers are, as a rule, intentionally malicious or studiously unfair in their attitude towards revolutionary themes. Undeniably, they are heartily, if sometimes furtively, on the side of the established order, but it does not make their definite anti-revolutionary bias any more pleasant to realize that it is the result of instinct and the box office, rather than of intentional malice. My point is that it is giving the Hollywood magnates credit for far too great a degree of intelligence to suspect any such conspiracy on their part. In their hearts they have, I firmly believe, intended to go in for the closest approximation of harmless, mid-Victorian liberalism they can hit upon. It merely happens that all of their handsome investments, all of their fears of censorship and legions of decency and the women's clubs, all their dreams of being big shots in a great industrial world—in fact, all of their instincts and emotions—make it subconsciously impossible for them to

be on the side of the exploited. They are not scheming villains.
They are just instinctive defenders of a system that has enabled
them to buy those swimming pools and tennis courts.[32]

More than a dozen years later, J. Parnell Thomas, as chairman
of the committee, disagreed with Watts and launched what he
intended to be a full-scale investigation of the "Red menace" in
the California cinema. It was suddenly truncated when some of
the same moguls whom Watts referred to came forth to
demonstrate the validity of his premise.

The dance is the other cultural phenomenon that employs
the use of a live audience and bears brief scrutiny as a device
that the radical left believed could engage the viewer in an
emotional appeal that might be translated into political action.

The art of the dance probably preceded all human physical
expression that could be called dramatic in intent. The dance
was used to encourage the gods to help yield a more bounteous
harvest long before its more realistic and ritualistic use in
ancient Greece and Italy. It was not until this century that the
dance became a clinically dissected tool of a revolutionary
political philosophy.

A dance group that is functioning properly in the radical
sense must fit into the overall concept of Socialist realism and
have five well-defined goals: (1) to dance before workers,
students, and the regular dance concert audience, (2) to dance
for the purpose of educating and stimulating the audience to
significant aspects of the class struggle, (3) to train new troops
to undertake this task, (4) to train the individuals who are to
make up the new troops, and (5) to have all the troops, new and
old, become part of the class struggle through practical and
theoretical education.[33]

The problem then arises for the radical dancer, after he has
thoroughly mastered his five points to revolution, what to
dance about? As in all totalitarian systems, there is an answer
for every problem. The class struggle was the main and only
focus of the dance as long as classes remained. Therefore "a
nature dance in a program may be just the nectar that a
fluttering, bourgeois butterfly may require to induce him to

alight"[34] and other such banal metaphoric admonitions were often advanced by the radical dance theorist of the thirties, theories that convinced him that through his art he could help create a political revolution.

The living theater's role in the cultural pattern of the 1930's was, as has already been suggested, more profound and emotionally cathartic for audiences than during any other decade in this century. The American social theater of that decade, although almost totally left of center in its productions and goals, should in no way be confused with the totalitarian left theater in Russia.

"The Russian Theatre deals with the very vitals of Russian life in its contemporary forms. . . . In the totalitarian economy every aspect of the life of the people is harnessed to specific forms of organization and to given purposes," observed economist James H. Shoemaker.[35]

In no way could the American theater of the left at any time be construed to be harnessed inextricably to any form of organization and certainly only most generally to purposes. There is no doubt that the social theater of the Depression was constantly, with varying degrees of success, penetrated by the then-burgeoning Communist Party, U.S.A.

In some cases this attempt at infiltration was overt and public, as we have observed in the Theatre Union. More often the social theater was beset by a more covert and less definable subversion. Particularly before 1930 this latter style of assault did not necessarily adhere to any specific Moscow party line. It was not even categorically anticapitalist in its intent, but nonetheless it was radical in its observations on the culture.

Specific assault upon the basic institutions of Western democracy, as currently propounded by the seventies' radicals, seemed hopeless to most of the revolutionary theorists of the thirties.

Social criticism in plays was more often directed at culture than at political organization. Contrasts between rich and poor were attempted in the theater for the purpose of ironic contemplation rather than violent destruction of the existing social order. If the rich were denigrated in the theater, it was because they were considered vulgar and intellectually and esthetically limited rather than for any reason attributed to defects in the capitalist system.[36]

After 1930, when the Depression was fully under way, the Communist Party made no attempt to disguise its desire to be a part of the mainstream of the American theater.

The agitprop play, usually very short, episodic, satiric, and employed for political *agit*ation and *prop*aganda, was first used by the Communists in 1930 in the German-speaking Prolet-buehne theater. Following this initial effort, the Workers Laboratory Theatre (WLT) and the Theatre Collective attempted to herald the coming of a Soviet America. In 1934, when the WLT was rechristened the Theatre of Action, it changed its policy and presentation, and "unlike the stylized agitprop, the new technique required the playwright to weave the Marxist ideas into a realistic plot."[37]

Leon Alexander, drama critic of the *Daily Worker*, the CP's official newspaper, vowed that the Theatre of Action would continue the production of the raw agitprop play against the desires of "some of our professionally minded comrades," but he indicated that the renamed company was on the look for more realistic material.[38]

The theater shortly moved to Broadway and in May, 1935, presented a three-act play, *The Young Go First*, which "was hailed by the Communist press more for the realism of the production than for the political correctness of the script," but historically it was probably more significant because its codirector was an up-and-coming young actor in the Group Theatre, Elia Kazan.[39]

The Theatre Collective was actually a subdivision of the WLT and was organized in order to stage full-length realistic plays in the normal Broadway manner.[40] Unlike the commercial theater, the Collective's plays were supposed to follow and be illustrative of the CP-U.S.A. line.[41]

These are but a few examples of the amateur Communist theaters that attempted to write and direct plays that would espouse the inherent wonders of collectivism as understood by the young artists who were sympathetic to the Soviet experiment. "These short-lived groups made but a slight impression on their radical audience and virtually no impression on the overall theatrical scene in New York." Despite the intention of the CP and the hope for a revolutionary theater that would rend the capitalist system asunder, they really did nothing revolutionary either theatrically or politically.[42]

The League of Workers Theatre (later renamed the New Theatre League) and the Labor Stage were probably the most well-known and overtly pro-Soviet semiprofessional theater groups in the thirties. There were many variations of these workers' theaters, both in and out of New York, but for the purpose of citing representative pro-Communist theaters they remain the best examples.

The New Theatre League proclaimed its philosophy for the American theater as "the most efficient use of drama as a weapon in the inevitable revolution"[43] when it published its new program:

> For mass development of the American Theatre to its highest artistic and social level. For a theatre dedicated to the struggle against war, fascism, and censorship.[44]

In addition to the WLT and the Theatre Collective, there arose an amateur theater which, because of its success in attracting audiences, became professional: the Labor Stage. Before the formation of Labor Stage the ILGWU (International Ladies' Garment Workers Union) made a few attempts at realistic drama, but until 1936, when Louis Schaeffer, an officer in the ILGWU's recreational program, presented Labor Stage's production of *Pins and Needles*, the left-wing theater had failed to find a broad audience.[45] *Pins and Needles* was performed more than 1,100 times in New York City alone. When it closed on June 20, 1940, it was the most successful musical revue of the decade.[46]

The Group and Federal were to be the most remembered theaters of the 1930's: the first because of its rich endowment of theater people who are still active today; the second because the government which created it with haste and the best of intentions dissolved it with equal dispatch and questionable judgment.

The reasons given by the committee for its decision to end

the Federal Theatre and the defense of the organization by the directors and the commercial show business world are the subject of the next chapter.

The inevitability of that confrontation seems now historically apparent when one considers the secondary role the American political right was forced to play during the New Deal's challenge to the Depression.

FOOTNOTES

1. Walter Goodman, *The Committee; the Extraordinary Career of the House Committee on Un-American Activities* (New York, Farrar, Straus & Giroux, 1968), pp. 492-93.
2. Raymond Moley, *The First New Deal* (New York, Harcourt, Brace & World, Inc., 1966), p. vii.
3. Allan Nevins and Henry Steele Commager, *A Short History of the United States*, 5th rev. ed. (New York, Alfred A. Knopf, 1966), pp. 476-77.
4. Goodman, *op. cit.*, p. 3.
5. *Ibid.*, p. 6.
6. *Ibid.*, pp. 8-9.
7. *New Republic*, January 14, 1931, p. 234.
8. Daniel and Gabriel Cohn-Bendit, *Obsolete Communism: The Left-Wing Alternative*, trans. by Arnold-Pomerans (New York, McGraw-Hill Book Co., 1968).
9. Arthur M. Schlesinger, Jr., *The Politics of Upheaval* (Boston, Houghton Mifflin Co., 1960), p. 69.
10. Nevins and Commager, *op. cit.*, p. 479.
11. Earl Latham, *The Communist Controversy in Washington* (Cambridge, Mass., Harvard University Press, 1966), p. 77.
12. *Ibid.*, p. 94.
13. Goodman, *op. cit.*, p. 6.
14. *Ibid.*, p. 21.
15. *Ibid.*, p. 23.
16. Cited in August R. Ogden, *The Dies Committee*, 2d rev. ed. (Washington, D.C., The Catholic University of America Press, Inc., 1945), p. 47.
17. New York *Times*, July 13, 1938.
18. *Ibid.*, July 20, 1938.
19. Martin Dies, *The Trojan Horse in America* (New York, Dodd, Mead & Co., 1940), p. 298.
20. "Theatre and Living," in *Declaration*, Tom Maschler, ed. (New York, E. P. Dutton & Co., Inc., 1958), p. 94.
21. Gerald Rabkin, *Drama and Commitment* (Bloomington, Indiana, Indiana University Press, 1964), p. 238.
22. New York *Times*, November 11, 1934, Sec. IX, p. 3.
23. Quoted in Anita Block, *The Changing World in Plays and Theatre* (Boston, Little, Brown and Co., 1939), p. 275.
24. Rabkin, *op. cit.*, p. 45.
25. *Ibid.*, p. 91.

26. *Ibid.*

27. *Ibid.*, p. 123.

28. V. I. Pudovkin, "Sound and the Future of the Cinema," *New Theatre*, March, 1934, p. 7.

29. *Ibid.*, p. 8.

30. *New Theatre*, March, 1934, p. 16.

31. Murray Kempton, *Part of Our Time: Some Monuments and Ruins of the Thirties* (New York, Dell Publishing Co., 1967), p. 192.

32. Richard Watts, Jr., "Hollywood Sees Pink," *New Theatre*, November, 1934, p. 14.

33. "The Dance: The New Dance Group; an Analysis," *New Theatre*, March, 1934, p. 17.

34. Ezra Freeman, "What to Dance About," *New Theatre*, March, 1934, pp. 18-19.

35. As quoted in Ben W. Brown, *Theatre at the Left* (Providence, R.I., Bear Press, 1938), Introduction.

36. Joseph Wood Krutch, *The American Drama Since 1918*, rev. ed. (New York, Braziller, 1967), pp. 227-28.

37. Morgan Y. Himelstein, *Drama Was a Weapon* (New Brunswick, New Jersey, Rutgers University Press, 1963), p. 17.

38. *Daily Worker*, May 27, 1935.

39. Himelstein, *op. cit.*, p. 18.

40. Jack Shapiro, "Theatre Collective," *New Theatre*, October, 1934, p. 15.

41. Himelstein, *op. cit.*, p. 19.

42. *Ibid.*, p. 22.

43. *Ibid.*, p. 33.

44. *New Theatre*, February, 1935, p. 3.

45. Himelstein, *op. cit.*, p. 76.

46. New York *Times*, May 30, 1941.

Chapter II

Martin Dies' 1938 Investigation of the Federal Theatre Project

MR. STARNES: You are quoting from this Marlowe. Is he a Communist?

MRS. FLANAGAN: I am very sorry. I was quoting from Christopher Marlowe.

MR. STARNES: Tell us who Marlowe is, so we can get the proper reference, because that is all that we want to do.

MRS. FLANAGAN: Put in the record that he was the greatest dramatist in the period of Shakespeare, immediately preceding Shakespeare.

MR. STARNES: Put that in the record, because the charge has been made that this article of yours is entirely communistic, and we want to help you.

MRS. FLANAGAN: Thank you. That statement will go in the record.

MR. STARNES: Of course, we had what some people call Communists back in the days of the Greek theater.

MRS. FLANAGAN: Quite true.

MR. STARNES: And I believe Mr. Euripedes [sic] was guilty of teaching class consciousness also, wasn't he?

MRS. FLANAGAN: I believe that was alleged against all of the Greek dramatists.

MR. STARNES: So we cannot say when it began. [1]

As the committee's Joseph Starnes (Democrat, Alabama) indicated, it may be somewhat difficult to trace the beginnings of class consciousness in dramatic literary history, but it is a

good deal easier to pinpoint the committee's first public interest
in the American drama of the thirties.

Description of the Hearings

On Tuesday, July 26, 1938, J. Parnell Thomas (Republican,
New Jersey), a member of the committee, announced that he
would call for the appearance before the committee of Mrs.
Hallie Flanagan to answer questions concerning purported
Communist activities in the Federal Theatre. Thomas indicated
she would be asked to explain why persons applying for jobs on
the project must first join the Workers Alliance, an organization
he described as Communist, and why employees of the theater
were allowed to hold protest meetings during regular working
hours. The Congressman noted that it was apparent from his
evidence that the theater not only was serving as a branch of the
Communist organization but also was a part of the New Deal
propaganda machine. Thomas concluded his attack by charging
that the entire Federal Theatre Project was "infested by radicals
from top to bottom."[2]

Mrs. Flanagan was quick to retort to the Congressman's
accusations and said the following day that "she would be glad
to answer any questions Representative Thomas . . . might wish
to ask her about the project and her own activities in it." She
further observed: "Some of the statements reported to have
been made by him are obviously absurd . . . of course no one
need first join or be a member of any organization in order to
obtain employment in a theatre project."[3]

Representative Thomas was not about to let Mrs. Flanagan
have the last public word on the matter prior to the beginning
of the hearings. He demanded a total cleaning of the project,
which he characterized as a "patronage vehicle" for the
Communist Party. Thomas said he would demand the resignation of various project officials because they were giving jobs to
Communists who had no prior theater training. In support of
this charge, the Congressman alleged that a Communist cham-
bermaid was given the leading role in a play despite the fact she
had never appeared on the legitimate stage—a situation that

would never have dismayed a Hollywood casting man as much as it apparently did Thomas.

After a three-week investigation, the Congressman stated that the project was completely dominated by Communists and therefore the American government was publicly funding the CP. He further asserted American World War veterans were being barred from the project solely because they were veterans and that virtually "every single play" was propaganda for Communism or the New Deal, because scripts attacked the United States judiciary system and one production, *Injunction Granted*, advocated "rioting and bloodshed."[4]

Thomas' arbitrary coupling of Communism and the New Deal indicated that one of the real motives of the committee was attacking the Roosevelt administration, not solely ferreting out Communists, as it claimed.

Such was the public case presented by the committee in the person of Congressman Thomas against the WPA's Federal Theatre Project.

Mrs. Flanagan quite rightly assumed that she would be subpoenaed to appear before the committee and drafted a letter saying she would be available on August 11. She noted that the date coincided with the meeting of the National Policy Board of the Federal Theatre and pointed out that six regional directors would then be present should the committee wish to interrogate them about projects throughout the country.[5]

Chairman Martin Dies rejected Mrs. Flanagan's request to testify but replied that Congressman Thomas apparently did intend to subpoena her, although it might be several weeks because the committee already had a heavy schedule of witnesses.[6]

On August 19, Thomas led off his attack on the Federal Theatre with ten witnesses headed by Hazel Huffman, "a former employee of the mail division of the WPA, who claimed to have been hired by the office of the New York City WPA administrator, Victor Ridder, as an investigator to read Federal Theatre mail" and who was subsequently fired when her dubious duties were discovered.[7]

Miss Huffman was followed by nine other persons associated

in tangential ways with the project and described as offering the "weirdest collections of evidence permitted before the Committee . . . at this stage," ranging from Communist activities, inefficiency, professional status debates, and the audacity of a Negro asking a white girl out.[8]

The case presented by the committee against the Federal Theatre, in addition to the aforementioned public utterances of Congressman Thomas, can best be summed up by briefly reviewing some of the testimony of the ten "friendly" former Federal Theatre employees.

Miss Huffman, in response to Thomas' question regarding what organization she represented, indicated that she was currently a member of the Committee of Relief Status Professional Theatrical Employees of the Federal Theatre Project in New York City.[9]

The witness stated that the Workers Alliance, an organization "closely allied with the Communist Party," currently dominated the Federal Theatre Project and had the cooperation and support of two of the national heads of the project, Aubrey Williams and Mrs. Hallie Flanagan.[10]

Miss Huffman described Mrs. Flanagan as a person who "was known as far back as 1927 for her communistic sympathy, if not membership" and went on to support her claim by testifying that Mrs. Flanagan had devoted 147 pages of her book *Shifting Scenes* to eulogizing the Russian theater.[11] Continuing her case, Miss Huffman presented as evidence an article written by Mrs. Flanagan for *Theatre Arts Monthly* of November, 1931. The article allegedly acknowledged Mrs. Flanagan's presence and participation in a meeting which had been called by the John Reed Club and *New Masses*.[12] Further, Miss Huffman said that Mrs. Flanagan, in cooperation with a Vassar student, coauthored a play, *Can You Hear Their Voices?*, from a story by Whittaker Chambers that was intended to picture all the countries of the world except Russia in a state of unrest and unemployment.[13]

"On one occasion when I was talking to Mrs. Flanagan, the subject came up of her being in Soviet Russia," according to Miss Huffman's testimony. She "was incensed over an article which had appeared against her in one of the magazines, and Mrs. Flanagan said that after they had treated her so royally and been so lovely to her, and produced a play which she had written for them, there was certainly no reason why she should not be sympathetic toward them."[14]

The balance of Miss Huffman's lengthy fifty-four-page testimony included her assertion that Mrs. Flanagan had appointed Elmer Rice, "a well-known leftist," as regional director of the New York City Federal Theatre Project. Mrs. Flanagan stated in 1936 "that though the project is set up for relief, our foremost consideration must be for the Federal Theatre Projects."[15] Miss Huffman concluded the case against Mrs. Flanagan by naming and describing a list of plays that she deemed to be anti-American and therefore pro-Russian and indicating just for good measure that in her judgment some of the plays took entirely too long to rehearse.

The next witness that day, William Harrison Humphrey, an actor who played Earl Browder, head of the Communist Party, U.S.A., in the Federal Theatre production of *Triple A Plowed Under*, declared that he left the play "because of the propaganda that was prevalent in the project."[16]

What precisely that propaganda was and how it was disseminated was never made clear. When Humphrey indicated he wanted to read a defense of the Earl Browder role he had played, the committee dismissed him.

On August 20, Francis M. Verdi was the first witness. He testified that 175 professional artists were dropped from the project in July, 1937, while nonprofessionals were held on. He implied that these nonprofessionals were members in many instances of the Workers Alliance and testified that Communist literature was handed out at many of the project theaters.[17]

Charles Walton followed Verdi and complained that he was unable to advance in the Federal Theatre projects because he was adamantly anti-Communist and despised anything that was un-American. Additionally, he testified, he was invited to a party by a Communist and at that party he saw colored men dancing with white girls.[18]

The next four who testified on August 20—Garland Kerr, Seymour Revzin, Sallie Saunders, and Henry Frank—followed by Wallace Stark and Leo Dawson on August 22, variously reported or corroborated the testimony of the preceding witnesses. Additionally, Miss Saunders said she had been telephoned by a Negro for a date, and the six further condemned the Federal Theatre because it had performed "pro-union plays, plays referring to Negro discrimination, and anti-Fascist plays."[19]

The last matter of moment occurred in the probe when the discussion of communications corroborating or denying charges made by the witnesses was raised. "Dies decided that to present them all would consume the entire appropriation and that the committee would have to consider later the question of people whom the committee could not afford to subpoena and who were unable to appear themselves."[20]

The case for the prosecution rested and the defense of the project by Mrs. Ellen Woodward and Mrs. Hallie Flanagan remained.

Mrs. Flanagan's natural inclination to respond immediately to the first collective public condemnation of her theater was somewhat vitiated by the WPA rule that only the Washington information division of that organization could answer press stories about those first hearings.[21]

On August 5, 1938, after Representative Thomas' first public proclamation against the Federal Theatre and before the above described hearings, Mrs. Flanagan began her efforts to cooperate with the committee by offering herself as a defense witness.[22] These efforts remained unsuccessful until December of that year when Mrs. Flanagan and Mrs. Woodward were allowed to testify in defense of the Federal Theatre Project.

Between August and December the public had been furnished stories about the project "that would hearten the most hard-boiled tabloid editor."[23] When witnesses returned to New York, they were met with reportage of their testimony from every newspaper vendor in the city. Headlines ran: "WPA Theatre Faces Probe As 'Hotbed' of Reds," "Flanagan a WPA 'Red,'" "Secretary of N.Y. Actors' Relief Group Tells House 'Hallie Is Communistic,'" and "Reds Urged 'Mixed Date,' Blonde Tells Dies Probers."[24]

Mrs. Flanagan was forced to defend herself against such lurid charges when she finally took the witness chair Tuesday, December 6, 1938.

The previous day the committee had a taste of what Mrs. Flanagan had in store for them when the assistant administrator of the WPA, Mrs. Woodward, first pleaded the case for the Federal Theatre.

Mrs. Woodward declared that she would carry the responsibility of the defense of the project, "although she herself," compared with Mrs. Flanagan, "had never been seriously attacked in the previous testimony."[25]

In contrast to the August hearings, the interrogation of Mrs. Woodward was an example of how all the relevant testimony should have been handled. Every remark that she made had to be documented, every word she said had to be clarified, and her qualifications as a witness were thoroughly examined. Mrs. Woodward was interrupted while reading her prepared accusatory statement in far more than a haphazard manner by the committee. Her cross-examination was provocative, with the committee "determined that nothing save that which could not be denied would be permitted to go into the record."[26]

Mrs. Woodward opened her testimony with an effort to present a prepared brief to the committee that defined the exact nature of the activities of the Federal Arts Projects under her jurisdiction. A debate between Chairman Dies and Congressman Thomas immediately ensued concerning the relevance of her statement to the investigation of un-American activities. Dies maintained that much latitude had been given other witnesses in the area of "things that didn't have anything to do with un-American activities. So let us be fair with her." Thomas rejoined: "But when they did talk about them, they were shut off."[27]

Nothing could have been further from the truth: In August the witnesses had ruminated over a wide diversity of subjects ranging from miscegenation to dramatic literary criticism.

Mrs. Woodward continued her statement, declaring that of the 924 plays produced in three years by the Federal Theatre, 26 had been charged by the previous witnesses as having "communistic propaganda" and none of the witnesses "could be qualified as an expert on the drama."[28]

She went on to say that the principal witness, Hazel
Huffman, "has so little theatrical experience that she could not
possibly qualify for employment on the project" and that Miss
Huffman was recently repudiated by Actors' Equity Association
in its official magazine which inveighed members against any
association with her or her committee in an article entitled
"Warning to H. Huffman & Co.: Keep Out. "[29]

Mrs. Woodward went on to name a number of artists who
had left the Federal Theatre and gone on to lucrative jobs in the
commercial theater and cinema. She also lauded Mrs. Flanagan
and documented her comments about the estimable quality of
the theater and its director with observations from such
distinguished critics as Brooks Atkinson, Archibald MacLeish,
and Burns Mantle.[30]

A long and heated debate followed concerning the mental
stability of a committee witness, the ability of Mrs. Woodward
to recognize her own signature, and her qualifications for
recognizing Communist infiltration in the agencies she headed.
Her assertion that there was something un-American in the way
in which the committee handled the charges against her project
led to an even more lively exchange.[31]

After the lunch recess Mrs. Woodward presented the next
section of her prepared statement. It dealt specifically with the
Federal Theatre Project and Mrs. Flanagan. Mrs. Woodward
attempted to refute four general accusations which had been
made directly or inferentially by previous witnesses. Number
one was "that the plays produced by the Federal Theatre are
either un-American or communistic, or subversive or propagandistic."[32]

Chairman Dies interrupted to point out that only some of the
plays produced by the project were under scrutiny, to which
Mrs. Woodward agreed. The second of the four allegations Mrs.
Woodward attempted to defend her project against was that the
audiences attending Federal Theatre plays were almost entirely
composed of Communistic or radical groups. She was once
again challenged by the chairman to give her reason for
believing that such a charge had been made against the project.
Mrs. Woodward, after a semantic joust with Dies over the
wording of the second accusation, was allowed to read the third

and, as it happened, the last point: "That a majority of the project's executives are communistic."[33]

She offered the committee a personal history sheet establishing the high qualifications of each of the directors, a record which the chair seemed uninterested in obtaining. Suddenly Representative Thomas decided it was time to discuss the twenty-six specific plays which had been introduced as being un-American in the August hearings.[34]

During the balance of the afternoon, Mrs. Woodward sought to prove the worth of the plays by producing drama critics' comments about their validity as significant theater truly representative of the times. The committee, in particular Dies and Thomas, sought to discredit the critics' evaluations by challenging their political leanings and military records, indicating that the Communist press was also favorably disposed toward the plays, implying that the critics gave good notices because the Federal Theatre advertised in their papers, debating the denotation of the word "propaganda," and finally questioning whether the democratic process was used in selecting the plays. The most interesting exchange, however, occurred when Mrs. Woodward used the phrase "capitalist press" and was immediately challenged by Thomas, Starnes, and Dies:

> MR. THOMAS: What press did you say?
> MR. STARNES: She said the capitalistic press.
> MR. THOMAS: What do you mean by the capitalistic press?
> THE CHAIRMAN: That is a communistic term.
> MRS. WOODWARD: You see, these big papers I named, some of them I have named, the Times—
> MR. THOMAS: Name some that you consider are members of the capitalistic press.
> MRS. WOODWARD: I mean papers that have big capital behind them, Mr. Congressman.
> MR. THOMAS: Just name some of them.
> MR. STARNES: Without prompting. Who is the third party here, this body?
> MRS. WOODWARD: This is Mr. Lavery.
> MR. STARNES: All right, let his name appear in the record.
> MRS. WOODWARD: The New York Times, the Herald Tribune, and many other papers where they have a lot of money.
> MR. THOMAS: And many others where they have a lot of money?

MRS. WOODWARD: Yes.

MR. THOMAS: What other ones do you have in mind?

MRS. WOODWARD: Well, papers that are capitalized—

MR. THOMAS: Do you include the Hearst papers?

MRS. WOODWARD: I think the Hearst papers have a great deal of capital behind them.

MR. THOMAS: Would you call a Scripps-Howard paper a capitalistic paper?

MRS. WOODWARD: Well, I really had reference to no particular paper.

MR. THOMAS: Would you include the New York Post, for instance?

MRS. WOODWARD: Would I include the New York Post?

MR. THOMAS: Yes.

MRS. WOODWARD: I would include any of the papers that had great capital behind them, or, perhaps, people that would be expected to be critical of what we were doing.

MR. THOMAS: Do you include the New York Post?

MRS. WOODWARD: I would not say whether I would or would not include the New York Post, because I do not know anything about their capital, but I would include some of those.

MR. THOMAS: We have the capitalistic press. What other kind of press have we got, Mrs. Woodward?

MRS. WOODWARD: I am sorry.

MR. THOMAS: We have the capitalistic press, and what other kinds of press do we have?

MRS. WOODWARD: I just used that colloquially. If you permit me, I will strike it out of the record.

MR. STARNES: Can you name any other papers in the country that are of the capitalistic press as you denominate?

MRS. WOODWARD: There are a lot of small papers in the country I would name there—

MR. STARNES: What about the New Masses, that is not a capitalistic paper, is it?

MRS. WOODWARD: I do not know much about the New Masses.

MR. STARNES: The Daily Worker is not a capitalistic paper, is it?

MRS. WOODWARD: Mr. Starnes, I probably chose my word very badly there.

MR. STARNES: I am afraid you did, Mrs. Woodward.

MRS. WOODWARD: I just mean papers that have not been very much interested in what we were doing, and would certainly come back and sock us between the eyes if we were doing communistic stuff.

MR. THOMAS: Mrs. Woodward, haven't you heard that term used by the Communist Party and the Communist press?

MRS. WOODWARD: I have just told you that I am not a member of the Communist Party.

MR. THOMAS: No one said you were; but haven't you heard this term used by the Communist Party or the Communist press?

MRS. WOODWARD: No; I do not remember reading anything in the Communist press.

MR. STARNES: If you take your two plays It Can [sic] Happen Here and Power, on page 7 of the Daily Worker, the issue of June 5, 1937, you will find out Earl Browder is quoted in his speech as stating:

> Two W.P.A. Federal Theater productions, It Can't Happen Here and Power, are among the plays which will be placed before delegates to the National Congress of American Writers this week as possibilities for the congress' award for the play of the greatest social significance produced during the year, it was announced yesterday by the League of American Writers.

MRS. WOODWARD: Do you think that is binding on us, Mr. Congressman?

MR. STARNES: No; but I am giving you the opinion of others.

THE CHAIRMAN: Now, Mrs. Woodward, before we go any further, we do not want you to be under a false impression here. Witnesses sometimes say something under stress that might be misconstrued. I am confident you have no such thing in mind. When you said capitalistic press, you just meant the big newspapers of the country?

MRS. WOODWARD: I just meant the big newspapers where they have a lot of money and can employ any kind of critics they want.

THE CHAIRMAN: You were not using it in the communistic sense or anything of the sort? I want to clear this thing up, because I am satisfied you had nothing in your mind with reference to the usual meaning of capitalistic press, which is used in all of the Communist papers, and by the speakers.

MRS. WOODWARD: I am willing to take my chance on that, Mr. Congressman, because I do not think anybody ever accused me of trying to embrace communistic language.

THE CHAIRMAN: I agree with you absolutely.

MRS. WOODWARD: Now, then, may I proceed?

THE CHAIRMAN: Yes, ma'am. [35]

The afternoon concluded with a silly and sad debate concerning the Federal Theatre children's play entitled *The Revolt of the Beavers*, a discussion that resumed the following day when Mrs. Flanagan was called to testify.

The committee had managed to establish a certain lack of credibility in Mrs. Woodward's testimony due to her admission that she had not read or seen some of the plays under discussion, including *The Revolt of the Beavers*. Hence, she was relying on the observations and criticisms of others relative to the social significance of the dramatic literature in the Federal Theatre.

Mrs. Flanagan, who had been in attendance during the afternoon questioning of Mrs. Woodward, arrived the following morning with a carefully prepared statement concerning the major allegations being debated: that the audiences, plays and personnel related to the Federal Theatre were Communistic.[36] Mrs. Flanagan summed up her statement by declaring that since the previous August witnesses before the committee had challenged her politics, she would state unequivocally that she had never been a Communist, that she was a registered Democrat, that she had never been involved with or belonged to any Red activities or organizations, and that she had contributed to many domestic periodicals and newspapers supporting her position that she "planned and directed Federal Theatre from the first as an American enterprise."[37]

Mrs. Flanagan's remarks about articles she had written were later to pique the committee, as they had Miss Huffman.

The Federal Theatre's national director described the scene that winter morning of Tuesday, December 6, 1939, in her moving memoir of the star-crossed project:

> Before me stretched two long tables in the form of a huge T. At the foot was the witness chair, at the head the members of the Committee. At long tables on either side of the T were reporters, stenographers, cameramen. The room itself, a high-walled chamber with great chandeliers, was lined with exhibits of material from the Federal Theatre and the Writers' Project; but all I could see for a moment were the faces of thousands of Federal Theatre people; clowns in the circus . . . telephone girls at the switchboards . . . actors in grubby rehearsal rooms . . .

> acrobats limbering up their routines . . . costume women busy
> making cheap stuff look expensive . . . musicians composing
> scores to bring out the best in our often oddly assembled
> orchestras . . . playwrights working on scripts with the skills of
> our actors in mind . . . carpenters, prop men, ushers. These
> were the people on trial that morning.
>
>   I was sworn in as a witness by Chairman Dies, a rangy Texan
> with a cowboy drawl and a big black cigar. I wanted to talk
> about Federal Theatre, but the Committee apparently did
> not. [38]

That the committee members did not want to talk about the
Federal Theatre was only partly true. They were interested in
Mrs. Flanagan's background and previous political sympathies,
but when they discussed facts concerning the project they were
even more demanding of specifics than they had been with Mrs.
Woodward. The committee in this sense cannot be faulted for
its efforts to obtain particulars concerning the project. But, as
distinguished from the antitheater testimony, one wonders why
at this juncture in the hearings the committee became particular. It seems somewhat mysterious that at this late date the
committee suddenly demanded facts on events observed by
witnesses when before they had allowed mass nondocumented
information in the record. Dies properly insisted that Mrs.
Flanagan had no right to refute information previously offered
by witnesses about Communist activities in the theater if she
was not present at the time of the alleged subversion. However,
what the chairman conveniently managed to overlook was the
fact "that he had already allowed thousands of pages of
testimony based principally on hearsay evidence."[39]

After being sworn in, Mrs. Flanagan, in response to Chairman
Dies' question on what the duties of her position were,
displayed her sense of the dramatic by answering, "Since
August 29, 1935, I have been concerned with combating
un-American inactivity."[40]

By this remark she meant that she had been about the
business of getting people off the relief rolls, a condition she
considered to be not historically American. The remark also
served notice on the committee that she was going to be a
somewhat more difficult witness than her predecessor, Mrs.
Woodward.

After routine questioning regarding how the project had been set up and what its purpose was, Congressman Starnes protested that getting people off relief rolls was a secondary issue to the welfare of the Federal Theatre Project. His accusation was based on Miss Huffman's testimony. Mrs. Flanagan denied the allegation, saying some 2,000 persons had been returned to private industry, and produced a letter substantiating her point that "My prime job is dealing with relief people, and always has been."[41]

Congressmen Thomas and Starnes then led Mrs. Flanagan through a recital of her background, educational achievements, and vocational chronology. Starnes brought out the fact that she was the first woman in America to receive the Guggenheim Foundation scholarship, an award which allowed her to go abroad to study the theater of Europe for fourteen months in 1926 and 1927. More important to the committee was that it put her in prolonged contact with the Russian theater. Starnes also elicited from the witness that she told the New York *Times* on September 22, 1935, that the Russian theater was "live and vital" compared with the Continental theater, which she called "a tiresome and boresome matter."[42]

Starnes was most interested to know why she found Soviet theater better than Europe's, or for that matter, America's. In answering Starnes, she stated that the Russians were gifted and temperamentally equipped for the theater. She did not deny that much of the work she had seen in the Soviet Union advocated the Soviet form of government. She further amplified her position by displaying a press-clipping book to the committee. The record of Mrs. Flanagan's hegira was embodied in a book entitled *Shifting Scenes,* and her clippings reviewing the work were from all over the world and every leading paper in the United States. She told the committeemen "that not one newspaper critic, when that book came out in 1927, not one critic picked out anything that was in that book that was subversive or un-American."[43]

A procedural argument immediately followed as to whether the witness was being responsive to the questioning. This tended to diminish the import of the book reviews Mrs. Flanagan had just cited.

Further questioning about Russia brought out that Mrs. Flanagan had returned there in 1931, that she did not see Elmer Rice there, that she had not been a member of any Russian organization, but that she had briefly served on a board that advocated the exchange of professors between Harvard and Yale and the University of Moscow. The Soviet Union phase of the interrogation was concluded.

In November, 1931, Mrs. Flanagan wrote an article for *Theatre Arts Monthly*, "A Theatre Is Born." Starnes criticized her for her attendance at a meeting where the Red banner was displayed and for her sympathetic handling of the subject matter—a workers' theater in America. Although Mrs. Flanagan dwelled heavily on the fact that it was a straight reporting job, it was this writer's impression, after a careful examination of the article, that it does indicate a less than objective evaluation of theater as a weapon in the revolutionary class struggle.

But Mrs. Flanagan properly assessed the argument when she accurately stated to Starnes that "no one picked up the point which you are trying to allege, which is, if I understand you—because the only possible point of reading it, of course, is to show that it has to do in some way with the Federal Theatre Project; and I claim that it has nothing whatsoever to do with it."[44]

Thomas followed Starnes' subsequent questioning about Christopher Marlowe's politics with a further interrogation of the witness on the subversive aspects of the children's play *The Revolt of the Beavers*.

Mrs. Flanagan responded that she was indeed disappointed that so estimable a critic as Brooks Atkinson had been disturbed by the play and additionally that the police commissioner had found the piece "poisoning the minds of youth."[45]

She pointed out that the play had not been written for Mr. Atkinson or the police commissioner and that the latter, to the best of her knowledge, had not seen the play. The play was written for children, and they enjoyed it immensely. To support this point, Mrs. Flanagan offered as evidence a survey conducted by the Department of Psychology of New York University on the Federal Theatre's children's projects and specifically *Beavers*. She sketched through the children's responses to the play:

> The play teaches us to never to be selfish; never to be selfish because you don't get anything out of it. . . . That it is better to be good than bad. That beavers have manners just like children. To teach that if you are unkind any time in your life, you will always regret it. Never to be selfish.[46]

Thomas found little poisonous subversion in the children's observations and moved on to a brief discussion of several other plays and their alleged anti-American content.

Chairman Dies concluded the questioning of Mrs. Flanagan with a lengthy and hard-hitting examination of the director vis-a-vis her views on the primary purpose in the production of plays, a rehash of the *Theatre Arts Monthly* article, profanity in the project's plays, and her specific refutation of charges made by the witnesses who testified in August. Dies made much of Mrs. Flanagan's claim that she was unable to speak personally about the politics of some 4,000 persons. Hence, he said, she was not a credible witness capable of denying the charges of Communist infiltration and activities in the project.

Mrs. Flanagan sums up her observations of that December morning:

> As the hearing broke up I thought suddenly of how much it all looked like a badly staged courtroom scene; it wasn't imposing enough for a congressional hearing on which the future of several thousand human beings depended. For any case on which the life and reputation of a single human being depended, even that of an accused murderer, we had an American system which demanded a judge trained in law, a defense lawyer, a carefully chosen jury, and above all the necessity of hearing all the evidence on both sides of the case. Yet here was a Committee which for months had been actually trying a case against Federal Theatre, trying it behind closed doors, and giving one side only to the press. Out of a project employing thousands of people from coast to coast, the Committee had chosen arbitrarily to hear ten witnesses, all from New York City, and had refused arbitrarily to hear literally hundreds of others, on and off the project, who had asked to testify. . . .

Congressman Thomas was jovial.

"You don't look like a Communist," he declared. "You look like a Republican!"

"If your Committee isn't convinced that neither I nor the Federal Theatre Project is communistic I want to come back this afternoon," I told him.

"We don't want you back," he laughed. "You're a tough witness and we're all worn out."[47]

The defense of the Federal Theatre was not exclusively in the hands of Ellen Woodward and Hallie Flanagan. In October, 1938, *TAC*, a monthly periodical of theater activities, published a statement condemning the committee's activities. *TAC*'s general proposition was that taxpayers' money, national newspaper space, and the efforts of a Congressional committee had been wasted on investigating alleged un-American activities while accepting and seemingly encouraging unauthenticated attacks on progressive groups, federal projects, government officials, trade unions, and cultural groups.

The periodical concluded its position by stating that "the very essence of our American democratic institutions is constantly subject to malicious falsification . . . therefore, that the investigation to date has failed its purpose, and urges the immediate dissolution of the Dies Committee."[48]

Hollywood and New York joined in attacking the committee, and many celebrities offered statements espousing their personal positions. A sampling of the Hollywood protest demonstrates the spectrum of opinions given for the issuing of the public statements against Dies and his colleagues:

Dashiell Hammett, chairman, Motion Picture Artists Committee:

We indignantly reject these irresponsible attacks. At this crucial time when the cooperation of all democratic forces is so essential, this attack throws a very dubious light on the character of the whole Dies investigation. It emphasizes the need for the greatest alertness on the part of all democracy-loving American people.

Lewis Milestone, director:

It seems to me that the hysteria of the Dies Committee's

investigations have only succeeded in strengthening public belief in the organizations and movements they have attacked. For myself, and for members of the motion picture industry, if our aid to democracies now victims of fascist aggression can be misinterpreted as un-American acts, then perhaps the Dies Committee has its own translation of the word democracy.

Fredric March, actor:

Every time during the last few years that I have felt impelled to protest an injustice, to cry out against man's inhumanity to man, or to espouse some social reform, I have been called a Communist. Because the founders of our country believed in justice, tolerance and the exercise of such social reform as would benefit the people at large, I insist upon the right to follow their example and still be recognized as a loyal American citizen.

John Ford, director:

May I express my whole-hearted desire to cooperate to the utmost of my ability with the Hollywood anti-Nazi League. If this be Communism, count me in.

Luise Rainer, actress:

I do not believe in the so-called revelations made by the Dies Investigating Committee. I believe their purpose is purely destructive, aimed at discrediting worthwhile peace and anti-fascist organizations, which are so much needed in these worried times.[49]

From New York a group comprised of Frances Farmer, Gertrude Niesen, Phoebe Brand, Artie Shaw, the dancer Tamiris, Robert Reed, and Michael O'Shea flew to Washington on a special chartered plane on January 16, 1939. They presented petitions signed by 200,000 persons protesting the scheduled dismissal of 1,526 WPA workers on the Federal Arts Project in New York City.[50]

TAC noted that "the daily press throughout the country, especially in Washington, where front-page pictures of the 'flying protest' were recorded for the benefit of Congress, was generous in bringing this news to the nation."[51]

The "flying pigeon protest" was another effort on the part of New York actors to save the project. In March, 1939, a group of

Broadway show girls assisted Leif Erickson, Janet Hill, and Nancy Stern in taking ninety-six carrier pigeons to Times Square, where the birds were released. Each pigeon wore a pink slip attached to its leg bearing the words: S.O.S. SAVE THE WPA.[52]

A subsequent rally at the Mansfield Theatre protesting the projected financial cuts of the arts projects brought out as speakers Frank Gilmore, president of the Associated Actors and Artistes of America; George Schreiber, artist; Jean Muir, Hollywood actress; Samuel Leibowitz, a prominent attorney; and New York Congressman Vito Marcantonio. A "living newspaper" production, *The Right to Live,* by Muni Diamond, "skillfully dramatized the achievements of the projects and provided an impressive argument for the continuation and expansion of the W.P.A."[53]

Radio, probably the most effective method of mass communication in the thirties, broadcast a number of memorable shows in an effort to save the Federal Theatre. One of the last programs was aired at midnight on Monday, June 20, 1939, and featured stars from both Hollywood and New York. Al Jolson, Dick Powell, Hugh Herbert, Gale Sondergaard, Joan Blondell, Ralph Bellamy, Walter Abel, Henry Fonda, James Cagney, and John Barrymore were among the artists endeavoring to stop Congress from cutting off appropriations for Mrs. Flanagan's project.[54] They were unsuccessful.

By act of Congress on June 30, 1939, Federal Theatre was ended. Who was responsible for this untimely death of such a seemingly worthwhile adjunct of the New Deal's Works Progress Administration? The director of the project's Play Bureau, Emmet Lavery, believed that the contributors to its demise were Congressman Dies, Congressman Clifton Woodrum (whose bill finally cut off appropriations), and the Workers Alliance (whose claim of infiltration of the project did little to help remove the "Red" cast).[55]

TAC laid the blame specifically on the shoulders of Dies. The magazine metaphorically claimed the Federal Theatre was destroyed by a "beater for the legislative hunting party gunning for the New Deal," Dies, who picked out the Federal Theatre "as the quickest game."[56]

Hallie Flanagan avoids assigning the blame for the end of her theater to any individual or group. With optimism rather than bitterness, she concluded that her theater created for citizens a medium for free expression that no other form of government could assure. In further offering people "access to the arts and tools of a civilization which they themselves are helping to make, such a theatre is at once an illustration and a bulwark of the democratic form of government."[57] Strangely pro-American words from a suspected un-American, who was a Democrat, Congregationalist, Grinnell (Iowa) College graduate out of Redfield, South Dakota.

Evaluation of the Hearings

The committee's first test of its ability to wave symbolically the Red flag above the theater artist, thereby denying him his right to work at his profession, was a stunning success.

The proper responsibility of the committee's investigation of the Federal Theatre Project should have been to determine if federal government funds were being paid to people who were consciously planning and plotting the overthrow of that government by nondemocratic means. That there were Communists and Communist sympathizers associated with the project is unquestionable in view of the social context of the times, the numbers of the personnel, and the inclination of some artists to support American liberal causes also allegedly championed by the Kremlin—e.g., civil rights, racial equality, brotherhood.

Out of nearly 1,000 plays produced during the four-year existence of the project, some were debatable on political grounds. But the contention of the committee that 26 Federal Theatre plays were un-American, anticapitalist, and therefore pro-Communist was never proved. Mrs. Flanagan's purported Russian sympathies were no more than one artist's respect for another's creation, regardless of the political system that tolerated that creativity.

On August 11, 1938, Mrs. Flanagan offered herself and her six regional policy directors to the committee in an effort to refute the sensational charges about Communism in the project made public the previous month by Representative Thomas. She was denied this opportunity by Chairman Dies.

Later that August, the ten friendly witnesses ruminated over a series of accusations about the Federal Theatre, few of which proved Communist domination of the project and none of which was challenged by the committee. Contrary to Chairman Dies' public utterances, communications from potential witnesses who might appear and challenge the credibility of the ten friendly witnesses were discounted by him as financially not feasible. His reasoning was that the monies allotted to the committee for its work were limited. In its coverage of the committee's investigation, the predominantly Republican anti-New Deal press gave the charges of Communist infiltration of the project inflated attention.

One is inclined to forgive Representative Starnes for his limited knowledge of Elizabethan playwrights, because he consistently tried to keep the investigation centered on Communism in the Federal Theatre.

Congressman Thomas' assertion that the plays produced by the Federal Theatre were propaganda for the Democratic administration was absurd. Quite the opposite was true. All the plays discussed by the ten friendly witnesses and Mrs. Woodward and Mrs. Flanagan were critical attacks on the failure of the New Deal to be responsive to the dire human needs and problems that beset America in the thirties.

Further, Thomas failed to prove that the project was part of a Communist organization and that radicals were the rule rather than the exception. He also failed to make good on his promise to demand the resignation of Federal Theatre officials.

The long time lapse between the charges made in August and the December defense of those charges indicated the administration's desire to play politics with the project. Had Washington allowed Mrs. Flanagan to answer the press stories immediately after their publication in August, the Federal Theatre might have had a longer existence.

With the New Deal suffering an economic recession and

setbacks in the 1938 Congressional elections, the elimination of federally sponsored show business was an overt appeasement to the foes of the Democratic administration.

The ability of the committee to investigate fairly was amply demonstrated by its interrogation of Mrs. Woodward and Mrs. Flanagan. That same ability was appallingly absent in the interrogation of the procommittee witnesses in August.

Representative Thomas' cavalier attitude, verbalized in his off-the-record remark about Mrs. Flanagan's looking more like a Republican than a Communist, suggests that his serious concern with Communism in the Federal Theatre may have been limited to self-serving publicity for himself and the committee. This awareness of the publicity value of Red probes was not limited to the times or the House of Representatives. Years later, Richard Rovere was to charge America's foremost hunter of Reds, Senator Joseph McCarthy, with a similar disinterest in Communism—unless it served his mania for publicity.[58]

The committee's later practice of including in its printed records only briefs friendly to its work was established when Mrs. Flanagan's carefully prepared statement, refuting charges made against her theater, failed to appear in the transcripts of the proceedings, despite the promise of the hearing's secretary.

Subsequently, more than 500 copies of her brief were sent to the office of WPA director of information David Niles for distribution to the members of Congress. He assured her the statements would be disseminated to the representatives. This was never done.[59]

Chairman Martin Dies stated publicly that he hoped to direct the committee's inquiries in a manner that would avoid publicity.[60] Slightly more than a month later, J. Parnell Thomas made public his damning accusations against Mrs. Flanagan's theater. For the remainder of that year the Dies committee received more press attention than any other organization in the country.[61]

Sallie Saunders' professed abhorrence at being telephoned by a Negro asking her for a date was but one example of the committee's failure to challenge the relevance of information to its inquiry into Communism in the project. The omission of the challenge strengthened the conservative charge that miscegenation was a plot fostered by the CP and the New Deal that would result in a breakdown of American traditions.

Although the majority of the press favored the committee's work, some decried its activities as another of the lunatic "Red hunts" that the country was prone to engage in from time to time.[62]

Paul Edwards, the New York Arts Projects administrator, made an exhaustive survey of the August witnesses' Federal Theatre personnel records. His findings would give one reason to challenge the worth of their testimony. Edwards revealed that nearly all of them were disgruntled employees who had been refused promotion by himself or Mrs. Flanagan.[63]

Shortly after the witnesses appeared in August, Dies charged that they had their wages docked in retaliation for their procommittee testimony.[64] This was true in the sense that when they traveled to Washington to testify they were not paid for the time they spent away from the project. But the Dies charge implied that Communists were responsible for the docking of the wages of the testifying anti-Communists, and so the case against the theater continued to grow in the public consciousness.

In November, 1938, Dies demanded the resignations of New Dealers Harold Ickes, Harry Hopkins, and Frances Perkins, claiming that their positions in the government impeded America's economic recovery. He charged that the three had associates who were Socialists, Communists, and "crack-pots."[65]

Mrs. Woodward and Mrs. Flanagan thus had reason to believe that anyone making such blatant accusatory statements against important public officials would show little mercy to any less significant figures in the Roosevelt administration. In the light of this knowledge, they both failed to arm themselves with sufficient data to present the best possible defense of their case. Mrs. Woodward's effort to condemn the witnesses in August as not being artistically qualified to testify about the project was properly challenged by the committee. Artistic training was not a requirement for recognizing subversion.

Mrs. Woodward, in her attempt to read favorable reviews of the so-called un-American plays, failed to defend the project

against the charges that the plays spread Communist doctrine.
She merely testified that they were reviewed as artistically
successful, not necessarily politically safe. She also was unable
to prove that she was familiar with all the plays or the
backgrounds of the authors or to produce evidence that the
people who bought tickets to the theater were not the radicals
Hazel Huffman charged them with being. The committee
refused to let her complete her opening statement; it also failed
to publish her remarks in its record of the hearings, as Dies had
promised.[66]

That Mrs. Flanagan had never seen Communist literature
distributed on the project did not mean that it had not
happened. Her testimony that she would have fired those who
attempted such an undertaking had she caught them hardly
satisfied the committee's need for proof of the pure American
nature of the project.

Though the director claimed her earlier sympathetic writings
on Russian theater and the American proletariat theater had no
influence on her direction of the Federal Theatre, the implication of her left leanings hampered her defense of the project.

It was the image of her political character that was also on
trial. The committee made the most of it.

Martin Dies seemed unable to tolerate Mrs. Flanagan's belief
that civil and social inequities should be material for drama—
even though he agreed they existed.

In conclusion, if the entire transcript of her testimony had
been front-page news, it would have shown her unable to refute
such charges made against the project as the distribution of
Communist literature, covert pressures exercised by such
Communist-dominated organizations as the Workers Alliance,
and her own left-of-center writings.[67]

This was more than sufficient evidence to condemn her in the
eyes of the 75 percent of the public that agreed with the work
of the committee.[68]

Dies' contention that the Communist Party did dominate the
Workers Alliance appears correct.[69] His charge that employment in the Federal Theatre was in some instances related to
membership in the Workers Alliance also was sound.[70]

Both the CP and Mrs. Flanagan were politically naïve. The

support of the Federal Theatre by the Communist press negated any possible Red dominance of the project. If the party wanted to infiltrate the project subtly, it would have served its purposes better to be less exuberant and complimentary about the theater's productions. Mrs. Flanagan's decision to use federal subsidies to produce plays condemning her subsidizer is another example of an impolitic decision that might have been avoided by less idealism or more political pragmatism.

The policy of exposure of evidence of Communist associations without allowing the accused refutation of the evidence had been established. It was a policy that would wreck hundreds of lives in the postwar period as insidiously as it returned to the relief rolls more than 8,000 living-theater artists in the summer of 1939.

Throughout the first twenty years of the committee's existence, investigations of the entertainment world were always a guarantee of maximum publicity for the chairman. Martin Dies, more remembered for his political pragmatism than his idealism, discovered this in 1938, and in 1947, J. Parnell Thomas, then chairman of the committee, began his tumultuous investigation of the Red menace in the most publicity-generating area of the entertainment world—Hollywood.

FOOTNOTES

1. U.S. Congress, House Committee on Un-American Activities, *Investigation of Un-American Propaganda Activities in the U.S.*, Hearings, Seventy-fifth Congress, Third Session, Vol. IV, pp. 2857-58. Hereinafter cited as *Propaganda Hearings*.
2. New York *Times*, July 27, 1938.
3. *Ibid.*, July 28, 1938.
4. *Ibid.*, August 10, 1938.
5. Jane DeHart Mathews, *The Federal Theatre, 1935-1939, Plays, Relief, and Politics* (Princeton, N.J., Princeton University Press, 1967), pp. 199-200.
6. *Ibid.*, p. 200.
7. *Ibid.*, p. 201.
8. August R. Ogden, *The Dies Committee*, 2d rev. ed. (Washington, D.C., The Catholic University of America Press, 1945), p. 63.
9. *Propaganda Hearings*, Vol. I, p. 775.
10. *Ibid.*, pp. 776-77.
11. *Ibid.*, p. 777.
12. *Ibid.*
13. *Ibid.*, p. 778.
14. *Ibid.*, p. 780.

15. *Ibid.*, p. 781.
16. *Ibid.*, p. 829.
17. *Ibid.*, pp. 833-39.
18. *Ibid.*, pp. 839-45.
19. Ogden, *op. cit.*, p. 63.
20. *Ibid.*
21. Hallie Flanagan, *Arena: the History of the Federal Theatre* (New York, Benjamin Blom, Inc., 1965), p. 335.
22. *Ibid.*, pp. 336-37.
23. Mathews, *op. cit.*, p. 205.
24. *Ibid.*
25. Ogden, *op. cit.*, p. 94.
26. *Ibid.*, pp. 94-95.
27. *Propaganda Hearings*, Vol. IV, p. 2733.
28. *Ibid.*, p. 2734.
29. *Ibid.*, pp. 2734-35.
30. *Ibid.*, p. 2736.
31. *Ibid.*, pp. 2750-89.
32. *Ibid.*, p. 2791.
33. *Ibid.*, p. 2793.
34. *Ibid.*, p. 2795.
35. *Ibid.*, pp. 2807-9.
36. Flanagan, *op. cit.*, p. 338.
37. *Ibid.*, p. 339.
38. *Ibid.*, p. 340.
39. Ogden, *op. cit.*, pp. 95-96.
40. *Propaganda Hearings*, Vol. IV, p. 2839.
41. *Ibid.*, p. 2842.
42. *Ibid.*, p. 2843.
43. *Ibid.*, p. 2845.
44. *Ibid.*, p. 2853-54.
45. *Ibid.*, p. 2859.
46. *Ibid.*
47. Flanagan, *op. cit.*, pp. 345-46.
48. *TAC*, October, 1938, p. 3.
49. *Ibid.*
50. *TAC*, February, 1939, p. 23.
51. *Ibid.*
52. *TAC*, March, 1939, p. 24.
53. *Ibid.*
54. *TAC*, July, 1939, p. 9.
55. Emmet Lavery, "Who Killed Federal Theatre?" *The Commonweal*, August 4, 1939, p. 351.
56. *TAC*, July, 1939, pp. 6-7.
57. Flanagan, *op. cit.*, p. 373.

58. Richard Rovere, *Senator Joe McCarthy* (New York, Harcourt, Brace & Co., 1959), p. 47. Most of Rovere's book supports this charge.

59. Flanagan, *op. cit.*, p. 346.

60. New York *Times*, June 19, 1938.

61. Mathews, *op. cit.*, p. 224.

62. St. Louis *Post-Dispatch*, August 17, 1938.

63. Mathews, *op. cit.*, p. 206.

64. New York *Times*, September 1, 1938.

65. *Ibid.*, November 25, 1938.

66. *Propaganda Hearings*, Vol. IV, pp. 2729-2730.

67. *Ibid.*, pp. 2838-85.

68. Washington *Post*, December 11, 1938, Sec. III, p. 1.

69. Irving Howe and Lewis Coser, *The American Communist Party, 1919-1957* (Boston, Beacon Press, 1957), p. 197.

70. New York *Times*, February 14, 1938.

Chapter III

J. Parnell Thomas' 1947 Investigation of Communist Infiltration in the Motion Picture Industry

LOUIS B. Mayer, head of Metro-Goldwyn-Mayer studios in 1947, is said to have drawn an analogy between the royal family and the personalities of the motion picture business. As the British people revered their kings and queens, Americans, according to Mayer, satisfied their deep human impulse to venerate by worshiping movie stars.[1]

Blacklisted writer Gordon Kahn believed that the analogy implied that "Hollywood Glamor . . . included the entire personnel of the studios, not just the stars whose images graced the household shrines of America."[2]

That this analogy has validity is open to scholarly debate, but if it is accepted by the reader in the most general of interpretations, then it is proper to add that it is "an essential tradition of constitutional monarchy that the reigning sovereigns be above politics and refrain from any significant expression of opinion whatsoever."[3]

Some Hollywood folk, according to the committee, were not above politics or opinions, and Chairman J. Parnell Thomas sought in 1947 to prove this contention.

Description of the Hearings

At nine o'clock in the morning, Monday, October 20, 1947,

the House Committee on Un-American Activities opened its much publicized and controversial hearings concerning Communist infiltration of the motion picture industry.

The first public postwar investigation of persons in the entertainment world occurred in the old House office building in Washington, D.C. More than one hundred news-gathering agencies from America and the rest of the world occupied the 40- by 80-foot room. The three major American radio networks were on hand. Eleven newsreel and television cameras were situated above the witness table. Some of the 300 spectator seats were occupied by the most well-known figures of the period. Many of the notables wore sunglasses, not for the purpose of incognizance but to protect their eyes from the harsh lighting necessitated by the cameras. Uniformed police were on guard outside the room to "manage the crowd of the curious and the ecstatic who sought to touch or at least to see a legendary figure from the magic mecca."[4]

From the moguls to the mummers, most of the friendly witnesses were indeed almost legendary figures—if not forever, at least in their own time.

Among the more illustrious in the spectrum of witnesses summoned by the committee to support its contention that there was Communist infiltration of the motion picture industry were Jack L. Warner, of the famous brothers Warner; Robert Taylor, the noted MGM profile; Louis Burt Mayer, production chief of Taylor's studio; Adolphe Menjou, a dapper "self-made expert on communism, Stalinism, Fabianism, Socialism and Marxism"[5] ; Thomas (Leo) McCarey, director of *Going My Way*; Robert Montgomery, actor and later speech writer and adviser to President Dwight Eisenhower; Walter E. (Walt) Disney, creator of Mickey Mouse; George L. Murphy, actor-dancer and later United States Senator from California; Ronald Reagan, actor and later Republican Presidential aspirant and governor of California; Lela Rogers, mother of actress Ginger Rogers; superstar Gary Cooper; and Ayn Rand, author of *The Fountainhead* and later the principal philosopher of Objectivism.[6]

Conducting the investigation was a subcommittee of the

House Committee on Un-American Activities. Its members were Representatives John McDowell of Pennsylvania, J. Parnell Thomas of New Jersey, chairman, Richard B. Vail of Illinois, John S. Wood of Georgia, and Richard M. Nixon of California.[7]

From Monday to Friday, October 20 to October 25, 1947, the members heard testimony from twenty-four friendly witnesses who variously asserted their patriotism and pleased the committee by indicating their awareness of the Communist menace in the film capital of the world.

The twelve quasi-legendary figures previously mentioned, ten men and two women, represented a fair cross section of the committee's friendly witnesses, and their testimony is briefly summarized here. Special attention is given to testimony that cites names of suspected Communists.

Jack L. Warner, accompanied by his counsel, Paul V. McNutt, former governor of Indiana and national commander of the American Legion, was the first witness of the day.[8]

Warner requested that he be allowed to read a statement and agreed that "similar to a degree, more or less," it was the same statement he had read to the committee in Los Angeles in the spring of 1947.[9] He was allowed to read the statement after Chairman Thomas declared it was pertinent to the inquiry.

Thomas' decision on pertinence, as we shall also observe with the unfriendly witnesses, seemed to revolve more around whether an opening statement was flattering to the committee's investigation than its relevance as information or evidence.

Warner was most complimentary to the committee, asserting: "It is a privilege to appear again before this committee to help as much as I can in facilitating its work."[10]

Robert E. Stripling, chief investigator for the committee, reminded Warner that in earlier testimony before the committee he had listed individuals he thought were injecting "un-American ideas" into scripts. He asked the producer if he still agreed that these writers were suspect. Warner declared he had reassessed the matter and felt that he would eliminate Guy Endore, Sheridan Gibney, and the twin brothers Julius and Philip Epstein from his subversive list, a list which originally included Alvah Bessie, Gordon Kahn, Howard Koch, Ring W.

Lardner, Jr., Emmet G. Lavery, John Howard Lawson, Albert Maltz, Robert Rossen, Irwin Shaw, Dalton Trumbo, John Wexley, and Clifford Odets.[11]

On May 15, 1947, when he offered his original list of names, Warner also stated that "Arthur Miller and Elia Kazan worked on Broadway where, he implied, they practiced some form of subversion."[12]

In summing up his position as the chief of production for a major film studio, Warner agreed with Congressman Vail that writers and actors with definite Communistic leanings should be eliminated from the industry, but he would never be guilty of trying individually or in association with others "to deprive a man of a livelihood because of his political beliefs."[13] He was to refute this position before the end of the year.

Spangler Arlington Brough, known to millions of adoring fans as Robert Taylor, denied that in his "preview" hearing in Hollywood in the spring he had said that he had been "forced" to play in *Song of Russia* by an emissary from President Roosevelt.[14]

On October 22, when the committee questioned Taylor about Communists in the Screen Actors Guild, the actor replied: "I can name a few who seem to sort of disrupt things once in awhile." The star named Howard da Silva and Karen Morley as contributing to a disruptive influence at guild meetings, but as to whether or not they were Communists he was not sure.[15]

Stripling asked if Taylor was acquainted with any writers whom he considered to be Communists or who followed the party line. He answered: "I know one gentleman employed at the studio at which I am employed, Mr. Lester Cole, who is reputedly a Communist. I would not know personally."[16] The exchange continued:

> MR. STRIPLING: Would you say that after Pearl Harbor the activities of the Communists in the motion-picture industry increased or decreased?
>
> MR. TAYLOR: I think quite obviously it must have increased. The ground for their work in this country was obviously more fertile. I would say "yes"; it did definitely increase following Pearl Harbor.

MR. STRIPLING: Mr. Taylor, have you ever joined any Communist-front organization?

MR. TAYLOR: No, sir; believe me.

MR. STRIPLING: Have you ever played in any picture with people whom you had any doubts about as to their loyalty to the Government?

MR. TAYLOR: Not that I know of. I have never worked with anyone knowingly who is a Communist. Moreover, I shall never work with anyone who is a Communist.

MR. STRIPLING: You would refuse to act in a picture in which a person whom you considered to be a Communist was also cast; is that correct?

MR. TAYLOR: I most assuredly would and I would not even have to know that he was a Communist. This may sound biased; however, if I were suspicious of a person being a Communist with whom I was scheduled to work, I am afraid it would have to be him or me, because life is a little too short to be around people who annoy me as much as these fellow travelers and Communists do.

MR. STRIPLING: You definitely consider them to be a bad influence upon the industry?

MR. TAYLOR: I certainly do; yes, sir.

MR. STRIPLING: They are a rotten apple in the barrel?

MR. TAYLOR: To me they are and I further believe that 99.9 percent of the people in the motion-picture industry feel exactly as I do.

MR. STRIPLING: What do you think would be the best way to approach the problem of ridding the industry of the Communists who are now entrenched therein?

MR. TAYLOR: Well, sir, if I were given the responsibility of getting rid of them I would love nothing better than to fire every last one of them and never let them work in a studio or in Hollywood again. However, that is not my position.

If I were producing a picture on my own and I hope I never do—but if I were, I would not have one of them within 100 miles of me or the studio or the script. I am sure the producers in Hollywood are faced with a slightly different problem. They are heads of an industry and as heads of an industry they might be slightly more judicial than I, as an individual, would be.

I believe firmly that the producers, the heads of the studios in Hollywood, would be and are more than willing to do everything they can to rid Hollywood of Communists and fellow travelers.

I think if given the tools with which to work—specifically, some sort of national legislation or an attitude on the part of

the Government as such which would provide them with the
weapons for getting rid of these people—I have no doubt
personally but what they would be gone in very short order.

MR. STRIPLING: Mr. Taylor, do you consider that the motion
picture primarily is a vehicle of entertainment and not of
propaganda?

MR. TAYLOR: I certainly do. I think it is the primary job of
the motion-picture industry to entertain; nothing more,
nothing less.[17]

Ironically, the authors of the *The High Wall*, the film Taylor
had just completed, were Sydney Boehm and—Lester Cole![18]

Louis Burt Mayer acknowledged that he was born in Russia, a
bit of information that "brought a score or more of random
spectators forward in their seats."[19] On October 20, Mayer,
after reading a prepared statement complimenting the work of
the committee and suggesting that it recommend to Congress
legislation regulating the employment of Communists in private
industry, attempted to establish MGM's patriotism by naming
two films produced to aid the war effort, *Joe Smith, American*
and *Mrs. Miniver.*[20]

In answer to the question: Were there any Communists at
MGM? Mayer responded that "they" had mentioned two or
three writers whom "they" had marked as Communists.[21] It
was never made clear who "they" were, but the production
chief indicated the names of the writers who were suspect:
Lester Cole, Dalton Trumbo, and Donald Ogden Stewart.[22]

Representative Vail was interested to know why people
earning "astronomical" salaries in the studios should wish to
denigrate the system that afforded them such affluence. The
Culver City lay analyst answered: "My own opinion is, Mr.
Congressman, which I have expressed many times in discussion,
I think they are cracked. It can't be otherwise."[23] Satisfied
with this diagnosis, Vail had no more questions.

Adolphe Menjou, "the screen's best-dressed mummer," told
the committee on October 21 that he had read more than 150
books on one subject, "an oriental tyranny, a Kremlin-
dominated conspiracy, Russia,"[24] and if other people would
only read and read and read they would wake up and no longer
be victims or innocent dupes of the Moscow politburo.[25]

MR. STRIPLING: Are you a member of the Screen Actors Guild?

MR. MENJOU: Yes, sir; I am.

MR. STRIPLING: Have you ever noticed any effort on the part of Communist individuals to gain influence in the Screen Actors Guild?

MR. MENJOU: I don't know any members of the Screen Actors Guild who are members of the Communist Party. I have never seen their cards. I am a firm believer that the Communist Party in the United States is a direct branch of the Comintern—which, in my opinion, has never been dissolved—direct from Moscow. It is an oriental tyranny, a Kremlin-dominated conspiracy, and it is against the interests of the people to admit that they are Communists. Very few admit it.

MR. STRIPLING: Do you have your very definite suspicions about some members of the Screen Actors Guild?

MR. MENJOU: I know a great many people who act an awful lot like Communists.

MR. STRIPLING: As an actor, Mr. Menjou, could you tell the committee whether or not an actor in a picture could portray a scene which would in effect serve as propaganda for communism or any other un-American purpose?

MR. MENJOU: Oh, yes. I believe that under certain circumstances a communistic director, a communistic writer, or a communistic actor, even if he were under orders from the head of the studio not to inject communism or un-Americanism or subversion into pictures, could easily subvert that order, under the proper circumstances, by a look, by an inflection, by a change in the voice. I think it could be easily done. I have never seen it done, but I think it could be done.

MR. STRIPLING: You don't know of any examples?

MR. MENJOU: I cannot think of one at the moment. No, sir.

MR. STRIPLING: Do you know Mr. John Cromwell?

MR. MENJOU: Yes, sir.

MR. STRIPLING: He was identified before the committee yesterday by Mr. Sam Wood as being one who sought to put the Screen Directors Guild into the Red river. Do you consider Mr. Cromwell to be a Communist?

MR. MENJOU: I don't know whether he is a Communist or not.

MR. STRIPLING: Does he act like one?

MR. MENJOU: In my opinion, he acts an awful lot like one.[26]

Citing other individuals, the self-proclaimed Soviet expert named John Howard Lawson and Herbert Sorrell, head of the

Conference of Studio Unions, as persons he believed or had heard were Communists.[27]

Menjou concluded his testimony with a panegyric that brought loud applause from his audience:

> I believe America should arm to the teeth. I believe in universal military training. I attended Culver Military Academy during the last war and enlisted as a private. Due to my military training I was soon made an officer and it taught me a great many things. I believe if I was told to swim the Mississippi River I would learn how to swim. Every young man should have military training. There is no better thing for a young man than military training for his discipline, for his manhood, for his courage, and for love of his country. I know it was good for me. It never did me any harm.[28]

The committee agreed. There were no more questions.

Unlike the previously mentioned witnesses, director Thomas (Leo) McCarey did not offer the committee any names of persons in the motion picture industry who were potential Communist infiltrators. Thomas asked the director the two key questions consistently posed to the friendlies:

> THE CHAIRMAN: Do you believe the industry should produce anti-Communist films in order to show the American people the dangers and the intrigue of the Communist Party here in the United States?
>
> MR. McCAREY: Well, Mr. Thomas, that is quite a question. I think basically the screen—I like to feel it is an art. I don't think pictures should be made that have much more than what the medium stands for. It is a great art. Pictures should be entertainment. I think that because of the number of people in all lands who see our pictures. I believe it only tends toward causing more enmity if we are partisan and take any sides in our pictures.
>
> For instance, Mr. Disney with his Donald Duck. Donald Duck is a great hero. The Three Little Pigs was very successful and the world is trying to tell us they want entertainment on the screen.
>
> THE CHAIRMAN: In other words, you believe we would be doing the same thing—
>
> MR. McCAREY: We would bring on more bitterness, I think.
>
> THE CHAIRMAN: We would be doing the same thing Soviet Russia is doing?

MR. McCAREY: That is right.

THE CHAIRMAN: The other question is with reference to outlawing the Communist Party. We have two bills before our committee, either one of which if passed would outlaw the Communist Party in the United States just the same as it is outlawed in Canada and outlawed in some South American countries.

As one of the leaders or spokesmen of your profession, spokesman for a great many people, do you believe the Congress should outlaw the Communist Party in the United States?

MR. McCAREY: I definitely do because I feel the party is not an American party. I think that within the confines of the United States we can have all the parties we want and have healthy debate on any subject for the betterment of all peoples but I don't think we should align ourselves with any foreign party.

THE CHAIRMAN: In other words, you think an American Communist is the agent of a foreign government?

MR. McCAREY: I definitely do and I hope something is done about it because at this time it is a very dangerous thing. It seems like in a way some people accuse us of being afraid of mentioning names. I would be very happy to mention names if we had a law with some teeth in it so that under the heading of—call it what you will; I am not a legislator and I am not a law maker—but somewhere along the line under the subdivision of "Treason," subdivision "D," or something like that, should label these people as truly un-American.

THE CHAIRMAN: So that if there was a law on the books making the Communist Party illegal you would not hesitate to name the persons whom you know and believe to be Communists?

MR. McCAREY: That is right.[29]

In response to Stripling's question about what pictures he had produced and directed, McCarey indicated:

Ruggles of Red Gap, the Awful Truth, Love Affair, Going My Way, and The Bells of St. Marys.

MR. STRIPLING: Were Going My Way and The Bells of St. Marys two of the most popular pictures which you have produced in recent years, according to the box office?

MR. McCAREY: According to the box office, they were both very successful.

MR. STRIPLING: They did very well?

MR. McCAREY: Yes, sir.

MR. STRIPLING: How did they do in Russia?

MR. McCAREY: We haven't received one ruble from Russia on either picture.

MR. STRIPLING: What is the trouble?

MR. McCAREY: Well, I think I have a character in there that they do not like.

MR. STRIPLING: Bing Crosby?

MR. McCAREY: No; God.[30]

Robert Montgomery, an actor probably most remembered for his performance as the insane killer Danny in *Night Must Fall* and a former president of the Screen Actors Guild, appeared on October 23 and read a resolution issued by the guild in 1946. The resolution had been introduced by Montgomery and its concluding sentence pleased the committee: "The guild in addition states that it has in the past, does in the present, and will in the future rigorously oppose by every power which is within its legal rights, any real Fascist or Communist influence in the motion-picture industry or in the ranks of labor."[31]

In response to Stripling's questions on Communist attempts to inject Red propaganda into scripts and his general opinion regarding Communism, Montgomery replied:

> I have heard these people [Communists] referred to as the lunatic fringe, and I quite agree with that definition. However, I do not think any of them would be crazy enough to try to inject Communist propaganda into a picture I had anything to do with . . . .
>
> Mr. Chairman, in common with millions of other men in this country in 1939 and 1940 I gave up my job to fight against a totalitarianism which was called fascism. I am quite willing to give it up again to fight against a totalitarianism called communism.[32]

There was applause.

Walter E. Disney testified on October 24 that films could be used successfully as propaganda; he cited six that were made by his studio that dealt with the Treasury Department, Air Power, and Hitler. He was for the first two and against the latter.[33]

The studio head said that there had been a strike at his studio, a strike that in Disney's opinion was instigated by the Communist Party. Disney identified Herbert K. Sorrell as the leader of the group initiating the alleged party takeover.[34]

Disney named David Hilberman, William Pomerance, and Maurice Howard as persons who, in his opinion, were Communists. Additionally, he averred that the League of Women Voters, the *People's World*, the *Daily Worker*, and "PM Magazine [sic] in New York" had smeared him and his pictures. That smear, according to Disney, also occurred in "Commie periodicals" in South America and throughout the world. In a subsequent letter to the committee, Disney corrected his allegation to read League of Women Shoppers, not League of Women Voters. His feelings about the CP remained uncorrected:

MR. SMITH: What is your personal opinion of the Communist Party, Mr. Disney, as to whether or not it is a political party?

MR. DISNEY: Well, I don't believe it is a political party. I believe it is an un-American thing. The thing that I resent the most is that they are able to get into these unions, take them over, and represent to the world that a group of people that are in my plant, that I know are good, 100-percent Americans, are trapped by this group, and they are represented to the world as supporting all of those ideologies, and it is not so, and I feel that they really ought to be smoked out and shown up for what they are, so that all of the good, free causes in this country, all the liberalisms that really are American, can go out without the taint of communism. That is my sincere feeling on it.

MR. SMITH: Do you feel that there is a threat of communism in the motion-picture industry?

MR. DISNEY: Yes, there is, and there are many reasons why they would like to take it over or get in and control it, or disrupt it, but I don't think they have gotten very far, and I think the industry is made up of good Americans just like in my plant, good, solid Americans.[35]

George L. Murphy, a former two-term president of the Screen Actors Guild and later Republican Senator from California, identified himself as an actor-dancer on October 23. He testified that to the best of his knowledge he had never

joined any subversive groups or organizations and that he was
"chairman of a political group lately formed in Hollywood.
Among the things it hopes to do is fight against communism
and fascism." The performer went on to assert his patriotism:

> MR. SMITH: Have you ever been called upon to give lines in a
> picture which you felt were communistic?
>
> MR. MURPHY: No; I have not.
>
> MR. SMITH: Supposing you were called upon to give such
> lines, what would be your position?
>
> MR. MURPHY: I am afraid, as they say in the theater, I would
> dry up, I wouldn't read the lines, nor would I play the part if
> I consider the part to be one that spread Communist
> propaganda.
>
> MR. SMITH: Do you feel that if things continue as they are the
> Communists might gain enough strength to control the
> industry?
>
> MR. MURPHY: There is much discussion about Communist
> propaganda. I think all who read the newspapers and the
> columns realize that the Communist Party in the past has
> appeared to be in no particular hurry about achieving its
> ends. I think to look for direct Communist propaganda in
> pictures at this particular moment might be a mistake. I
> think we should be well on our guard that the infiltration
> maybe is taking place at this time so that after the
> infiltration has reached a saturation point later on the screen
> may be used in a manner inimical to the best interests of our
> country.
>
> MR. SMITH: Do you believe the Communist Party is an agency
> of a foreign enemy?
>
> MR. MURPHY: I have no way of proving this, but from the
> reading that I have done, and listening to the radio, I believe
> that the Communist Party members are agents of a foreign
> country.[36]

Murphy indicated that if the government of the United States
decided that the Communist Party was taking orders from a
foreign government, the party could be considered as acting as
an agent of a foreign government and not as an American
political party. If this differentiation were made public to the
people, he concluded, "the great American public would tell the
Congress of the United States very quickly and without
question what action they think should be taken."[37]

The actor-dancer informed the panel he had been called a Fascist, but he made it clear that he did not mind the cognomen because he felt the time had come when anyone who disagreed with a Communist was labeled a Fascist, and he certainly disagreed.[38]

He stepped down and made way for a future Republican Presidential contender and governor of California, Ronald Reagan. Reagan at the time of his testimony before the committee on October 23 was the president of the Screen Actors Guild and a liberal Democrat given to quoting Thomas Jefferson.[39]

The actor explained how he had been led into sponsoring a drive to raise money for the All-Nations Hospital in Los Angeles and how he had subsequently found out that a recital for the hospital was under the auspices of the Joint Anti-Fascist Refugee Committee and that the "principal speaker was Emil Lustig, Robert Burman took up a collection, and the remnants of the Abraham Lincoln Brigade were paraded to the platform." He added that he did not see one mention of the hospital in the newspaper account he had read. Reagan acknowledged that solid information existed regarding CP members in the actors union:

> MR. STRIPLING: As a member of the board of directors, as president of the Screen Actors Guild, and as an active member, have you at any time observed or noted within the organization a clique of either Communists or Fascists who were attempting to exert influence or pressure on the guild?
>
> MR. REAGAN: Well, sir, my testimony must be very similar to that of Mr. Murphy and Mr. Montgomery. There has been a small group within the Screen Actors Guild which has consistently opposed the policy of the guild board and officers of the guild, as evidenced by the vote on various issues. That small clique referred to has been suspected of more or less following the tactics that we associate with the Communist Party.
>
> MR. STRIPLING: Would you refer to them as a disruptive influence within the guild?
>
> MR. REAGAN: I would say that at times they have attempted to be a disruptive influence.
>
> MR. STRIPLING: You have no knowledge yourself as to

whether or not any of them are members of the Communist
Party?

MR. REAGAN: No, sir; I have no investigative force, or
anything, and I do not know.

MR. STRIPLING: Has it ever been reported to you that certain
members of the guild were Communists?

MR. REAGAN: Yes, sir; I have heard different discussions and
some of them tagged as Communists.

MR. STRIPLING: Have you ever heard that from any reliable
source?

MR. REAGAN: Well, I considered the source as reliable at the
time.[40]

After Richard M. Nixon, his future opponent for the 1968
Republican Presidential nomination, said that he had no
questions, Reagan summed up his 1947 political position about
Communism and democracy:

> I detest, I abhor their [the Communists'] philosophy, but I
> detest more than that their tactics, which are those of the fifth
> column, and are dishonest, but at the same time I never as a
> citizen want to see our country become urged, by either fear or
> resentment of this group, that we ever compromise with any of
> our democratic principles through that fear or resentment. I
> think democracy can do it.[41]

Gordon Kahn noted that the committee acted with "Bourbon punctilio toward the two 'friendly ladies' whom it had
subpoenaed—Miss Ayn Rand and Mrs. Lela Rogers. Neither was
asked to tell her age."[42]

Mrs. Rogers told the committee on October 24 that she was
one of the original members of the Motion Picture Alliance for
the Preservation of American Ideals and that in her capacity as a
script reader for RKO Studios she was able to render assess-
ments of movie material and its value as Communist propaganda. She proudly stated that *None but the Lonely Heart*,
starring Cary Grant and written and directed by Clifford Odets,
"lent itself to propaganda, particularly in the hands of a
Communist." The person she made reference to was Odets,
whom she had heard was identified January 8, 1936, by
columnist O. O. McIntyre as a member of the Communist Party.

She had never seen the charge denied. Mrs. Rogers was less
certain of how Odets got his Red propaganda into one of his
own pictures:

> MR. McDOWELL: Mrs. Rogers, you have devoted many years
> to the reading of manuscripts and the study of pictures in
> general. You make the statement here that there was Com-
> munist propaganda, as you detected it, in this film None But
> the Lonely Heart. I haven't heard any description of Com-
> munist propaganda in these films yet except that a banker
> was shown occasionally as being a no-good, and so forth.
> Well, of course, I know many fine bankers, many patriotic
> men. I also know some stinkers that should have been in jail
> 30 years ago. That doesn't necessarily constitute the Com-
> munist propaganda. What would you describe in this film as
> being Communist propaganda?
>
> MRS. ROGERS: In None But the Lonely Heart?
>
> MR. McDOWELL: Yes.
>
> MRS. ROGERS: I can't quote the lines of the play exactly but
> I can give you the sense of them. There is one place in
> which—it is unfair, may I say, to take a scene from its
> context and try to make it sound like Communist propa-
> ganda, because a Communist is very careful, very clever, and
> very devious in the way he sets the film. If I were to give you
> a line from that play straight out you would say "What is
> wrong with that line?" unless you knew that the Communist
> is trying in every way to tear down our free-enterprise
> system, to make the people lose faith in it, so that they will
> want to get something else—and the Communists have it
> waiting for them.
>
> I will tell you of one line. The mother in the story runs a
> second-hand store. The son says to her, "You are not going
> to"—in essence, I am not quoting this exactly because I can't
> remember it exactly—he said to her, "You are not going to
> get me to work here and squeeze pennies from people poorer
> than we are.". . . Many people are poorer and many people
> are richer.
>
> As I say, you find yourself in an awful hole the moment
> you start to remove one of the scenes from its context.
>
> MR. McDOWELL: Well, unfortunately for an intelligent discus-
> sion, I didn't see the picture, so I am at a complete loss.[43]

Representative McDowell concluded the examination of Mrs.
Rogers by noting that she was not merely "a disturbed lady

who in the course of her activities in Hollywood has stumbled across the fingers of this conspiracy against the American Government, but that long ago she discovered it and that she has become, in my opinion, one of the outstanding experts on communism in the United States, and particularly in the amusement industry."[44]

On October 23, Gary Cooper, the committee's friendly superstar, testified there was a lot of Communist word-of-mouth at social gatherings in Hollywood and he observed that he had been diligent in ferreting out scripts "tinged with communistic ideas."[45]

He was unable to elucidate on the precise titles of the scripts. Chairman Thomas evidenced concern for the star's memory loss, but Cooper maintained that he usually read the material at night and what he didn't like he didn't finish and by implication did not remember.[46]

Two documents in pamphlet form from the Communist parties of Italy and Yugoslavia were introduced. The leaflets placed Cooper in Philadelphia, where he purportedly made a speech before 90,000 persons denigrating Rockefeller, Ford, Rothschild, and Senator Bilbo. The CP literature also had Cooper and actor Tyrone Power carrying the coffin of swimmer-actor Buster Crabbe, who had been machine-gunned on the corner of Broadway and Seventh Avenue for his leftist leanings.

Cooper observed quite accurately that these documents were untrue and that Mr. Crabbe was alive and healthy. He was not quite sure of the validity of investigator H. A. Smith's claim that it would be hard "getting 90,000 people out in Philadelphia for anything."[47]

Ayn Rand left her native USSR in 1926 during a period of Soviet bureaucratic relaxation, and in more than two decades that had elapsed since her emigration she had developed a "gloveless hand of iron," which she demonstrated to the committee by her sociopolitical criticism of L. B. Mayer's *Song of Russia*.[48]

On October 20, she assessed the MGM picture as a complete and naïve propaganda film about life in Russia prior to and including World War II. She threaded the film's storyline carefully through her own observations on what it was like to live under totalitarian Communism. In her emotional and lengthy 3,000-word statement, she made it amply clear to the committee that Mayer's film was a useless war effort device that would have been far more useful to Soviet-American relations if it had not been made.

Miss Rand observed with rigid objectivism:

> I don't believe that the morale of anybody can be built up by a lie. If there was nothing good that we could truthfully say about Russia, then it would have been better to say nothing at all.

In closing questions of this testimony, Representative John McDowell of Pennsylvania expressed a somewhat more relaxed curiosity about Russia than was ordinarily displayed at these hearings:

MR. McDOWELL: You paint a very dismal picture of Russia. You made a great point about the number of children who were unhappy. Doesn't anybody smile in Russia any more?

MISS RAND: Well, if you ask me literally, pretty much no.

MR. McDOWELL: They don't smile?

MISS RAND: Not quite that way; no. If they do, it is privately and accidentally. Certainly, it is not social. They don't smile in approval of their system.

MR. McDOWELL: Well, all they do is talk about food.

MISS RAND: That is right.

MR. McDOWELL: That is a great change from the Russians I have always known, and I have known a lot of them. Don't they do things at all like Americans? Don't they walk across town to visit their mother-in-law or somebody?

MISS RAND: Look, it is very hard to explain. It is almost impossible to convey to a free people what it is like to live in a totalitarian dictatorship. I can tell you a lot of details. I can never completely convince you, because you are free. It is in a way good that you can't even conceive of what it is like. Certainly they have friends and mothers-in-law. They try to live a human life, but you understand it is totally inhuman. Try to imagine what it is like if you are in constant terror from morning till night and at night you are waiting for the doorbell to ring, where you are afraid of anything and everybody, living in a country where human life is nothing,

less than nothing, and you know it. You don't know who or
when is going to do what to you because you may have
friends who spy on you, where there is no law and any rights
of any kind.

MR. McDOWELL: You came here in 1926, I believe you said.
Did you escape from Russia?

MISS RAND: No.

MR. McDOWELL: Did you have a passport?

MISS RAND: No. Strangely enough, they gave me a passport to
come out here as a visitor.

MR. McDOWELL: As a visitor?

MISS RAND: It was at a time when they relaxed their orders a
little bit. Quite a few people got out. I had some relative here
and I was permitted to come here for a year. I never went
back.[49]

During the first week of the hearings, the remaining twelve
friendly witnesses were H. A. Smith, A. B. Leckie, and Louis J.
Russell, committee investigators; Samuel (Sam) Grosvenor
Wood, producer; John (Jack) Charles Moffitt, writer and
motion picture critic; writers Morrie Ryskind, Fred Niblo, Jr.,
Richard Macaulay, and Rupert Hughes; James K. McGuinness,
MGM script supervisor; Howard Rushmore, an editor of the
New York *Journal-American*; Oliver Carlson, writer and teacher;
and Roy M. Brewer, representative of both the International
Alliance of Theatrical Stage Employees (IATSE) and Motion
Picture Machine Operators of the United States (MMO).

They variously described and reported incidents and names
they felt were significant to the committee in its search for
Communist encroachment in the motion picture industry.

The first five days of testimony were completed and, "With
only one week of a promised three-week hearing concluded, the
House Committee on Un-American Activities stood ready to
take the testimony of those individuals who had, from the very
beginning, declared themselves to be the sworn enemies of
everything the House Committee stood for."[50]

The unfriendly witnesses were next.

October 27, 1947, marked the beginning of the second week
of the hearings. Since then the terms "Unfriendly Ten" and
"Hollywood Ten" have become quite well known in Holly-

wood, but there were in fact eighteen persons who had publicly stated in advance of the hearings that they would refuse to answer certain questions. They were Alvah Bessie, Herbert Joseph Biberman, Lester Cole, Richard Collins, Edward Dmytryk, Gordon Kahn, Howard Koch, Ring W. Lardner, Jr., John Howard Lawson, Albert Maltz, Lewis Milestone, Samuel Ornitz, Larry Parks, Irving Pichel, Robert Rossen, Waldo Salt, (Robert) Adrian Scott, and Dalton Trumbo.[51]

This study will concentrate on the testimony of the ten who appeared, were recalcitrant, and subsequently went to jail for contempt of Congress.

Robert W. Kenny, the attorney for the Unfriendly Eighteen, requested permission to argue a motion to quash their subpoenas, but Chairman Thomas, after fifteen minutes in executive session, denied the request.[52]

The opening testimony of the second week, October 27, was from writer John Howard Lawson, who was somewhat surprised when he heard himself called first, since he had been named third in the order of witnesses cited to appear.[53] Lawson requested the right to make an opening statement. It was denied. Lawson indicated that the committee had allowed Warner, Mayer, and others to make opening statements, to which Thomas replied, in reference to Lawson's document, "That statement is not pertinent to this inquiry."[54]

When Stripling asked him if he was a member of the Screen Writers Guild, Lawson replied that the raising of any question in regard to his membership, political beliefs, or affiliations was beyond the powers of the committee. However, he did indicate that his membership in the guild was a matter of public record.[55]

After extracting a list of Lawson's film credits, Stripling went directly to the big question that was to be the nemesis for committee witnesses for more than a decade to come. "Mr. Lawson, are you now, or have you ever been a member of the Communist Party of the United States?"[56]

Lawson's reply was emotional and adamant:

> MR. LAWSON: In framing my answer to that question I must emphasize the points that I have raised before. The question

of communism is in no way related to this inquiry, which is an attempt to get control of the screen and to invade the basic rights of American citizens in all fields.

MR. McDOWELL: Now, I must object—

MR. STRIPLING: Mr. Chairman—

(The chairman pounding gavel)

MR. LAWSON: The question here relates not only to the question of my membership in any political organization, but this committee is attempting to establish the right—

(The chairman pounding the gavel)

MR. LAWSON (continuing): Which has been historically denied to any committee of this sort, to invade the rights and privileges and immunity of American citizens, whether they be Protestant, Methodist, Jewish, or Catholic, whether they be Republicans or Democrats or anything else.

THE CHAIRMAN (pounding gavel): Mr. Lawson, just quiet down again.

Mr. Lawson, the most pertinent question that we can ask is whether or not you have been a member of the Communist Party. Now, do you care to answer that question?

MR. LAWSON: You are using the old technique, which was used in Hitler Germany in order to create a scare here—

THE CHAIRMAN (pounding gavel): Oh—

MR. LAWSON: In order to create an entirely false atmosphere in which this hearing is conducted—

(The Chairman pounding gavel)

MR. LAWSON: In order that you can then smear the motion-picture industry, and you can proceed to the press, to any form of communication in this country.

THE CHAIRMAN: You have learned—

MR. LAWSON: The Bill of Rights was established precisely to prevent the operation of any committee which could invade the basic rights of Americans.

Now, if you want to know—

MR. STRIPLING: Mr. Chairman, the witness is not answering the question.

MR. LAWSON: If you want to know—

(The chairman pounding gavel)

MR. LAWSON: About the perjury that has been committed here and the perjury that is planned.

THE CHAIRMAN: Mr. Lawson—

MR. LAWSON: You permit me and my attorneys to bring in here the witnesses that testified last week and you permit us to cross-examine these witnesses, and we will show up the whole tissue of lie—

THE CHAIRMAN (pounding gavel): We are going to get the answer to that question if we have to stay here for a week.

Are you a member of the Communist Party, or have you ever been a member of the Communist Party?

MR. LAWSON: It is unfortunate and tragic that I have to teach this committee the basic principles of American—

THE CHAIRMAN (pounding gavel): That is not the question. That is not the question. The question is: Have you ever been a member of the Communist Party?

MR. LAWSON: I am framing my answer in the only way in which any American citizen can frame his answer to a question which absolutely invades his rights.

THE CHAIRMAN: Then you refuse to answer that question; is that correct?

MR. LAWSON: I have told you that I will offer my beliefs, affiliations, and everything else to the American public, and they will know where I stand.

THE CHAIRMAN (pounding gavel): Excuse the witness—

MR. LAWSON: As they do from what I have written.

THE CHAIRMAN (pounding gavel): Stand away from the stand—

MR. LAWSON: I have written Americanism for many years, and I shall continue to fight for the Bill of Rights, which you are trying to destroy.

THE CHAIRMAN: Officers, take this man away from the stand—

(applause and boos)

THE CHAIRMAN (pounding gavel): There will be no demonstrations. No demonstrations, for or against. Everyone will please be seated.[57]

He was removed from the stand by guards.

Stripling then received permission for a nine-page memorandum to be read into the hearings detailing Lawson's alleged affiliations with the Communist Party, charges that Lawson was given no opportunity to refute.

If the committee found Lawson a somewhat truculent witness, it found in writer Dalton Trumbo a "veritable ring-tailed tiger." [58]

His opening statement was turned down by the committee and after the panel made five attempts to find out whether the writer was a member of the Screen Writers Guild, Trumbo asserted the question had a specific design. It was, according to the writer, "to identify me with the Screen Writers Guild; secondly, to seek to identify me with the Communist Party and thereby destroy that guild. . . ."[59]

Next came the big question regarding Communist Party membership:

> THE CHAIRMAN: Are you or have you ever been a member of the Communist Party?
> MR. TRUMBO: I believe I have the right to be confronted with any evidence which supports this question. I should like to see what you have.
> THE CHAIRMAN: Oh. Well, you would!
> MR. TRUMBO: Yes.
> THE CHAIRMAN: Well, you will, pretty soon.
> (Laughter and applause)
> THE CHAIRMAN (pounding gavel): The witness is excused. Impossible.
> MR. TRUMBO: This is the beginning—
> THE CHAIRMAN (pounding gavel): Just a minute—
> MR. TRUMBO: Of an American concentration camp.
> THE CHAIRMAN: This is typical Communist tactics. This is typical Communist tactics.
> (Applause).[60]

Committee investigator Louis Russell then read into the record nine pages of Trumbo's alleged Communist Party affiliations. Like Lawson, Trumbo was not there to refute them.

The policy of not allowing unfriendly witnesses to make an opening statement was abruptly and for no apparent reason reversed when writer Albert Maltz took the stand on the afternoon of October 28. The following is the entirety of Maltz's prepared statement and part of the subsequent exchange with the committee that sent him to prison on contempt charges:

> I am an American and I believe there is no more proud word in the vocabulary of man. I am a novelist and a screen writer and I have produced a certain body of work in the past 15 years. As with any writer, what I have written has come from the total fabric of my life—my birth in this land, our schools and games, our atmosphere of freedom, our tradition of inquiry, criticism, discussion, tolerance. Whatever I am, America has made me. And I, in turn, possess no loyalty as great as the one I have to

this land, to the economic and social welfare of its people, to the perpetuation and development of its democratic way of life.

Now at the age of 39, I am commanded to appear before the House Committee on Un-American Activities. For a full week this committee has encouraged an assortment of well-rehearsed witnesses to testify that I and others are subversive and un-American. It has refused us the opportunity that any pickpocket receives in a magistrate's court—the right to cross-examine these witnesses, to refute their testimony, to reveal their motives, their history, and who, exactly, they are. Furthermore it grants these witnesses congressional immunity so that we may not sue them for libel for their slanders.

I maintain that this is an evil and vicious procedure; that it is legally unjust and morally indecent—and that it places in danger every other American, since if the rights of any one citizen can be invaded, then the constitutional guaranties of every other American have been subverted and no one is any longer protected from official tyranny.

What is it about me that this committee wishes to destroy? My writings? Very well, let us refer to them.

My novel, The Cross and the Arrow, was issued in a special edition of 140,000 copies by a wartime Government agency, the armed services edition, for American servicemen abroad.

My short stories have been reprinted in over 30 anthologies, by as many American publishers—all subversive, no doubt.

My film, The Pride of the Marines, was premiered in 28 cities at Guadalcanal Day banquets under the auspices of the United States Marine Corps.

Another film, Destination Tokyo, was premiered aboard a United States submarine and was adopted by the Navy as an official training film.

My short film, The House I Live In, was given a special award by the Academy of Motion Picture Arts and Sciences for its contribution to racial tolerance.

My short story, The Happiest Man on Earth, won the 1938 O. Henry Memorial Award for the best American short story.

This, then, is the body of work for which this committee urges I be blacklisted in the film industry—and tomorrow, if it has its way in the publishing and magazine fields also.

By cold censorship, if not legislation, I must not be allowed to write. Will this censorship stop with me? Or with the others now singled out for attack? If it requires acceptance of the ideas of this committee to remain immune from the brand of un-Americanism, then who is ultimately safe from this committee except members of the Ku Klux Klan?

Why else does this committee now seek to destroy me and others? Because of our ideas, unquestionably. In 1801, when he was President of the United States, Thomas Jefferson wrote:

Opinion, and the just maintenance of it, shall never be a crime in my view: nor bring injury to the individual.

But a few years ago, in the course of one of the hearings of this committee, Congressman J. Parnell Thomas said, and I quote from the official transcript:

I just want to say this now, it seems that the New Deal is working along hand in glove with the Communist Party. The New Deal is either for the Communist Party or it is playing into the hands of the Communist Party.

Very well, then, here is the other reason why I and others have been commanded to appear before this committee—our ideas. In common with many Americans, I supported the New Deal. In common with many Americans I supported, against Mr. Thomas and Mr. Rankin, the antilynching bill. I opposed them in my support of OPA controls and emergency veteran housing and a fair employment practices law. I signed petitions for these measures, joined organizations that advocated them, contributed money, sometimes spoke from public platforms, and I will continue to do so. I will take my philosophy from Thomas Payne, Thomas Jefferson, Abraham Lincoln, and I will not be dictated to or intimidated by men to whom the Ku Klux Klan, as a matter of committee record, is an acceptable American institution.

I state further that on many questions of public interest my opinions as a citizen have not always been in accord with the opinions of the majority. They are not now nor have my opinions ever been fixed and unchanging, nor are they now fixed and unchangeable; but, right or wrong, I claim and I insist upon my right to think freely and to speak freely; to join the Republican Party or the Communist Party, the Democratic or the Prohibition Party; to publish whatever I please; to fix my mind or change my mind, without dictation from anyone; to offer any criticism I think fitting of any public official or policy; to join whatever organizations I please, no matter what certain legislators may think of them. Above all, I challenge the right of this committee to inquire into my political or religious beliefs, in any manner or degree, and I assert that not only the conduct of this committee but its very existence are a subversion of the Bill of Rights.

If I were a spokesman for General Franco, I would not be here today. I would rather be here. I would rather die than be a shabby American, groveling before men whose names are Thomas and Rankin, but who now carry out activities in America like those carried out in Germany by Goebbels and Himmler.

The American people are going to have to choose between the Bill of Rights and the Thomas committee. They cannot have both. One or the other must be abolished in the immediate future.

THE CHAIRMAN: Mr. Stripling (pounding gavel).

MR. STRIPLING: Mr. Maltz, what is your occupation?

MR. MALTZ. I am a writer.

MR. STRIPLING: Are you employed in the motion-picture industry?

MR. MALTZ: I work in various fields of writing and I have sometimes accepted employment in the motion-picture industry.

MR. STRIPLING: Have you written scripts for a number of pictures?

MR. MALTZ: It is a matter of public record that I have written scripts for certain motion pictures.

MR. STRIPLING: Are you a member of the Screen Writers Guild?

MR. MALTZ: Next you are going to ask me what religious group I belong to.

THE CHAIRMAN: No, no; we are not.

MR. MALTZ: And any such question as that—

THE CHAIRMAN: I know.

MR. MALTZ: Is an obvious attempt to invade my rights under the Constitution.

MR. STRIPLING: Do you object to answering whether or not you are a member of the Screen Writers Guild?

MR. MALTZ: I have not objected to answer that question. On the contrary, I point out that next you are going to ask me whether or not I am a member of a certain religious group and suggest that I be blacklisted from an industry because I am a member of a group you don't like.

(The chairman pounds gavel)

MR. STRIPLING: Mr. Maltz, do you decline to answer the question?

MR. MALTZ: I certainly do not decline to answer the question. I have answered the question.

MR. STRIPLING: I repeat, are you a member of the Screen Writers Guild?

MR. MALTZ: And I repeat my answer, sir, that any such

> question is an obvious attempt to invade my list of organiza-
> tions as an American citizen and I would be a shabby
> American if I didn't answer as I have.
> MR. STRIPLING: Mr. Maltz, are you a member of the
> Communist Party?
> MR. MALTZ: Next you are going to ask what my religious
> beliefs are.
> MR. McDOWELL: That is not answering the question.
> MR. MALTZ: And you are going to insist before various
> members of the industry that since you do not like my
> religious beliefs I should not work in such industry. Any
> such question is quite irrelevant.[61]

When Stripling repeated the question about Communist Party
affiliation, Maltz deliberately replied, "I have answered the
question, Mr. Quisling. I am sorry. I want you to know—"[62]

Representative McDowell immediately objected to the comparison by innuendo of the committee's chief investigator with
the World War II Norwegian traitor. Chairman Thomas excused
the witness, saying that his testimony was "typical Communist
line." Maltz retorted before he left the stand, "Let's get on with
the rigged record."[63]

The peppery writer's dossier was subsequently read into the
record by Russell, again with no opportunity for refutation
accorded the witness.

Later that day, Thomas and writer Alvah Bessie reached a
compromise on the writer's opening statement. The chairman
wanted only the two opening paragraphs read. Bessie opted for
the last two also—and won. As with Maltz, the entire statement
of the fourth writer was placed in the record. Lawson and
Trumbo had not been afforded the same courtesy.

Stripling moved immediately to the two key questions, the
second of which he was now calling the $64 question.[64]

In reply to the chief investigator's question about Communist
Party affiliation, Bessie rejoined that General Eisenhower had
refused to reveal his political affiliations and what was good
enough for the general was good enough for him.[65]

After Thomas derisively excused Bessie to go out and "make
a speech under a big tree," the chairman commented to large
applause on the Eisenhower remark:

It is my belief that if General Eisenhower were a witness before this committee and he was asked the question, "Are you a member of the Communist Party?" he would not only be very responsive to the question, but would be absolutely insulted, and solely for this reason: A great man like General Eisenhower would not ever think or dream or stoop to ever being a low-down Communist.[66]

The now established procedure of Russell's reading of the witness's dossier into the record with no possibility of argument was followed with Bessie.

Writer Samuel Ornitz was the fifth of the Unfriendly Ten called to testify. In a reversal of the position taken on Maltz and Bessie, Thomas declined to allow Ornitz to read his opening statement on October 29, calling it "just another case of vilification."[67]

In reply to the first question, concerning Ornitz's membership in the Screen Writers Guild, the fifth witness indicated that to answer properly would not be a simple matter because it involved his conscience versus constitutional rights. The writer stated, "I say you do raise a serious question of conscience for me when you ask me to act in concert with you to override the Constitution."[68]

After responding negatively to the $64 question by insisting he had a right to belong to any party he saw fit to join, Ornitz was removed from the witness stand.

His unchallenged list of alleged Communist affiliations was read into the record while Herbert Joseph Biberman prepared for his moment before the tribunal on that same October morning.

Biberman's opening statement was rejected, but the film and theater producer-writer-director answered Stripling's question about when and where he was born with patriotic pride and splendid specificity: "I was born within a stone's throw of Independence Hall in Philadelphia, on the day when Mr. McKinley was inaugurated as President of the United States, March 4, 1900, on the second floor of a building at Sixth and South, over a grocery store."[69]

Stripling was most complimentary to Biberman for his

answer. The investigator hoped that statement would be a forerunner of similar detailed responses from the witness. He was wrong on both the accuracy of the answer and the subsequent responses to the two key questions. McKinley was inaugurated March 4, 1901, not 1900, and Biberman was no more inclined than his predecessors to reveal his membership in either the Screen Writers Guild or the Communist Party.

After a heated exchange he did, however, apologize to the committee, an apology that the preceding unfriendly witnesses had not felt compelled to make.

"Mr. Stripling, I apologize for one thing and that is raising my voice. I had no intention of doing so."[70]

The chairman had had enough of Biberman, and as he pounded his gavel there was laughter, the witness was excused, and his dossier of alleged Communist affiliations was read into the hearing record.

Gordon Kahn, who attended the hearings and was one of the eighteen unfriendly witnesses originally subpoenaed, believed Edward Dmytryk and Adrian Scott were summoned to testify because they had respectively directed and produced a film attacking anti-Semitism, *Crossfire*.[71] His evidence for this observation was that Stripling inadvertently addressed Scott as Dmytryk.

Director Dmytryk was the first witness at the afternoon session on October 29. He stated that he was born in Canada and nationalized as an American citizen in 1939. His opening statement was disallowed.

He was asked whether he was a member of the Screen Directors Guild, as the preceding witnesses had been asked if they were members of the Screen Writers Guild. Dmytryk told Stripling that it would take much less than five minutes to answer the question about his membership. He added that should he be allowed sufficient time to answer in his own way, he hoped in so doing he would not bore the chairman.[72]

When questioned about his membership in the Communist Party, the director, in concert with his predecessors, claimed constitutional immunity. The witness was excused, and the proficient committee investigator Louis Russell read into the record the attestations against Dmytryk. Once again the charges would remain unanswered by the defendant.

Scott, the other half of the *Crossfire* team, followed Dmytryk and told the chair that his opening statement had to do with that film and anti-Semitism. Chairman Thomas, after reading the statement, ruled against its admission to the record. Said Thomas, "This may not be the worst statement we have received, but it is almost the worst."[73]

The two key questions were then asked the producer, to which he replied, "I believe it is a question which invades my rights as a citizen. I do not believe it is proper for this committee to inquire into my personal relationships, my private relationships, my public relationships."[74]

Thomas and Scott sparred briefly on whether the committee had the right to inquire into what a person thought. Thomas held that was not the purpose of either key question; Scott retorted that he believed he had answered satisfactorily. The chairman stated that from what Scott had said it was not clear to him whether or not he was a member of the Communist Party. Thomas said, "I must be terribly dumb, but from your answer I can't tell whether you are a member or not." In a splendid display of benevolence, Scott disagreed: ' I don't think you are."[75]

The producer was excused and cited for contempt prior to Russell's reading of the assertions against him.

Writer Ring W. Lardner, Jr., best-known name of the unfriendly witnesses at the time of the hearings, struck a bargain on October 30 with the chairman on his opening statement. He would be allowed to read it at the conclusion of his testimony.[76]

After Lardner refused to answer yes or no to the two key questions, J. Parnell Thomas stated that if the writer maintained that position his statement would not be read. He did—and it wasn't.

When the irate chairman repeated the Communist Party membership interrogatory the fourth time, the witness replied ironically, "It depends on the circumstances. I could answer it, but if I did I would hate myself in the morning."[77] This allusion he later explained to the New York *Herald Tribune*: "I have always associated the words I'll hate myself in the morning with a situation in which a previously chaste woman is succumbing to the indecent blandishment of a scoundrel and very likely launching herself on the road to prostitution. That is the analogy I wished to suggest."[78]

Apparently the analogy needed no explanation. Thomas demanded that the sergeant at arms forcibly remove the writer from the hearing room. There was applause when Lardner was led out of the chamber. The record does not state whether it was for or against the writer.

Stripling's assistant, Russell, submitted the unrefuted reading of the allegations against Lardner.

Whether Chairman Thomas was aware that October 30, 1947, would be the last day of the hearings in the capital is not certain. "But that morning he breakfasted well in his suite at the Mayflower Hotel and arrived at the hearing room looking like a man with a delicious secret. His mood was affable and expansive, in a pink sort of way."[79]

The last of the Unfriendly Ten who eventually went to jail for contempt of Congress was writer Lester Cole.

His opening statement on October 30 was declined by the chairman, who called it "clearly another case of vilification and not pertinent at all to the inquiry."[80]

Cole likewise refused to answer the two main questions, his membership in the Writers Guild and in the Communist Party. He was excused, his alleged record of Communist affiliation was recorded by Russell, and the hearing room was then ready to hear the only non-American witness to come before the committee, playwright and poet Bertolt Brecht. The German writer, accompanied by a committee-chosen interpreter, explained that he was not a citizen of the United States but had filed his first papers toward the end of 1941.[81]

Brecht's testimony revealed that he left Germany in 1933 when Hitler took power. From Germany he went to Denmark, then to Sweden, and finally to Finland to await his visa for the United States. His connection with Hollywood was through the sale of his story *Hangmen Also Die* to an independent producer.[82]

He was not a member of the Screen Writers Guild, so the committee was able to move on immediately to the big question. For once the members apparently were surprised by the answer. Brecht replied:

> Mr. Chairman, I have heard my colleagues when they considered this question not as proper, but I am a guest in this country and do not want to enter into any legal arguments, so I will answer your question fully as well as I can. I was not a member or am not a member of any Communist Party.[83]

Later, the observation was made that Brecht *was* a Communist, albeit not a card-carrying member, at least "in his total life commitment," as his biographer Martin Esslin informs us.[84]

Three additional witnesses who also require brief scrutiny appeared during the second week of the inquiry. They were Eric Allen Johnston, president of the Motion Picture Association of America (MPAA); Emmet G. Lavery, playwright, screenwriter, and member of the bar of New York State; and Dore Schary, then executive in charge of production at RKO.

The three were not unfriendly to the point of being cited for contempt, but they did evidence disapproval of the tactics of the committee.

The pertinence of Johnston's opening statement on October 27 was deemed in order and he proceeded to read a zigzagging combination of kudos for the committee and brickbats against its arbitrary methods, a style he also used in his subsequent testimony. His most cogent comment centered on his conviction that it was necessary to expose Communism, but "don't put any American who isn't a Communist in a concentration camp of suspicion. We are not willing to give up our freedoms to save our freedoms."[85]

Before the end of the year the president of the MPAA was to enter into an agreement with the producers to do exactly what he had admonished against in his opening remarks at the October hearings.

Lavery, then president of the Screen Writers Guild, remarked to Stripling on October 29 that he was "delighted and proud" to answer the question about his membership in the guild. He added that he felt it was something that each witness should decide for himself.

Lavery was granted permission to make several brief motions, due undoubtedly to the fact that his opening answers were what the committee wanted to hear.

The writer requested Jack Warner be recalled to testify so that the committee could examine him about his claim that he had fired Lavery. The request was turned down. Lavery denied he had been fired by Warner, an assertion made by the production chief in the previous week's testimony.

Next he requested permission to correct statements made by writers John C. (Jack) Moffitt, Morrie Ryskind, and Rupert Hughes. Lavery denied allusions the trio made about his Communist Party affiliations when they testified.[86]

He also denied any knowledge of Lawson's or Trumbo's Communist Party memberships. He added that he had sued Billy Wilkerson, publisher of the *Hollywood Reporter*, for similar unsubstantiated allegations about himself. The publisher subsequently printed a two-page retraction at his own expense, stated Lavery.[87]

Lavery then noted that he had sued Lela Rogers for libel and slander and the $1,000,000 suit was currently pending in the superior court of California.[88]

The chair refused to permit the writer-attorney to read his statement, and the balance of his testimony failed to bring forth any new names of suspected show business Communists.

Producer Dore Schary admitted knowing suspected Communist Hans Eisler but said he was not responsible for employing the composer and musician. The executive told the committee on October 29 that until such time as a man was proved to be a Communist he would continue to hire him. If the suspect was verified as a person dedicated to the overthrow of the government by force, Schary would not have hired him.[89]

Stripling pursued the questions relating to Eisler. He wanted to know if Schary would hire him based on what he had read about his pro-Soviet activities in the newspapers. Schary replied that he was not capable of answering the question for two reasons. First, he did not know Eisler's qualifications as a musician and, second, the United States Supreme Court had ruled that an employer could not arbitrarily refuse a man work because of his political convictions.

The chairman asked: ". . . assuming that Hans Eisler is a great artist; assuming also that he is a Communist, you would not hesitate to rehire him?" Schary retorted, "I would not hesitate to rehire him if it was not proven that he was a foreign agent. I would still maintain his right to think politically as he chooses."[90] In subsequent testimony that day he recanted and declared if all Stripling said about the composer was true he would not hire Eisler.

Schary stated that although he was not responsible for hiring Dmytryk and Scott, he would continue to employ them at RKO until they were proved to be foreign agents. He added that Brecht, to his knowledge, was never employed by RKO.

Stripling wanted to know if the executive was aware that his company was producing a film written by Howard Fast and that the writer was a publicly avowed Communist. Schary replied that these circumstances had occurred before he came to the studio and after reviewing the Fast script, he found it "a very charming story, not political whatsoever."

The chairman terminated the inquiry by reminding the witness of Rip Van Winkle, an allusion to an analogy he made earlier about the committee's efforts to awaken America from its long sleep in disregarding the facts of internal and external Communist aggression and expansion. The remarks of the chairman drew laughter from the crowded chamber.[91]

The general conclusions drawn from the total testimony are worth noting.

Chairman Thomas never produced the list of pro-Communist films he promised. The films that were mentioned by the friends of the committee were nothing for the American public to be concerned about. Though denying it, the committee did make a sustained effort to persuade Hollywood to make anti-Communist pictures. The dossiers of the ten unfriendly

witnesses did authenticate that there were Communists in
Hollywood. A total of thirty-five individuals were named as
Communist Party members during the hearings. Eleven had the
opportunity to reply. Lavery was not a Communist and said so.
Brecht probably was but denied it.

The committee accepted much testimony at face value with
no opportunity for many of those named as Communists to
reply. The Screen Writers Guild was damaged by the hearings.
The press forced the hearings to end prematurely. The entire
proceedings were conducted in a circuslike atmosphere. The
committee was arbitrary in allowing witnesses to read prepared
statements, usually determined by whether they were in sympathy with the investigation.

Many harmless associations in the dossiers were presented as
"proof of subversion," although there were "valid bits of
information about the Hollywood Ten which did tend to prove
their membership in the Communist Party."[92] Walter Goodman
asserts that all the "Ten" were members of the CP.[93] The
copies of the party membership cards were never shown to the
press or "anyone else."

Finally, the contention that those identified as being affiliated with the Communist Party were capable of subverting the
American moviegoer by injecting pro-Soviet propaganda into
their work was never proved by the Committee.[94] On the
contrary, the leaders of the film industry unanimously testified
that no Communist propaganda had been able to get through
them.

How the American theater was affected by these hearings is
perhaps more in the province of the psychologist than the
historian. The fact that a Congressional body was allowed to be
the catalyst that sent men to jail for contempt because they
refused to reveal private and political associations undoubtedly
gave those artists that were later subpoenaed much room for
soul-searching. These witnesses and their decisions on handling
the committee's Communist Party membership question will be
discussed in the following chapter.

Nine of the ten men who went to jail for periods of six
months to one year were blacklisted when they were released.

They were unable to work in the Hollywood studios under their own names and were forced to earn their postprison livings in circuitous ways. The tenth man, director Dmytryk, became a friendly witness when he was released; he resumed his career almost immediately.[95]

After prison, only a few of the nine wrote for the theater.

Ornitz died in 1957 after completing one unsuccessful novel.

Scott worked in England as executive assistant to the head of production at MGM's Boreham Wood Studio until August, 1968, when he returned to Hollywood as a producer at Universal Studios. Lawson, the only prominent playwright before the 1947 investigation, after serving his time, wrote a play, *Thunder Morning*, which delineated black ghetto life. It was never produced. He wrote a historical study while in prison, *The Hidden Heritage*.

In the fifties, Cole wrote two plays, both of which were produced in Europe only. In 1961, he wrote two more plays, one of which was produced in England and the other in Prague. In 1962, Lardner collaborated with Ian Hunter on the Bert Lahr musical *Foxy*, which found its way to Broadway two years later. Maltz, while living in Mexico, wrote a play under a pseudonym; Biberman and Bessie wrote nothing for the theater. Biberman died in 1971. Dalton Trumbo, now by far the most successful film writer of the ten, wrote a play, *The Biggest Thief in Town*, which played briefly in New York and then opened in London, where it ran two years.[96]

What the ten did not or could not write, produce, or direct for the theater following their release from prison is a matter for speculation. The fact that their latitude for creation was significantly diminished by the committee's 1947 investigation is not open to argument.

Evaluation of the Hearings

Failure to affirm or deny advocacy of the most widely held political doctrine in the world—Communism—sent ten creative artists to jail. The republic that recognized the right of men to belong to the *legal* Communist Party, U.S.A., incarcerated them for using the founding fathers' First Amendment mandate protecting the privacy of political beliefs.

Reaffirmation of that right to privacy occurred in this century and Ring Lardner, Jr., believed he and the remainder of the ten based part of their decision to defy the committee on the 1943 Supreme Court decision which read: "If there is any fixed star in our constitutional constellation, it is that no official, high or petty, can prescribe what shall be orthodox in politics, nationalism, religion or other matters of opinion, or force citizens to confess by word or act their faith therein."[97]

The legality of the contempt of Congress charges and the ultimate jail sentences of the Hollywood Ten is a subject of debate for juridical scholars and therefore outside the scope of this study. The use of prehearing publicity by the committee and the method of its investigation which created the contempt charges are well within this researcher's discipline and are briefly summarized here.

In 1938, it was Martin Dies and J. Parnell Thomas who shared the prehearing public accusations about Communism in the entertainment world. In 1945, similar charges were leveled by Representative John Rankin of Mississippi, a virulent anti-Semite who opposed the creation of the committee until he was certain it would not be chaired by Samuel Dickstein.[98]

With an inexplicable lack of prudent impartiality, Rankin declared he had information that "one of the most dangerous plots ever instigated for the overthrow of this government has its headquarters in Hollywood." He pursued his melodramatic harangue: "The information we get is that this is the greatest hot bed of subversive activities in the United States. We're on the trail of the tarantula now, and we're going to follow through. The best people in California are helping us."[99]

The committee's policy of accuse, expose, and thereby indict in the eyes of much of the public was even more unjustified and incredible in the hands of the Mississippian than it had been with Dies or Thomas.

Either Rankin decided at the time of the October investigation that the Hollywood Commie crisis had passed or Thomas refused to appoint the flamboyant Southerner to the subcommittee because of the possibility that his presence might take the spotlight away from the chairman.[100]

After his strident exhortations, it is a strange anticlimax that Rankin was not permitted to appear as a member of the subcommittee in Washington.

Rankin attended none of the hearings.

In addition to the debatable propriety of the preinvestigation publicity, the press coverage attendant to the hearings was, as Robert K. Carr suggests in his assessment of six diverse newspapers, arguable on grounds of confusion and distortion of what actually took place.[101]

After a careful examination of original clippings from the six Los Angeles and Hollywood daily newspapers of October, 1947, Carr's observations in the following areas appear substantially accurate.[102] The reporting job, although given prominent attention and space, was only average. The photographic coverage was more than adequate. The committee's charge that there were Communists in Hollywood was well covered by the press. The failure of the committee to prove its allegations that films contained specific propaganda and that the Roosevelt administration had pressured Hollywood to make pro-Soviet films was largely ignored by the Los Angeles press. The specific import and content of the Communist dossiers of the Hollywood Ten, even if only partially true, appeared nowhere save the hearing record. The Communist Party registration cards of the ten cited by the committee received scant attention.

The volatile and supercilious style of testifying employed by the ten, a manner that is apparent in reading the transcript of the proceedings, was also largely overlooked by the fourth estate of Hollywood and its environs.

Chairman Thomas even used the pulp-fiction device of announcing a mystery witness who would produce "sensational" evidence supposedly pertaining to the hearings.[103] The awesome testament finally came from the committee's omnipresent investigator Louis Russell, who discussed wartime atomic espionage that took place in Berkeley, California—not Hollywood Communism.

The methods and procedures utilized by the committee were,

as previously described in the 1938 hearings, equally dubious in 1947.

The friendly witnesses were allowed to read lengthy opening statements, while only two of the unfriendly ten were granted a forum for their opinions. Albert Maltz read all of his prepared remarks; Samuel Ornitz managed to interject a portion of his text.

Eight of the Hollywood Ten were writers. The committee could easily have proved they conspired to advocate the overthrow of the government by force and violence by producing words written by them to that effect. The Congressmen did not, because undoubtedly no such writings exist. Charges made by Jack Warner regarding the subversion of Broadway theater by Arthur Miller and Elia Kazan were, as hundreds of other allegations, left unchallenged by the committee.

The spring, 1947, preview testimony of the friendly witnesses in Hollywood was only alluded to in the October hearings; it was never publicly released in its entirety. Jack Warner and Robert Taylor denied in October specific charges they had made earlier in the year.

Although it is doubtful that the committee could have elicited any direct or meaningful answers from the Hollywood Ten, it should have tried. To broach the $64 question so early in each man's interrogation eliminated any possibility of significant disclosures of Red activities in Hollywood.

The record clearly indicates that the inquisitors were primarily interested in forcing the unfriendly witnesses into contempt charges rather than investigating Communism in the American cinema.

Subsequent investigations in the 1950's would reveal that high-paid Hollywood artists contributed heavily to the CP causes; this would have been a proper field of inquiry in 1947. It was not touched upon.

Chairman Thomas' revelation that he had the names of seventy-nine prominent Hollywood Communists in his files, sixty-nine of whom presumably remained at large as Hollywood subversives, seemed to bother very few patriots.[104] Resumption of a full-scale investigation of show business Reds did not occur until almost four years after the abrupt conclusion of the 1947 probe.

There can be little argument that the American people did have the right to know if Communist writers, producers, and directors were working in a communications medium of such significant impact as the movies.

Totalitarianism, the greatest revolutionary force of the twentieth century, has found its dual deputies, Fascism and Communism, to be most effective in societies which deny the public knowledge of diasgreement within their authoritarian regimes.

The activities of the suspected subversives should have been the proper thrust of the committee's investigation. The simplistic exposure of people as American Communists contributed negligibly to our purported national death struggle with the Kremlin.

Considering the enormous attention given the 1947 Hollywood hearings, it is inexcusable that the committee filed only a one-sentence summary of its findings in a review of the events of 1947-48. It stated: "While the committee could not within the limits of its time and resources examine every single phase of Communist activity in the industry, the outlines and the pattern of such activity was clearly disclosed."[105]

The later annual reports, detailing findings of the committee's 1950's investigations, were specific about affiliations, activities, and goals of Communists and Communism in the entertainment world.

When it appeared their livelihoods might be endangered, Eric Johnston and Dore Schary shared honors for reversing their antipathy toward the committee's work.

After much solemnizing during the October, 1947, hearings about never conspiring to deprive a man of work because of his private political convictions, both men did precisely that before the end of the year.

The moral dilemma, to say nothing of the practical expediency, of how to answer the committee's questions without informing on one's friends and yet avoid the blacklist faced hundreds of witnesses in the 1950's. This conundrum was also faced by the Hollywood Ten, and the answer broke down generally into these alternatives: If a man was a Communist and denied it before the committee, he went to jail for perjury. If he admitted he was a Communist, he was then asked to inform on his friends; if he refused, he went to jail for contempt because he had already waived protection of the Bill of Rights when he answered in the affirmative to the first question.

Also, once he admitted being a Communist and stood pat without further admissions, he could expect to return from jail blacklisted from his career, friends, associates, and acquaintances. The Bill of Rights "was not conceived for the powerful and popular who have no need for it," declared Dalton Trumbo. "It was put forth to protect even the most hated member of the most detested minority from the sanctions of the law on the one hand, and of public disapproval on the other."[106]

Robert Carr drew on a theatrical analogy for the hearings, commenting that there was a first act consisting of the friendly witnesses, a second act composed of the unfriendly witnesses, and a third act that was seemingly written and rehearsed but not performed.[107]

To extend the analogy, the hearings also had a few other theatrical ingredients, besides the stars. The investigation had "rising action" as the friendly witnesses prepared the audience for the unfriendly; the conflict of emotion between the committee and the Hollywood Ten; the rendering of moral decisions by the principal players when answering the $64 question; a denouement of sorts in the contempt convictions; and, somewhat belatedly, after the poor second-act curtain, a dash of the ironic during the elongated intermission.

In 1950 Ring Lardner, Jr., was sent to the Federal Correctional Institution at Danbury, Connecticut. His prison job was that of a stenographer in the office of classification and parole. That same year the somewhat less exotic job of caretaker of the chicken yard was held by a former government employee imprisoned for putting nonworkers on the government payroll and appropriating their salaries for himself. The chicken custodian was—J. Parnell Thomas.

FOOTNOTES

1. Gordon Kahn, *Hollywood on Trial* (New York, Boni and Gaer, Inc., 1948), p. 186.

2. *Ibid.*

3. *Ibid.*

4. Howard Suber, *The 1947 Hearings of the House Committee on Un-American Activities into Communism in the Hollywood Motion Picture Industry* (Unpublished master's thesis, University of California at Los Angeles, 1966), pp. 5-6.

5. Los Angeles *Daily News*, October 21, 1947.

6. U.S. Congress, House Committee on Un-American Activities, *Hearings Regarding the Communist Infiltration of the Motion Picture Industry*, Eightieth Congress, First Session. Hereinafter cited as *Motion Picture Hearings*, 1947.

7. *Ibid.*, pp. ii, 1.

8. *Ibid.*, p. 7.

9. *Ibid.*, p. 9.

10. *Ibid.*

11. Suber, *op. cit.*, pp. 10-11.

12. *Ibid.*

13. *Motion Picture Hearings,* 1947, p. 53.

14. Kahn, *op. cit.*, p. 53.

15. *Motion Picture Hearings*, 1947, p. 166.

16. *Ibid.*, p. 167.

17. *Ibid.*, pp. 167-68.

18. Kahn, *op. cit.*, p. 55.

19. *Ibid.*, pp. 27-28.

20. *Motion Picture Hearings*, 1947, pp. 70-71.

21. *Ibid.*, p. 72.

22. *Ibid.*, p. 72-73.

23. *Ibid.*, p. 79.

24. Kahn, *op. cit.*, pp. 47-50.

25. *Motion Picture Hearings*, 1947, p. 103.

26. *Ibid.*, pp. 94-95.

27. *Ibid.*, pp. 97-98.

28. *Ibid.*, pp. 107-8.

29. *Ibid.*, p. 227.

30. *Ibid.*, p. 225.

31. *Ibid.*, p. 204.

32. *Ibid.*, p. 205.

33. *Ibid.*, p. 281.

34. *Ibid.*, p. 282.

35. *Ibid.*, pp. 283-85.

36. *Ibid.*, pp. 208-12.

37. *Ibid.*, p. 212.

38. *Ibid.*, p. 213.

39. Kahn, *op. cit.*, p. 59.

40. *Motion Picture Hearings*, 1947, pp. 214-16.

41. *Ibid.*, p. 218.

42. Kahn, *op. cit.*, p. 43.

43. *Motion Picture Hearings*, 1947, pp. 230-34

44. *Ibid.*, p. 237.

45. *Ibid.*, p. 220.
46. *Ibid.*
47. *Ibid.*, pp. 221-23.
48. Kahn, *op. cit.*, pp. 32-33.
49. *Motion Picture Hearings*, 1947, pp. 82-90.
50. Suber, *op. cit.*, p. 85.
51. *Ibid.*, p. 86.
52. *Ibid.*, pp. 86-88.
53. Kahn, *op. cit.*, p. 63.
54. *Motion Picture Hearings*, 1947, p. 290.
55. *Ibid.*, p. 291.
56. *Ibid.*, p. 293.
57. *Ibid.*, pp. 293-95.
58. Kahn, *op. cit.*, p. 78.
59. *Motion Picture Hearings*, 1947, p. 333.
60. *Ibid.*, p. 334.
61. *Ibid.*, pp. 364-67.
62. *Ibid.*
63. *Ibid.*, p. 367.
64. *Ibid.*, p. 386.
65. *Ibid.*
66. *Ibid.*, pp. 387-88.
67. *Ibid.*, p. 403.
68. *Ibid.*, p. 404.
69. *Ibid.*, p. 412.
70. *Ibid.*, p. 414.
71. Kahn, *op. cit.*, p. 105.
72. *Motion Picture Hearings*, 1947, pp. 460-61.
73. *Ibid.*, p. 466.
74. *Ibid.*
75. *Ibid.*
76. *Ibid.*, p. 480.
77. *Ibid.*, p. 482.
78. New York *Herald Tribune*, January 7, 1948.
79. Kahn, *op. cit.*, p. 113.
80. *Motion Picture Hearings*, 1947, p. 486.
81. *Ibid.*, p. 492.
82. *Ibid.*, pp. 492-93.
83. *Ibid.*, p. 494.
84. Suber, *op. cit.*, p. 288.
85. *Motion Picture Hearings*, 1947, p. 308.
86. *Ibid.*, pp. 420-22.
87. *Ibid.*, pp. 444-45.
88. *Ibid.*, p. 445.
89. *Ibid.*, pp. 470-71.

90. *Ibid.*, pp. 471-72.

91. *Ibid.*, pp. 473-78.

92. Suber, *op. cit.*, pp. 285-97.

93. Walter Goodman, *The Committee; the Extraordinary Career of the House Committee on Un-American Activities* (New York, Farrar, Straus & Giroux, 1968), p. 301.

94. Suber, *op. cit.*, pp. 285-97.

95. C. Robert Jennings, "The Hollywood Ten, Plus Twenty," Los Angeles *Times, West Magazine*, September 3, 1967, p. 12.

96. *Ibid.*, pp. 12-14.

97. Ring Lardner, Jr., "My Life on the Blacklist," *Saturday Evening Post*, October 14, 1961, p. 38.

98. Goodman, *op. cit.*, p. 19.

99. New York *Herald Tribune*, July 1, 1945.

100. Goodman, *op. cit.*, p. 222.

101. Robert K. Carr, *The House Committee on Un-American Activities, 1945-1950* (Ithaca, New York, Cornell University Press, 1952), pp. 368-84.

102. No Los Angeles newspaper was included in the six analyzed by Carr.

103. Washington *Post*, October 23, 1947.

104. *Motion Picture Hearings*, 1947, p. 529.

105. U.S. Congress, House Committee on Un-American Activities, Eigthieth Congress, Second Session, *Report*, December 31, 1948, p. 9.

106. Dalton Trumbo, *The Time of the Toad* (Hollywood, The Hollywood Ten, n. d. [1949?]), p. 18.

107. Carr, *op. cit.*, p. 58.

Chapter IV

John S. Wood's Marathon Ten-Part 1951-1952 Investigation of Communism in the Entertainment Field

THE "ism" that was to be affixed to the name McCarthy had not yet become part of the American lexicon when J. Parnell Thomas closed his 1947 investigation of Communist infiltration of the motion picture industry. But the factors that made Senator Joseph McCarthy's astonishing position in American history possible were apparent in the period immediately following World War II.

The half-dozen years from 1939 to 1945 had given the nation a brief respite from hating Communism. The Russians had been our allies and the Germans and Japanese our enemies. Suddenly these positions were reversed. In Europe, formidable Fascism was over and we were helping our recent enemies with vast amounts of economic aid. The USSR was no longer inhabited by friendly Russians. It harbored the enemy—Communists. In 1947, the Truman Doctrine committed America's might to the defense of Greece and Turkey, two Middle East countries threatened by Communist expansion. In 1948, the Berlin airlift saved that city from Joseph Stalin.

Extreme unrest was the mood of the nation and damning Communism was the principal occupation of many of the leading figures of the period. During the Depression years many people joined groups that were to be listed later as Red tinged. They had joined with the hope of bettering the human condition, not, with few exceptions, as advocates of the violent dismantling of the American system. Unfortunately, many of the joiners were inevitably to be so categorized "by the loudest voices of demagoguery."[1]

Before 1949 was over, some 462,000,000 Chinese could see the Red flag of Communism raised over their ancient Asian land. In June, 1950, North Korean Communist troops marched across the thirty-eighth parallel, and the United States was, for the third time in the first half of the twentieth century, at war. The atmosphere in America was rife with persons being called Communists by anyone with whom they disagreed.

Shortly before the outbreak of the Korean War, Senator McCarthy was invited to speak to the Ohio County Women's Republican Club at Wheeling, West Virginia. ". . . it was there that he either did or did not wave a piece of paper—reports were contradictory—and say that it contained the names of 205 Communists in the State Department."[2] McCarthyism was born at that moment and it did not die with its creator's demise in 1956.

The vehicle McCarthy used in the Senate for his investigations was the cumbersomely titled Permanent Sub-Committee on Investigations of the Senate Committee on Government Operations of the United States Senate. It was more familiarly known to the public as the McCarthy Committee because of the imprint made by its chairman.

The proper purpose of a Congressional committee, be it McCarthy's in the Senate or the House Committee on Un-American Activities, is to investigate how existing laws work and to either amend or draft new laws. A Congressional committee was never intended to "conduct quasi trials with power of punishment."[3]

McCarthy's personal publicity as a hunter of Communists, his flair for theatrics, his perception of the timing of news releases, his ability to discredit by implication some of the most significant men in the government in the early 1950's all made the work of the committee in the House that much easier and, to the public, significant.

The refusal to assist a Congressional committee in its at-

tempts to investigate gives Congress the power to punish for
contempt. In the case of the Hollywood Ten, the First Amendment was used as protection.

By 1951 the protective cover was the Fifth Amendment,
which broadly states, ". . . when a witness in his own opinion
considers that the answer to a question might tend to incriminate him, he cannot be compelled to be a witness against
himself and made to answer."[4]

The shield offered to a witness under the Fifth Amendment
became quite the opposite. Instead, abuse and distortion caused
the words "the Fifth Amendment" to become scatological.
Congressional committees exposed people for nonconformity of
thought and action, one of the hallmarks of a robustious
republic. The fear of being subpoenaed to appear before one of
these investigating committees "silenced many people whose
unorthodox and controversial views would be healthy elements
in a democratic society."[5]

While McCarthy was busy conducting his Senate investigations, the House committee was once again certain that there
was Communist infiltration of the entertainment industry.

Description of the Hearings

At 10:30 a.m., March 8, 1951, in room 226 of the old House
Office Building in Washington, D.C., Chairman John S. Wood
set about the business of clearing the Reds out of the studios
and stages of America.

In addition to Wood, committee members present were
Representatives Francis E. Walter, Morgan M. Moulder, Clyde
Doyle, James B. Frazier, Jr., Harold H. Velde, Bernard W.
Kearney, and Charles E. Potter.

Staff members present were Frank S. Tavenner, Jr., counsel;
Louis J. Russell, senior investigator; John W. Carrington, clerk;
and A. S. Poore, editor.[6]

The first witness on March 8 was the Communist Party's
cultural chieftain, Victor Jeremy Jerome.[7] In 1947, Jerome
published his observations on Eugene O'Neill's thesis of life:

In the theatre, dead-end futility is bodied forth in Eugene

O'Neill's The Iceman Cometh. O'Neill builds his drama on the thesis that life is a struggle between illusion and reality, in which illusion is indispensable to life, while reality is unbearable and means death.[8]

V. J. Jerome's struggle that first morning before the committee was far more significant for its constitutional dogmatism than for anything as lofty as life. He invoked the Fifth Amendment on self-incrimination 113 times![9]

The distinguished constitutional historian Leonard W. Levy, in his brilliant study of the Fifth Amendment, concluded:

> The framers of the Bill of Rights saw their injunction, that no man should be a witness against himself in a criminal case, as a central feature of the accusatory system of criminal justice. While deeply committed to perpetuating a system that minimized the possibilities of convicting the innocent, they were not less concerned about the humanity that the fundamental law should show even to the offender. Above all, the Fifth Amendment reflected their judgment that in a free society, based on respect for the individual, the determination of guilt or innocence by just procedures, in which the accused made no unwilling contribution to his conviction, was more important than punishing the guilty.[10]

Actor Howard da Silva was the next witness to take the constitutional refuge implied in Levy's historical summation.[11] Before notifying the committee of his intention to take the Fifth, the actor asked if he might read a statement when he took the stand on March 21. Chairman Wood denied his request because the actor had released his remarks to the press shortly before 10 a.m. that day. The chairman noted that it was now after 3 p.m. "In the light of the fact it has been given this wide publicity, I see no purpose in burdening the record with a repetition of it."[12]

Counsel Tavenner asked Da Silva about his affiliations with the Civil Rights Congress, the Joint Anti-Fascist Refugee Committee, the Actors' Laboratory, a statement in the Daily Worker which bore his name, and then wanted to know if he had been a member of the Communist Party:

MR. DA SILVA: I refuse to answer the question on the

following basis: The first and fifth amendments and all of
the Bill of Rights protect me from any inquisitorial procedure, and I may not be compelled to cooperate with this
committee in producing evidence designed to incriminate me
and to drive me from my profession as an actor. The
historical origin of the fifth amendment is founded in the
resistance of the people to attempts to prosecute and
persecute individuals because of—

MR. WOOD: Will you please wait a moment? Please ascribe to
the committee the intelligence to determine these questions
for itself, and don't argue about it.

MR. DA SILVA: I don't care to argue about it, but I wish to
clarify my position.

MR. WOOD: You need not teach this committee a class in law.

MR. DA SILVA: It is not my position. It is my position to
uphold the law and to make sure the committee does.

MR. WOOD: If you say you decline to answer for the reasons
given, it will be understood.

MR. TAVENNER: Do you refuse to answer the question?

MR. DA SILVA: I refuse to answer the question on the basis of
my statement here, on the basis that my answer might,
according to the standards of this committee, tend to
incriminate me.

He refused, on the same basis, to admit being associated in a
gala Communist function with actor Will Geer, who was,
according to the evidence, director of a play honoring Mother
Bloor, a celebrated Red (and incidentally his grandmother-in-
law), on her seventy-fifth birthday.

Da Silva defended his position from the point of view of
"peace":

MR. KEARNEY: Are you in favor of the Communist-inspired
peace marches on Washington?

MR. DA SILVA: Mr. Kearney, my opinions on peace have been
many, and I have made them over a period of many years.

MR. KEARNEY: No further questions.

MR. DA SILVA: But today, when the purpose is to link the
word "peace" and the word "subversive" all over America, I
refuse to answer this question on the basis previously stated.

MR. WOOD: Mr. Velde?

MR. VELDE: Do you think this is a legally organized committee of Congress?

MR. DA SILVA: A legally organized committee of Congress?

MR. VELDE: Yes.

MR. DA SILVA: I think its actions have been decidedly illegal. I think its actions have been for the specific purpose of pulling wool over Americans' eyes.

MR. VELDE: Do you think the Congress has a right to inquire into subversive activities in the United States of America?

MR. DA SILVA: I think that Congress has many rights. The least of its rights are the freedom to wage war today.

MR. VELDE: I would appreciate a specific answer.

MR. DA SILVA: Would you voice your question again?

MR. VELDE: Do you believe that the Congress has a right to inquire into subversive and disloyal activities in the United States?

MR. DA SILVA: Well, this is obviously what this committee is doing at present.

MR. VELDE: Do you believe that we have that right?

MR. DA SILVA: I think that the overwhelming majority of the American people want peace and don't want to drop an atom bomb. I think that is the most pressing issue of the day. I think that any attempt to investigate so-called subversive organizations is an attempt to pull wool over the American people's eyes, the old Army game, to say, "Look what is happening there, and meanwhile we pick your pockets and drop atom bombs." That is the real function.

MR. VELDE: I think you are not answering the question.

MR. DA SILVA: I am answering the question as specifically as I can. It has been said before. This is part of the same thing. I heard Mr. Walter say it sounds like the Daily Worker. I recognize that every statement made which is on peace or on any issue that you find in your disfavor is called an issue that sounds like the Daily Worker or an issue that is subversive or an issue that is questionable. To me the question of peace today is not a subversive issue.[13]

The first actress to win the Oscar as best supporting player, Gale Sondergaard (for her role in *Anthony Adverse*), was also refused permission by the chair to read her prepared statement on March 21. Chairman Wood said the committee would file her remarks for the record after she was examined. In private life the actress was the wife of Herbert J. Biberman, the writer, director, producer, and member of the Unfriendly Ten.

In reply to Tavenner's question about what "guilds or

organizations" she had "been identified with in Hollywood," the actress responded that she had "read a long, long list of organizations" branded subversive by the committee and other governmental bodies. She further explained:

> I have a feeling if you will ask me what organizations I belonged to that you probably would like me to tie myself into one of these, and there I must refuse to answer the question on the grounds of the fifth amendment, that it might tend to incriminate me.[14]

The counsel disclosed that the committee was in possession of a card dated December 1, 1944, indicating that the actress was registered as a Communist and her membership card bore the number 47328 for the year 1945. Miss Sondergaard refused to comment upon this documentary evidence and all subsequent efforts by the committee to link her with Communist fronts and organizations.[15]

Actor and entertainer Will Geer told the committee on April 11 that although he had completed college in 1926, he was still a student of philosophy and he pursued agriculture and horticulture as hobbies. After a homey exchange concerning a hen, an egg, and the actor's blueberry farm, Geer refused to tell Tavenner if he had signed a Communist Party nominating petition on July 23, 1942. He also refused to answer whether or not he was a member of the Communist Party. Not satisfied with Geer's illusive answers, Wood and Velde pressed him further:

> MR. WOOD: I want to know what your conception is about what incriminates you to tell the truth before this committee, if it is the truth, that you are not a member of the Communist Party. That wouldn't in any sense incriminate you, would it?
>
> MR. GEER: I really believe, sir, that the best answer to that, that I'm just allergic to meetings and things of that sort, and I stand on the advice of my counsel that—
>
> MR. WOOD: And decline to answer that question?
>
> MR. GEER: In this particular day, April 11, 1951, I do, sir, with the situation of the world as it is. It's a hysterical situation.
>
> MR. WOOD: That's all.

MR. GEER: Thank you, sir.

MR. VELDE: I have one more question. Did I understand you to say that you felt the Communist Party was a legal party?

MR. GEER: I understand so. I believe that.

MR. VELDE: You understand it is?

MR. GEER: To my understanding.

MR. VELDE: Would it be any crime to admit your membership in a legal party, then?

MR. GEER: In this day of hysteria it is, sir.[16]

Screenwriter Robert Lees followed Geer and was as unfriendly to the committee as his predecessor. In refusing to answer questions about organizations to which he had belonged or to name individuals with whom he had worked, he adopted the premise taken by Miss Sondergaard. The writer testified:

> Well, I know this: That there are a great number of organizations that this committee has deemed to be subversive and my connections with any individual that can be connected with these organizations can tend to incriminate me, and for this reason I have declined to answer that question.[17]

Referring to the First Amendment, Lees remarked, "I feel that any infringement on perhaps opinions or thoughts which this committee or some other future committee might deem suddenly un-American becomes a very dangerous thing in this country. Very dangerous."[18]

Waldo Salt, later scenarist for the 1969 hit film *Midnight Cowboy* concurred with Lees and Miss Sondergaard, pointing out that the committee had labeled 643 organizations subversive. He refused on April 13 to answer if he was "at any time a member of the board of directors or other governing body of Actors' Laboratory, Inc." He based his refusal on his contention that California State Senator Jack Tenney had already investigated the organization and labeled it subversive.[19]

Paul Jarrico, collaborator with Richard Collins on *Song of Russia*, the film that had so offended Ayn Rand in 1947, was next to testify that day. In response to Representative Doyle's question if Jarrico felt that the committee "was controverting and destroying the rights of American citizens" by its investigation, the writer emotionally replied:

I am certain that Congress had no such intention. However, 10 of my friends, very dear friends, have gone to jail for coming before this body and saying that Congress may not investigate in any area in which it may not legislate, and since the Constitution of the United States specifically states that Congress shall make no law restricting the freedom of speech, and since countless decisions of the courts have held that this provision of the Constitution means that Congress cannot investigate into areas of opinion, of conscience, of belief, I believe that in asking that those men be cited for contempt of Congress and in successfully sending these men to jail, that this committee has subverted the meaning of the American Constitution; yes.

In his statement, Jarrico was alluding to the contempt charges invoked by the use of the First Amendment. He declined to answer committee questions, basing his refusal on the Fifth, and as a result it was he who was publicly suspect of subverting the Constitution. Representative Doyle asked for a definition of advocacy:

MR. DOYLE: I will ask you another question, Mr. Jarrico, and if you think the form of my question is not fair I want you to tell me so, because I am trying in good faith to be fair. I am not trying to take any advantage of you or lay any groundwork for any persecution.

I think you said that you believed that the American citizen had the right to advocate anything he wished to?

MR. JARRICO: That's correct.

MR. DOYLE: Do I understand, therefore, that you think an American citizen has the right to advocate the forceful overthrow of our constitutional form of government?

MR. JARRICO: I believe he may advocate it. I believe that it is unlikely he will get a great response to such a thing. I want to make it clear that I am personally opposed to the overthrow of this Government by force and violence and to the use of force and violence. However, President Lincoln said that the people of this country have the right to revolution, if necessary, if the democratic processes are clogged, if the people can no longer exercise their will by constitutional means.

MR. DOYLE: Do you know of any organization in the United States that is regulated from within the United States that advocates the forceful overthrow of the constitutional form of government? Do you know of any organization that does?

MR. JARRICO: Well, the McCarran Act, the Smith Act—

MR. DOYLE: I am asking you about an organization. Do you know of any organization?

MR. JARRICO: I am answering that question, sir. I am saying that various acts passed by the United States Congress have defined certain organizations as organizations which advocate the overthrow of this Government. I do not necessarily agree with these definitions.

MR. DOYLE: I am not asking you whether you agree with the definition or not. I am asking you as man to man in good faith whether or not you know any such organization. I am assuming that you as an American citizen are interested in protecting our American form of government against forceful revolution. If my assumption is wrong, of course the basis of my question is wrong. I am not asking you whether or not you are a member of any such organization, you notice. I am not asking that question. You have stood on your constitutional right under the fifth amendment. I am not asking you in that area. But I am just assuming as man to man that you, if you know of any organization in America that favors that policy, in good faith will come out and tell us so.

MR. JARRICO: Well, sir, this committee—

MR. DOYLE: Do you know of any such organization?

MR. JARRICO: According to this committee, every organization that has advocated peace in this country—

MR. DOYLE: Just a minute. That question can be answered "Yes" or "No." We have other witnesses from Hollywood here. We want to have them be heard, too, so they can get home over the weekend.

MR. JARRICO: By your definition, sir, every organization that has stood for decency and progress, the New Deal, against discrimination, for peace, and so on—these organizations are all allied with an organization which advocates the overthrow of this Government. I do not accept that definition.

MR. DOYLE: In other words, you don't accept the definition of Mr. Webster's dictionary.

MR. JARRICO: Yes, I do accept the definition of Mr. Webster.

MR. DOYLE: I am asking you whether or not, under the definition of Mr. Webster, you know of any organization in this country that advocates what Mr. Webster says is subversive conduct, that's all. That is what I am asking you. I am assuming that you want to help protect the American Government.

MR. JARRICO: If I knew of such an organization, sir, I should help you to expose it.

MR. DOYLE: Do you know of any individual that is interested in that?

MR. JARRICO: If I knew of such an individual, sir, I should help you to expose him.

MR. DOYLE: All right. Now, one more question. In answer to our counsel you stated that you believed that our functioning as a committee was to form the basis of a blacklist. Why do you believe this committee is interested in blacklisting people so they can't get employment, if they are honest, patriotic citizens? Is that your statement?

MR. JARRICO: You are not interested in that end, but you had better revise your methods, because your methods have had that end. I know of many people who are blacklisted in Hollywood as a result of the hearings in 1947, and I know that today the basis is being laid for an increase of that blacklist, so that anyone who has advocated anything progressive is going to be a suspect. And the Motion Picture Alliance for the Preservation of American Ideals, quaintly named, is going to be the organization in Hollywood that decides who shall work and who shall not work, what pictures shall be made and what pictures shall not be made, and this is an organization that upholds this committee and thinks it is doing a splendid job in exposing so-called "Reds."

MR. DOYLE: What is the name of that committee?

MR. JARRICO: The Motion Picture Alliance for the Preservation of American Ideals. You should know it very well, Mr. Doyle.

MR. DOYLE: But I don't happen to know it, sir. You see, there are many of us, Mr. Jarrico, in spite of your assumption, that are just as much interested as you are in protecting the rights of American citizens and are just as progressive and just as patriotic toward liberal thinking, whether you believe it or not.

I wish to state—I know for myself, and I state it for myself and I state it for every member of the committee—that we are not interested in blacklisting anyone. I wouldn't be true to my duty as a citizen if I allowed you to charge that we are without denying it. But I will say this: My own belief is that you gentlemen who come to this committee and unalterably claim the fifth amendment and the first amendment when we get into the area of questioning you about the organizations you have been or are members of, are making it very difficult for this committee as a committee of Congress to function.

MR. JARRICO: I feel I am defending the Constitution, sir, and not hiding behind it. I feel that sincerely. And I feel that if you were sincere in your declarations against blacklisting that you should make it plain that people who claim their constitutional privileges should not be discriminated against in Hollywood, because Hollywood has the impression that you intend everyone who is called before this committee and who does not cooperate with this committee to be driven from the industry.[20]

Actors Victor Kilian, Jr., and Fred Graff testified before the committee on April 13, 1951, the last of the unfriendly witnesses to appear during the first of the ten-part, two-year, second investigation of Communist infiltration of the Hollywood motion picture industry. Kilian was told by Tavenner that the committee had information that he had been issued a numbered registration card in the Communist Party in 1945. Graff was informed by Tavenner that he held a numbered registration card in the Communist Political Association dated 1941. Both men took the Fifth.[21]

Chairman Wood closed the session by announcing:

> . . . that any person whose name has been given in these public hearings as having been affiliated with the Communist Party or any other organization that may have been cited by either the committee or the Attorney General of America as being a subversive or front organization, who desires to do so, we will certainly welcome their presence here at such time as the committee may be able to make the proper arrangements, to make whatever reply or response they desire in connection therewith.[22]

And there had been many names mentioned during this first phase of the investigation, not only by the committee in its dialogue with the unfriendly witnesses, but also by the friendly witnesses, commencing with the strange and pitiful testimony of actor Larry Parks.

After a thirteen-day layoff following V. J. Jerome's uncooperative appearance, the committee reconvened on the first day of spring, Wednesday, March 21, 1951, at 10:35 a.m. It is certain that Parks does not remember the day as one of seasonal awakening but rather as one of moral deadening—as did Paul Jarrico.

On March 24 of that year, Jarrico told the New York *Times*, "If I have to choose between crawling in the mud with Larry Parks or going to jail like my courageous friends of the Hollywood Ten, I shall certainly choose the latter."[23]

Parks was the first entertainer in 1951 who was forced to soul-search for the proper moral answer to the question that was to face all of the subpoenaed show business witnesses who followed him.

The dilemma was: "If they took the Fifth Amendment, their Hollywood careers would, for the foreseeable future, be ended. But to testify about their friends was for some a repugnant as well as an uncertain means of salvation."[24]

Additionally, due to the 1947 Hollywood investigation, there was the specter of prison beclouding the decision.

These confusing problems and possibilities prompted Parks to try to avoid any conclusive, specific answers to the majority of the committee's questions.

After some gentle prodding by Counsel Tavenner, Parks admitted: "I'm familiar with the Actors' Laboratory . . . I'm familiar with the Actors' Lab."

Further probing by the committee counsel elicited from the actor who had starred in *The Jolson Story*: "For a time I was sort of honorary treasurer of this organization." When Tavenner asked if he had served in 1949 and 1950, the actor had another lapse of memory. "Well, I can't recall the exact date. I don't believe it was in 1950. I believe it was before that. I can't tell you the exact date."

He thought he was a member of some of the other organizations on the subversive list handed him by Tavenner. He did not believe he held any official position in any of them. He asked Tavenner to "refresh" his memory. It was "possible," the actor said, that he had appeared at a meeting of the Civil Rights Congress—and he might have been one of the speakers. Yes, the actor acknowledged, there were Communists attached to some of the organizations with which he had been affiliated—"the Actors' Lab, for instance. . . ."

Finally, Parks conceded, "I was a member of the Communist Party. . . ." He joined in 1941. "And to the best of my recollection I petered out about the latter part of 1944 or 1945." He joined because membership "fulfilled certain needs of a young man that was liberal in thought, idealistic, who was for the underprivileged, the underdog."[25]

On the question of naming names of alleged Communists, Parks beseechingly demurred:

> MR. PARKS: Well, Counsel, these—I would prefer not to mention names, if it is at all possible, of anyone. I don't think it is fair to people to do this. I have come to you at your request. I have come and willingly tell you about myself. I think that, if you would allow me, I would prefer not to be questioned about names. And I will tell you everything that I know about myself, because I feel I have done nothing wrong, and I will answer any question that you would like to put to me about myself. I would prefer, if you will allow me, not to mention other people's names. . . .
>
> MR. WOOD: Just a moment. At that point, do you entertain the feeling that these other parties that you were associated with are likewise guiltless of any wrong?
>
> MR. PARKS: The people at that time as I knew them—this is my opinion of them. This is my honest opinion: That these are people who did nothing wrong, people like myself. . . .
>
> And it seems to me that this is not the American way of doing things—to force a man who is under oath and who has opened himself as wide as possible to this committee—and it hasn't been easy to do this—to force a man to do this is not American justice.
>
> I perhaps later can think of more things to say when I leave, but this is in substance I guess what I want to say.[26]

Representatives Wood and Walter respected the actor's plea largely because, as it was later made clear in testimony, the committee already knew the names it was trying to get the witness to divulge. Parks was let off on the condition that he would testify fully in executive session. This he did, and "Parks was left with his career in limbo, the film he was scheduled to do for Columbia Studios having been canceled when he received his subpoena."[27]

The longest testimony of the first part of the investigation was given on April 10 by actor and friendly witness Sterling Hayden, another former member of the Communist Party. He, unlike Parks, was not hesitant to name names of alleged Communists publicly, before the committee and the nation. He was the first of many who elected to put the continuance of their careers ahead of personal and professional friendships.

After a lengthy explanation of how he had, through his daring war exploits behind the German lines, become enraptured by the Partisans of Yugoslavia and how he concomitantly became exposed to Communist ideology and Communists, he told the committee he joined the Communist Party in Hollywood "approximately between the 5th and 15th of June, 1946, but that may not be accurate."[28]

He named Bea Winters, a secretary, as the woman who was responsible for asking him to join the Communist Party. She was the first of a list of show business persons named by Hayden as Communists, ex- or current. The list included writer-director Abraham Polonsky, actress Karen Morley, her husband-actor Lloyd Gough, and writer Robert Lees. Hayden implied that Howard da Silva was a Communist because of his "behavior" before the committee the previous month. He mentioned that some of the meetings of the Communist group to which he belonged occurred at the home of actor Morris Carnovsky, although Carnovsky was never present. Hayden additionally furnished the committee investigators with a list of people he conjectured were Communists. His reason for doing this was summed up by Chairman Wood: "Your purpose in furnishing the list of names to the investigators was that by proper investigation on the part of the investigators of the committee and the committee itself, that their connection with the Communist Party might be revealed with reference to some of them?" The actor replied in the affirmative!

> MR. DOYLE: I am going to ask you this question. I don't know if it was asked by any other member of the committee when I went to the floor to vote or not. You are here before a committee of the United States Congress, a duly constituted committee of the House of Representatives, every Member of which is elected every 2 years by the American people. What is your opinion of the jurisdiction, the purpose, the functioning of this committee, before which you have testified 3 hours today? Is it, in your judgment, serving a

useful purpose? Is it serving a necessary purpose? If so, to what extent, and if not, why? Is that a fair question?

MR. HAYDEN: Yes.

MR. DOYLE: I am really asking for your honest-to-God truthful opinion. I have never asked that question before, but I think in view of the manner in which you have come before this committee, and the apparent frankness with which you have answered questions, if you have any criticism of the manner in which this committee functions, I would like to know what that criticism is. You have now been before us 3 hours.

MR. HAYDEN: I think of no criticism whatever.

MR. DOYLE: Have you any suggestions to make of ways and means in which we might be more helpful in meeting this problem of the determination of the Communist Party of the United States to overthrow, if necessary by force, our Government?

MR. HAYDEN: I think that the request and suggestion that was made by the chairman of the committee, of which I was apprised by the counsel of the committee, that people come up and speak up, is the thing I came here today thinking it was an extremely fine thing, a constructive thing.

I don't mean to attach any importance to myself as an individual who is out of balance, but I have had the feeling that my appearance before the committee could serve a very useful purpose. I hope it does.

MR. DOYLE: Thank you.[29]

Hayden was excused by the committee and subsequently by the majority of the nation's press, but not by the actor himself. He wrote later:

Not often does a man find himself eulogized for having behaved in a manner that he himself despises. I subscribed to a press-clipping service. They sent me two thousand clips from papers east and west, large and small, and from dozens of magazines. Most had nothing but praise for my one-shot stoolie show. Only a handful—led by *The New York Times*—denounced this abrogation of constitutional freedoms whereby the stoolie could gain status in a land of frightened people.[30]

The first Hollywood pigeon of the genus "stoolie" had sung publicly, and before Chairman Wood had concluded his ten-part marathon investigation on November 13, 1952, many more voices would be raised in a cacophony of naming names.

On April 12, 1951, screenwriter Richard J. Collins took the witness stand. Collins recounted that in 1936 he was introduced to a class in Marxism by a man who had been to Russia and "was very enthusiastic about it." The traveler was writer Budd Schulberg. Collins admitted to Counsel Tavenner that he had been a Communist. He named John Howard Lawson as a former leader of the Communist Party in Hollywood. Ring Lardner, Jr., was identified by the witness as having been a member of his Communist Party cell. Collins continued: Albert Maltz had been a Communist; Samuel Sillen, one of the editors of the *New Masses*, Collins presumed, had been a Communist; Lester Cole was a Communist; Paul Jarrico had been; Louis B. Mayer was not; Robert Rossen had been but had sent a letter to Harry Cohn, head of Columbia Pictures, saying that he was no longer a member of the party; Schulberg had been; screenwriter Martin Berkeley had hosted a cell meeting at his home; also in attendance was Hollywood Ten writer Samuel Ornitz; silent movie actor Herbert Blache had attended a cell meeting where Collins was present; the witness had recruited writer Waldo Salt as a Communist; writer John Bright was a Communist; Gertrude Purcell, a member of the board of the Screen Writers Guild in 1938 and 1939, might have been; writers Gordon Kahn and Leonardo Bercovici had been Communists; Elizabeth Leech Glenn had been a Communist and may have worked at a studio; her husband Charles Glenn had co-led with Salt a section of the Communist Party; Frank Tuttle had been a Communist; and writer Dudley Nichols was not.[31]

This comprised Collins' list of persons associated in one way or another with Hollywood who were, had been, or were not Communists.

In response to Representative Donald Jackson's questions, Collins estimated that the peak membership of the Communist Party in Hollywood during the Second World War was "several hundred," of whom he knew twenty. The witness supposed that of the latter group, "about" 25 percent had broken with the party "in various degrees." Collins agreed that the balance of 75 percent "might be considered to belong actively or to be in the fellow-traveler classification."[32]

Richard Collins, the second friendly witness before the committee (he had also been subpoenaed in 1947 but was not called to testify), summed up his reasons for stating why he would not have been a friendly witness in the J. Parnell Thomas investigation and why now, in 1951, he was:

> It would be because at that time it seemed to me that purely on American democratic constitutional grounds there was a question of the propriety of asking a man his political beliefs. Without going into the question of its propriety today, there has been a marked change in the world situation since 1947, and there has been as great a change in me. It is hard to tell where one thing begins and the other ends.[33]

It was less difficult for Paul Jarrico, Collins' writing collaborator and friend for fourteen years, to tell where friendship ends and personal expediency begins.

Ten days before Collins' testimony, Jarrico telephoned his friend and asked if he might see him. Jarrico asked his host if he would give his personal assurance that he would not give any names when called to testify. Collins resisted at first but then attempted to strike a bargain. He would not name names if Jarrico would promise he would do nothing to help the Soviet Union in the event of war between the United States and the Soviet Union. Jarrico could not agree to this proposition, and Collins refused to alter his original offer of compromise. In Collins' words, ". . . since we would not lie to each other, we had no further conversation."[34]

"It was," as Walter Goodman points out, "but one of many friendships that were shattered in the course of these hearings."[35]

The remaining friendly witness in the first session of Wood's investigation was Mrs. Meta Reis Rosenberg, former head of the literary department of Berg-Allenberg, a motion picture agency. She spoke up when on April 13 she identified persons she had seen at Communist Party meetings who were previously cited publicly by witnesses before the committee. She also introduced into the "Red" record such personages as actress Dorothy Tree and her husband, writer Michael Uris, writer Francis

Faragoh, film maker Carleton Moss, artist Edward Biberman (Herbert's brother), and agent George Willner. The woman literary agent's dossier also included Madelaine Ruthven, ex-writer and CP functionary in Hollywood and its environs.[36]

Nunnally Johnson, a producer-writer at Twentieth Century-Fox Studios at the time of Mrs. Rosenberg's testimony, sent her a telegram which she presented to Tavenner at the conclusion of her testimony. The committee counsel graciously decided to read it aloud, "to save the witness a little embarrassment":

> Mrs. Meta Rosenberg
> Statler Hotel, Washington, D.C.
>
> I trust this will convince you that politics is no business for a fetching girl. Politics is for flat-chested girls.
>
> (Laughter.)[37]

It is certain that those persons whose names were cited publicly for the first time by Mrs. Rosenberg as having been in attendance at Communist meetings agreed with Nunnally Johnson.

Round two of ten opened April 17, 1951, with a dozen new witnesses appearing and two former figures from the 1947 hearings testifying for the second time, labor leader Roy Brewer and Edward Dmytryk. This time director Dmytryk was as friendly as Brewer had been in the earlier investigation, a situation occasioned undoubtedly by time, prison, reflection, and a personal reassessment of the moral question of naming names in order to continue working above ground at his career.

As discussed in the preceding chapter, after prison the remainder of the First Amendment unfriendly witnesses were forced underground until the anti-Communist public passions cooled toward the end of the fifties. But this was the beginning of that decade and the first three witnesses before the committee that April day were Fifth Amendment unfriendlies.

They were writers Sam Moore and Harold Buchman and Academy Award winner actress Anne Revere, who were sworn in April 17. Miss Revere won the Oscar for "best supporting female player" in *National Velvet*.

Moore declined to answer any questions regarding his association with the Hollywood Writers Mobilization, claiming that the organization had been listed as a "so-called subversive group" by the committee and others.[38]

Counsel Tavenner told the witness the committee had information that he was a member of the Communist Party in 1944 and 1945 and cited the number of his CP registration card for the latter year. Moore once again claimed his constitutional privilege of not incriminating himself.[39]

Buchman, for reasons similar to Moore's, refused to answer questions regarding the Hollywood Writers Mobilization. The writer informed the committee that he had taken a "grand tour" for five months in 1937 and 1938 and that he had spent five or six weeks in the Soviet Union. Tavenner told Buchman the committee had information that the writer held cards in the Communist Political Association in 1944 and the Communist Party in 1945 and cited their registration numbers.

After refusing to comment on the CP membership cards, Buchman explained to Representative Doyle that he had "applauded" his election many years ago and that he believed Doyle was "sincere" in his "desire to understand what was going on here."

"But I could find a stack of very conservative opinion, Mr. Doyle, to the effect that this committee is not a good committee." The Congressman did not choose to comment on the committee's goodness and Buchman was followed by Miss Revere.[40]

The "Bourbon punctilio" of the committee, as Gordon Kahn described the interrogators in 1947, was practiced in 1951 by Tavenner when the counsel asked the actress the place of her birth. She facetiously replied, "Thank you for not asking me when. . . . Occasionally I play grandmothers, and it might jeopardize my professional standing."

In response to a question regarding her former membership in the Actors' Laboratory, Miss Revere refused to answer and gave the committee her interpretation of what constituted an attempt to overthrow the American system:

Mr. Tavenner and gentlemen, this would seem to me, based

upon my observation in the course of the week in which I have listened to these testimonies, to be the first in a possible series of questions which would attempt in some manner to link me with subversive organizations; and as the Communist Party is a political party—legal political party—in this country today, and as I consider any questioning regarding one's political views or religious views as a violation of the rights of a citizen under our Constitution, and as I would consider myself, therefore, contributing to the overthrow of our form of government as I understand it if I were to assist you in violating this privilege of mine and other citizens of this country, I respectfully decline to answer this question on the basis of the fifth amendment, possible self-incrimination, and also the first amendment.

Miss Revere requested to see the document Tavenner held, establishing her numbered Communist Party registration cards for the years 1944 and 1945. Satisfied that the counsel seemed to have such evidence, she refused to answer whether she recognized the card he handed to her.[41]

The next two unfriendly witnesses appeared a week later, on April 24, 1951, writers' agent George Willner and actor Morris Carnovsky.

When asked if he had been the business manager of the *New Masses* in New York from 1936 to 1939, Willner refused to answer because the publication was listed as "subversive" in the committee's guide and the members were therefore "trying to link" him with an organization already categorized as Red.

Representative Morgan M. Moulder summed up his observations on the agent's subsequent refusal to answer questions about people, organizations, and events":

> Mr. Willner, the record would reveal that you have refused to answer probably 99 percent of the questions propounded to you, for the alleged reason that it would tend to incriminate you. . . . And under the Federal statutes any testimony you may give here could not be used against you. Therefore, your refusal to testify so consistently leaves a strong inference that you are still an ardent follower of the Communist Party and its purpose. That's all.

It was not *all* the dialogue for the day, however. Carnovsky was next and gave the committee a detailed recital of his academic and professional background before claiming his constitutional immunity on questions concerning his relationship with the Group Theatre, the Joint Anti-Fascist Refugee Committee, the Civil Rights Congress, the Progressive Citizens of America, the Council of the Arts, Sciences, and Professions, the American Peace Mobilization, and a 1944 Communist Party membership book numbered 48975. Regarding the CP card, Representative Walter inquired:

MR. WALTER: As I understand your position, you feel that if you would admit that you were the holder of that Communist Party card you might be prosecuted in a criminal case for what you have admitted here. Is that correct?

MR. CARNOVSKY: I feel that under the fifth amendment I have the right to decline to answer that statement and that question, and I stand on it.

MR. WALTER: But, now, let's get this straight. You are fearful, and that is why you invoke the protection given by the fifth amendment to people charged with crimes, that the testimony adduced here might be used against you in a criminal proceeding. Is that correct?

MR. CARNOVSKY: That is as I understand it, sir; yes.

MR. WALTER: Don't you know under the law any testimony given here cannot be used anywhere else?

MR. CARNOVSKY: That is not the fact, Mr. Walter.

MR. WALTER: Do you get your legal opinions from the New Yorker, also?

MR. CARNOVSKY: I get my legal opinions basically from the Constitution of the United States and the Bill of Rights.

MR. WALTER: Of course, the statute that I have referred to is a law enacted under the Constitution and the Bill of Rights. It was enacted for the very purpose of affording protection to people who come forward and assist congressional committees in fulfilling their obligation to the Congress and to the people of the United States. There is a statute that expressly protects the witness from any use of any testimony he gives in any other proceeding.

MR. CARNOVSKY: Mr. Walter, it seems you have not read the recent case passed upon the Supreme Court.

MR. WALTER: What case was that? Why don't you answer, Mr. Popper?

MR. POPPER:* I think that is a good idea, sir, because I know
you were a distinguished lawyer long before you were in
Congress. The fact of the matter is the Supreme Court of the
United States has repeatedly said, and said very recently,
that there is no such thing as an immunity statute.

MR. WALTER: I am not so certain this exact question has been
passed upon.

MR. POPPER: Oh, yes. May I refer you to United States
against Bryan.

MR. WALTER: Yes. I know the case.

    You still decline to answer because you are afraid you
might be prosecuted criminally for any testimony you give.
Is that correct?

MR. CARNOVSKY: I refuse to answer, because this might tend
to incriminate me.[43]

On the following day writer Abraham Polonsky was the first
witness. When confronted with the testimony of friendly
witnesses Sterling Hayden, Mrs. Meta Rosenberg, and Richard
Collins, persons who had identified Polonsky as a member of
the Communist Party, he invoked the Fifth Amendment. He
subsequently refused to answer whether his wife, Sylvia Marrow, was a member of the Communist Party.[44]

On succeeding days of the following months, May 16 and 17,
1951, writer Leonardo Bercovici, actors Alvin Hammer and
Lloyd Gough, and Bea (Bernadette) Winters, former secretary
to Meta Reis Rosenberg, completed the list of unfriendly
witnesses during the second part of the committee's 1951-52
investigation.[45]

In addition to the two committee investigators, William A.
Wheeler and Thad Page, one major film star, John Garfield, one
character actor, Marc Lawrence, an unfriendly Hollywood Ten
member who recanted, Edward Dmytryk, and a recurring
witness, labor leader Roy Brewer, made up the remainder of
persons friendly to the investigative body during part two of the
hearings.

The sensitive, able, and much-loved actor John Garfield
sprang to fame as the star of *Golden Boy* on Broadway; his

---

* Carnovsky's attorney.

many notable performances in motion pictures included *Body and Soul*. But before the committee, the intelligent performer "did his best to make himself appear a simpleton, marvelously naive about politics, who had helped support a variety of Communist fronts despite his firm hatred of Communism."[46]

He appeared before the austere panel on April 23, 1951, and consumed an entire morning (from 10:25 a.m. to 1:15 p.m.) with his account of what he described as his "open-book" life and his hatred of Communism.

He did not know any Communists in Hollywood, past or present; he was, in his own words, an "outstanding liberal," who had never joined any parties other than the Democratic and the Liberal. He was a backer of Henry Wallace for the Presidency on a third party ticket, until he saw how the Communists were "capturing" the ex-Vice President. Garfield could not recall introducing actor-singer Paul Robeson at a dinner for the Joint Anti-Fascist Refugee Committee. He did admit being a member of the Committee for the First Amendment. He believed the Communist Party should be outlawed; he did not support the Moscow trials; and he was for Finnish war relief.

The actor talked on, as the committee probed his background. Yes, Garfield recalled having a drink on a Russian ship in Los Angeles Harbor with Constantine Semenov, a Russian playwright invited to the United States by the State Department; director Lewis Milestone and actor Charles Chaplin and their wives had been aboard the ship. Finally, Representative Donald L. Jackson became dissatisfied with the star's lack of "accuracy" and failure to cooperate with the committee.[47]

The Congressman commented:

> And you contend that during the 7½ years or more that you were in Hollywood and in close contact with a situation in which a number of Communist cells were operating on a week-to-week basis, with electricians, actors, and every class represented, that during the entire period of time you were in Hollywood you did not know of your own personal knowledge a member of the Communist Party?

Garfield said that was "absolutely correct. . . ." Jackson

pursued the questioning: "Have you been approached to assist at Communist Party functions, or functions of Communist-front organizations when you knew they were front organizations?" The actor returned: ". . . I would have run like hell."

Jackson summed up his feelings to Representative Wood:

> MR. JACKSON: I must say, Mr. Chairman, in conclusion, that I am still not satisfied.
>
> One more question. I have before me a letter from the National Counsel of the Arts, Sciences and Professions, which states:
>
>> The Eighty-first Congress has a primary obligation to protect the civil rights of the American people. For years now the constitutional rights, the reputations, the jobs, and the private lives of many of our citizens have been recklessly attacked by the irresponsible Committee on Un-American Activities.
>>
>> This committee has been denounced by the President, by Members of the Congress, and by American leaders throughout the country. In its hearings it has failed to observe the most basic concept of Anglo-Saxon law. It has consistently used headline scare tactics to intimidate and to induce an atmosphere of fear and repression which is repugnant to our most precious American traditions. Its entire history has been one of flagrant violation of common decency and human liberty and has been an affront to one of the greatest institutions in our democracy—the American Congress.
>>
>> The Eighty-first Congress can and must abolish the Committee on Un-American Activities. We urge immediate action toward this end.
>
> You are listed as one of a number of signers. Did you or did you not sign it?
>
> MR. GARFIELD: May I ask the date of that, please?
>
> MR. JACKSON: The date of the letter is—the date is not given. Yes; it was received in January 1949. Is that right?
>
> MR. NIXON: That is the date we received it.
>
> MR. GARFIELD: I don't recall signing it.
>
> MR. JACKSON: You do not recall signing it?

MR. GARFIELD: I do not recall signing it.

MR. JACKSON: Do you subscribe to the statements made in the letter?

MR. GARFIELD: No.

MR. JACKSON: You repudiate the statements made in the letter?

MR. GARFIELD: Yes.

MR. JACKSON: That is all, Mr. Chairman.[48]

The chairman waived the rule which forbade the reading aloud of statements by witnesses when he learned that Garfield's prepared remarks numbered only a few sentences. The star vocally assessed his political position:

> When I was originally requested to appear before the committee, I said that I would answer all questions, fully and without any reservations, and that is what I have done. I have nothing to be ashamed of and nothing to hide. My life is an open book. I was glad to appear before you and talk with you. I am no Red. I am no "pink." I am no fellow traveler. I am a Democrat by politics, a liberal by inclination, and a loyal citizen of this country by every act of my life.[49]

Actor Marc Lawrence was next, on Tuesday, April 24. He proved not quite as amnesic as Garfield. However, he did complain of getting "headaches" in the thirties listening to speeches at Communist group meetings. He identified some of his fellow participants who had been mentioned before by previous friendly witnesses—Lester Cole, Robert Rossen, Richard Collins, Lionel Stander, Gordon Kahn, J. Edward Bromberg, John Howard Lawson, Morris Carnovsky, Karen Morley, Sterling Hayden, Larry Parks, Anne Revere, Howard da Silva, and Lloyd Gough.

Lawrence amplified: "Now, I don't know if these people were members of the Communist Party, but it was supposed to have been a closed cell. I couldn't identify these people."

He was on more certain ground where Lionel Stander was concerned. Stander had introduced Lawrence into the Communist Party. "He was the guy that said to me, 'Get to know this stuff and you will make out more with the dames.' "[50]

Lawrence also distinctly remembered actor Jeff Corey as a

person who attended meetings of a CP group within the Actors' Lab.[51]

Committee member Jackson was pleased with the aggregate of names new and old. He commended the witness—sarcastically. "I congratulate you upon your splendid memory. You should have less difficulty in learning scripts than some of the people who have appeared here."[52]

The only one of the unfriendly Hollywood Ten ever to assume the cloak of friendliness before the committee was Edward Dmytryk. The director delivered his roster of names of persons he knew as members of the CP on April 25, 1951.

His reason for his change of mind since 1947: "The situation has somewhat changed." Dmytryk clarified this comment to Tavenner, explaining that before 1947 he had never heard anyone say he would refuse to fight for America in a war against the Soviet Union. Now CP members were boasting that they would not fight for the United States. The director thought that the Soviet Union and Communist China supported the North Koreans in their attack on South Korea. The Communists of the world were not interested in peace. ". . . there is a Communist menace . . . and the Communist Party in this country is a part of that menace."

As a third reason for recanting, Dmytryk alluded to the spy trials of Alger Hiss and Judith Coplon, incidents which caused the director to remark, "I don't say all members of the Communist Party are guilty of treason, but I think a party that encourages them to act in this capacity is treasonable. For this reason I am willing to talk today."[53]

Dmytryk said that what the Communist Party was after in Hollywood was (1) money, (2) prestige, and (3) control of the content of pictures by taking over the guilds and unions:

> The chief effort was in the craft unions. I want to say that in my opinion the Communist Party never had any control over any major executive in any major studio, nor did they at any time have any effective control over the contents of pictures. It is true that somebody may have slipped in a line or something that made them happy, but that is not the kind of thing that would be effective in the least degree, and certainly they never had any control over any major executive that I know of.

But in the craft unions they were successful in organizing a group called the Conference of Studio Unions that did have a great deal to do with the policies. They eventually got so strong that they risked a strike against the IATSE. However, they lost the strike after a very, very long and serious battle, and that attempt came to nothing.

Dmytryk named seven of the 225 or 230 members of the Screen Directors Guild he knew to be Communists: Frank Tuttle, Herbert Biberman, Jack Berry, Bernard Vorhaus, Jules Dassin—"and myself."

Turning to the Screen Writers Guild, he named John Howard Lawson, Lester Cole, Gordon Kahn, John Wexley, Adrian Scott, Richard Collins, Paul Trivers, Albert Maltz, Alvah Bessie, Arnold Manoff, Michael (Mickey) Uris, Leonardo Bercovici, Francis Faragoh and his wife, Elizabeth, and George Corey as ex- or current Communists.

After the lunch break, Dmytryk proceeded with reeling off the names, singling out Ben Margolis, an attorney for some of the unfriendly witnesses, as having hosted a Communist committee meeting at his home which the director attended. Present also were writer Henry Blankfort and George Pepper, described by the committee as "an employee of Communist-front organizations." Writers Sam Moore and Maurice Clark also attended CP fraction meetings, Dmytryk testified.[54]

The witness offered up his definition of an "informer." He had even consulted a dictionary to make sure of its meaning, he told Representative Jackson.

I know that there have been comments—I don't mean Communists but even among certain progressives and liberals—that people who talk are in effect informers. I heard that so much that I went to the dictionary and looked up the word. An informer, roughly speaking, is a man who informs against colleagues or former colleagues who are engaged in criminal activity. I think the Communists, by using this word against people, are in effect admitting they are engaged in criminal activity. I never heard of anybody informing on the Boy Scouts.[55]

Roy M. Brewer, IATSE (International Alliance of Theatrical

Stage Employees) international representative for Hollywood, who was a friendly witness in 1947, was the last of the friendly persons to appear before the committee in part two of its 1951 hearings. His discourse, rendered on May 17 and 18, was the lengthiest of the session. It dealt almost exclusively with the efforts of the CP to take over the trade unions in Hollywood. Brewer managed, however, to delve into blacklisting of anti-Communists in cinemaland. Writers Fred Niblo and Jack Moffitt, who had been friendly witnesses in 1947, had "practically no work since that time," according to the crafts union chief.[56]

Brewer said there was a Communist group in 1945 that waged a character assassination program that "was so effective that it is beyond my power to describe it. . . ."[57]

When asked by Representative Potter if there were any records that would bear out his testimony about character assassination, the witness replied:

> I do not think the opinion of one man is of much value, but I think if you could document the employment records of those individuals that were not acceptable to the Communist group as against those individuals who were in the forefront of it, I think you would find a rather substantial indication that there were influences at work. Those influences work in many, many ways. Lots of times the opinion of a secretary or of a clerk in a casting bureau can make the difference between whether one man is hired or another man is hired. I can see, from my standpoint, knowing the set-up in Hollywood, how easy it would be for an underground movement to use influence in such a way that an individual without such protection would be at a disadvantage, and I am of the definite opinion that was the case. I think it can be proven by records. I haven't attempted to do that, but in my judgment it could be done. [58]

It was Brewer's impression that John Garfield had been aligned with Communist-front groups, and contrary to the actor's testimony, Brewer felt it was impossible for a man to be in the position the actor was and not be aware that there was a Communist movement in Hollywood.[59] Brewer was correct.

The week before John Garfield's death at thirty-nine years of age in May, 1952, the actor was said to be preparing a statement admitting that he had lied to the committee about his former affiliations. He admitted that he belonged to thirty-two Redfront organizations and had signed twelve petitions on behalf of Red causes and groups.[60]

Part three of the committee's investigation began May 22, 1951, with the appearance of that year's Oscar-winning star Jose Ferrer.[61] He was represented by Abe Fortas, who was later to serve for a brief time as a Supreme Court Justice. The actor's presence before the committee constituted the longest testimony of the third session, covering almost two days.

In the forties, Ferrer had been among the more active theater people who eventually were subpoenaed to appear before the committee in the fifties.

He had enjoyed long runs both on Broadway and nationally in such plays as *Othello, Cyrano de Bergerac*, and *The Silver Whistle*.

In responding to questions, Ferrer tried basically the same tactics Garfield and others affected in their appearances before the committee.

Ferrer had a very poor memory about places, meetings, dates, and suspected Communist fronts and organizations he was alleged to have supported by his name or appearance. The actor explained:

> I would like to tell you that my memory in these matters is controlled largely by association. If I can see where a function took place and who was there, then I am able to tell you accurately my participation.[62]

Ferrer, like Garfield, avoided taking the Fifth Amendment and avoided naming names. After looking at an article supplied by Counsel Tavenner that indicated he had sponsored a Communist for the New York City Council, the actor and Representative Kearney jousted about Ferrer's memory:

> MR. FERRER: I am sorry to say, Mr. Tavenner, that this does not refresh my memory. I repeat that among these people are many many people whom I know, whom I have worked

with, and it is possible and even probable that I did allow the use of my name, but I cannot in all honesty tell you that I remember doing so.

MR. WOOD: Mr. Kearney, did you have a question to ask?

MR. KEARNEY: Yes. I would like to call your attention, Mr. Ferrer, to the letter that the chairman spoke about, under date of May 21, 1951, directed to him, of which I believe all members of the committee received a copy.

I am simply searching for the truth. I can't reconcile your statement with that portion of your letter which states: "I also permitted my name to be used in support of the candidacy of Benjamin Davis as councilman of New York City."

MR. FERRER: Mr. Tavenner just asked me about that, Mr. Kearney, and I told him that when I am now asked under oath, do I remember, I cannot honestly say "I do remember." The reason I wrote this this way—and I still say it was careless on my part—was that I come here to testify before you gentlemen assuming that most of the charges leveled against me are true.

MR. KEARNEY: Is this true: "I also permitted my name to be used in support of the candidacy of Benjamin Davis as councilman of New York City."

MR. FERRER: I don't remember, but I say it probably was, Mr. Kearney. Under oath I don't want to say it was. For the purposes of brevity and simplicity, in this letter I said it was true.

MR. KEARNEY: We want to know if it was true.

MR. FERRER: I can't honestly, completely say it was true.

MR. KEARNEY: This letter was written 2 days ago.

MR. FERRER: Yes.

MR. KEARNEY: A lot of the matters you testified about occurred in 1942, 1943, 1944, and 1945.

MR. FERRER: Yes.

MR. KEARNEY: Here, only 2 days ago, you stated definitely that you permitted your name to be used to further the candidacy of Benjamin Davis as councilman of New York City.

MR. FERRER: Yes, sir.[63]

Kearney was later astonished by the star's vagueness about an article that appeared in the April 22, 1946, issue of the *Daily Worker*, which indicated Ferrer supported the forthcoming May Day parade. The Congressman asked, "Mr. Ferrer, do you want this committee to believe that during all the years you lived in

New York City, that you never knew that May Day was the Communist Party day in the city of New York and all over the nation?" He got this naïve reply from the actor: "I would like them to believe, but even if they don't, it is the truth." In the closing moments of his second appearance before the committee he continued in his attempt to make this quite clear to the committee. Not without some duress.

MR. JACKSON: I don't believe you are a member but I do believe that you have given aid and comfort to the Communist Party. . . .

MR. FERRER: I wrote a letter to this committee offering all my records and checks. I had an informal hearing before appearing formally, at my request. I have done my very best to help you. I believe in what you want to do. I am against the Communist Party. I don't want it. And however negligent I may have been, my actions have never been other than anti-Communist and pro-American.

MR. JACKSON: I think that is a splendid statement.

MR. FERRER: It is also true, Mr. Jackson.

MR. JACKSON: Splendid and probably true. It would have carried twice as much conviction a year ago as it carries today, when your presence before this committee follows service of a subpoena. I very frankly cannot place credence in some of the statements that you have made.

MR. FERRER: That I have just made?

MR. JACKSON: No; in your testimony.

MR. FERRER: In other words, I perjured myself?

MR. JACKSON: That I do not say. I say I can't place credence in some of the things you have said. That is as much my constitutional right as the constitutional privilege claimed by some of the witnesses in refusing to testify.

MR. FERRER: I am not questioning your constitutional right.

MR. JACKSON: That is all.

MR. WALTER: Mr. Kearney.

MR. KEARNEY: Mr. Ferrer, have you ever known an individual who was a member of the Communist Party?

MR. FERRER: I didn't know him to be a member of the Communist Party, Mr. Kearney.

MR. KEARNEY: Anyone?

MR. FERRER: At the time I did not know him to be.

MR. KEARNEY: Have you ever known anyone to be?

MR. FERRER: I now know Mr. Davis is a member of the Communist Party.

MR. KEARNEY: Any others?

MR. FERRER: I can't think of any at the moment. There may
have been. If you tell me Mr. Da Silva is a member of the
Communist Party, I know him. I know Mr. Geer. I know
these men, but I never knew them as members of the
Communist Party.

MR. KEARNEY: That is all.

MR. JACKSON: I think the record should show I did not say
that Mr. Da Silva and Mr. Geer were members of the
Communist Party. I said they refused to testify.

MR. FERRER: I said if you did say.

MR. MOULDER: This may be repetition. Are you now or have
you ever been a member of the Communist Party?

MR. FERRER: No.

MR. MOULDER: Have you ever been sympathetic to Communist or subversive activities?

MR. FERRER: No, sir. [64]

On May 23, writer Budd Schulberg succeeded Ferrer in the
witness chair and demonstrated to the committee a considerably greater grasp of his fact-retention prowess than had his
predecessor. In a telegram received by the committee on April
14, 1951, Schulberg stated: ". . . my recollection of my Communist affiliation is that it was approximately from 1937 to
1940. . . ."[65]

After reiterating the names of a number of persons the
committee had already heard described as Communists, the
witness explained his reason for leaving the party: He could not
write what he wanted as an individual and still follow the
Communist Party dictum of writing for propaganda purposes
only. The writer supported this position by stating:

> . . . it was suggested that I talk with a man by the name of V. J.
> Jerome, who was in Hollywood at that time.
>
> I went to see him. Looking back, it may be hard to
> understand why, after all these wrangles and arguments, I
> should go ahead and see V. J. Jerome. But maybe every writer
> has an insatiable curiosity about these things; I don't know.
>
> Anyway, I went. It was on Hollywood Boulevard in an
> apartment. I didn't do much talking. I listened to V. J. Jerome.
> I am not sure what his position was, but I remember being told
> that my entire attitude was wrong; that I was wrong about
> writing; wrong about this book, wrong about the party; wrong

about the so-called peace movement at that particular time; and I gathered from the conversation in no uncertain terms that I was wrong.

I don't remember saying much. I remember it more as a kind of harangue. When I came away I felt maybe, almost for the first time, that this was to me the real face of the party. I didn't feel I had talked to just a comrade. I felt I had talked to someone rigid and dictatorial who was trying to tell me how to live my life, and as far as I remember, I didn't want to have anything more to do with them.

Tavenner substantiated Schulberg's point concerning the domination of the party over its members, and particularly its writers, when two reviews of the witness's book *What Makes Sammy Run?* were cited by the committee counsel:

To emphasize clearly the way in which the Communist Party changed and followed the dictates of some directing authority, I want to read into the record, just very briefly, some of those outstanding points which you mentioned in the course of your testimony. What I am going to read now is from the Daily Worker of April 7, 1941, being the favorable review of Charles Glenn. This is his language:

"For slightly fewer years than they have awaited the great American novel, whatever that may be, American bibliophiles and critics have been awaiting the Hollywood novel. While they may argue its merits and demerits I've a feeling that all critics, no matter their carping standards, will have to admit they've found the Hollywood novel in Budd Schulberg's What Makes Sammy Run?"

Now, in the retractive statement of Charles Glenn published in the People's World of April 24, 1941, this is what he says, and I quote:

"The first error I made was in calling the book the Hollywood novel."

And I quote again, from the Daily Worker of April 23, 1941:

"Recently I wrote a review on Budd Schulberg's book, What Makes Sammy Run? I said it was the story of a Hollywood heel and could be regarded as the Hollywood novel. On the basis of quite lengthy discussion on the book, I've done a little reevaluating, and this helps me emphasize the points I've tried to make here."

He then makes various criticisms, and adds:

"Can it then be termed 'the Hollywood novel'?"

I want the record to also show one or two other points, so
that it may be plain. I quote from the Daily Worker of April 7,
1941, and the People's World of April 2, 1941, which was the
favorable review:

"Former works on the film city have been filthy with
four-letter words, spoken and implied * * * None of these
things hold true for Schulberg's novel.

"There is nothing vulgar in what he says, nothing super-
ficially vulgar, that is. * * *

"Writing in the first person, Schulberg tells of the good as
well as the bad."

Then, after the meeting, from the Daily Worker of April 23,
1941, appears this statement:

"We do not intend to go into all the aspects of the
conscience of a writer, a conscience which allows him (with full
knowledge of the facts) to show only the dirt and the filth."

And from the People's World again, of April 24, 1941, after
the meeting I quote:

"In a full-drawn portraiture of either Sammy Glick or
Hollywood, the people must be seen in action, living the lives
they lead. Even more effective would the filth of Sammy Glick
become when counterposed to the cleanliness of the
people."[66]

Director-writer Frank Wright Tuttle was the next witness
appearing on May 24 in Washington. Like Schulberg, he was
friendly to the committee's operation. Richard Collins had
described Tuttle as a Communist. The witness had seen Collins'
allegation in the press and had contacted the committee,
indicating he wanted to testify.

Tuttle named seven directors who had been Communists,
including himself, and added that he thought two of them,
Michael Gordon and Jules Dassin, had left the party.[67]

After informing on more than two dozen more persons
associated with the Communist Party, Tuttle explained his
reasons for so doing:

I believe that there is a traditional dislike among Americans
for informers, and I am an informer, and I have thought about
this constantly. I believe all decent people who share this
dislike for informers, if they think about this carefully, will
agree with me that at this particular moment it is absolutely
vital. In a case like this, with ruthless aggression abroad in the

world, the aggressors, I believe, are as ruthless with their own people as they are with those they consider their enemies; and I feel that today it is absolutely necessary for Americans to be equally ruthless.[68]

Director Robert Rossen, in his first appearance before the committee on June 25, 1951, attempted to be both a friendly and unfriendly witness. He would not name names. He did respond to Tavenner's comment that he had been named as a Communist before the committee (and by implication therefore was one) and to the question: Did the fact of his being a Communist influence his decision to change from being a writer to a producer? Rossen answered:

> Without conceding the validity of your statement, sir, I should like to say that my interest in becoming a director and producer was primarily one in which (1) I thought I could express my ability; (2) I thought I could get increased prestige and whatever economic gains I could get coincident with this rise of mine in the film industry.[69]

He admitted that he had directed a three-act play in 1932, *Steel*, under the auspices of the *Daily Worker*, and in answer to Tavenner's question about whether he was now a member of the Communist Party, Rossen replied:

> I should like to emphatically state that I am not a member of the Communist Party. I am not sympathetic with it or its aims. I can't believe in any divided loyalty, and in the event this country goes to war I stand ready now, as I always have, to bear arms in its defense and to serve in whatever capacity the country may call on me, against any and all of its enemies, including the Soviet Union.
>
> MR. TAVENNER: You state you are not sympathetic with the aims of the Communist Party. Has that always been true?
>
> MR. ROSSEN: I shall have to decline to answer that question on the grounds it may tend to incriminate and degrade me, and thus violate my rights under both the first and fifth amendments.
>
> MR. TAVENNER: Information has come to the attention of the committee that the Communist Party may have reregistered its members on June 4, 1951. Were you a member of the Communist Party on June 3, 1951?

MR. ROSSEN: I decline to answer that question on the grounds previously stated.

MR. TAVENNER: Were you a member of the Communist Party on June 5, 1951?

MR. ROSSEN: I decline to answer that question on the same grounds.

MR. TAVENNER: I understand you to say you are not now a member of the Communist Party?

MR. ROSSEN: I said I am not a member of the Communist Party.

MR. TAVENNER: Were you a member of the Communist Party at the time you entered this hearing room?

MR. ROSSEN (after conferring with his counsel): No.

MR. TAVENNER: Were you a member of the Communist Party yesterday?

MR. ROSSEN: I decline to answer that question on the same grounds.[70]

Less than two years later, on May 7, 1953, Rossen appeared again and answered all questions posed by the committee regarding his former membership in the Communist Party.[71]

Actor J. Edward Bromberg was on June 26, 1951, the last and only totally unfriendly witness in part three of the committee's investigation.[72]

He declined to answer virtually every question submitted by Tavenner and the Congressmen. The actor died later that year in London at the age of forty-seven, while preparing to appear in the West End production of Trumbo's *The Biggest Thief in Town.*

On December 15 and 16, 1969, under the auspices of the American National Theatre Academy, *Dream of a Blacklisted Actor* played at the Theatre DeLys in New York. It was written by Conrad Bromberg, son of the late actor.

For the next three parts of its investigations the committee members moved to the place that was the object of the 1947 investigation, the city containing Hollywood—Los Angeles.

Over a ten-day period in September, 1951, the committee heard forty-nine witnesses, some of whom had little or nothing to do with the entertainment field. The testimony of the few witnesses who, in the opinion of this author, were most identified with the theater is generally assessed here. The remaining witnesses are identified as to occupation and whether they were friendly or unfriendly.

On September 17, stage and film director Michael Gordon rebuffed questions concerning his affiliation with groups on the "subversive" list of the Attorney General of the United States. He likewise declined to comment on his "alleged acquaintance" with Frank Tuttle, the director who had named Gordon as a former Communist. In the event of war with the Soviet Union, the witness indicated he would fight for the United States, but he would disclose nothing about his "personal opinions" on the actions of the United States in the Korean War.[73]

From the testimony of Larry Parks to the appearance of writer Martin Berkeley was only slightly more than six months in time; it was a millennium in the business of naming names. Berkeley was accompanied by attorney Edward Bennett Williams, who later represented Senator Joseph McCarthy in his Senate censure hearings. In his nonstop performance, the writer identified 162 persons as current or ex-Communists.[74]

Williams opened the discussion on September 19, 1951, by noting that Berkeley and his family had been threatened the night before. A phone call had promised repercussions if the writer disclosed "names of members of the Communist Party which had not been known or disclosed prior to this session."[75]

Throughout his testimony, Berkeley admitted he had been a Communist but now presented himself as one of the most vigorous anti-Communists in the United States. The writer stated that Carl Foreman was then on the Screen Writers Guild board and, to Berkeley's knowledge, Foreman had never "disavowed his communism."[76] The witness summed up his staunch patriotism when he replied to Representative Potter's question about his past and present experiences with Communism. He said, "Mr. Potter, I believe that anyone who was then a member of the party or joined the party since 1945 and who retains his membership today is a traitor."[77] Berkeley completed his name-naming later that day, behind closed doors, in an executive session of the committee.

Actor Jeff Corey was the first witness to apply a new color term to his professional work status. He appeared on September 21, 1951. Earlier that year his fellow actor, Marc Lawrence, had identified Corey as a person who had attended Communist meetings. In answer to Counsel Tavenner's question about whether the actor was employed in his profession in California, Corey replied:

> I am really not, sir. My name was brought up at an earlier committee hearing and since then I have been gray-listed, if not completely black-listed. Hitherto I had been quite busy as an actor, but my professional fortunes have waned considerably, coincident with the mentioning of my name.[7][8]

When Corey was asked if he knew Lawrence, he answered ironically: "I know him as an actor who played an informer; with great verisimilitude, in a picture called *Asphalt Jungle*." Corey did not elect to inform and took the First and Fifth amendments. Furthermore, on being questioned about standing also on the First Amendment, Corey stated, "I do feel . . . that my rights of freedom of conscious thought, as embodied in the Bill of Rights, are violated by my being summoned and interrogated in front of this hearing." Representative Jackson challenged the actor on this issue:

> MR. JACKSON: Has your freedom of speech been abridged in any way, Mr. Corey?
> MR. COREY: Well, it isn't—I think that probing into one's thoughts and conscience—I will put it this way. I believe that no one can bargain for the key to my brain wherein is stored multitudinous attitudes about life, religion, politics, and art. You may try to ferret it out against my consent, but—
> MR. JACKSON: You are afraid freedom of speech is going—
> MR. WIRIN: May he continue to answer the question?
> MR. JACKSON: No, I have heard the speech 50 times.
> MR. WIRIN: Not this one, sir.
> MR. JACKSON: The same one, with variations. That's all.

Then Mr. Wood, contrary to the avowed position of the committee, added:

> . . . I don't want to speak for the remaining members of this committee, but if, by any action of this committee, we could

be instrumental in eliminating from the field of public entertainment the views of people—particularly the youth of this
country being moved to a large extent—people who decline to
answer a question as to whether or not they are members of the
Communist Party, it would make me extremely happy.[7][9]

Writer-producer Carl Foreman, whom Berkeley had named as
a Communist only five days previously, declined to answer
questions during his appearance before the committee on
September 24, 1951.[80]

The cleverest witness in the ten-day period was writer-
producer Sidney Buchman, who admitted being a Communist
from 1938 to 1945, but evaded naming names and also avoided
taking the Fifth Amendment when he made his public confes-
sion on September 25.[81] Buchman was eventually cited for
contempt.

"In contempt he indubitably was, and the House approved
the citation by a vote of 316-0. He was found guilty and given a
one-year suspended sentence and a fine of $150," Walter
Goodman writes. The committee, he added, "had gotten its
man, but the really interesting question, on the naming of
names, remained unsettled."[82]

Twelve friendly witnesses and thirty unfriendly witnesses
completed the September, 1951, investigation of the film
industry. In addition, Karl Tunberg, president of the Screen
Writers Guild, told the committee on September 25 that only a
small fraction of his group's 1,200 members were Communists.[83]

The dozen who responded graciously to all committee questions were all admitted former members of the Communist
Party. They appeared at ease in naming names. Two of them
appeared in executive session—Eugene Fleury, artist and art
instructor, on September 10, and Robert Shayne (Robert Shaen
Dawe), actor, on September 11.

Two other cooperative witnesses made their identifications of
other Communists in sworn statements given to investigator
William A. Wheeler on September 10. They were Miss Anne
Ray, writer and wife of writer Melvin Frank, and Miss Eve
Ettinger, story editor for a movie studio.

The balance of the helpful ex-Communists made their identifications at the public hearings. They were Harold J. Ashe,
magazine writer and CP functionary, and his former wife,
Mildred. Mrs. Ashe was described by the committee as a
"communist party organizer." The Ashes spoke their piece on
September 17. On the following day, Leo Townsend, a writer,
gave the committee the names of more than a score of show
business figures who were party members.

On September 20, 1951, the friendly witnesses who publicly
put the finger on the Reds in Hollywood were composer David
Raksin and publicist William Frank Blowitz. The next day the
committee heard from writer Elizabeth Wilson (Mrs. Richard
Wilson), who was also able to present the names of more than
ten theatrical figures whom she knew to be Communists.

Mrs. Bernyce Polifka Fleury, an artist and wife of Eugene
Fleury, was able on September 24 to give the names of
Communists not even identified by her spouse in the earlier
secret session. Writer George Beck rounded out the list of
friendly September witnesses on the twenty-fifth day of that
month.

Three of the thirty unfriendly witnesses that September
appeared in executive session on the twelfth. They were Prokop
Jack Prokop (also known as Jack Frank), who was associated
with a dry-cleaning business; Mrs. Hannah Schwartz Donath,
who listed herself as a "nonprofessional" and who was the wife
of actor Ludwig Donath (Donath was later to be named a
Communist by actor Lee J. Cobb); and Miss Bella Lewitzky
(Mrs. Newell Reynolds), a dancer.

On September 17, in public hearings, the unfriendly witnesses were Charles Daggett, a publicist and former newsman (on
January 21, 1952, he became friendly); and Percy Solotoy,
furniture manufacturer, who was identified by Mildred Ashe on
that day as a CP member.

On September 18, the committee had to content itself with
learning virtually nothing about Hollywood Reds from the
witnesses, but that was offset by the plethora of names announced by Leo Townsend. Those who were mute about the
CP on that day were Henry Blankfort, writer; Howland

Chamberlin, actor; Mrs. Helen Slote Levitt (Mrs. Alfred Levitt), former executive secretary of the Actors' Laboratory, former secretary to actor John Garfield, and described by the committee as a "functionary" of the CP; her husband, Alfred Levitt, studio reader and also a writer; Miss Bess Taffel, writer; and Herbert Arthur Klein, writer and publicist.

The following day marked the appearance of no friendly witnesses; the committee was confronted with four uncooperative persons. They were Philip Edward Stevenson, writer; Daniel Lewis James, writer; Lilith James (Mrs. Daniel L. James), writer; and Georgia Backus (Mrs. Hy Alexander), actress.

September 20 was indeed a full day for the solons in Hollywood. There were two friendly witnesses (Raksin and Blowitz) to counterbalance the balky seven under public scrutiny: Robert L. Richards, writer; and his wife, Ann Roth Morgan Richards, former secretary, Screen Writers Guild; Mrs. Ellenore Abowitz (wife of Murray Abowitz, MD), a lady who was termed by the committee a "functionary" of the CP; Miss Marguerite Roberts, Michael Wilson, and John Sanford, all writers; and Miss Herta Uerkvitz, architectural researcher for the motion picture studio.

Four uncooperative witnesses made a reluctant appearance on September 21: Max Howard Schoen, DDS, a friend of John Howard Lawson; Miss Mary Virginia Farmer, actress; Miss Louise Rousseau, writer; and Murray Abowitz, MD, member of the Hollywood Independent Citizens' Committee of the Arts, Sciences, and Professions. (Meanwhile, the committee had ex-Red writer Elizabeth Wilson on hand that day to aid in identification.)

September 24 saw the last of the month's—and the year's—unfriendly show business personages sworn in: Reuben Ship, radio writer; Donald Gordon, editor, story department, motion picture studio; Josef Mischel, writer and studio story editor; and Lester Koenig, writer and associate producer.[84]

In the nation's capital in the winter and spring of 1952, the committee members of the second session of the Eighty-second Congress heard the testimony of ten show business witnesses, three of whom were among the most illustrious names in the

American theater—director Elia Kazan and writers Lillian Hellman and Clifford Odets. The gentlemen were friendly; the lady was not.

Kazan appeared initially before a private executive session of the committee on January 14, 1952, and then again in executive session on Thursday, April 10, 1952.

In the latter appearance Kazan submitted a statement declaring that he had been a member of the Communist Party and announced: "I want to tell you everything I know about it."[85]

His statement told about his nineteen-month membership in the Communist Party, 1934-36, the names of the members of the Group Theatre who were Communists, and how he came to leave the party. Kazan reported he left after he was asked to apologize and be repentant for refusing to fall in with the party line. The director in his statement said, "I had had a taste of police-state living and I didn't like it."[86]

Kazan described the duties of CP members as fourfold:

1. To "educate" ourselves in Marxist and party doctrine;

2. To help the party get a foothold in the Actors Equity Association;

3. To support various "front" organizations of the party;

4. To try to capture the Group Theatre and make it a Communist mouthpiece.

The witness's statement noted that numbers two and four were failures and numbers one and three only semisuccessful. Kazan concluded his prepared remarks with a complete listing of the plays and films he had directed and his assessment of the political significance of each.[87]

On two consecutive days, May 19 and 20, 1952, the foremost social playwright of the thirties, Clifford Odets, told the committee about his experiences as a member of the Communist Party. (Odets had testified in secrecy at an executive session on April 24, 1952.) The morning testimony of the first day revealed few new show business names and dealt largely with the playwright's financial contributions to the *New Masses* and various other left-wing periodicals and his trip to Cuba in June, 1935, as chairman of the American Commission to Investigate Labor and Social Conditions in Cuba.[88]

The afternoon session revealed that Odets' disillusion with the Communist Party was essentially the same as Kazan's. He believed he was writing plays that dealt with the real problems of America in the thirties. The Communist Party, through its organ the *Daily Worker*, criticized the playwright for not writing "progressive plays" and, in effect, said Odets, told its readers, "He is stupid, he has too much talent. He is wasting his time writing about ordinary, middle-class life when he could be writing a glorious play about the war in Spain."[89]

Opening the second day of testimony on May 20, Counsel Tavenner suggested to Odets that the committee records show that he had had connections with various Communist-front organizations after he claimed he had left the party; further, these connections continued until June 22, 1950.[90]

Tavenner asked: "How do you reconcile your statement that your break with the Communist Party was complete and final with this record of affiliation with Communist-front organizations as shown by these exhibits?" Odets summed up the tangled problem of the American liberal:

> Well, I will say again, as I said before, Mr. Tavenner, that the lines of leftism, liberalism, in all of their shades and degrees, are constantly crossing like a jangled chord on a piano. It is almost impossible to pick out which note is which note. I have spoken out on what I thought were certain moral issues of the day, and I found myself apparently in line with your documentation, I have found myself frequently on platforms with Communists that I did not know about then but evidently are now known Communists. I have said before that many of these people have some very good tunes. They have picked up some of our most solemn and sacred American tunes and they sing them. If I as an American liberal must sometimes speak out the same tune, I must sometimes find myself on platforms, so to speak, with strange bedfellows. I have never wittingly, since these early days, have ever wittingly, joined or spoken on an exclusively Communist program or platform, not to my knowledge. I see that one must do one of two things. One must pick one's way very carefully through the mazes of liberalism and leftism

today or one must remain silent. Of the two, I must tell you
frankly I would try to pick the first way, because the little that
I have to say, the little that I have to contribute to the
betterment or welfare of the American people could not permit
me to remain silent.[91]

Lillian Hellman, America's most prominent woman playwright, attempted in advance of her appearance before the
committee on May 21 to make a "trade" with Chairman John
S. Wood. The exchange of letters between Miss Hellman and
Wood was introduced and read to the committee by Tavenner:

> Dear Mr. Wood: As you know, I am under subpena to appear
> before your committee on May 21, 1952.
> I am most willing to answer all questions about myself. I
> have nothing to hide from your committee and there is nothing
> in my life of which I am ashamed. I have been advised by
> counsel that under the fifth amendment I have a constitutional
> privilege to decline to answer any questions about my political
> opinions, activities, and associations, on the grounds of self-
> incrimination. I do not wish to claim this privilege. I am ready
> and willing to testify before the representatives of our Govern-
> ment as to my own opinions and my own actions, regardless of
> any risks or consequences to myself.
> But I am advised by counsel that if I answer the committee's
> questions about myself, I must also answer questions about
> other people and that if I refuse to do so, I can be cited for
> contempt. My counsel tells me that if I answer questions about
> myself, I will have waived my rights under the fifth amendment
> and could be forced legally to answer questions about others.
> This is very difficult for a layman to understand. But there is
> one principle that I do understand: I am not willing, now or in
> the future, to bring bad trouble to people who, in my past
> association with them, were completely innocent of any talk or
> any action that was disloyal or subversive. I do not like
> subversion or disloyalty in any form and if I had ever seen any I
> would have considered it my duty to have reported it to the
> proper authorities. But to hurt innocent people whom I knew
> many years ago in order to save myself is, to me inhuman and
> indecent and dishonorable. I cannot and will not cut my
> conscience to fit this year's fashions, even though I long ago
> came to the conclusion that I was not a political person and
> could have no comfortable place in any political group.
> I was raised in an old-fashioned American tradition and there

were certain homely things that were taught to me: To try to tell the truth, not to bear false witness, not to harm my neighbor, to be loyal to my country, and so on. In general, I respected these ideals of Christian honor and did as well with them as I knew how. It is my belief that you will agree with these simple rules of human decency and will not expect me to violate the good American tradition from which they spring. I would, therefore, like to come before you and speak of myself.

I am prepared to waive the privilege against self-incrimination and to tell you everything you wish to know about my views or actions if your committee will agree to refrain from asking me to name other people. If the committee is unwilling to give me this assurance, I will be forced to plead the privilege of the fifth amendment at the hearing.

A reply to this letter would be appreciated.

Sincerely yours,
Lillian Hellman

The answer to the letter is as follows:

Dear Miss Hellman: Reference is made to your letter dated May 19, 1952, wherein you indicate that in the event the committee asks you questions regarding your association with other individuals you will be compelled to rely upon the fifth amendment in giving your answers to the committee questions.

In this connection, please be advised that the committee cannot permit witnesses to set forth the terms under which they will testify.

We have in the past secured a great deal of information from persons in the entertainment profession who cooperated whole-heartedly with the committee. The committee appreciates any information furnished it by persons who have been members of the Communist Party. The committee, of course, realizes that a great number of persons who were members of the Communist Party at one time honestly felt that it was not a subversive organization. However, on the other hand, it should be pointed out that the contributions made to the Communist Party as a whole by persons who were not themselves subversive made it possible for those members of the Communist Party who were and still are subversives to carry on their work.

The committee has endeavored to furnish a hearing to each person identified as a Communist engaged in work in the entertainment field in order that the record could be made clear as to whether they were still members of the Communist Party. Any persons identified by you during the course of committee hearings will be afforded the opportunity of appearing before the committee in accordance with the policy of the committee.

Sincerely yours,
John S. Wood, *Chairman* [92]

Wood commented on the substance of his letter to the playwright: ". . . it is in my view that in the function of this committee we cannot be placed in the attitude of trading with the witnesses as to what they will testify to. . . ."[93] Miss Hellman declined to comment or answer and also refused to respond to the committee's questions when she appeared.

A gentleman with an "implied clearance" in the winter-spring investigation of 1952 was Hollywood tough guy Edward G. Robinson.[94] He had appeared before the committee previously, but unlike Kazan and Odets, publicly rather than privately. His earlier appearances were on October 27 and December 21, 1951. In the October appearance he was questioned by members of the committee's investigative staff because the Congressmen were in their districts preparing for the November 7 elections. In December, 1951, he appeared before the regular committee, as he did again April 30, 1952.

The actor on all three occasions was not a friendly witness in the sense of offering the committee names or information about the operations of the Communist Party. On the other hand, in answering questions he was not unfriendly to the point of invoking the Bill of Rights.

The actor explained that his voice was hoarse due to having just completed 250 stage performances of *Darkness at Noon.* "It is, perhaps," said Robinson, certifying his Americanism, "the strongest indictment of communism ever presented."[95]

Robinson denied he had ever been a member of the Communist Party but admitted that on occasions he had been duped into contributing to Communist-front organizations:

> . . . May I add that of the very many civic, cultural, philanthropic, and political organizations of which I have been a

member and a contributor, but a small percentage I later discovered were tinged with the taint of communism.

It is a serious matter to have one's loyalty questioned. Life is less dear to me than my loyalty to democracy and the United States. I ask favors of no one. All I ask is that the record be kept straight and that I be permitted to live free of false charges.

I readily concede that I have been used, and that I have been mistaken regarding certain associations which I regret, but I have not been disloyal or dishonest.

I would like to find some way to put at rest the ever-recurring innuendoes concerning my loyalty. Surely there must be some way for a person falsely accused of disloyalty to clear his name once and for all. It is for this purpose that I come again voluntarily before this committee to testify under oath. What more can I do?

Anyone who understands the history of the political activity in Hollywood will appreciate the fact that innocent, sincere persons were used by the Communists to whom honesty and sincerity are as foreign as the Soviet Union is to America. I was duped and used. I was lied to. But, I repeat, I acted from good motives, and I have never knowingly aided Communists or any Communist cause.

Congressmen Jackson and Moulder declared that they did not believe the actor was a Communist. Moulder commended the actor for "patriotic service for our great country."[96]

Robinson, "humble past the point of embarrassment,"[97] said:

Thank you sir. You are very kind to say that.

What I am most jealous of, after good theatrical notices, is my Americanism, and I am very happy to hear that coming from you.

Believe me, Congressman Jackson, when you said that you didn't believe that I am a Communist, it made me feel good.[98]

Playwright Hyman (Hy) Solomon Kraft was the only other unfriendly witness of the ten entertainment figures subpoenaed in the first half of 1952. He was called before the committee on March 20.[99] His position on answering the committee's questions came to be known as the "diminished fifth," meaning that he was not then a Communist but declining to say whether he ever had been.[100]

The remaining friendly witnesses were writers Melvin Levy, Michael S. Blankfort, Isobel Lennart, and Stanley Roberts, and musician, composer, and arranger George Bassman.

In the last half of 1952, Chairman Wood closed his marathon investigation of Communism in the entertainment world by hearing only four witnesses—writers Bernard C. Schoenfeld and Roy Huggins, actress Karen Morley, and director-performer and Broadway play doctor Abram S. (Abe) Burrows. The writers were friendly, the actress was not, and Burrows was evasive.

Schoenfeld's testimony on August 19 was in the familiar pattern of a liberal Democrat seeking another outlet for his frustrations about the slowness of social change. He joined the Communist Political Association, believing that since it had supported Roosevelt for reelection in 1944, it "would continue to work within the framework of the existing Democratic Party."[101] His reasons for leaving the Communist Party also followed familiar lines established by earlier show business writers—that is, Schoenfeld found he was unable to function as an individual artist and still satisfy the rigid orthodoxy of Communist Party propaganda.

Huggins, on the other hand, had been dabbling with Communism since the late thirties, when as an undergraduate at the University of California at Los Angeles he "became a Marxist."[102] From that time until the mid-forties he was in and out of the Communist Party. His final reason for withdrawal dealt with a larger and certainly more meaningful concept to the committee than a writer's freedom to create.

Huggins stated his "basic reason for" his "withdrawal" when he appeared on September 29, 1952: He felt that "the party had finally reached a point where you simply could not be a member of the Communist Party and consider yourself to be an American citizen. It was that simple. . . ."

Huggins, a Phi Beta Kappa from UCLA, tried to explain to the committee his views on Communism:

> . . . Marxism has a wonderful thing about it, in that, being a closed system of thought, if you feel great despair about the

world or are having difficulty understanding it, Marxism does something for you. It suddenly allows the whole universe to fall into a nice simple pattern. There are no unanswered questions once you become a Marxist. It is a nice feeling, particularly if your field is political philosophy, and you like to feel that you do know all of the answers. . . .

I realize, like all closed systems of thought, once you find a hole in it, then you realize that it is all wrong, because that is the nature of a closed system of thought. You must either accept it all without question, or you do not accept any of it, and this is recognized by the Communists.

There are no Communists who say, "Well, I am a Marxist, but I don't accept this particular theory of Marx," and if you don't accept that theory, you are not a Marxist, and you are not a Communist if you don't go along with every bit of the theory.

So I think it is in the nature of the things that once you find one big flaw, then you suddenly realize that that is just a resultant flaw of other flaws. . . .

So I think that to the Communist, capitalism is going to be in a sense an easy thing to overthrow, eventually, I suppose, because we do have a tendency to fail to fight our enemies properly, but I suppose one of the reasons for that is that it would be a terrible thing if we were to fight tyranny by becoming a tyranny ourselves, isn't that so? This would be a terrible thing if we are anti-Communist because we feel that Communists destroy individual freedom and liberty, and in fighting communism, we destroy individual freedom and liberty. This would be a fight in vain.

So I think that is why I say this committee is in a terrible spot, because I think that subversive elements must be fought, and I think democracy has to fight for its life, and it can't just sit back and say, "Well, history will take care of us." It has got enemies and it has to fight those enemies but it has to fight them within the framework of the democratic system, or it might as well not fight at all, because it loses the battle in the means it chooses to use to fight that battle.[103]

Abe Burrows, coauthor of the hit Broadway musical *Guys and Dolls*, attempted on November 12, 1952, to avoid any conclusive statements to the committee about his Communist Party affiliations or friends by establishing his personality as that of a vagabond piano player who just liked to go to parties and "ham" it up.[104] It appeared from the testimony of previous friendly witnesses that many of these parties that engaged Burrows' talent were of the Communist variety. The witness admitted contributing money to support the *New Masses* and the *People's World* but denied ever having written anything for a Communist Party publication.[105] The thrust of his lengthy testimony was obtuse and yet cooperative.

Chairman Wood asked if Burrows had ever been a member of the CP:

> MR. BURROWS: Well, as far as I have ever been, as I said, I have never applied for party membership; if there is a party card with my name, I know nothing about it, but, as I said, I did associate with these fellows.
>
> MR. WOOD: I know, but you can answer that question in your own express way as to whether or not you have ever been or considered yourself as a member of the Communist Party.
>
> MR. BURROWS: I was considered a Communist.
>
> MR. WOOD: You so considered yourself, too?
>
> MR. BURROWS: I was considered a Communist. In my own heart I didn't believe it, but I think I was considered a Communist, and that was the whole thing of my coming here to talk about Mr. Vinson's testimony. [Radio director Owen Vinson testified on October 2, 1952, that Burrows was a member of the CP.]
>
> MR. WOOD: You say you were considered by others to be. You know yourself whether or not you were, don't you?
>
> MR. BURROWS: Well, you see, sir, by all of the actions I did, all of the material things, all of the facts, I guess I committed enough acts to be called a Communist. I am testifying here under oath.
>
> MR. WOOD: Well, what would you call yourself? Would you have called yourself a Communist at that time?
>
> MR. BURROWS: Not in my own heart, sir. But I am here under oath, and I am here to tell the truth, the whole truth, and nothing but the truth, and there is an element of truth in the statement that I was a Communist, but there is also an element of untruth, and I am left in that position.
>
> MR. WOOD: We understand your position in that respect, but now can't you answer on your own as to whether or not you were ever a member of the Communist Party?
>
> MR. BURROWS: Well, I don't see how I could answer it any differently from how I did answer it. I would like anybody's help in this if I could have it, sir.
>
> MR. WOOD: I understand about the witness who gave the

testimony. You have given a clear answer to that, but you have not expressed yourself clearly as to what you have to say about it.

MR. BURROWS: Well, sir, let's put it this way: I don't deny the truth of the accusations of the witness.

MR. WOOD: Any other questions?

MR. TAVENNER: I might make one comment. You stated that you desired to use your weapons against communism.

MR. BURROWS: Yes, sir.

MR. TAVENNER: I might say, our observations have been that ridicule is about one of the most effective weapons against members of the Communist Party.

MR. BURROWS: They can't take it. I know in Russia, I read daily about what happens with writers there, and about Stalin likes an opera or doesn't like an opera, and he likes it to be serious. I read one item somewhere where they don't like jokes, they don't like funny stuff.

MR. WOOD: May I resume? I cannot understand how at this time you can emphatically say you are not now a member of the Communist Party and why you cannot so clearly express yourself in the same manner as to whether or not you have ever been.

MR. BURROWS: Because of my associations, sir, and the fact that I was around with those fellows, and I did go to meetings with them, and attended things with them. I have to go on this case by the objective facts of what other people thought and what it looked like. I was, by association—by association, sir, I can't under oath deny that.

MR. WOOD: Well, that is the point. You are not necessarily a Communist by association; I mean you weren't.

MR. BURROWS: I didn't say I was by association. But I say they thought me one, and I was assumed to be one, and I am not denying they had a right to.

MR. WOOD: You mean to say that to a full extent you conducted yourself and participated in all of the Communist activities at that time with a reservation in your own heart?

MR. BURROWS: Yes, sir. That is very well put.

MR. VELDE: And you did attend Communist Party meetings, knowing them to be such?

MR. BURROWS: Well, I attended meetings at which Communists were present. I still don't know whether study groups were Communist Party meetings, HICCASP meetings, radio writers' meetings; it is all kind of jelled together in my mind. Those were very bad years for me in the terms of personal trouble, and my mother and father both died, and I, as a matter of fact, had to seek help from a psychiatrist, and that whole period is kind of a painful, very painful period to me.

MR. WOOD: I am sorry to pursue this line of thought further, but your participation in those organizations, you say, cast some suspicion upon you, as I understand it, that others considered you a Communist, but were you actually a member of the Communist Party or any of those organizations?

MR. BURROWS: I have answered that, sir.

MR. WOOD: I do not mean Communist-front organizations or any other activities that would cast a reflection on you, but actually attend Communist Party meetings of Communist members.

MR. BURROWS: As I say, I was at meetings which had Communists at them, and I was at these study groups I have told you about.

MR. WOOD: And they were Communist Party meetings?

MR. BURROWS: I imagine they could be called Communist Party meetings. I imagine so. I really am very vague on that. I am sorry if I sound overvague.

MR. WOOD: Any more questions, Mr. Tavenner?

MR. TAVENNER: No, sir.[106]

Evaluation of the Hearings

Economic determinism, not democratic patriotism, created the blacklist that fell like a shroud over the entertainment world in the first years of the 1950's.

If the movies employed blacklisted artists, they were subject to boycott by sundry civic and church organizations. If television hired the political untouchables, it was in the equally compromising position of being on the receiving end of ostracism by commercial sponsors.

The blacklist was a public relations gimmick in motion pictures and in television but not to any significant extent in the living theater. How, when, and where a theater blacklist operated is discussed in Chapter VII. Why such a list was so meaningful in most entertainment media and not in the theater is briefly examined here.

The blacklist in Hollywood did not start with the Hollywood Ten or end with John Wood's extended investigation of Communism. Certainly the number of witnesses called by Wood and the resultant names offered by the friendly testaments produced many new movie and television undesirables, but blacklisting was not always a response to controversial political ideas. Negroes as performers or workers in Hollywood studios were members of a tacit blacklist until the sixties. In the twenties movie stars such as Fatty Arbuckle, Mary Miles Minter, and Mabel Normand were *persona non grata* on the screen—for their morals, not their politics. The reason—economics, fear of boycott by organizations that might pressure the ticket buyer into staying away from the movie theater.

By the time the Hollywood Ten had returned from jail Communist China in 1949 and North Korea in 1950 had become political threats that stimulated American demonologists into renewed interest in ferreting out Commies of the homegrown variety. But whereas in the early fifties the movie producer or television sponsor lived in dire fear of picketing or boycott, the entire history of the liberal New York theater audience and the Broadway stage militated against political blacklisting. Therefore, the committee was forced to turn again to the movies and to television not only because they were the most vulnerable of the entertainment media but also because they were infinitely more valuable from a publicity angle than the theater.

All the big living-theater names appearing before Chairman Wood—Kazan, Odets, Garfield, Ferrer, Robinson, and to a lesser extent, Schulberg, Burrows, and Miss Hellman—were known to the mass public because of their identification with movies and theater and success.

This latter condition—success—undoubtedly contributed heavily to their respective decisions to be friendly with the committee in varying ways and degrees ranging from informing and ineptitude to intellectuality and integrity.

The lesser luminaries from the theater who also worked in the movies—Da Silva, Geer, Corey, Carnovsky, Bromberg, Gordon, Sondergaard, and Revere—were as one in their reluctance to cooperate with the committee's objectives.

With the exception of friendly witness Marc Lawrence, those

theater and film people who had the most to lose by being blacklisted managed, each in his own way, to avoid the problem. The already less fortunate artists stood fast against the committee and then saw their careers and incomes in virtually every case diminish to almost nothing for a decade.

Approximately eighty-five witnesses appeared before John Wood, with forty-eight categorized as unfriendly, thirty-two friendly, and the remainder in a limbo of vague cooperation without outright defiance.

Elia Kazan, after his testament before the committee, returned to a career in films and the theater. However, his most prolific and vital work on the New York stage preceded his appearance as an informer. Budd Schulberg, a friendly witness, did not return to any significant work in the theater after his appearance before the committee. Kazan and Schulberg subsequently teamed up to write and direct a hit movie in the mid-fifties—*On the Waterfront*—dealing with a theme they had recent knowledge of—informing. Blacklisted Michael Gordon directed ten theatrical productions from 1951 to 1958, when he returned to films. Howard da Silva managed to sustain himself during the fifties in New York on and off Broadway as an actor-director and teacher. In the fall of 1969 he starred as Benjamin Franklin in the hit Broadway musical *1776*.

Larry Parks and Marc Lawrence appear to have been the victims of a reverse blacklist, and although they gave the committee names of alleged Communists, their film and theatrical careers came to an abrupt halt along with the unfriendly blacklistees. Odets remained active in films and the theater after his appearance before the committee and died in 1963.

Abe Burrows went on to greater success as an author, television celebrity, and Broadway play doctor. Jose Ferrer continued his career on Broadway and in films, as did Lillian Hellman. Miss Revere worked intermittently in the theater on both coasts and Miss Sondergaard did not return to films until after her appearance in *Uncle Vanya* on stage in Los Angeles in the fall of 1969. Will Geer became "hot" in 1970 when he was featured in the film version of William Faulkner's *The Reivers*. Blacklisted actor Morris Carnovsky worked and taught in the

New York theater during the fifties, and his 1963 performance as King Lear at Stratford, Connecticut, was widely acclaimed.

Actor Jeff Corey became the most celebrated drama teacher in Hollywood during the fifties and was always graciously accepted within the studio gates as a talent observer and critic as well as coach, but never as an actor. He did one play at the Circle Theatre in Hollywood during this period and in 1959 played at La Jolla, California, in a production of *A View from the Bridge*. He is currently working full-time again in movies and television, as well as continuing his active career as a drama instructor.

Besides the heinous conditions caused individual artists by the blacklist, the majority of the respondents to my questionnaire concurred on the theory that the work of the committee not only destroyed careers in the early fifties but also significantly reduced controversial creativity in writing for both films and the theater. There was little reason for an established writer to attempt a subject he felt no Broadway producer would tangle with, and few if any producers encouraged anti-establishment efforts by tyro playwrights. Undoubtedly, this dearth of provocative realistic writing gave rise to the absurdist school which avoided not only social or political themes but theme itself.

The matter of the time factor in playwriting, political positions, and the intellectual history of the liberal movement in the United States in the twentieth century should have been considered by the committee in its 1951-52 investigation of Communism in the entertainment field. It was not. Virtually all the unfriendly artists who appeared before John Wood were blacklisted for opinions and positions they held in the past, notably in the distant past of the prewar social ferment of the thirties. As in the case of the Hollywood Ten, the majority of the unfriendly witnesses in the early fifties shared Schulberg and Kazan's disenchantment with Communism, but unlike the writer and the director, they refused to prove their reformation by informing on their friends.

If it was possible in the thirties to be an American Communist and believe in a coalition government of democratic and socialist elements, it was equally possible in 1947 to surrender that belief when Czechoslovakia became the last East European country to have such a coalition destroyed by Soviet machinations. The committee's failure to research and develop the anti-Communist backgrounds of the witnesses it deemed hostile was manifest in the transcript of the 1951-52 hearings.

No doubt, in the thirties many of the unfriendly witnesses of the fifties were sympathetic to Marxism and truly ignorant of prewar Stalinism in the Soviet Union. Later, when the crimes and purges of the Soviet ruler and system became public knowledge, it is certain many of these same people denounced Russian totalitarianism as they had once railed against Nazi totalitarianism.

One of the consistent curiosities that threads through much of the hearings is the reliance of the committee on Communist periodicals to support its case against the hostile witnesses. While sometimes intimating and more often stating flatly that Communists lied to achieve their evil ends, the committee continuously cited the voice of the party, the *Daily Worker*, and Red periodicals, such as *New Masses* and *Mainstream*, as publications verifying the investigators' charges of Communism in show business.

Lillian Hellman's carefully reasoned correspondence and her subsequent dialogue with the committee was a splendid example of the manner in which unfriendly witnesses might have avoided taking constitutional immunity and risking the resultant blacklist.

It is apparent that the overwhelming majority of the attorneys for the unfriendly witnesses failed to prepare properly; it is patent in the transcripts that they neglected to advise their clients on the possible variables available when answering the committee's questions.

Surely Miss Hellman's prestige and intellectual gifts were helpful in her appearance as a committee witness. It is equally certain, however, that a significant number of unfriendly witnesses had a sufficient amount of intellect and confidence to challenge the interrogators' questioning procedures. Why they did not and why they were not so counseled by their lawyers remains a mystery.

The committee usurped the functions of the grand jury without the protective secrecy of that body by making charges publicly in a purported effort to obtain information. The committee was able to punish people for acts or associations that would not be regarded as crimes in a court of law. The punishment was the loss of their livelihood and the annihilation of their reputations.

In this sense the committee conducted trials rather than hearings, and the jury that sat in judgment on the guilt or innocence of the witnesses was a public court made up of such self-appointed watchdogs of the nation's security as the right-wing faction of the anti-Communist American Legion.

Outspoken liberal and left-wing anti-Communist watchdogs are also necessary for the security of a democracy; the committee's constant bellicose overstating of the significance of Communist subversion in show business must have enraged the liberal intellectuals and thus weakened their rational interest in the real nature of the problem.

As mentioned in the Introduction of this book and of primary significance and totally disregarded by the Wood investigation was the fact that Communism, as that word is understood in this century, has developed in a revolutionary sense only in countries devoid of a strong middle class and fraught with economic extremes, whose governments are administered by a minuscule ruling elite dominating an oppressed peasant majority.

Whether any committee member had this understanding of what factors are involved in Communism as a radical method of social change is debatable. What is apparent from a careful reading of the John Wood investigation is that no committee member revealed any such understanding.

This failure to comprehend the historical perspective of Communism as a revolutionary force served the committee well in the sense that it could deal with the problem of internal subversion in a manner that was sufficiently simplistic for the public to understand and sympathize with. When national interest in and fear of Communism began to diminish at the conclusion of the Korean War, public sympathy for the committee's work likewise diminished. Why interest and fear waned in the mid-fifties is discussed in the evaluation of the following chapter, which deals with that period.

In its 1952 *Annual Report*, the committee managed to conclude mistakenly that because it exposed certain persons as Communists, this led to a marked diminution of Red influence in Hollywood films. Obviously, if the unfriendly witnesses were blacklisted, their incomes were resultantly diminished; hence, there was less money for the Commie coffers. Since the committee never proved there was any significant Red propaganda in films, the report's contention that because of this exposure the blacklistees had less chance of injecting their philosophy into films was meaningless.[107]

At no time during the Thomas, Wood, or subsequent investigations of Hollywood film content was the committee ever able to establish conclusively that Communist Party dogma managed to find its way to the American people via the American cinema.

Rather than exorcising the Red spirits from the silver screen, the Wood investigation was another personalized persecution of entertainment people.

FOOTNOTES

1. Charles E. Potter, *Days of Shame* (New York, Coward-McCann, Inc., 1965), pp. 55-56.
2. *Ibid.*, p. 57.
3. *Ibid.*, p. 56.
4. *Ibid.*
5. *Ibid.*, p. 57.
6. U.S. Congress, House Committee on Un-American Activities, *Communist Infiltration of Hollywood Motion-Picture Industry*, Hearings, Eighty-second Congress, First Session, 1951, Part I, p. 55. Hereinafter cited as *Motion Picture Hearings*, 1951.
7. Walter Goodman, *The Committee; the Extraordinary Career of the House Committee on Un-American Activities* (New York, Farrar, Straus & Giroux, 1968), p. 307.
8. V. J. Jerome, *Culture in a Changing World* (New York, New Century Publishers, Inc., 1947), p. 16.
9. *Motion Picture Hearings*, 1951, Part I, pp. 56-76.
10. Leonard W. Levy, *Origins of the Fifth Amendment* (New York, Oxford University Press, 1968), p. 432.
11. *Motion Picture Hearings*, 1951, Part I, p. 115.

12. *Ibid.*, pp. 113-20.
13. *Ibid.*, pp. 114-21.
14. *Ibid.*, p. 122.
15. *Ibid.*, p. 123.
16. *Ibid.*, pp. 177-93.
17. *Ibid.*, p. 199.
18. *Ibid.*, p. 214.
19. *Ibid.*, p. 262.
20. *Ibid.*, pp. 278-81.
21. *Ibid.*, pp. 296-302.
22. *Ibid.*, pp. 301-2.
23. New York *Times*, March 24, 1951.
24. Goodman, *op. cit.*, p. 301.
25. *Motion Picture Hearings*, 1951, Part I, pp. 79-83.
26. *Ibid.*, pp. 87-90.
27. Goodman, *op. cit.*, p. 302.
28. *Motion Picture Hearings*, 1951, Part I, p. 139.
29. *Ibid.*, pp. 139-65.
30. Sterling Hayden, *Wanderer* (New York, Alfred A. Knopf, Inc., 1963), p. 392.
31. *Motion Picture Hearings*, 1951, Part I, pp. 222-54.
32. *Ibid.*, pp. 257-58.
33. *Ibid.*, p. 258.
34. *Ibid.*, pp. 255-56.
35. Goodman, *op. cit.*, p. 307.
36. *Motion Picture Hearings*, 1951, Part I, pp. 286-89.
37. *Ibid.*, p. 296.
38. *Motion Picture Hearings*, 1951, Part II, p. 305.
39. *Ibid.*, p. 310.
40. *Ibid.*, pp. 314-18.
41. *Ibid.*, pp. 318-20.
42. *Ibid.*, pp. 377-85.
43. *Ibid.*, pp. 390-93.
44. *Ibid.*, pp. 400-3.
45. *Ibid.*, pp. 441-71.
46. Goodman, *op. cit.*, p. 304.
47. *Motion Picture Hearings*, 1951, Part II, pp. 328–59.
48. *Ibid.*, pp. 358-59.
49. *Ibid.*, p. 362.
50. *Ibid.*, pp. 367-70.
51. *Ibid.*, p. 370.
52. *Ibid.*, p. 374.
53. *Ibid.*, pp. 410-11.
54. A list of show business persons named as Communists before the committee and the former Communists who identified them appears in Appendix A.
55. *Motion Picture Hearings*, 1951, Part II, p. 437.

56. *Ibid.*, Part II, pp. 488-89.
57. *Ibid.*, p. 489.
58. *Ibid.*, pp. 489-90.
59. *Ibid.*, p. 516.
60. *Newsweek*, June 2, 1952, p. 27.
61. For the film *Cyrano de Bergerac*.
62. *Motion Picture Hearings*, 1951, Part III, p. 538.
63. *Ibid.*, p. 552.
64. *Ibid.*, pp. 560-67.
65. *Ibid.*, p. 583.
66. *Ibid.*, p. 588-94.
67. *Ibid.*, p. 629.
68. *Ibid.*, p. 637.
69. *Ibid.*, p. 680.
70. *Ibid.*, pp. 676-77.
71. *Ibid.*, pp. 719-38.
72. Howard Suber, *The 1947 Hearings of the House Committee on Un-American Activities into Communism in the Hollywood Motion Picture Industry* (Unpublished master's thesis, University of California at Los Angeles, 1966), p. 233.
73. *Motion Picture Hearings*, 1951, Part IV, pp. 1482-87.
74. Richard English, "What Makes a Hollywood Communist?" *Saturday Evening Post*, May 19, 1951, p. 40.
75. *Motion Picture Hearings*, 1951, Part IV, p. 1576.
76. *Ibid.*, p. 1599.
77. *Ibid.*, p. 1612.
78. *Motion Picture Hearings*, 1951, Part V, p. 1733.
79. *Ibid.*, pp. 1735-36.
80. *Ibid.*, pp. 1753-71.
81. *Ibid.*, pp. 1856-80.
82. Goodman, *op. cit.*, p. 306.
83. *Motion Picture Hearings*, 1951, Part V, p. 1835.
84. All testimony and identifications of the forty-three persons who took part in the September session are from *Motion Picture Hearings*, 1951, Parts V and VI.
85. *Motion Picture Hearings*, 1952, Part VII, p. 2408.
86. *Ibid.*, p. 2411.
87. *Ibid.* pp. 2408-14.
88. *Motion Picture Hearings*, 1952, Part VIII, pp. 3453-73.
89. *Ibid.*, p. 3476.
90. *Ibid.*, p. 3508.
91. *Ibid.*, pp. 3510-11.
92. *Ibid.*, pp. 3545-46.
93. *Ibid.*, p. 3545.
94. New York *Times*, February 10, 1951, and February 23, 1951.
95. *Motion Picture Hearings*, 1952, Part VII, p. 2417.
96. *Ibid.*, p. 2417-32.

97. Goodman, *op. cit.*, p. 304.
98. *Motion Picture Hearings*, 1952, Part VII, pp. 2432-33.
99. *Ibid.*, pp. 2395-2405.
100. English, *op. cit.*, p. 40.
101. *Motion Picture Hearings*, 1952, Part IX, p. 4251.
102. *Ibid.*, p. 4266.
103. *Ibid.*, pp. 4266-80.
104. *Motion Picture Hearings*, 1952, Part X, p. 4477.
105. *Ibid.*, pp. 4480-91.
106. *Ibid.*, pp. 4500-2.
107. U.S. Congress, House Committee on Un-American Activities, *Annual Report*, Eighty-Second Congress, Second Session, December 28, 1952, p. 40.

Chapter V

Harold H. Velde and Francis S. Walter's 1953-54-55 Entertainment Hearings and the Committee's 1956 Investigation of the Fund for the Republic's Report on Blacklisting

CONTAINING international Communism by investigating domestic Communism was not the American national pastime in 1953 and 1954, but such inquiries certainly took up an inordinate amount of time in the Eighty-third Congress. With Senators William E. Jenner and Joseph McCarthy leading the Senate inquisitions, the committee's new chairman in the House, Harold H. Velde, a former FBI agent who was elected to Congress on the slogan "Get the Reds out of Washington and Washington out of the Red," conducted 178 days of taking testimony from more than 650 witnesses, most of whom took the Fifth Amendment.[1]

In contrast to the general barrage of Congressional investigations, the Velde committee seemed to feel no specific obligation to extend itself much past John S. Wood's lengthy 1951-52 examination of the entertainment industry.

Description of the Hearings

After a brief sojourn in Los Angeles in March, 1953—a trip that netted only one unfriendly screenwriter, Ben Maddow,[2] and one friendly but little known actor, Roy Erwin—the committee returned to New York to hear on consecutive days in May the testimony of bandleader Artie Shaw, Broadway chore-

ographer Jerome Robbins, actor Lionel Stander, and the re-
cantation of Robert Rossen.

On Monday morning, May 4, 1953, in Room 1105 of the
United States courthouse, Foley Square, New York, committee
members Donald L. Jackson, Kit Clardy, Gordon H. Scherer,
Clyde Doyle, James B. Frazier, Jr., Bernard W. Kearney, and
Chairman Velde heard witness Shaw weep "with remorse over
having been duped by the Communists."[3]

The bandleader told the Congressmen he first came into
national prominence overnight in 1938 on the basis of a record
called *Begin the Beguine.* Suddenly he was being called upon to
lend his name and talents to many variegated causes, some of
which, the witness admitted, were Communist fronts. He denied
every having joined the CP. "I can only emphatically state I am
against the objectives of the Communist Party in the United
States," he solemnly averred.

During Shaw's long testimony, Tavenner questioned him
about his exposure to Marxist philosophy:

> MR. TAVENNER: So, . . . you attended four of these meet-
> ings?
> MR. SHAW: Three meetings and one lecture.
> MR. TAVENNER: Over what period of time—
> MR. SHAW: Well, during—
> MR. TAVENNER (continuing): Were those meetings held?
> MR. SHAW: During the period I told you about—as I say, from
> a month to 6 weeks previous to July 1946. At this lecture
> meeting there was a lot of, oh, large—an awful lot of
> large—there were a lot of large statements made about
> international, policy, and so on and so forth, and I wasn't
> very concerned with it. I mean, I just didn't care about it one
> way or another. It didn't mean very much to me. It didn't
> interest me very much, and I sat there for about an hour, an
> hour and a quarter, and listened to this man talk. At the end
> of that time, I left. I informed someone I wasn't coming
> back to these things any more, and that was the end of any
> of these meetings.

Shortly after that Shaw confessed,

> . . . And I am at the point now where I am afraid to join any
> organization. I haven't joined any organization for 3 years

because I don't know what any word stands for any more.

Further on Shaw reiterated this dilemma:

> MR. SHAW: . . . I am at a point today if someone says, "Here is
> a committee for personal freedom," I don't want any part of
> it. I don't know what these things mean any more.
> MR. JACKSON: They have been used by the Communist Party
> to the detriment of those words.
> MR. SHAW: I am afraid that is true. I used to think I knew
> what freedom and democracy meant.
> MR. CLARDY: The meaning has been pretty well destroyed?
> MR. SHAW: I am afraid so.

At one point Shaw's testimony inspired enthusiastic applause from the audience:

> MR. SHAW: . . . I had this discussion with a man not long ago,
> when he asked me how I could have been naive enough to
> join the congress—the World Peace Congress—put my name
> on that. I said to him, "Do you know of any other peace
> congress I can join? I want peace."
> He says, "That is the Communist-inspired one." I said,
> "Get me a Republican Party-inspired one and I'll join that. I
> don't care which one"—
> MR. VELDE: The committee must have order—
> MR. SHAW: That wasn't meant—
> MR. VELDE (continuing): In the hearings, and we will counte-
> nance no further demonstrations, favorable or unfavorable.
> MR. SHAW: I wasn't bidding for any applause, I assure you.
> MR. VELDE: I am sure you weren't, Mr. Shaw.[4]

Approximately five years earlier, in her divorce petition, Kathleen Winsor, Shaw's former wife, stated that Shaw confessed he had become a registered member of the Communist Party and he tore up his card immediately upon its being issued to him.[5]

The following day, May 5, was highlighted by the appearance of dancer-choreographer and friendly witness Jerome Robbins. Velde, "like a frugal housewife, squeezed out a last few names to fatten the industry blacklist," and Robbins helped amiably in the verbal decoction.[6]

At the time of his appearance before the committee, Robbins was represented on Broadway by *The King and I*. His previous New York productions were *On the Town, Million-Dollar Baby, High Button Shoes, Call Me Madam, Miss Liberty,* and *Two Is Company*. His ballets included *Fancy Free, Interplay, Facsimile, Age of Anxiety, The Pied Piper,* and *The Cage*.

He admitted that he had been a member of the Communist Political Association from 1944 to 1947 and that his unit was known as the "theatrical transient group," a part of the cultural division. At one of the earliest meetings Robbins attended he was asked "in what way did dialectical materialism" help him in his ballet *Fancy Free*. Since the choreographer had prepared *Fancy Free* before attending any CP meetings, he told Counsel Tavenner he "found the question a little ridiculous and a little outrageous."[7]

Robbins felt that Soviet dictates undermined the basic freedom of the artist:

> I could not understand how the Soviet musicians could be accused of writing—I think the word—formalistic music and bourgeois music, having to repent publicly and then get a benediction to move on and continue composing.
>
> I found this intolerable to an artist. I feel that they must be allowed to say what they want to say as they feel it, and that the minute they become subject to any dictums they're being false.[8]

Robbins cited his reasons for joining the Communist Political Association: It was fighting Fascism and, therefore, anti-Semitism and it "was striving to make out of communism an American form of communism and [he believed] that it would coordinate with other political parties rather than be as secretive a thing as the Communist Party became when it changed back again."[9]

The witness admitted he was wrong on both assumptions and that he terminated his affiliation with the party for these reasons and

> that the artist was not free; that he wasn't—that he became a

puppet to the Communist line, Communist propaganda. There was the attempt to move everything that way.[10]

In bizarre juxtaposition to Robbins' disdain for having his work used as a tool for political propaganda were his last words with Representative Doyle before leaving the witness chair:

> MR. DOYLE: Now, I have a very personal question—and I have never met you; I have never talked with you before, have I?
>
> MR. ROBBINS: No, sir.
>
> MR. DOYLE: Well, then, let me ask you: What is it in your conscience, or what was it in your experience, that makes you certainly one of the top men in your profession, one who has reached the pinnacle in your art, willing to come here and in spite of the fact that you knew some other people, who claim to be artists or authors or musicians, would put you down as a stoolpigeon, and voluntarily testify as you have today?
>
> MR. ROBBINS: I've examined myself. I think I made a great mistake before in entering the Communist Party, and I feel that I am doing the right thing as an American.
>
> MR. DOYLE: In other words, you feel you are doing the right thing as an American?
>
> MR. ROBBINS: Yes, sir.
>
> MR. DOYLE: Well, so do I.
>
> Again I want to compliment you.
>
> Now, let me say this, too: You are in a wonderful place, through your art, your music, your talent, which God blessed you with, to perhaps be very vigorous and positive in promoting Americanism in contrast to communism. Let me suggest to you that you use that great talent which God has blessed you with to put into ballets in some way, to put into music in some way, that interpretation.
>
> MR. ROBBINS: Sir, all my works have been acclaimed for its [sic.] American quality particularly.
>
> MR. DOYLE: I realize that, but let me urge you to even put more of that in it where you can appropriately.[11]

The next unfriendly witness was every bit as hostile as Robbins had been cooperative. Not since October, 1947, when the committee first heard articulate, emotional, sardonic, and unfriendly witnesses Lawson, Trumbo, and their First Amendment brethren of the Hollywood Ten, had the Congressmen faced such a tough show business personality as actor Lionel Stander. He "whipped up a furious storm in the course of taking the Fifth Amendment,"[12] a storm interspersed with enough good humor to keep him on the stand somewhat longer than the usual uncooperative witness.

Stander was sworn in on the morning of May 6, 1953, and immediately asked that the lights and television cameras be turned off because as "a professional performer," he only appeared "on TV for entertainment or for philanthropic organizations." His presence before the committee fell into neither category. The actor added that if his appearance and entire testimony were seen live before the American public—"just the way I make it"—he did not think he "would have as strenuous objections; but I still might object."[13]

Chairman Velde said that such a request had been honored before when the cameras and lights might have made the witness nervous and interfered with the testimony. Stander replied, "I am not exactly calm this morning."[14]

To support his request, he said that as an actor he liked to give a good performance and in order to perform, it was necessary to rehearse; this he had not been able to do. The cameras and lights were turned off only after Stander agreed to answer the questions put to him by counsel.

Stander had appeared before the special committee on Tuesday, August 27, 1940, in executive session and "denied having been a member of the Communist Party and stated that he never intended to be," according to a statement made by his attorney at the 1953 session.[15]

From the appearance of actor Marc Lawrence on April 24, 1951 (the friendly witness who identified Stander as a Communist), to Stander's performance was more than two years, a period during which the witness claimed he was blacklisted. Throughout the two-year period the witness had consistently requested to appear before the tribunal to refute Lawrence's charges and also condemn the informer as a "psychopathic" and a perjurer.[16]

He further charged that in 1948 or 1949 he was forced to make a nightclub personal appearance because he had been blacklisted by the major studios "by merely newspaper accusation, without anybody charging me with anything."[17]

Stander supported this thesis, remarking that

> through newspaper headlines people get peculiar attitudes. Mere appearance here is tantamount—not just appearance; the mere fact, in my case, I was subpenaed, is tantamount—to being blacklisted because people say, "What is an actor doing in front of the Un-American Activities Committee?"[18]

When Chairman Velde later observed that the witness was apparently "excited and nervous," Stander, paraphrasing an allegation he made earlier, wryly commented, "Not as nervous as Marc Lawrence, who came out of a mental institution."

Stander, throughout his testimony, maintained a great verbal energy and managed to outtalk the entire Congressional committee. On one occasion the actor turned the hearings into what can only be called a satire:

> MR. STANDER: Does this committee charge me with being a Communist?
>
> MR. VELDE: Mr. Stander, will you let me tell you whether you are charged with being a Communist?
>
> Will you be quiet just for a minute while I will tell you what you are here for?
>
> MR. STANDER: Yes; I would like to hear.
>
> MR. VELDE: You are here to give us information, facts and information, which will enable us to do the work that was assigned to us by the House of Representatives, which is a duty imposed upon us to investigate reports regarding subversive activities in the United States.
>
> MR. STANDER: Well, I am more than willing to cooperate—
>
> MR. VELDE: Now, just a minute.
>
> MR. STANDER: Because I have—I know of some subversive activities in the entertainment industry and, elsewhere in the country.
>
> MR. VELDE: Mr. Stander, the committee is interested—
>
> MR. STANDER: If you are interested, I can tell you some right now.
>
> MR. VELDE: (continuing): Primarily in any subversive knowledge you have—
>
> MR. STANDER: And I have knowledge of some subversive action.

MR. VELDE (continuing): In the overthrow of the Government.

MR. STANDER: I don't know about the overthrow of the Government. This committee has been investigating 15 years so far, and hasn't even found one act of violence.

MR. VELDE: Now, the record will speak for itself.

MR. STANDER: Well, I have been reading the record.

MR. VELDE: That is entirely—

MR. STANDER: I know of some subversion, and I can help the committee if it is really interested.

MR. VELDE: Mr. Stander—

MR. STANDER: I know of a group of fanatics who are desperately trying to undermine the Constitution of the United States by depriving artists and others of life, liberty, and pursuit of happiness without due process of law.

    If you are interested in that, I would like to tell you about it. I can tell names, and I can cite instances, and I am one of the first victims of it; and if you are interested in that—and also a group of ex-Bundists, America Firsters and anti-Semites, people who hate everybody, including Negroes, minority groups, and most likely themselves—

MR. VELDE: Now, Mr. Stander, let me—

MR. STANDER: And these people are engaged in the conspir acy, outside all the legal processes, to undermine our very fundamental American concepts upon which our entire system of jurisprudence exists—

MR. VELDE: Now, Mr. Stander—

MR. STANDER: And who also—

MR. VELDE: Let me tell you this: You are a witness before this committee—

MR. STANDER: Well, if you are interested—

MR. VELDE (continuing): A committee of the Congress of the United States—

MR. STANDER (continuing): I am willing to tell you—

MR. VELDE (continuing): And you are in the same position as any other witness before this committee—

MR. STANDER (continuing): I am willing to tell you about these activities—

MR. VELDE (continuing): Regardless of your standing in the motion-picture world—

MR. STANDER (continuing): Which I think are subversive.

MR. VELDE (continuing): Or for any other reason. No witness can come before this committee and insult the committee—

MR. STANDER: Is this an insult to the committee—

MR. VELDE (continuing): And continue to—

> MR. STANDER (continuing): When I inform the committee I
> know of subversive activities which are contrary to the
> Constitution?
>
> MR. VELDE: Now, Mr. Stander, unless you begin to answer
> these questions and act like a witness in a reasonable,
> dignified manner, under the rules of the committee, I will be
> forced to have you removed from this room.
>
> MR. STANDER: Well, I—
>
> MR. CLARDY: Mr. Stander, may I say—
>
> MR. STANDER: I am deeply shocked, Mr. Chairman.
>
> MR. CLARDY: Mr. Stander, let me—
>
> MR. STANDER: Let me explain myself. I don't mean to be
> contemptuous of this committee at all.
>
> MR. VELDE: Will you—
>
> MR. STANDER: I want to cooperate with it.
>
> You said something—you said you would like me to
> cooperate with you in your attempt to unearth subversive
> activities. I know of such subversive activities. I began to tell
> you about them, and I am shocked by your cutting me off.
> You don't seem to be interested in the sort of subversive
> activities I know about.[19]

The next friendly witness had been uncooperative during his first appearance before the committee. Writer-director Robert Rossen indicated on June 25, 1951, that if he changed his mind about naming names he would get in touch with the committee.

On May 7, 1953, the day following Stander's testimony, Rossen returned to the witness chair and "testified that he had been a Communist from 1937 to 1947 and had contributed about $40,000 to Party causes; he gave fifty-seven names, most all of them well worn by now from Committee handling."[20]

Earlier that day, Lee Sabinson, who produced *Finian's Rainbow* and Dalton Trumbo's *Biggest Thief in Town* on Broadway and such Hollywood films as *Home of the Brave, Trio*, and *Counter-Attack*, appeared before the committee. He emphasized that although he was not now a Communist, he would claim his privilege under the Fifth Amendment when questioned about past membership.[21]

Sabinson, when confronted with documentation showing his name aligned with Communist-front groups, usually replied that he had no recollection of such associations, but even so he would do the same thing today.

Following the same line of reasoning, the producer, who was accompanied by his attorney Osmund K. Frankel, dumbfounded the committee members and their counsel, Robert Kunzig, during this exchange:

> MR. KUNZIG: ... I have a photostatic copy of a page of the Daily Worker of Monday, February 16—
>
> MR. FRANKEL: What year?
>
> MR. KUNZIG (continuing): Marked "Sabinson Exhibit No. 6" for identification. It states in a headline: "Eighty City Leaders Ask Council Seat Gerson; Issue Up Today." It lists Lee Sabinson, producer, as one of those who wanted to seat Simon W. Gerson to the city council seat made vacant by the death of Councilman Peter C. Cacchione, Brooklyn Communist. Are you the Lee Sabinson listed in that article?
>
> MR. FRANKEL: You didn't give the date, or the year.
>
> MR. KUNZIG: Will you put the year in? I'm sorry.
>
> MR. FRANKEL: 1948.
>
> MR. SABINSON: I most likely was the Lee Sabinson. Since the people elected Cacchione, I thought his successor most likely should be a Communist, since the people of New York City elected the man.
>
> MR. CLARDY: Witness, may I ask you this: You said you "most likely"—
>
> MR. SABINSON: Yes; I—
>
> MR. CLARDY: Did you mean that to be an affirmation that you were the person so identified?
>
> MR. SABINSON: I have no recollection of this, but most likely this is true because I would today do the same thing.
>
> MR. CLARDY: In other words, you are in no position to say you were not?
>
> MR. SABINSON: I am in no position to say I was not.
>
> MR. SCHERER: You said today you would urge it?
>
> MR. SABINSON: If the people elected a Communist, and that Communist died, then I think he should be replaced by a Communist.
>
> MR. CLARDY: Today?
>
> MR. SABINSON: Yes, if the people elected the man. That is the will of the American people, in this instance.
>
> MR. KUNZIG: So, if the will of the American people were to elect Communists and have a completely Communist government of the United States of America, that would be entirely satisfactory to you?
>
> MR. SABINSON: Whatever the will of the American people is [is] perfectly satisfactory to me.

MR. KUNZIG: Including a Communist government in New
York, Washington, or anywhere?

MR. SABINSON: Whatever the will of the American people is
[is] perfectly satisfactory with me, because the people are
sovereign.

MR. KUNZIG: I think you have made your position completely clear.[22]

In replying to Congressman Doyle's request for cooperation
with the committee in the area of subversive activities, Sabinson
generously responded:

If I am familiar with any subversive activities, I will cooperate.

And at this point may I tell you that in 86th Street in New
York City on Friday night there was a Bundist meeting, at
which Senator McCarthy was "heiled," and again at [sic.] this
Friday there is going to be such a meeting.[23]

There was laughter.

Acting Chairman Kit Clardy, who had the dehumanizing
habit of calling any witness "Witness" instead of by his name,
thundered, "There will be no laughter in this hearing room
during the time I am chairman or you will all be expelled from
the room—and I mean all."[24]

Whether all meant disbanding the proceedings Clardy did not
clarify. But there was no more laughter.

Other unfriendly show business witnesses appearing during
those four days in May were television and theater director
Mortimer Offner, writer Cedric Henning Belfrage, playwright
and screenwriter Arnaud d'Usseau, and songwriter Jay Gorney.

Writer-actress-director Carin Kinzel Burrows, wife of Abe,
was a friendly witness on May 5, 1953, and a good deal less
oblique in her testimony than her husband. The committee
asked her to name names. She did, but no questions were asked
about her husband. She admitted joining the CP in 1940. She
believed she quit in 1946. She testified in executive session; her
testimony was released by the committee on the same day.

At one point Mrs. Burrows explained what triggered her
departure from the Communist Party:

MRS. BURROWS: There was a man named Albert Maltz, whom I admired a great deal. You see, one of the greatest appeals the party had for artists and people in the show business was that being a good artist in itself was being a good citizen, and was contributing something of value to the country and to the community. Now a discussion arose in which, I believe, Mr. Maltz took the position that an artist should write and create the truth as he saw it and felt it, and that political knowledge was not necessary to know the truth or to state the truth. I think he gave examples of authors who had been actually reactionary, and still had been fine artists, and that was also true as I saw it. One of the examples which sticks in my mind was Balzac. He wrote of this in an article which I read, and I liked it very much. I respected Mr. Maltz very much. I didn't really know him personally, but had read some of his books and admired him greatly.

MR. TAVENNER: In that article, did he take the position that art should not be used as a weapon?

MRS. BURROWS: I think that was certainly the gist of what was said. I don't, of course, recall the exact words. I think I have said that I respected Mr. Maltz very much as an artist, and a creative man, and a man of dignity and stature in his world. After he wrote that article, he was severely reprimanded—I don't remember by whom—some bigwig in the Communist Party—and he was told that he was so wrong—that art is a weapon and that it must be used, and it must be slanted, and it is very important for the artist to incorporate in his work his political views. At any rate, I know they were very much against what Mr. Maltz had said.

He was forced to, or allowed himself to be forced to publicly recant his position. I attended a large meeting in Hollywood in which Mr. Maltz got up and made a speech and said how wrong he had been, and blamed himself for having fallen into such a grave error and said art was a weapon and had to be used as a weapon. He publicly disgraced and humiliated himself. It was a terrible spectacle to see a man I had always respected behave in this way. I decided that, with the constant changes taking place in the Communist Party, it was impossible to be a Communist and have freedom of thought and dignity as a human being. It was a dictatorship, and as such, was degrading to the people in it. I left the party after that.[25]

At 4:30 p.m., Tuesday, June 2, 1953, in Room 1117 of the

Hollywood Roosevelt Hotel in the film capital, the distinguished actor Lee J. Cobb became an informer.

His statement was given to committee investigator William A. Wheeler in executive, or private, testimony later released by the full committee. It was brief and not notable for any new information other than that John Howard Lawson had attempted to adapt Konstantin Stanislavski's acting precepts to prevailing Communist ideology. Cobb described this extraordinary venture thus: "The excuse was that however good Stanislavski was, he would be so much better if he were a Communist, and so the purpose was to add the Communist portion to Stanislavski which he was not endowed with by God."[26]

Several weeks later, on June 15, 1953, in Washington, D.C., actress Jean Muir volunteered to come before the committee to explain why she had not worked since August 25, 1950, and why she had sent a greeting to the Moscow Art Theatre:

> MR. KUNZIG: Do you recall sending a greeting to the Moscow Art Theater? According to the Daily Worker of November 1, 1948, you did that.
>
> MISS MUIR: Yes; I did. I sent that telegram to Constantine Stanislov [sic] of the Moscow Art Theater, because that theater represents to the actors just about the best theater we have had in the past 100 years. It has had a tremendous influence on the training of actors. I didn't send it because it was a Communist organization. It was not. Stanislov [sic] was able to successfully put on plays which no other theater in Russia was allowed to do. He stood up against the regime from the first, according to my recollection. His reputation was so great—his world reputation was so great, that he was allowed to do this. A play like Czar Theodor, for instance, which was banned all over Russia, he succeeded in putting on. This was an artistic thing which I did, and just because the title of the theater was the Moscow Art Theater I don't think I could be called a Communist for that.

Miss Muir testified that she had been signed to play the part of Mrs. Aldrich in *The Aldrich Family* television show. The show was canceled and she was fired, according to the actress, because NBC had received approximately ten telephone calls and two telegrams regarding her alleged Communist affiliations.[27] NBC put the number of phone calls at more than twenty but fewer than thirty.[28]

Whatever the number of calls, they were the work of former FBI man Theodore C. Kirkpatrick, who was also secretary-treasurer of American Business Consultants, a group that published the weekly newsletter *Counterattack* whose aim "was to expose the Communist menace."[29]

Three months before Miss Muir lost her job, Kirkpatrick's group had also published a book called *Red Channels, the Report of Communist Influence in Radio and Television*. The publication listed 151 names associated with the industry, along with the so-called Communist or Communist-front organizations with which each had been affiliated. Miss Muir's had been one of the names in *Red Channels*, together with nine subversive allegations.[30]

Testifying before the committee, Miss Muir made no attempt to deny that she had supported organizations that had been labeled subversive by the Attorney General, but she did flatly deny that she had ever been a Communist.[31]

With the exception of actress Lucille Ball's neutral appearance, the committee's relationship with the world of entertainment was, for the remainder of 1953, relatively uneventful.[32] And 1954 was no different. Reports released by the committee indicate that Chairman Velde's group investigated only three persons on three different days, with almost a year elapsing between the appearance of the first two witnesses and the third.[33]

On January 13, 1954, writer Allan E. Sloane was added to the list of people deemed friendly to the committee's work. Sloane had been listed in *Red Channels* and admitted to the committee his former CP membership and also his association with Communist-front groups.

As a newspaperman he began to be disenchanted when he was told to hawk the *Daily Worker* on street corners. Sloane rebelled. He said this order was beneath him, but it was explained to him that this was all part of "Party discipline."

The witness described the unique use of Communist code words when introducing people who were not acquainted with each other:

It involves the use of Aesopian language. When, for instance, in this particular meeting of the MWC, Lampell introduced me to the lyric writer, he described him as a terrific guy. When a Communist introduces somebody to you as a terrific guy it means you are being introduced to somebody who is a fellow Communist. When he is called a good guy it means you are being introduced to somebody who is known to be a fellow traveler, or not unsympathetic to your being a Communist. When you refer to somebody or ask about him and are told he is a bastard that does not mean he is of illegitimate parentage but an active anti-Communist and to watch your step. Therefore, I say I was introduced at one of these meetings to this lyric writer who was described to me as a terrific guy, which meant a green light for an all-out discussion of things of a dialetic materialism viewpoint. In other words, this is a brother Communist.

MR. VELDE: Was this usage of words you have just referred to common in your own group or in all groups?

MR. SLOANE: This was common in the circles we people moved in—the writers of radio and TV material. Any fellow writer was also in our social circle. If you would go to a party, you would meet somebody. You would tell somebody you met that person and he would say "He is a terrific guy." He meant, specifically, a Communist, and it was a sort of signal. When you hear somebody in a conversation use the word "terrific" you can sense that the person is almost sending out signals. You have heard when a male butterfly sends out vibrations the females hear them. The same way if you heard the words "terrific guy" come out and if the conversation was political, you would bet your last dollar that person referred to was a Communist.[34]

Sloane later explained how he and a lyric writer, whom he did not identify, wrote a children's playlet under the direction of the cultural wing of the CP:

. . . Then another time they called, and this time they said "We would like a little playlet suitable for presentation by the school children," so another person and I sat down and figured out this Divide and Conquer thing. It told how a lot of children were to be on a stage playing marbles, and along came a big bully who said "Let me play," and the children said "No." So he called one of the children aside and said "You can't play with them because you are a Negro." So they chased the Negro

away. Then he said "You can't play with him because he is a
Jew." So they chased the Jew away. Then before long there
was no one left to play. He divided them all. Then they all
came out and chased him away. He was supposed to be Hitler,
and so the person I am speaking of and I combined our talents
and figured out the playlet in this manner.

  This almost perfectly shows the cultural aspects of the
Communist Party. . . .[35]

Much to the satisfaction of the committee, and not without a
basis in fact, the witness compared art under capitalism and
Communism:

  This is the vicious thing about communism, capturing an artist.
  I would also say there is no such thing as a Communist artist,
  because communism involves slavery and art involves freedom
  and you can't have an enslaved free man.[36]

In 1948, after Sloane had left the CP and was still believed by
Communist-front organizations to be a fellow traveler,[37] he
co-wrote with another fellow traveler, Millard Lampell, the
acceptance speech of the Presidential candidate of the Progressive Party, Henry Wallace.[38]

Sloane testified that he had once named an old merchant
marine character in a radio show Pop Silverman to please his
father. (Sloane's real name was Allan Silverman and was legally
changed.) The director of the show demanded the name be
changed, saying, " 'that old Communist line' " and " 'Everybody has to have a Jewish name in the script, or an Italian
name—why do you have to do that?—fix that.' " And Sloane
did.[39]

The following Monday, January 18, 1954, Broadway and
Hollywood stage designer Howard Bay refused to answer all
self-incriminating questions submitted to him by the committee
and added that because he refused, "No inference need be
drawn as to my guilt."[40]

The committee disagreed, as it had so many times before, but
the witness maintained his stance and did not cooperate with
the Congressmen.

Slightly less than a year later, on December 14, 1954, the

committee heard the testimony of a most cooperative actor-
writer-director, Nicholas Bela.

Near the end of Bela's testimony, Counsel Kunzig posed a
question based on the rumor that since the exposé of Communist activity in the motion picture industry, the residue of the
Communist left wing had secreted itself in the legitimate stage
in New York. Counsel wanted to know if the witness had any
information on that.

Bela responded that it would be a question of guessing, but
he did not think the rumor was correct, except for a few, like
Waldo Salt, for example, who wrote the book for the musical
comedy *The Sand Hog*, which was running off-Broadway.[41]

Having admitted to the committee that he had been a
Communist, the witness generously sprinkled his testimony
with expressions of grieving remorse, concluding his appearance
by asking to be allowed to stand while he publicly repented his
errors:

> I feel if I am allowed I would like to stand. That the House
> of Representatives represents the country, and the committee
> of the House of Representatives is also, therefore, a representa-
> tion of this country. So I want to thank you for hearing me. I
> want to humbly apologize for the grave error which I have
> committed, and beg of you to forgive me.
> Thank you.[42]

For four consecutive days during August, 1955, the committee's new chairman, Francis E. Walter, heard testimony from
twenty-three witnesses, mostly actors, who "were several steps
below star rank."[43] These were the only investigations conducted by the Walter committee that dealt exclusively with the
living theater and the New York stage.

When Chairman Walter was asked to reveal the reason for the
investigation, "he referred vaguely to Communist infiltration of
the entertainment unions and to the filling of Communist
coffers with Broadway salary checks, but neither line was
pursued."[44]

On Monday morning, August 15, 1955, the committee
returned to Foley Square, New York City, and heard actor
George Tyne decline to answer questions regarding his private

and political beliefs. He did not indicate a specific constitutional amendment as the reason for his position.[45] He and actor Elliott Sullivan were cited for contempt and acquitted in 1961, "when the district court found their indictments 'fatally defective' because the government had not submitted the Committee's resolution ordering the hearing."[46]

The next witness, actor John Randolph, started his career in the late thirties in the Federal Theatre. When Counsel Tavenner asked the witness about his knowledge of "a group of Communist Party members within the Federal Project," the actor invoked both the First and Fifth amendments.[47] He explained that he had engaged in much television work until 1952, when he was blacklisted by the vigilante anti-Communist publication, *Counterattack*, and AWARE, Inc. Again he took the First and Fifth amendments.[48]

Actor Lou Polan was next to testify, and like the opening witness, George Tyne, he refused to answer questions not on the basis of a constitutional amendment but for personal reasons. Polan said, "I wish to put this committee on notice that I will not assist you in your lawless efforts to censor the legitimate theatre or control the entertainment field which, in my opinion, are the real aims of this committee."[50] The actor insisted that he wanted to give his reasons for being uncooperative. Tavenner "permitted" him only legal reasons. The witness said his reasons were legal. The chair, without hearing Polan's reasons, said they were not legal. Polan's counsel said they were. The chair said he could refuse to answer on the grounds that he did not have to answer. And the witness was excused. He was not cited for contempt.[51]

Unfriendly witnesses actor Phil Leeds and actress Sarah Cunningham, wife of John Randolph, completed the first day's testimony.

The following morning marked the appearance of the second witness who would be called in contempt of Congress during the four-day period, August 15-18. Actor Elliott Sullivan made no effort at constitutional refuge when he was sworn in by Chairman Walter on August 16. The actor was advised by Congressman Gordon H. Scherer that he was in contempt.

Chairman Walter responded: "I don't think it makes any difference to him. So why tell him?"

Sullivan emotionally replied:

> Of course it makes a difference, and I have a wife and two children, and I am very anxious to work and this is a big waste of time as far as I am concerned. The harassment that is involved in this is utter nonsense, and when you make a statement such as you don't think it makes any difference to me, I beg to differ with you very strongly about that. It makes a serious difference to my entire life, my appearance here, and I resent that remark.[52]

Commenting on the fear that was extant in America during the early and mid-fifties, the witness explained the significance of a skit he participated in at a summer camp:

> The purpose was to entertain an audience there by satirizing a condition which exists in this country today, and I believe the best musical theater of the past has always been the kind which has satirized current events. In my estimation this sketch falls into that category. The fact that you are asking me about a 2-minute sketch that takes place 80 miles away from New York would lead me to believe that there is [sic] some censorship notions about your raising the question. Is it your province to examine material that goes on the stage anywhere, and to comment on it in such a way that it may discourage people from making comments about things that go on today?
>
> This again seems to me to be contrary to the stated purposes of this committee, and it very clearly indicates what I have said in my statement here that this committee encourages censorship, and it encourages fear to produce this kind of material. In my estimation this is as good a piece of American theater as you could possibly get. It presents two men who are selling the Bill of Rights to each other, and then the minute each of them buy it, they disclose themselves as being members of the FBI, or some other Government agency, and they arrest each other. Of course, this is exaggerated, but such is the nature of humor on the stage. However, it is not terribly exaggerated when you consider the fact that a newspaper reporter some time ago attempted to get signatures to the very Bill of Rights itself, and out of 125 people, I believe, he succeeded in getting one

signature, and the rest were afraid to sign it or considered him to be some sort of a subversive, as several of them actually said.[53]

Three unfriendly witnesses on the fringe of the theater, folk singer Lee Hays, composer Irma Jurist, and artist Susan d'Usseau, completed the second day's questioning.

Actor Geroge Hall, an admitted former Communist and the only friendly witness during the Broadway hearings, testified the following morning. He explained to Tavenner on August 17 why he now said that having joined the Communist Party was "a mistake" and why using the Fifth Amendment was wrong and therefore, by implication, why he was friendly to the committee's investigation:

> A mistake in the sense that I concluded that it is a distortion of the simple truth of democratic processes. For instance, it was said, or the fifth amendment was used or "invasion of privacies" was used as an excuse for not answering, and one of the reasons was that someone's ancestors came to this country many, many years ago, and signed the declaration, and what have you, and the witnesses testified that they were following what they felt the ancestors would want them to do. But I don't think the point was made clear that those specific ancestors fought, died, and created this country on the basis of a 2-party system, and I think they would be twirling in their graves if they thought this ancestor of today was fighting for a 1-party dictatorship.
>
> That is what I want to avoid most specifically, and I learned to realize that was coming about, and it was a one-party dictatorship, which is more of an invasion of privacy than any use of any [gun] which this Constitution gives to citizens of this country.
>
> The 1-party dictatorship completely deprives, let us say, 50 percent of those who may choose to vote or are eligible to vote, by directing that there is only 1 choice. Our system provides us a choice to be right or wrong and to change our minds if we so choose to do so.[54]

After announcing that he was going to investigate a New York theater blacklist against non-Communists which created a preference of employment for "people who were either members of the Communist Party or who adhered to the leadership of the Communist Party," Chairman Walter made this astonishing appraisal of actor Hall's testimony:

> ... Every patriot in the history of America has been proud of the enemies that he has made, and I am sure that you will be proud as you go along in life of the enemies that you have made. Your contribution here cannot be appraised. It may well be that it is equal to that of a division of infantry, and nobody knows in this cold war to what extent this sort of a revelation has contributed to ultimate victory—and the victory will be ultimate.[55]

The transcript of the hearing does not indicate there was applause.

Actress Madeline Lee, wife of actor Jack Gilford, used four amendments in her declination to answer the committee inquiries on August 17. She said:

> I am declining on the basis of the first amendment, that you are prying into my personal affairs, beliefs, and opinions, and on the basis of the fourth amendment, that this is an illegal search and seizure of my property, and deprivation by due process of law of the only thing I have to sell in this industry—my talent and my good name. I also decline on the basis of the eighth amendment, that this is a cruel and unusual punishment that you are inflicting without due process of law, and on the basis of the fifth amendment, that you may not compel me to be a witness against myself.[56]

Theatrical producer Peter Lawrence, actors Joshua Shelley, George Keane, Albert M. Ottenheimer, Alan Manson, and Tony Kraber, public relations counsel Ivan Black, motion picture production employee Harold J. Salemson, and theatrical stage manager David Kanter constituted the remainder of the August witnesses who refused to answer questions on the basis of constitutional immunity.

Peter (Pete) Seeger, "bard of the Wallace movement and a popular figure in Communist-front activities," testified on August 18, 1955, the final day of the Broadway hearings, and "put on a folksy manner in the witness chair," but soon "dropped the stage business and objected calmly and succinctly to the intrusion on his privacy."[5][7]

During his testimony, Seeger not only defended his right to sing his songs, but felt that such songs transcended political implications:

> ...I am proud that I have sung for every American, Americans of every political persuasion, and I have never refused to sing for anybody because I disagreed with their political opinion, and I am proud of the fact that my songs seem to cut across and find perhaps a unifying thing, basic humanity....
>
> MR. TAVENNER: Did you hear Mr. George Hall's testimony yesterday in which he stated that as an actor, the special contribution that he was expected to make to the Communist Party was to use his talents by entertaining at Communist Party functions? Did you hear that testimony?
>
> MR. SEEGER: I didn't hear it; no.
>
> MR. TAVENNER: It is a fact that he so testified. I want to know whether or not you were engaged in a similar tune of service to the Communist Party in entertaining at these features.
>
> (Witness consulted with counsel)
>
> MR. SEEGER: I have sung for Americans of every political persuasion, and I am proud that I never refuse to sing to an audience, no matter what religion or color of their skin, or situation of life. I have sung in hobo jungles, and I have sung for the Rockefellers, and I am proud that I have never refused to sing for anybody. That is the only answer I can give along that line.

In answering the committee's questions on August 18, Seeger followed the examples of George Tyne and Elliott Sullivan and avoided using the Fifth Amendment refuge.[5][8] As a result, he was also cited for contempt and sentenced to a year in prison after a trial in which Chairman Walter was put on the stand. Six years later the court of appeals reversed the conviction on the grounds that his indictment was defective. The reason for the reversal was much the same as it had been the previous year in the cases of Tyne and Sullivan—failure of the government to submit the committee's resolution ordering the hearings.[5][9]

Seeger did not appear on television between his 1950 listing in *Red Channels* and September, 1967, when at the urging of television satirist Dick Smothers he was allowed to perform on the CBS variety show *The Smothers Brothers Comedy Hour*. He was not allowed to sing the folk song "Knee Deep in Big Muddy," which is critical of the Vietnam War and President Lyndon Johnson. Ironically, the following year the television series was peremptorily canceled for reasons Dick Smothers believed to be political, not theatrical.

The last and most varied talent to be investigated by the Walter committee in 1955 was subpoenaed to the August hearings, but because of professional commitments, he did not testify until Friday, October 14, of that year. In Hollywood, unfriendly witness Sam (Zero) Mostel told committee counsel Frank Tavenner he had acquired his nickname as the result of his "financial standing in the community," a reference no doubt to his loss of income as the result of being accused by Martin Berkeley of Communist affiliations. Mostel denied ever knowing or meeting his accuser.[60]

In June, 1956, the two-volume *Report on Blacklisting* by John Cogley, former executive editor of *Commonweal*, saw publication. The cost of the reports was underwritten by the Fund for the Republic, Inc., headed by the erstwhile president of the University of Chicago, Robert M. Hutchins. A teacher of legal procedure and evidence before he became an academic administrator, Hutchins undoubtedly riled the committee toward the end of the previous year when he was quoted as saying, "I wouldn't hesitate to hire a Communist for a job he was qualified to do provided I was in a position to see he did it."[61]

The reports charged that blacklisting because of political affiliation was prevalent in all areas of the entertainment field except the New York theater. They further asserted that the leaders of the show business world had given the task of judging and clearing accused Reds to such organizations as the American Legion, publications like *Red Channels, Counterattack*, and groups like AWARE, Inc., and staunch anti-Communist columnists George Sokolsky and Victor Riesel.[62] The irony of this was that the above "judges" were cocontributors, with the committee, in creating the blacklist. These organizations and publications relied heavily on the committee hearings and reports as the basis for their newsletters and press releases substantiating Communism's grip on the entertainment world.

The month after the issuance of the Cogley reports the committee decided to investigate the value of the blacklisting analysis. For many of the same reasons that the committee's work was often chastised, the reports were equally vulnerable. Cogley's examination relied heavily on anonymous informers, the use of Miss X and Mr. M in place of names, and citing individually inadequate investigation to support a whole concept of inefficient inquiry. Probably the greatest failure of the reports was their insistence on avoiding the key issue regarding the blacklisted person's right to work—national security.[63]

In Washington, D.C., on July 10, 1956, the committee opened its "Investigation of So-Called Blacklisting in the Entertainment Industry" by subpoenaing John Cogley as its first witness.

The interrogation was conducted by the former investigator for the Senate Internal Security Subcommittee, Richard Arens. He was a tough and sarcastic inquisitor who intimated that Cogley's former employer, *Commonweal*, a liberal Catholic publication, was not Catholic at all. He charged the investigation with being researched by persons who were debatable patriots and accused Cogley of being soft on the Communist affiliations of the "sad cases" contained in the report.[64] This attack was not altogether unjustified, since Michael Harrington, one of the researchers, although an outspoken anti-Communist, was a publicly confessed Socialist, bitterly critical of the inequities of capitalism.[65]

Further, the vast majority of those blacklisted were or had been Communists "or had done their darndest to pass as such," and Cogley avoided mentioning this rather than defending the right to work of the suspected persons, regardless of political persuasion.[66]

Repeatedly paraphrasing the argument, "This is the way I wrote the book," Cogley proved to be not only an inept

defender of the report but also the only defense witness called
by the committee.[67]

In Cogley's chapter on blacklisting on Broadway he made this
observation, which provoked Arens to ask the witness why he
would not describe Paul Robeson as a Communist rather than a
"political person":

> In general the few actors who have found it difficult to find
> work on Broadway are people so politically active that their
> "unemployability" is based on the fact that they are a nuisance
> to work with. Producers who are quite willing to hire actors
> "listed" in *Red Channels* or even those who refuse to cooperate
> with Congressional Committees, draw the line in cases where
> they feel a performer is primarily a "political person" who also
> acts, rather than an actor who happens to take an interest in
> politics. But these cases are relatively few in number. The
> exclusion of such performers is not based on the existence of
> any kind of a "list." Paul Robeson is a good example.[68]

Cogley's explanation was that other people "who had refused
to cooperate with the committee by taking" the Fifth Amendment were employed on Broadway but Robeson was not
because he had become secondarily an actor and primarily a
controversial political figure and therefore "a nuisance to the
rest of the cast."[69]

Arnold Forster, general counsel for the Anti-Defamation
League of B'nai B'rith, appeared before the committee on July
11 and acknowledged that he was possibly the "New York
public-relations expert" referred to in Volume II of the Cogley
report.[70] Forster was somewhat ambiguous about his role in
guiding blacklisted persons to those who might clear or rehabilitate them, although he did admit that such people did exist and
that writers George Sokolsky, Frederick E. Woltman, Victor
Riesel, and American Legion representative James F. O'Neil
were among them.

Woltman was the next witness and denied his role in assisting
to rehabilitate blacklisted performers, referring emphatically to
the instance of humorist Henry Morgan. Contrary to the
implication that the witness had made a deal to plant a
favorable story on Morgan, Woltman claimed he wrote a straight

news story about a union meeting where the humorist spoke and damned Communists.[71]

Talent consultant Vincent W. Hartnett testified the following day that Cogley's assertion that he was in the business of exposing and then clearing people for fees was an "outrageous falsification."[72] He accused Cogley of "McCarthyism in reverse," because he cropped evidence the way "some unscrupulous politicians crop photographs."[73]

In further testimony Hartnett insinuated that J. Edward Bromberg had kidded the committee by pleading a heart attack and then went to Ann Arbor to work. Bromberg's son Conrad recently wrote:

> ... there's no question that five and a half years of semi-employment will have some deleterious effect on a man's mental and physical health. His appearance before the Committee was postponed once because of a heart attack sustained a month earlier. Letters from physicians were introduced stating that such an appearance and the accompanying tension and anxiety would be dangerous to his health. He suffered from rheumatic heart disease and its concomitant cardiac decompensation, so that any prolonged cardiac demand for greater output (such as we find in times of tension) would further weaken an already weakened heart. But the heart beats harder not only at hearings, but sitting at home waiting for the phone to ring. (As you well know, the phone is the actor's lover-enemy, because it either rings with work or silently witholds it.) It's hard to pin down in terms of months or years how much his life was curtailed by the blacklist and its effects. I feel it was, to a measurable degree.[74]

An old face from the 1947 Thomas and 1951-52 Wood hearings came forth again as a witness on July 12, 1956. He was labor leader Roy M. Brewer. He also denied any hand in clearing blacklisted artists, charges made by Cogley in his investigation. His attestation said:

> I did not want, I did not seek, I do not want now, any power over anyone. As I said, any influence that I had came from the fact that I was willing to work at the job of countermanding the influence of what I consider to be a very evil force.[75]

The witness later made the observation that he believed persons identified as Communists by the committee were working on Broadway in the top plays.[76]

Paul R. Milton[77] and Godfrey P. Schmidt[78] represented AWARE, Inc., at the investigation of the Cogley report and generally concurred with the committee about shortcomings of Cogley's inquiry, as did Francis J. McNamara, spokesman for *Counterattack.*[79]

George E. Sokolsky and Victor Riesel submitted statements that further challenged the accuracy of Cogley's investigation.

On July 17 and 18, 1956, the committee moved to Philadelphia for the purported reason of hearing testimony about blacklisting from an actress and an actor who had been mentioned in the Cogley report as having been victims of the process, Gale Sondergaard and Jack Gilford.

The interrogation of both quickly moved from discussion of blacklisting to an accusatory posture by Arens. He started to bring up the alleged Communist affiliations of the two artists and provoked Miss Sondergaard into taking the Fifth Amendment for the second time in that decade and Gilford for the first. The result was that no information pertinent to defending or condemning the Cogley report was forthcoming on the last day of the committee's investigation of the two-volume document.[80]

Evaluation of the Hearings

Once again, the familiar pattern of cooperation with the committee by the witnesses who had the most to lose was repeated. Famous bandleader Artie Shaw, film director Robert Rossen, and from the New York theater actor Lee J. Cobb and choreographer Jerome Robbins were the biggest and most successful names to come before the committee during the Velde years, and their friendly stance allowed them to maintain or regain their vaunted positions in the entertainment industry.

Lee Sabinson, a well-established and successful film and Broadway producer, was the exception to the pattern and emerged as the most courageous living-theater artist to appear before the investigators during 1953-54. Not only was he uncooperative with the investigators, but Sabinson's candor undoubtedly astounded the committee when he stated that if the sovereign people of New York, Washington, or America wished to elect a Red government, that choice was satisfactory to him.

Writer Allan E. Sloane was one of the few friendly witnesses who responded to my request for cooperation in the study. Additionally, his correspondence waived the anonymity promised him, saying "Frankly, I don't give a damn anymore."[81]

Although the three-page letter received from Sloane was not significant as far as theater information was concerned, it was important because of its human angle. Many unfriendly witnesses who responded to the survey questionnaire indicated strong personal vilification directed at them for their position, including violence. Sloane was alone in stating that "midnight phone calls" and "flight and institutionalization" of a member of his family and "public disavowal by a church" resulted from his friendly contact with the committee. He also notes that the foreshortening of J. Edward Bromberg's life was related to the committee's activities. Lastly, Sloane states that when actor Everett Sloane appeared as a witness in radio celebrity John Henry Faulk's lawsuit against AWARE, Inc., actor Sloane replied to attorney Louis Nizer's question on how he happened to be blacklisted that his name had been confused with that of a writer named Allan Everett Sloane. Actor Sloane later received an FBI clearance for his work on a United Nations radio show but when Paul Milton of AWARE, Inc., wanted him to meet with Vincent Hartnett for their clearance, the actor told Milton to "Go fly a kite."[82]

The August, 1955, entertainment hearings in New York were obviously one of the committee's last efforts to scrape the bottom of the publicity barrel in search of headlines. Hollywood had borne the brunt of the Red investigations for almost a decade and that particular medium was bankrupt of attention-getting names. What good purpose was served by the committee's investigations of the twenty-three actors was not clear. The only friendly witness had previously delivered his

names to the FBI and received "absolution from the committee,"[83] and the three witnesses who did not invoke the
protection of any constitutional amendment risked jail sentences, but the nation was certainly no more secure because of
their decision. Even if Chairman Walter had proved Broadway
salary checks were finding their way to Communist purses,
which he did not, the twenty-three subpoenaed witnesses'
living-theater salaries were certainly far too modest to present a
threat to the republic's sovereignty.

As previously mentioned, uncooperative Broadway witnesses
did not always enjoy complete immunity from a blacklist.
During the fifties, actress Florida Friebus, cochairman with
Margalo Gilmore of the Actors' Equity antiblacklist committee,
stated that there were three cases of actual blacklisting in the
theater during this period which were reversed by the committee she cochaired.

There was an agreement between the League of New York
Theatres and Actors' Equity Association that they would not
tolerate blacklisting in the theater. This agreement was honored
in the first blacklisting case to come before Miss Friebus'
committee. The situation involved a New York director who
was being harassed in Baltimore by an American Legion group
and a local radio columnist as he was preparing a play for a
pre-Broadway opening. After a meeting involving all concerned,
the director returned to work without further trouble from the
Legion or the columnist.

Miss Friebus indicated she did not remember the circumstances regarding the other two cases but admitted that her
group did not stand behind an actor who had been blacklisted
out of a reading after the circumstances surrounding the case
had been thoroughly reviewed by both the antiblacklist committee and the artist involved. Though the actor could have
pressed his case and would have been supported by Equity, he
elected not to, based on his own assessment of his then
politically radical views.[84]

There seems to be no question that the work of the House
committee did give sustenance to a group of self-appointed
protectors of the state such as AWARE, Inc., *Red Channels*, the

American Legion, and others investigated in the Cogley report. The month before the August, 1955, hearings, one such evangelist checked on the patriotism of actress Uta Hagen, who was about to open in a play in Chicago:

Anti-Subversive Committee
Cook County Council
The American Legion
Edward Clamage, Chairman
1313 W. Randolph Street
Chicago 7, Illinois

July 19, 1955

Mr. E. J. Reynolds, Acting General Manager
Edgewater Beach Hotel
5349 N. Sheridan Road
Chicago, Illinois

Dear Mr. Reynolds:

My attention has been directed to a forthcoming play to be staged in the Playhouse at the Edgewater Beach Hotel, August 2, 1955. Among the cast members will be Uta Hagen, who has drawn protest from a great number of people due to her activities which a great portion of it is included in the attached report from the "INFORMATION FROM THE FILES OF THE COMMITTEE ON UN-AMERICAN ACTIVITIES," U.S. House of Representatives.

We never hurriedly draft a complaint for the purpose of having persons punished in any form. There is however, one thing for sure, that those who have been giving aid to the enemy, and those of being disloyal citizens, certainly are not entitled to our respect.

We believe that it is incumbent of Miss Hagen to seek a clearance from proper U.S. Governmental Agencies from the charges appearing on attached report, and if granted should proceed without interruptions to seek a livelihood.

I am quite impressed with the cartoon appearing on the editorial page of the Chicago American, Thursday July 14, 1955. It deals with the three "Turncoats", who were captured by the Red Chinese, and now being returned home. The caption reads, "WASH YOUR HANDS FIRST". If we are to take this attitude toward our American soldiers then by the same token we should treat all others alike. I read all types of publications, including Confidential which I am not in a position to share their views or condone their work. There is, however, in the current issue a scandalizing item about Uta Hagen.

Edgewater Beach Hotel enjoys a great reputation. As a lifelong Chicagoan, I am rather proud of the sterling reputation they enjoy, and it should be kept that way. I trust that you will make your own examination, and determine whether or not our information is correct before making a final decision to allow Hagen being broadcasted around the nation as a member of the cast appearing at the Edgewater Beach Hotel.

Yours very truly,

Edward Clamage, Chairman
Anti-Subversive
Cook County Council[85]

The committee's investigation of the John Cogley report on entertainment blacklisting descended to an all-time low for procedural inequity. Not only was Cogley the only defense witness subpoenaed, but also he was treated with caustic severity by the committee's new staff director, Richard Arens. It is clear from the transcripts that even if Cogley had been an able defender of his two-volume report—which he was not— Arens and Chairman Walter were more interested in condemning Cogley and the sponsor of the report, the Fund for the Republic, than seriously examining the volumes. The 1938 precedent of encouraging the pro-committee witnesses to declaim and ramble at will was once again invoked in 1956 when the vanguard of the country's foremost blacklisters followed Cogley to the witness chair.

As Walter Goodman properly remarked, Chairman Walter's condemnation of the Fund for the Republic report could easily have been delivered in advance of the committee's investigation, instead of at its conclusion, when he publicly scored it as a "partisan, biased attack on all persons and organizations who are sincerely and patriotically concerned in ridding the movie industry and radio and television of Communists and Communist sympathizers."[86]

For varying political reasons the problem of Reds in the entertainment industry was ebbing well before the issuance of the Cogley report. The starboard political tides of 1952 swept the Grand Old Party into the Presidency and the dominance of both houses of Congress. Communism, the subject that had been a whipping boy for two decades for Republicans and Southern conservative Democrats, was no longer political grist for the "out-party" mill. A great war hero, Dwight David Eisenhower, was in the White House, largely because of his promise to end the increasingly unpopular Communist-capitalist war in Korea. And only the proverbial heartbeat away from the Presidency was the second most celebrated hunter of Reds during the cold war—Richard M. Nixon.

Now that the GOP was at the helm, the two decades of waiting had made the Republicans wary of an unnecessary rocking of the political ship of state, such as subversion in show business. In 1948, the "outs" had almost captured 1600 Pennyslvania Avenue, only to have Harry Truman wrest the prize from Thomas E. Dewey in the last few days of the heated quadrennial election.

Political historian Earl Latham concluded that "the frustration of twenty years had been eased. Although it had seemed desirable and even necessary for the more aggressive and less liberal Republicans, when they were on the sidewalk looking in, to throw rocks at the house they hoped to occupy, they were now inside and had an interest in keeping the property intact."[87]

From 1951 to 1952, when John Wood was conducting his voluminous investigation of Communism in the entertainment world, there was a corresponding decline in films dealing with social themes. According to film analyst Dorothy B. Jones, Hollywood had started to move away from controversy after the Thomas investigation in 1947, and this movement produced a return to escapist fare and films of an anti-Communist nature. This avoidance of controversial themes continued during the Harold Velde years of 1953-54. Miss Jones points out antithetically that the two most successful films from both an artistic and a commercial standpoint for those years, *From Here to Eternity* and *On the Waterfront*, were "inclined toward the tradition of social realism."[88]

The last event contributing to Velde's disinterest in scouting for show business Commies occurred on December 2, 1954, when the Senate voted to "condemn" Joseph McCarthy for contempt of the elections subcommittee, abuse of its members, and insults to the Senate during his censure proceedings. And by April, 1955, preceding the August New York entertainment hearings, it was remarked that "Senator McCarthy has faded away quite satisfactorily, but the inanities to which he gave his name still find their voice in the United States Senate."[89]

Thus, four factors were conducive to the Velde committee's lack of concern about Communism in the world of entertainment:

> 1. John Wood's exhaustive 1951-52 examination of nearly all suspect Communist theatrical artists in the committee's files.
> 2. The new Republican administration in the White House and the GOP majority in both houses of Congress.
> 3. The tepid themes of Hollywood films in the years 1953-54.
> 4. The decline of America's leading threat to the Reds, Joseph McCarthy, as a national symbol of superpatriotism.

The committee's chairman in 1955, Francis Walter, did manage to find a voice for McCarthy's "inanities" in his House investigation of Broadway.

Of the approximately two dozen show business witnesses called by the committee in August, 1955, only Elliott Sullivan revealed any vaguely suspect patriotism in his testimony. Counsel Frank Tavenner somehow managed to imply that the sale of the Bill of Rights for one dollar in the summer camp skit mentioned by Sullivan was ridiculing that document, and Chairman Walter inanely described the satire as "an attempt to discredit this form of government."[90]

Such "inanities" lent little weight to the committee's importance as a defender of the nation or as a significant sleuth in the uncovering of entertainment Reds.

Rather, efforts such as attempting to equate political satire with subversion only served to diminish further the credibility of the committee's *raison d'être* and overall image. And by mid-1955, as Joseph McCarthy's image continued to tarnish, the committee needed more provocative publicity for its face than Broadway was able to muster.

FOOTNOTES

1. Walter Goodman, *The Committee; the Extraordinary Career of the House Committee on Un-American Activities* (New York, Farrar, Straus & Giroux, 1968), pp. 321-22.
2. Coauthor of the 1969 film success *The Secret of Santa Vittoria.*
3. Goodman, *op. cit.*, p. 323.
4. U.S. Congress, House Committee on Un-American Activities, *Investigation of Communist Activities in the New York City Area*, Hearings, Eighty-third Congress, First Session, Part I, May 4, 1953, pp. 1151-93. Hereinafter cited as *Hearings, New York City.*
5. New York *Sun*, August 10, 1948.
6. Goodman, *op. cit.*, p. 323.
7. *Hearings, New York City*, Part I, May 4, 1953, pp. 1314-17.
8. *Ibid.*, p. 1319.
9. *Ibid.*, pp. 1320-21.
10. *Ibid.*, p. 1321.
11. *Ibid.*, pp. 1324-25.
12. Goodman, *op. cit.*, p. 323.
13. *Hearings, New York City*, Part I, May 4, 1953, pp. 1343-44.
14. *Ibid.*, p. 1344.
15. *Ibid.*, p. 1345.
16. *Ibid.*, pp. 1346-47.
17. *Ibid.*, p. 1354.
18. *Ibid.*, p. 1355.
19. *Ibid.*, pp. 1352-69.
20. Goodman, *op. cit.*, pp. 323-24.
21. *Hearings, New York City*, Part I, May 4, 1953, p. 1429.
22. *Ibid.*, pp. 1432-33.
23. *Ibid.*, p. 1439.
24. *Ibid.*, p. 1440.
25. *Ibid.*, pp. 1327-38.
26. U.S. Congress, House Committee on Un-American Activities, *Investigation of Communist Activities in the Los Angeles Area*, Hearings, Eighty-third Congress, First Session, Part VI, June 2, 1953, p. 2350. Hereinafter cited as *Hearings, Los Angeles.*
27. *Hearings, New York City*, Part I, June 15, 1953, pp. 1-18. (Miss Muir testified in executive session on that day. Her testimony was released by the committee on May 25, 1955, Eighty-fourth Congress First Session.)
28. Merle Miller, *The Judges and the Judged* (Garden City, N.Y., Doubleday & Co., Inc., 1952), p. 38.

29. *Ibid.*, pp. 35-36.

30. *Ibid.*, p. 36.

31. *Hearings, New York City*, Part I, June 15, 1953, p. 11.

32. *Hearings, Los Angeles*, Part VII, pp. 2561-72. ("Lucy" appeared in executive session before committee investigator Wheeler on September 4, 1953, and confessed that she had registered to vote Communist in 1936 to make her Socialist grandfather happy. She swore that she did not ever vote Communist.)

33. U.S. Congress, House Committee on Un-American Activities, *Communist Methods of Infiltration (Entertainment)*, Hearings, Eighty-third Congress. Second Session, Part I, January 13 and 18, 1954; Part II, December 14, 1954. Hereinafter cited as *Entertainment Hearings*

34. *Entertainment Hearings*, Part I, pp. 3863-64.

35. *Ibid.*, p. 3864.

36. *Ibid.*, p. 3867.

37. The term "fellow traveler" in this instance meant to the Communist Party that a person was not a member of that party but was knowingly and openly sympathetic and supportive of many of the goals of Communism. This was the definition from the left. The right tended to use the term in the collective as a synonym for dupe, comsymp, fool, traitor, and tool of the international Communist conspiracy.

38. *Entertainment Hearings*, Part I, p. 3869.

39. *Ibid.*, p. 3874.

40. *Ibid.*, p. 3881.

41. *Ibid.*, Part II, p. 7269.

42. *Ibid.*, p. 7270.

43. Goodman, *op. cit.*, p. 375.

44. *Ibid.*

45. *Entertainment Hearings*, Part VI, pp. 2262-75.

46. Goodman, *op. cit.*, p. 378.

47. *Entertainment Hearings*, Part VI, pp. 2276-79.

48. *Ibid.*, pp. 2284-85.

49. *Ibid.*, Prager testimony, pp. 2286-2300; Wolfson testimony, pp. 2300-10.

50. *Ibid.*, pp. 2311-12.

51. *Ibid.*, pp. 2312-14.

52. *Ibid.*, p. 2330.

53. *Ibid.*, p. 2345.

54. *Ibid.*, p. 2384.

55. *Ibid.*, pp. 2386-87.

56. *Ibid.*, p. 2394.

57. Goodman, *op. cit.*, p. 378.

58. *Entertainment Hearings*, Part VII, pp. 2447-60.

59. Goodman, *op. cit.*, p. 378.

60. *Entertainment Hearings*, Part VIII, pp. 2492-93.

61. New York *Times*, November 8, 1955.

62. John Cogley, *Report on Blacklisting*, Vol. I, *Movies*; Vol. II, *Radio-Television* (New York, Fund for the Republic, 1956).

63. Goodman, *op. cit.*, p. 382.

64. U.S. Congress, House Committee on Un-American Activities, *Investigation of So-Called "Blacklisting" in Entertainment Industry—Report of the Fund for the Republic, Inc.*, Hearings, Eighty-fourth Congress, Second Session, Part I, July 10, 1956, p. 5193. Hereinafter cited as *Blacklisting Hearings*.

65. Michael Harrington, *The Other America; Poverty in the United States* (New York, Macmillan, 1962).

66. Goodman, *op. cit.*, p. 383.

67. *Blacklisting Hearings*, Part I, p. 5194.

68. Cogley, *op. cit.*, Vol. II, p. 214.

69. *Blacklisting Hearings*, p. 5189.

70. *Ibid.*, p. 5229.

71. *Ibid.*, p. 5242.

72. *Ibid.*, Part II, p. 5292.

73. *Ibid.*, p. 5300.

74. Based on personal correspondence between Conrad Bromberg and the author, November 6, 1969.

75. *Blacklisting Hearings*, Part II, p. 5323.

76. *Ibid.*, pp. 5324-25.

77. *Ibid.*, pp. 5329-53.

78. *Ibid.*, pp. 5353-67.

79. *Ibid.*, pp. 5368-88.

80. *Ibid.*, Part III, pp. 5390 ff.

81. Based on personal correspondence between Allan Sloane and the author. March 5, 1970.

82. John Henry Faulk, *Fear on Trial* (New York, Simon and Schuster Inc., 1964), p. 254.

83. New York *Times*, September 4, 1955, Sec. 2, p. 1.

84. Based on personal taped interview between Miss Florida Friebus and the author, November 11, 1969.

85. Copy on file with the author.

86. Goodman, *op. cit.*, p. 384.

87. Earl Latham, *The Communist Controversy in Washington, from the New Deal to McCarthy* (Cambridge, Mass., Harvard University Press, 1966), p. 400.

88. Dorothy B. Jones, "Communism and the Movies, A Study of Film Content," in Cogley, *op. cit.*, Vol. I, pp. 218-21.

89. "The Senator and the Economist," *Commonweal*, April 1, 1955, p. 669.

90. *Entertainment Hearings*, Part VII, pp. 2346-47.

Chapter VI

The Paul Robeson-Arthur Miller Passport Investigations, 1956, and the Most Recent 1957-58 Show Business Hearings

Eddie: (He is angering.) Didn't you hear what I told you?

Alfieri: (With a tougher tone.) I heard what you told me, and I'm telling you now, I'm warning you—The law is nature. The law is only a word for what has a right to happen. When the law is wrong it's because it's unnatural, but in this case it is natural and a river will drown you if you buck it now. Let her go. And bless her. (*A phone booth begins to glow on the opposite side of the stage D.L.; a faint, lonely blue. Eddie stands up, jaws clenched.*) Somebody had to come for her, Eddie, sooner or later. (*Eddie starts turning to go and Alfieri rises with new anxiety.*) You won't have a friend in the world, Eddie! Even those who understand will turn against you, even the ones who feel the same will despise you! (*Eddie moves off up ramp and off U.R.*) Put it out of your mind! Eddie! (*Eddie is gone. The phone is glowing in light now. Light is out on Alfieri. Eddie at the same time appeared beside the phone booth from off L.*) Eddie: Give me the number of the Immigration Bureau. Thanks. (*He dials.*) I want to report something. Illegal immigrants. Two of them. That's right. 441 Saxon Street, Brooklyn, yeah. Ground floor. Heh? (*With greater difficulty.*) I'm just around the neighborhood, that's all. . . . [1]

This dialogue from the play *A View from the Bridge* was written by one of America's most distinguished playwrights,

Arthur Miller, not long before he appeared before the committee. The work dealt with a New Jersey longshoreman, Eddie Carbone, who, in his zeal to keep his niece from leaving his home, defies one of the basic tenets of the Italian character: He becomes an informer.

The theme of the play is that when a man knowingly betrays his own moral code, his desire to live diminishes with each day and may lead him to suicide.[2] Eddie, stricken with shame, finally precipitates his own death at the hands of one of those he informed on. Through the character of Alfieri, Miller makes an observation that the playwright was later able to champion personally and publicly.

Miller, under much pressure to inform before the committee, declined, undoubtedly remembering full well his words, "Even those who understand will turn against you, even the ones who feel the same will despise you!"

Miller and America's foremost black living-theater actor, Paul Robeson, appeared before the committee in June, 1956, to defend their right to retain their United States passports. The two witnesses are among the elite of the American theater. For this reason their contribution to that medium and their divergent involvement with Communism, as indicated in their testimony, is given special attention here.

Robeson, son of a Methodist minister who was a former slave, was born April 9, 1888, in Princeton, New Jersey. Following All-American honors as a football star at Rutgers and membership in Phi Beta Kappa, he earned his LLB at the Columbia University Law School in 1922. The year prior to his graduation from Columbia he made his New York theatrical debut in *Simon the Cyrenian* at the Lafayette Theatre. Before the end of the twenties, Robeson had starred in London and New York in such hits as *Taboo, The Emperor Jones, All God's Chillun Got Wings, Black Boy, Porgy and Bess,* and *Showboat.*

In the thirties the actor-singer concertized extensively throughout Britain and Europe and added *Othello* and *The Hairy Ape* to his living-theater successes. He repeated his role of Othello in New York and on tour in America from 1943 to 1945. Opposite him, in the role of Iago, was another committee witness, Jose Ferrer. Robeson repeated the role in 1959 at the Shakespeare Memorial Theatre, Stratford-on-Avon, England.

Honors proffered him that unquestionably gave the committee members pause were the Stalin Peace Prize and his being named honorary professor at the Moscow State Conservatory of Music.[3]

Description of the Hearings

In Washington, D.C., on June 12, 1956, nine days before Miller's testimony, Robeson gave one of the most emotional, pro-Russian exhortations of any entertainment figure who had ever appeared before the committee.

Richard Arens acted as chief interrogator of the witness, and Chairman Francis E. Walter presided over the heated session until he was forced to conclude, "I have endured all of this that I can."[4]

Robeson's obvious hostility to the committee was immediately apparent when he demanded that Arens identify himself by name and position. Arens politely complied and proceeded with dispatch to pose the $64 question about Robeson's CP membership.

The witness replied:

> What do you mean by the Communist Party? As far as I know it is a legal party like the Republican Party and the Democratic Party. Do you mean—which, belonging to a party of Communists or belonging to a party of people who have sacrificed for my people and for all Americans and workers, that they can live in dignity? Do you mean that party?[5]

Robeson then invoked the Fifth Amendment and supported his right to do so without inference or criminality by citing Chief Justice of the Supreme Court Earl Warren.

When Arens asked the witness if he had ever been known under the name of "John Thomas," Robeson testily replied, ". . . my name is Paul Robeson, and anything I have to say or stand for I have said in public all over the world, and that is why I am here today."[6]

When Representative Gordon Scherer complained that the witness talked very loudly when he was making a speech but almost inaudibly when invoking the Fifth Amendment, Robeson bragged that he had medals for his voice and diction.[7] He continued his refusal to answer questions until the name Manning Johnson was mentioned. The actor observed that he had read newspaper reports that Johnson was dismissed from the FBI and concluded, "He must be a pretty low character when he could be dismissed from that."[8]

The issue of racism in the committee chairman's personality was obliquely tendered by the lawyer-turned-actor when he asked Walter to identify himself:

> MR. WALTER: You are speaking to the chairman of this committee.
> MR. ROBESON: Mr. Walter?
> THE CHAIRMAN: Yes.
> MR. ROBESON: The Pennsylvania Walter?
> THE CHAIRMAN: That is right.
> MR. ROBESON: You are the author of all of the bills that are going to keep all kinds of decent people out of the country.
> THE CHAIRMAN: No, only your kind.
> MR. ROBESON: Colored people like myself from the West Indies and all kinds, just the Teutonic Anglo-Saxon stock that you would let come in.
> THE CHAIRMAN: We are trying to make it easier to get rid of your kind, too.
> MR. ROBESON: You do not want any colored people to come in?
> THE CHAIRMAN: Proceed.[9]

Pursuing the racial implications that were perhaps unavoidable in Robeson's appearance, Arens asked the witness if he had ever told an audience in Paris that the American Negro would never go to war against the Soviet government. The actor retorted:

> Listen to me, I said it was unthinkable to me that any people would take arms in the name of an Eastland [Democratic Senator James O. Eastland of Mississippi] to go against anybody, and gentlemen, I still say that. What should happen

would be that this United States Government should go down
to Mississippi and protect my people. That is what should
happen.[10]

He later hedgingly admitted he had made the remark, but in
America.[11]

Robeson unreservedly proclaimed his adoration for the
Soviet Union, where for the first time he felt "like a full human
being." Congressman Scherer inquired why he did not stay
there. The witness's reply was:

> Because my father was a slave, and my people died to build
> this country, and I am going to stay here and have a part of it
> just like you. And no Fascist-minded people will drive me from
> it. Is that clear? I am for peace with the Soviet Union and I am
> for peace with China, and I am not for peace or friendship with
> the Fascist Franco, and I am not for peace with Fascist Nazi
> Germans, and I am for peace with decent people in the
> world.[12]

When Arens asked Robeson if he had recently changed his
mind about Joseph Stalin, whom he had once called "a great
man," the actor responded in a fashion that more than a decade
later would be the clarion call of the Black Panthers' Bobby
Seale and Eldridge Cleaver, and of Stokely Carmichael, one of
the founders of the Student Non-Violent Coordinating Committee. The accusatory response was, "You are responsible and
your forebears for 60 million to 100 million black people dying
in slave ships and on the plantations, and don't you ask me
about anybody, please."[13]

Arens responded by asking the witness if while he was in the
Soviet Union he had asked to see any slave-labor camps.
Robeson said that as far as he knew, such camps held "Fascist
prisoners who had murdered millions of the Jewish people and
who would have wiped out millions of the Negro people could
they have gotten a hold of them."[14]

Robeson "brought a stormy morning session to a sudden
close" by raising his resonant bass voice to shouting pitch" and
condemning the committee as "non-patriots" and "un-
Americans." Chairman Walter "immediately conferred with the

three other members present, and they unanimously voted the contempt action."[15]

Robeson was "inordinately contemptuous" in his appearance before the committee, but the decision reached by that body was not "to give him yet another stage for his resonant defiance"; the contempt citation was dropped.[16] The committee's ostensible purpose in subpoenaing the actor, his right to hold a passport, was hardly mentioned in the testimony.

On the first day of summer, June 21, 1956, Pulitzer Prize winner Arthur Miller's appearance before the committee was, in striking contrast to Robeson's, "notable for its air of sober amiability."[17]

The playwright and novelist was born October 17, 1915, in New York City. He received an AB from the University of Michigan in 1938. His first New York play, *The Man Who Had All the Luck*, opened at the Forrest Theatre on November 23, 1944. *All My Sons* followed in 1947, and the Pulitzer winner, *Death of a Salesman*, opened at the Morosco Theatre in New York City, February 10, 1949. Other plays include *The Crucible*, 1953; *A View from the Bridge*, 1955; *After the Fall*, 1964; *Incident at Vichy*, 1965; and *The Prize*, 1968. His novels include *Situation Normal*, 1944; *Focus*, 1945; and *The Misfits*, which was made into a film in 1961 starring his wife, the late Marilyn Monroe.[18]

Miller was accompanied by attorney Joseph Rauh, Jr., "who was identified with Americans for Democratic Action rather than with the National Lawyers Guild."[19]

The National Lawyers Guild has often been considered a controversial, if not subversive, organization by various private and governmental agencies.

On the Saturday preceding his appearance before the committee, Miller had received an honorary doctor of humane letters from the University of Michigan and proudly attached the award of his educational resumé for the committee.

The writer stated he had received his first passport in 1946; in 1954, his most recent request for renewal was refused. He admitted he had been affiliated with organizations that were cited as Communist-dominated but denied that he was ever "under the discipline of the Communist Party or the Communist cause."[20]

Investigator Arens then ran through a list of organizations, petitions, individuals, and meetings deemed subversive by the committee; Miller acknowledged that he had supported or had been aligned with them in some way.

Using the technique of pleading intellectual vacuity outside of his art form, Miller agreed that he had in the past opposed the committee's work. "I know really very little about anything except my work and my field, and it seemed to me that the then prevalent, rather ceaseless, investigating of artists was creating a pall of apprehension and fear among all kinds of people."[21]

For the leading intellectual playwright of the American postwar theater to demean his considerable knowledge of the world about him was a technique of defense more aptly believed if it had come from a Lionel Stander or an Abe Burrows. Continuing in this self-deprecatory vein, Miller agreed that although he had denounced poet Ezra Pound for his anti-Semitism, he had made no similar denunciation of anti-Semitism in the Soviet Union, although he concurred with Nikita Khrushchev about Joseph Stalin's prejudice:

> Now I have ceased these kinds of statements, as I said, which were befitting the frame of mind I was in. I ceased issuing statements right and left except when I am personally involved because I found I was being tangled in stuff that I was really not prepared to defend 100 percent, and I am ashamed to say that I should have and I did feel I was not completely ignorant of this. It isn't a matter of Khrushchev. I knew this before Khrushchev.[22]

Miller had signed a statement in defense of twelve Communists who were convicted in Foley Square in New York City in 1952 for violation of the Smith Act. The playwright defended his action in an exchange with Representative Scherer:

> MR. MILLER: I am opposed to the Smith Act and I am still opposed to anyone being penalized for advocating anything. I say that because of a very simple reason.

I don't believe that in the history of letters there are many great books or great plays that don't advocate. That doesn't mean that a man is a propagandist. It is in the nature of life and it is in the nature of literature that the passions of an author congeal around issues.

You can go from War and Peace through all the great novels of time and they are all advocating something. Therefore, when I heard that the United States Government wanted to pass a law against the advocacy without any overt action, I was alarmed because I am not here defending Communists, I am here defending the right of an author to advocate, to write.

MR. SCHERER: Even to advocate the overthrow of this Government by force and violence?

MR. MILLER: I am now speaking, sir, of creative literature. These are risks and balances of risks.[23]

At this point Chairman Walter called a recess of five minutes; when testimony resumed, it was clear that the committee had a unanimity of interest in pursuing Miller's distinction between advocacy and action.

The argument centered on the committee's apparent desire to compel the witness to say he was in favor of the prosecution of anyone who would advocate, teach, and urge the overthrow of the United States government by force and violence. Miller tenaciously clung to his position that punishment for mere advocacy without overt and clearly defined action could carry over into literature as well as politics, thus placing the United States under the restrictions that prevailed in Nazi Germany and the Soviet Union.

Borrowing from the appeal of an author of the eighteenth century, Miller looked at the problem of the artist's freedom of action through the eyes of Tom Paine:

I think a work of art—my point is very simple. I think that, once you start to cut away, there is a certain commonsense in mankind which makes these limits automatic. There are risks which are balanced. The Constitution is full of those risks. We have rights, which, if they are violated, are rather used in an irresponsible way, can do damage. Yet they are there and the commonsense of the people of the United States has kept this in sort of a balance. I would prefer any day to say, "Yes, there should be no limit upon the literary freedom," than to say "you can go up this far and no further," because then you are getting into an area where people are going to say, "I think that this goes over the line," and then you are in an area where there is no limit to the censorship that can take place.[24]

Miller vouchsafed that nothing of value had been written in the Soviet Union for twenty-five years because of the repression of literature that was not sympathetic to Communism. In justification for the writer's freedom from political limitations, Miller tried delicately to distinguish the position of the artist from that of the people.

In answer to Representative Kearney's question—was the witness putting the artist and literature in a preferred class?— Miller explained in distinctly nonegalitarian terms:

> I thought we were going to get to this and it places me in a slightly impossible position, and I would be lying to you if I said that I didn't think the artist was, to a certain degree, in a special class. The reason is quite simple and maybe absurd but, if you are asking me what I think, I will tell you. . . .
>
> Most of us are occupied most of the day in earning a living in one way or another. The artist is a peculiar man in one respect. Therefore, he has got a peculiar mandate in the history of civilization from people, and that is he has a mandate not only in his literature but in the way he behaves and the way he lives. . . .
>
> The artist is inclined to use certain rights more than other people because of the nature of his work.
>
> Most of us may have an opinion. We sit once or twice a week or we may have a view of life which on a rare occasion we have time to speak of. That is the artist's line of work. That is what he does all day long and, consequently, he is particularly sensitive to its limitations.[25]

Betraying his feigned intellectual limitations, Miller answered Kearney's statement on the artist's living in a different world from anyone else with what Miller had learned from Socrates:

> No, he doesn't, but there is a conflict I admit. I think there is an old conflict that goes back to Socrates between the man who is involved with ideal things and the man who has the terrible responsibility of keeping things going as they are and

protecting the state and keeping an army and getting people fed.[26]

The witness was even more dignified and proper when the name of ex-Communist Elia Kazan was introduced into the testimony. Miller acknowledged that he knew Kazan as a director of two of his plays and that he had been a friendly witness before the committee. The playwright refused to agree with Arens' assertion that he had publicly condemned the director for his being an informer and speculated that Kazan might direct one of his plays in the future.[27]

Miller explained to the committee that after his passport had been denied, he was besieged by foreign newspapermen from the right and center press. He was forced to hide out in his Roxbury, Connecticut, home to avoid them. Miller's reason: "I do draw a line between criticism of the United States in the United States and before foreigners."[28]

Much to the playwright's surprise, Arens asked him if he had coauthored a play. Miller did not remember any such endeavor until his interrogator reminded him of a one-act drama he had written in 1939 with Norman Rosten, *Listen My Children*. Arens proceeded to read an excerpt from the work:

Curtain slowly opens. The committee members are engaged in activity of an extraordinary variety, amid an equally extraordinary environment. Profuse flag bunting over the walls. There are several huge clocks ticking ominously. Also a metronome which is continually being adjusted for tempo change.

Secretary, at desk, pounds typewriter and, as alarm clock rings, she feeds the committeemen spoonsful of castor oil.

In center of room, in rocker, sits a man. He is securely tied to chair, with a gag in his mouth and a bandage tied over his mouth. Water, coming from a pipe near ceiling, trickles on his head.

Nearby is a charcoal stove holding branding irons. Two bloodhounds are tied in the corner of room.[29]

When Miller described the play as a "farce," Arens asked if his play *You're Next*, attacking the House Committee on Un-American Activities, was also "just a little farce" and if he knew that it was reproduced by the Communist Party. The witness replied "No."[30]

Arens asked if Miller was aware that his play *The Crucible* "was the case history of a series of articles in the Communist press drawing parallels to the investigations of Communists and other subversives by congressional committees?" The author responded that the comparison was inevitable and that the non-Communist press had the same reaction.[31]

Miller wanted a passport so that he could travel to England to discuss a British production of *A View from the Bridge* and to be there with the woman he would marry on July 13, Marilyn Monroe.[32]

The playwright's contempt citation, issued July 25, 1956, was occasioned by his reply to Arens' effort to get him to name names. Miller's answer was in keeping with Lillian Hellman's refusal to inform. He said:

> Mr. Chairman, I understand the philosophy behind this question and I want you to understand mine.
> When I say this I want you to understand that I am not protecting the Communists or the Communist Party. I am trying to and I will protect my sense of myself. I could not use the name of another person and bring trouble on him. These were writers, poets, as far as I could see, and the life of a writer, despite what it sometimes seems, is pretty tough. I wouldn't make it any tougher for anybody. I ask you not to ask me that question. . . .
> I will tell you anything about myself, as I have.[33]

Miller carried his case to the court of appeals, which found in September, 1958, that he had not been properly informed that he was risking contempt if he refused to answer questions based on conscience alone. The contempt charge was dropped. "Thus the court managed, without becoming involved with the substantive issues, to escape the embarrassment of sending an international celebrity to jail."[34]

An interesting footnote to the matter involved Miller's alleged CP membership card:

> As Miller brought his appeal, the Committee released a reproduction of a card, dated 1943, in which "A. Miller," a "writer"

of 18 Schermerhorn Street, Brooklyn—a former address of the playwright—applied for membership in the Communist Party. The card was not signed by Miller, who described it as "either a forgery or . . . done unknown to me." In the place set aside for the name of the person proposing the new member was the signature of "Sue Warren," a one-time acquaintance of Miller's, who declined to answer any of the Committee's questions. Miller called the release of the ambiguous card "a transparent attempt to influence the course of my appeal," and so it was.[35]

During 1957, the committee heard only one witness related to the entertainment world, actress Lee Grant (Mrs. Arnold Manoff). She appeared in executive session in Washington on April 1 of that year; her testimony was released in 1958.

Arens, who had displayed little "Bourbon punctilio" throughout his tenure as interrogator, asked Miss Grant her real name and where and when she was born. She answered that her true name was Lyova Rosenthal and that she was born in New York City in 1926.

After outlining her educational and professional background, the actress stated that she was currently in the Broadway production *Hole in the Head.*[36]

In answer to the $64 question, Miss Grant took the "diminished fifth," claiming that she was not then a member of the CP, but refusing to answer whether she ever had been in the past or any other questions relating to her former affiliations.[37]

An interesting exchange between Miss Grant, her counsel, Leonard B. Boudin, Congressman Scherer, and Arens concluded with a clean bill of patriotic health for one of President Dwight D. Eisenhower's advisers and speechwriters:

> MR. ARENS: Was your employment in the production *Danger* procured for you by any person who, at any time, was known to you to have been a Communist?
>
> MR. BOUDIN: Could I have a word with the witness? Will you excuse me a second, Mr. Congressman?
>
> MR. DOYLE: Yes.
>
> (Counsel conferred with the witness.)
>
> MR. BOUDIN: The answer with respect to that, and generally, would have been the same, namely, that Miss Grant got the job through the routine way and is not

prepared to say who were and who were not members of the Communist Party.

MR. ARENS: Danger was a series of productions, was it not, or was it a single production?

MISS GRANT: Yes.

MR. ARENS: Danger.

MISS GRANT: You want to know what Danger is?

MR. ARENS: Yes, ma'am.

MISS GRANT: Do I answer this? You don't know the nature of the television show?

MR. ARENS: No, I don't. At least this record doesn't reflect it.

MISS GRANT: Danger is like any other of the television shows that appears from week to week on a certain day.

MR. ARENS: It is a serial?

MISS GRANT: No, it is not a serial. It is a series, like Alcoa.

MR. ARENS: It is a series then?

MISS GRANT: Yes.

MR. ARENS: Which ran for how long?

MR. SCHERER: Who was it that played in that? I have forgotten.

MISS GRANT: There was no lead in Danger.

MR. SCHERER: A different cast?

MISS GRANT: A new show every week like all these shows. Alcoa or Montgomery or Philco.

MR. SCHERER: Didn't you yourself play it regularly?

MISS GRANT: No.

MR. ARENS: Were you in just one show?

MISS GRANT: No.

MR. ARENS: Did you participate in more than one show?

MISS GRANT: Yes.

MR. ARENS: There were other actors and actresses who appeared in it more than once?

MISS GRANT: Yes. You see in all these shows, such as Mr. Montgomery, for instance, likes an actor, and he finds in a certain particular play he played a father best, and another play he does the boy best, so then he will hire him once every 6 months, you know.

MR. ARENS: But Mr. Montgomery didn't have anything to do with this series entitled, Danger?

MISS GRANT: No, I am giving you a going example.

MR. ARENS: I just wanted the record to be clear that Mr. Montgomery had nothing to do with the series.[38]

Shortly before its most recent public entertainment hearings, on June 18 and 19, 1958, the committee heard on May 8, 1958, in executive session the unfriendly testimony of free-lance writer Louis Solomon. His appearance was notable for its brevity, two and one-half pages of printed testimony, and that no specific Communist affiliations were mentioned. Only the big CP membership question was posed.[39]

In all, nineteen persons testified during the two days in June, a dozen of whom were related to show business, with seventeen invoking the Fifth Amendment, one the First Amendment, and a former official of the CP, John Lautner, on hand as the only cooperative witness.

Stage manager Bernard Gersten, employed by the American Shakespeare Festival in Stratford, Connecticut, was the first of the seventeen witnesses to take the Fifth Amendment when he came before the committee on June 18. When staff director Arens asked Gersten the usual preliminary questions about his past employment record, the stage manager gave a lengthy answer about the "legislative purpose" of the committee. Provoked by the uncooperative and evasive response, Arens sardonically replied, "Perhaps it would help if we had another preliminary question. Are you now a member of the Communist Party?"[40]

When asked if actor Will Geer was a member of the Shakespeare festival, Gersten wryly commented that there were twenty-four actors in the company, listed alphabetically; they had equal billing clauses in their contracts and he could not remember all their names; therefore, he could not mention the name of one player without listing all of them. He finally confessed that Geer was a member of the company but indicated he knew him only "as an actor" and in "no other way."[41]

Actor-director-teacher Paul Mann, also testifying on June 18, 1958, read an opening statement that charged among other things that the committee had "investigated nearly everybody—from Shirley Temple at the age of 10 to ex-President Truman."[42]

In rebuttal, when the above testimony was published, the committee made the following remarks:

> The case of Paul Mann was typical. He falsely accused the committee of having "investigated" Shirley Temple when she was only 10 years of age. The truth, of course, is that this committee has never investigated Shirley Temple. The facts of the Shirley Temple incident are as follows:
>
> Twenty years ago, an expert witness, in the course of his testimony before the Special Committee on Un-American Activities, explained how the Communist Party uses prominent non-Communists to promote Moscow's line, relying on the willingness of many such people (or their agents) to sign statements without bothering to read them. As an example of what he meant, he pointed out that, on the occasion of its first anniversary, a French Communist Party newspaper had recently featured greetings from three of America's best-known male movie stars (whose names he gave) "and even Shirley Temple."
>
> The witness had prefaced this example of how the Communist Party uses non-Communists and anti-Communists to promote its cause with these words: "I am not trying to make these persons' names stand out in any odious manner whatsoever." A reading of the full testimony of the witness in question—a recognized authority on communism—makes it clear that he had no intention of implying or hinting that Shirley Temple or any of the other persons whose names had been used by the French Communist newspaper were Communists, pro-Communists, or fellow travelers.
>
> Yet Paul Mann attempted to use the testimony of this witness to give new and wider circulation to the tale that this committee had "investigated" Shirley Temple, a fable that has been repeatedly used by Communists and their sympathizers in their efforts to discredit committees of the Congress investigating communism.[43]

The alleged investigation of President Harry S. Truman was not mentioned in the committee's retaliatory defense of Mann's charges.

On June 18, actor Earl Jones (not to be confused with actor James Earl Jones) constitutionally declined to state whether he had appeared in theater productions of *Strange Fruit* and *The Iceman Cometh* and a television production of *Green Pastures*. He further maintained his unfriendly stance when questioned about his association with a number of Communist-front organizations.[44]

Actor-teacher-director Will Lee followed Jones. He obviously resented Arens' rehashing questions the actor had answered in a preview hearing held in closed session.[45] Before citing the First and Fifth amendments, he introduced into the inquiry his Brooklyn education in American history. Lee said:

> I have been born in Brooklyn; and in Brooklyn, in Public School 144 that I went to, I was always told that an individual had a right to select what he wants to be part of, speak freely, his associations, and that this was also clearly pointed out to us as inseparable from the Bill of Rights.
>
> I will not cast any shadow over the Bill of Rights; and in raising this question, I stand on the right as given to us by James Madison and his associates. . . .[46]

Television director Charles S. Dubin was next and, using his Bill of Rights privilege, refused to answer questions about his possible membership in the CP, the Stage for Action, the National Council of the Arts, Sciences, and Professions, and if he had been a signer of the nominating petition on behalf of George Blake Charney, former head of the CP in New York State.[47]

Actress Adelaide Klein Annenberg, who had just closed the previous Saturday night in *Jane Eyre* at the Belasco Theatre in New York, was another unfriendly witness on June 18. She refused to answer questions concerning her association with the CP, the People's Radio Foundation Inc., Howard Fast, and Martin Berkeley. She refused to tell whether she had taken a public stand on the recent Communist purges in Hungary and earlier ones in the Soviet Union.[48]

Living-theater publicist James D. Proctor was the first unfriendly witness on the second day of the 1958 public hearings, June 19.

Proctor, employed then by producer Kermit Bloomgarden for the Broadway production of *Look Homeward Angel*, had previously served as publicist for *The Diary of Anne Frank* and Arthur Miller's *A View from the Bridge*.

In contrast to the 1947 hearings, the 1958 committee

allowed the witnesses to read an opening statement. Proctor's remarks were generally representative of the tenor of the other entertainment figures subpoenaed that year. Replying to Arens' $64 question, the publicist said:

> I am going to read a short statement, Mr. Arens, in reply to that question.
>
> I refuse on several grounds to answer your question.
>
> First, I consider your question improper. You are asking it, seeking to pry into my private opinions and associations. A concomitant of the right of free speech is the right to remain silent about one's thinking, and I have the right—in fact the obligation—to resist any such invasion of my rights, to refuse to discuss or divulge my opinions and associations. I, therefore, exercise my constitutional rights under the first amendment to refuse to answer.
>
> Second, I do not think this committee has the right, the authority, or the power to require an answer to the question. There can be no legitimate purpose. The only possible results of the inquiry are to cause me to lose employment since, as you know, anyone called before this committee alone is considered controversial and, therefore, a candidate for the blacklist.
>
> And, to publicly assist the members of this committee as a professional publicist, I cannot publicly recognize the techniques employed by the committee in that respect. The committee cannot claim it is seeking information, since it has already questioned me in closed session.
>
> The committee cannot pretend after so very many years of investigation that there can be any legitimate reasons for the continuance of the investigation at this time. I consider the first two reasons adequate and sufficient. I know, however, if I rest on them alone I shall be subject to harassment and [the] expense of defending contempt proceedings, which I cannot afford.
>
> I, therefore, also invoke my fifth amendment rights to refuse to be a witness against myself and on that ground, also, refuse to answer the question.
>
> I will add—not because this committee has any right to know, but only because under the circumstances my failure to make a statement may injure my associates—that I am not a member of the Communist Party.[49]

Representative Scherer, "the alleged Birchite,"[50] challenged the right of the publicist to invoke the Fifth Amendment:

". . . He is not invoking the amendment in good faith, and not because it will incriminate him but because he will probably face contempt charges and put him to great expense."[51] The witness chose to disregard Scherer's admonition. He was not, however, charged with contempt.

During the June, 1958, hearings, the lengthiest testimony of an unfriendly witness came from producer Joseph Papirofsky, known professionally as Joe Papp. The witness, who was producing Shakespearean plays in Central Park, gave the committee his dissenting point of view on June 19.

As a student under the GI Bill of Education, Papp had been employed by the Actors' Laboratory Theatre in California for two years and later by CBS as a stage manager, a position he still held at the time of the hearings. The witness denied current membership in the CP but took the Fifth Amendment on the years preceding 1957.[52]

In an exchange somewhat reminiscent of the discussion by the Dies Committee of Christopher Marlowe, Arens, Congressman Moulder, and Papp debated the influence of Marlowe's great contemporary and Papp's potential as a Shakespearean producer to infuse the product with the Red line:

MR. MOULDER: At any time during your professional career or in connection with the work that you are doing at the present time, do you have the opportunity to inject into your plays or into the acting or the entertainment supervision which you have, any propaganda in any way which would influence others to be sympathetic with the Communist philosophy or the beliefs of Communism?

MR. PAPIROFSKY: Sir, the plays we do are Shakespeare's plays. Shakespeare said, "To thine own self be true," and various other lines from Shakespeare can hardly be said to be subversive or influencing minds. I cannot control the writings of Shakespeare. He wrote plays 500 years ago.

I am in no position in any plays where I work to influence what the final product will be, except artistically and except in terms of my job as a producer.

MR. MOULDER: My point is, do you intentionally control the operation of the entertainment which you produce or supervise for the purpose of influencing sympathy toward communism? That is my point.

MR. PAPIROFSKY: The answer to that is obviously "No." The plays speak for themselves. I began to mention the plays that we did. Maybe some of these plays might be considered propagandistic.

MR. ARENS: We are not concerned with the plays and you know we are not, and there is no suggestion here by this chairman or anyone else that Shakespeare was a Communist. That is ludicrous and absurd. That is the Commie line.

The inquiry of this committee is solely with reference to Communist activities, Communist propaganda, the extent to which Communists, people in the Communist Party, have used their prestige in the theatre to promote Communists; and for you to twist this testimony in the presence of the public press here to give an implication that the chairman is trying to elicit information from you that Shakespeare was subversive or this committee is investigating Shakespeare, investigating that type of thing, is not only ludicrous, but it is highly unfair.[53]

Musician-singer Paul Villard, writer Richard Sasuly, actor Clifford Carpenter, and writer-editor-publicist Irwin Silber comprised the last of the unfriendly witnesses to appear before the committee during its most recent probe into the role of Communism in the entertainment world.[54]

Evaluation of the Hearings

In their appearances before the committee, Paul Robeson and Arthur Miller represented not only widely diversified attitudes toward Communism but also vastly different emotional approaches to the investigators' questions.

Robeson was in the best theatrical tradition of the Hollywood Ten, demonstrating sarcasm, irascibility, rudeness, and generally unsavory and unacceptable behavior publicly before a Congressional committee. On the other hand, the 1956 Walter committee proved no more adept at handling obstreperous witnesses than had the 1947 Thomas aggregate.

One of the purported reasons for the untimely conclusion of the first Hollywood hearings was the fact that the press was having a field day with the witnesses' bad manners and, more importantly, the committee's response in kind. Undoubtedly sensing the possibility of a repetition of this bad publicity, the Walter committee wisely decided to avoid allowing Robeson a return performance on the public stage and dropped his contempt citation. If there was one area the committee consistently showed a sensitivity for, it was publicity.

The vast majority of those persons interviewed for this book indicated they believed the committee's real purpose was not hunting dangerous Red show business subversives but rather publicizing the patriotism of the investigators for their own political expediency.

In contrast, the investigators were at their best and most docile when confronted with a calm witness of intellectual and literary reputation—such as Lillian Hellman or Arthur Miller.

Though Miller endeavored to present himself to the committee as an artist somewhat removed from and above the world of domestic politics, his efforts were not entirely successful. Miller, because of his celebrated position in American letters, was in a better situation than any previous witness to develop the historical time factor in the Communist movement in America. By 1956 his writing career had covered more than two decades and his testimony alluded sporadically to his own metamorphosis as a progressive who, as he matured, became increasingly disenchanted with Communism.

Miller's admission of his youthful affiliation with groups that were later named by the committee as having been Red-dominated was the ideal circumstance for an in-depth discussion by the playwright of the constantly changing attitudes toward Communism evidenced by the American liberal.

Also, Miller obviously knew he would be confronted with the above charges. In view of the fact that he had already written *The Crucible*, which severely condemned the practice of witch-hunting in early Massachusetts, this point in his testimony was the perfect juncture for the playwright to present a prepared statement about his feelings relevant to the committee's real, not purported, role in American history. Rather than take this opportunity, he simply admitted he had opposed the committee's work in the past because the investigations caused fear and apprehension in artists as well as other people.

In Miller's subsequent discussion with the committee regarding the distinction between advocacy and action, the playwright missed a second opportunity to clearly enunciate a position on changing *ideas* he held over the years and the action he had taken to implement those ideas. His general observations on advocacy and action were valid; however, the playwright's failure to put those observations in the perspective of his own public life and professional career, particularly as they related to his changing views on Communism, was another improper choice made by the witness.

On the asset side of the playwright's appearance was Miller's sensitive, though occasionally snobbish, observations on the historical role of the artist in society. His general theme that men such as he were in a special class because they dealt with opinions and a view of life that the common fellow had no time for may not have endeared him to the committee, but the thesis must certainly have buoyed his followers in the intellectual community. Lastly, and much to the playwright's credit, was his refusal to name names or to deprecate publicly his old friend Elia Kazan for acting as an informer.

Not to be disregarded in assessing Arthur Miller's decisions during and before his testimony is the rather human fact that he was then about to marry the foremost sex symbol of modern motion pictures, Marilyn Monroe, and any unnecessary provocation of the committee might have delayed their honeymoon in England.

The dozen unfriendly show business witnesses called in June, 1958, represented the end of the rope for the committee's twenty-year on-again-off-again investigation of Communism in the entertainment field. None of the subpoenaed persons were anywhere near star status and therefore were incapable of producing headlines for the always publicity-conscious committee.

In its *Annual Report* for 1958, the committee noted it was struck by the "agility" of the June witnesses

> as they protected the Communist conspiracy and the identity
> of its members. They [the witnesses] were more concerned
> with villifying [*sic*] the committee than with providing the

Congress with the sort of information that would be of help in
enacting legislation vital to the security of the nation.

The report went on:

They [the witnesses] interjected into the hearings statements
designed to arouse sympathy for themselves as persecuted
martyrs, attempted to becloud the real issues and made un-
founded statements in their efforts to discredit this committee.

The summation obliquely concluded: "By indirection, however, they unwittingly supplied the committee with valuable
information."[55]

The committee had a continuing responsibility to report on
the current status of the alleged menace they always referred to
as the Communist conspiracy. Was this conspiracy international
in scope in 1958 in the same way the committee believed it to
be in 1938? And if so, were these dozen minor show business
persons truly being directed from the Kremlin in any destructive or meaningful manner that would in any way seriously
jeopardize the interests of America? The answer is "unlikely" in
both cases. Were these witnesses in possession of any information that might have helped the committee in enacting legislation *vital to the security* of the nation? The answer again is if
the dozen did have such crucial information and had chosen to
reveal it to the committee, it is also unlikely that the Congressmen would have proposed any legislation significant to the
security of the republic.

Through thousands of investigations over a twenty-year
period, in and out of the entertainment world, no law or laws
remotely essential to the security of the nation ever resulted
from the committee's work.

FOOTNOTES

1. Arthur Miller, *A View from the Bridge* (New York, Dramatists Play Service, Inc.,
   1957), II, 51. The play was originally copyrighted by Miller in 1955 under the
   title *From Under the Sea.*
2. This author directed the play at Los Angeles State College in Summer Session,
   1960. It featured James Coburn as Alfieri.
3. Walter Rigdon, ed., *The Biographical Encyclopaedia and Who's Who of the
   American Theatre* (New York, James H. Heineman, Inc., 1966), p. 779.

4. U.S. Congress, House Committee on Un-American Activities, *Investigation of the Unauthorized Use of United States Passports*, Hearings, Eighty-fourth Congress, Second Session, Part III, June 12, 1956, p. 4509. Hereinafter cited as *Passport Hearings*.

5. *Ibid.*, p. 4494.

6. *Ibid.*, p. 4495.

7. *Ibid.*, p. 4496.

8. *Ibid.*, p. 4497.

9. *Ibid.*, p. 4498.

10. *Ibid.*, p. 4501.

11. *Ibid.*, p. 4502.

12. *Ibid.*, p. 4504.

13. *Ibid.*, p. 4506.

14. *Ibid.*

15. New York *Times*, June 13, 1956.

16. Walter Goodman, *The Committee; the Extraordinary Career of the House Committee on Un-American Activities* (New York, Farrar, Straus & Giroux, 1968), p. 391.

17. *Ibid.*, p. 392.

18. Rigdon, *op. cit.*, p. 682.

19. Goodman, *op. cit.*, p. 391.

20. *Passport Hearings*, Part IV, June 21, 1956, p. 4660.

21. *Ibid.*, p. 4668.

22. *Ibid.*, p. 4672.

23. *Ibid.*

24. *Ibid.*, p. 4674.

25. *Ibid.*, pp. 4675-76.

26. *Ibid.*, p. 4676.

27. *Ibid.*, pp. 4677-78.

28. *Ibid.*, p. 4680.

29. *Ibid.*, pp. 4681-82.

30. *Ibid.*, p. 4683.

31. *Ibid.*, p. 4684.

32. New York *Times*, June 22, 1956.

33. *Passport Hearings*, Part IV, p. 4686.

34. Goodman, *op. cit.*, p. 394.

35. *Ibid.*

36. U.S. Congress, House Committee on Un-American Activities, *Communism in the New York Area (Entertainment)*, Hearings, Eighty-fifth Congress, Second Session, April 1, 1957, p. 2595. Hereinafter cited as *1957-58 Entertainment Hearings*.

37. *Ibid.*, pp. 2595-96.

38. *Ibid.*, pp. 2598-99.

39. *1957-58 Entertainment Hearings*, pp. 2591-93. Solomon's closed-door testimony before the committee's subcommittee in New York City was made public later in 1958.

40. *Ibid.*, p. 2480.

41. *Ibid.*, p. 2483.

42. *Ibid.*, p. 2500.

43. *Ibid.*, pp. 2475-76.

44. *Ibid.*, pp. 2514-16.

45. *Ibid.*, pp. 2517-18.

46. *Ibid.*, p. 2519.

47. *Ibid.*, pp. 2523-27.

48. *Ibid.*, pp. 2534-37.

49. *Ibid.*, p. 2544.

50. Goodman, *op. cit.*, p. 443. The John Birch Society is an organization founded by Robert Welch of Massachusetts. Its purported purpose is to furnish information about the international Communist conspiracy.

51. *1957-58 Entertainment Hearings*, p. 2546.

52. *Ibid.*, pp. 2551-52.

53. *Ibid.*, pp. 2556-57.

54. *Ibid.*, pp. 2656 ff.

55. U.S. Congress, House Committee on Un-American Activities, *Annual Report*, 1958, Eighty-sixth Congress, First Session, p. 29.

Chapter VII

The 1969-70 New Primary Data Gathered from Correspondence, Questionnaires, and Personal Taped Interviews

APPENDIX I of this book contains the names of seventy-two friendly witnesses and the approximately three hundred and twenty-five persons they identified as Communists. On January 15, 1970, one hundred requests (roughly 25 percent of the above total) for new information were mailed to seventy persons named as Communists before the committee who did not subsequently appear as friendly witnesses, twenty friendly witnesses, and ten nonwitnesses. The requests contained a cover letter, questionnaire, and a return self-addressed stamped envelope bearing my name.* On February 15, 1970, a reminder was sent to those persons who had not yet responded to the first mailing. March 14, 1970, was the last date new information was incorporated into this book.

The twenty friendly witnesses and the seventy persons identified as Communists were chosen (1) on the basis of my professional theatrical knowledge of the artists whose careers seemed most linked to the living theater, and (2) because the figures of twenty and seventy constitute roughly 25 percent of the total of each group identified in Appendix I. The remaining ten nonwitnesses were selected on the basis of particular information they might offer to the study due to their occupations or unique insights into the subject matter of the book.

* A sample copy of the cover letter and questionnaire appears in Appendix IV.

This latter group of ten was also selected on the basis of my professional judgment.

Additionally, twelve persons were interviewed personally on tape by me. They were selected on the same basis as the ten nonwitnesses and where possible were given copies of the questionnaire in advance of the interview.

Thirty-six persons responded to the cover letter and questionnaire, with twenty-two filling out the questionnaire and fourteen answering by letter only. No friendly witnesses answered the questionnaire. Only one friendly witness was found who was willing to discuss the subject of this book with me.

The forty-seven persons who responded to this researcher's request for information were writers Albert Maltz, Lester Cole, John Howard Lawson, Ring Lardner, Jr., Budd Schulberg, Paul Jarrico, Isobel Lennart, Frank Tarloff, David Lang, Allan Sloane, Louis Solomon, Pauline Townsend, Elizabeth Wilson, Melvin Levy, Wilma Shore, Silvia Richards, Michael Blankfort, Robert Lees, Robert Richards, Hy Kraft, Howard Dimsdale, Harold Buchman, and Ben Barzman; actors Jeff Corey, Mary Virginia Farmer, Will Geer, Lloyd Gough, Rose Hobart, Victor Kilian, Martin Wolfson, Marsha Hunt, Howard da Silva, Florida Friebus, Frank Maxwell, Ralph Bellamy, Adelaide Klein Annenberg, and Georgia Backus; directors Herbert Biberman, Michael Gordon, Vincent Sherman, Carl Foreman, and Elia Kazan; producers Shepard Traube and Adrian Scott; drama critic John Crosby; actor's agent Jack Fields; and professional informer Harvey Matusow.

One director, one producer, and seven writers indicated in their letters that they felt they could offer little information about the living theater. One writer's office stated he was out of the country and the matter would be turned over to him when he returned, and another writer evidenced a vacillating interest in the study for highly personal and emotional reasons and promised information eventually. No subsequent response from either was available at the time of this writing. A director replied that he was planning a book on his experiences with the committee and therefore did not wish to simplify the matter for this study. And lastly, a writer declined to cooperate, stating, "This whole problem is so long ago and so distasteful to me that even at this period I find little empathy in any further investigation in the matter."

The majority of the thirteen persons mentioned in the preceding paragraph, who decided not to cooperate in this study, appeared before the committee as cooperative witnesses.

All the following answers to the queries posed in the questionnaire were paraphrased for brevity and clarity except where direct quotes were deemed significant.

Presentation of the Data

Under the category of "probable effects of the committee's work on the American theater," the following observations were made regarding the achievement of that council's purposes as stated on page 15 of this study and page 1 of the questionnaire.

A blacklisted writer believed the purpose of the committee was unconstitutional because what it succeeded in doing in part was to pervert the Constitution. He further stated that the committee frightened writers from writing what they might have wanted to write, thus keeping from the audience points of view which the investigators opposed.

A witness who appeared in executive session and relied on constitutional privilege when asked to name names felt the committee was exclusively a "publicity-getting group of men who had no morality or real principles except to get their names into print." The witness further observed that "attacking Hollywood stars was juicy stuff for making headlines" and that "Martin Dies and all of his successors were of the same stripe, small-minded men of little integrity and conscience who made national reputations out of the great Red scare."

An actor who was an unfriendly witness stated the committee never defined what "un-American" meant. The actor also shared an observation with a blacklisted writer concerning the fact that the committee did not propose a single piece of legislation during the twenty-year period analyzed in this study.

A blacklisted writer commenting on the committee's purposes declared that "attacking private enterprise and advocating socialism or government ownership is a change in *economics*, not necessarily a change in the form of government." He then offered the question, "Would propaganda for publicly owned power be deemed subversive?"

A member of the Hollywood Ten thought the committee's intention to investigate propaganda was patently illegal because it involved "an attempt to impose political censorship on the expression or circulation of ideas, opinions, beliefs—activities which are the right of every citizen, a right clearly protected by the First Amendment."

A writer who took the diminished Fifth said that the committee was not interested in the Communist Party of the United States, but rather its interest was primarily and almost exclusively in the so-called front organizations and individual liberals. The writer believed that the committee did succeed in the sense that it liquidated a number of progressive organizations and immobilized individuals through blacklist and imprisonment. However, he concluded, it never proved any link between American progressive organizations and propaganda instigated by foreign countries.

Another blacklisted writer felt that since Congress cannot legislate in the area of opinion, according to the First Amendment to the Constitution, it should not be allowed to investigate in that area. He further observed that although the committee had a lack of success in achieving its stated purposes, that did not prevent it from achieving an unstated purpose, "the suppression of dissent." In that, he said, "it was quite successful, and for quite a long time."

A blacklisted director observed that the stated purposes of the committee were ambiguous and that words like "un-American" and "subversive" were generalizations that defy precise and objective definitions.

A blacklisted writer who was not a witness replied that if there were any foreign subversion, it would certainly have been under attack by J. Edgar Hoover.

An actor who took the Fifth Amendment felt that the

rhetoric describing the committee's function was only relevant in "an environment of intense subversion and incipient treason," which was not "the context of the world the committee presumed to investigate and therefore the resolution was so much demagogy."

Another blacklisted writer and witness concluded the investigators succeeded brilliantly in their real aim, "to completely silence the millions of liberal Americans—not the comparative handful of Communists."

Another member of the Hollywood Ten asserted that no Communist propaganda was ever found in films, radio, or television because it was not there and that the "search" was "phony and thoroughly political" and they (the committee) "attacked *labeled* individuals and damned their work along with their labeling."

A nonwitness believed the committee's record was a serious blight on the history of Congress and felt the final proof of that statement was the committee's 1969 request to change its name because "it had become anathema wherever it was heard."

A blacklisted writer who was forced to leave the country to secure work stated that the real targets of the committee were those who "on the international level had opposed the rise of Nazism and Fascism, and on the domestic level who had fought against minority discrimination, rights of union organization etcetera." He concluded, ". . . the committee showed a complete unwillingness to discuss what might or might not be in the American tradition, and consistently refused to deal with actual issues."

Finally, a blacklisted writer in the most definitive answer to this question had the following to say:

> In my opinion the Committee could not achieve its purposes since the Congressional law empowering it was alien to both the letter and the spirit of the Constitution. When I say this, I want to make it clear that I do not oppose the right of Congressional committees to investigate for purposes of proposing legislation. However, whatever the personnel of the House Committee on Un-American Activities or however it conducted its hearings, its stated purpose in the legislation empowering it did, and must, involve an invasion of the civil rights of citizens. There are laws

to cover crimes. There are law enforcement agencies to arrest and try citizens who commit crimes. But this Committee, by its history and by its policy—openly stated in the Congress by one of its members, Congressman Carl Mundt—operated not in the field of crime but in the field of ideas. By its very history and by its open policy it operated in the very field forbidden to it by the Constitution and the Bill of Rights.

It is precisely for this reason that in the nine years of its existence up until March 1948 this Committee succeeded in having only one case of legislation passed by the Congress—and the bill was immediately declared unconstitutional by the Supreme Court.

Since the purpose of Congressional investigation is precisely to gather information on the basis of which Committee members then propose new legislation to the country at large, this zero batting average on the part of the Committee should in itself, in my opinion, render its efforts highly suspect.

Question B under "probable effects" concerned the decision of whether to answer the committee's questions or not. It asked, "If you were a witness and therefore were confronted by this alternative, please describe your resolution. If you were not a witness, and were aware you might be, how were you prepared to resolve this choice?"

A member of the board of the Actors' Laboratory Theatre felt that the committee was getting at the "Lab," not individuals, and therefore the group voted to refuse to answer certain questions. According to the actress, none of the group took the Fifth Amendment.

An unfriendly witness stated he was

unwilling to purchase personal immunity at the expense of others, and reluctant to invite the inevitable contempt citation by describing my own activities but refusing to recite a list of names, on the advice of council [sic] I availed myself of my constitutional prerogative under the Bill of Rights and stood mute.

An actor and unfriendly witness said, "Few people realize that if you answer any questions you open the door to all others. I had no wish to name my friends and make them vulnerable."

The longest answer to this question came from a witness who took the Fifth Amendment and said he would never do so again, citing the fact that the Fifth position was "good law but lousy public relations." He went on to say:

> The rationale for the 5th was this: by court-established rules of the game the witness could not be selective in refusal to answer questions protected by the 5th. In practice this meant that one could not admit CP membership and then refuse to name names, result being citation for contempt. Nor would "I don't remember" suffice. The witness then would be confronted by an informer who would swear, perhaps truthfully, that the witness knew *him*. Result, perjury and a possible 5 yrs.
>
> The public could scarcely be expected to understand these legal ramifications. The natural reaction: "If they won't talk they must have something to hide." The witness was in the impossible posture of standing mute while the Committee convincingly pled for information on an International Conspiracy dedicated to the destruction of the nation.
>
> If on the other hand the witness had taken the position that he would answer to anything *except* names, the Committee would have been faced with two alternatives (1) to let the witness speak freely of his reasons, valid, naive or even opportunistic for CP membership or (2) to shut him up with an immediate question about names and a citation for contempt, thereby exposing the punitive purpose for its existence as opposed to the legislative function which it claimed.
>
> In the first of these alternatives I do not know of any witness who had anything of a remotely "conspiratorial" nature to hide. (The testimony of the "cooperative" witnesses, at least in the Theatre and allied fields, may perhaps be judged by the fact that not a single one to my knowledge "volunteered" his testimony but only came forth after massive threats to his economic and professional life.) In the second alternative surely one might reasonably have expected a public reaction. "They say they want them to give information, but all they're doing is throwing them in jail."
>
> Of course many witnesses, with family responsibilities etc., doubtless were in no position to accept such punitive measures. In my own case, in retrospect, I can think of no overwhelming hardship to myself or anyone else override the possibility of dulling, if not pulling, the Committee's teeth. If enough of us had done this I believe that such a possibility was a very real one.

An actor who was an unfriendly witness said that although he knew his material well-being would be affected by his refusal to answer the committee's questions, he was faced with his "own dignity and self-esteem as well as the future of my child."

An unfriendly witness in 1947 felt then and now that he was performing a patriotic service in denouncing the committee's attempt to ask about Communist Party membership or belief. He said, "I answered questions which (as I understood it) did not violate my elementary rights of conscience and association."

A writer who was not a witness said he would have refused to answer because he felt that after the committee had finished dealing with individuals who provided a large "harvest of publicity," they

> would then turn to less-rewarding (publicity-wise) fields such as schools and universities. I felt I, like many others in the theatre and screen, was better able to defend myself than school teachers and university professors might be.

A writer and unfriendly witness called the committee a "cancer within the American body politic." He said he had watched the committee "month after month and year after year attacking everything that I considered humane and progressive in American life—the New Deal, Welfare legislation of all sorts, Liberal and Radical groups, and I had seen it give open forum to such reactionaries as Gerald K. Smith." He further observed that the Hollywood Ten's appeal of their contempt citations would have been reversed at the Supreme Court level if the two most liberal members of the court had not unexpectedly died during the summer of 1950. He concluded that the court that ruled on the Hollywood Ten's petition for reverse of the contempt citation was differently constituted than the court that had been in existence when the ten first challenged the committee in 1947.

A nonwitness who thought he might be a witness said he had thought the situation over for many many hours and was never able to arrive at a conclusion regarding how to answer the committee's questions. He felt he was lucky that he never had to face the situation, but he has still not been able to decide how he would have responded had he been forced into that predicament.

An actress who was an unfriendly witness said the only alternative she ever considered was the First Amendment, which did not appear to offer quite such safe grounds constitutionally as the Fifth, and she never considered the alternative of answering questions.

A writer and unfriendly witness stated that ten years after he took the Fifth Amendment his private position was beautifully summarized by the English writer E. M. Forster: "If I ever have to choose between my country and my friends, I hope I have the courage to choose my friends."

An actor and unfriendly witness who took the Fifth Amendment regretted the unfortunate impression the Fifth Amendment made in the public eye. He said, "I sometimes thought it might have been better to risk a prison term and answer questions that you were disposed to answer and simply refuse to answer questions you chose not to. . . ."

Another actor who was an uncooperative witness answered the query by simply saying, ". . . the question is mildly insulting."

A writer who took the Fifth Amendment said he would have been willing to overlook his philosophical opposition to the committee in order to avoid the blacklist and loss of opportunity to support his family by talking about his own "involvement," particularly since he believed that involvement was humanitarian in its motivations and certainly not in his opinion un-American. However, the writer concluded:

> . . . it was absolutely clear that the committee wanted more; wanted names of others "involved," and that was something I was never prepared to do. Having no alternative except jail, I reluctantly took the "Fifth."

Under "possible effects of the committee's work," question A asked if the committee had any constructive influence on the American theater. The answer was a unanimous "No" from the questionnaires and the interviewees. One writer allowed for the possibility that the creation of a few plays, such as *The Crucible*, might not have occurred were it not for the committee's work. An actor who did not respond directly to the question did observe that individuals may have been "strengthened through their willingness to 'take it' but it did not make their lives, personal or professional, richer. . . ."

Another actor said in response to this question, "In its clumsy way, the committee brought home to American theatre people that 'It Can Happen Here,' Fascism, that is."

A blacklisted director concurred that there were no constructive effects from the committee's activities on the American theater and stated that it was his

> belief the theatre has never recovered from the blow struck by the committee. For its greatest injury was done to the American audience. Ideas became suspect. They disappeared for decades. Writers, audiences and producers surrendered to the intimidation.

And from a director who went back to acting after twenty years, the following remarks came:

> Are you not aware that this question is a joke? The committee must have been aware that there was no way for them to make any headway in the American theatre, which please understand was and is New York City where no boycott of any production had ever been in the least successful and couldn't be for the simple reason that the public in New York is too special and diffuse and impersonal. Therefore, they never even made any attempt to question the loyalties in the American theatre.

Question B under "possible effects" asked for comments on any destructive influences the committee's activities may have had on the American theater.

A blacklisted writer felt that since plays are produced with an eye toward film and television, he was sure that money to back a play written by a blacklistee would make the financing difficult, if not impossible. He speculated that in the period when the blacklist was in total effect in Hollywood it must have affected production and casting in the theater.

Another blacklisted writer said if he had an idea for a play that he felt might be considered "dangerous" by the committee, he probably would not have written it, and he imagined that this actually happened to a number of writers.

An actor who took the Fifth Amendment cited the cases of Elia Kazan and Clifford Odets, who "capitulated, they made no contribution to the theatre comparable to that which they had made before. Fear is not conducive to a healthy theatre—the Committee spread fear."

A New York theater person believed that

> as a result of Senator McCarthy and HUAC, many of our playwrights created their own self-censorship and began writing bland plays, trivial plays. Our theatre did suffer in this respect. In England, the writers had no such sword hanging over their heads and the British theatre flourished as a result.

A First Amendment witness agreed that the committee's activities closed the Federal Theatre and said:

> It so happens that in my opinion the only unique contribution to theatre form that the United States has given to the world was that of the Living Newspaper as it evolved in several plays presented by the WPA Theatre. I believe that it required a subsidized theatre such as the WPA to present theatre in the form of the Living Newspaper and that the educational effects of the Living Newspaper plays were benign and important. This form of theatre died when the WPA theatre died.

He went on to say that he does not believe it is the proper function of any government to legislate what people may or may not produce in the theater. The writer concluded his observations on this question with the following statement:

> There is no way of proving the intimidating effects that the committee's activities had upon various individual theatre producers who may have declined play scripts because they were afraid of being attacked by the committee or one of its members in Congress. However, the general effects of governmental intimidation are very clear. One may only imagine what the effect upon Russian writers is today of the imprisonment of a small number of writers and expulsion of several others from the Writers Union to realize what this would produce by way of self-censorship amongst writers themselves as well as intimida-

tion of theatre producers and directors. I feel certain that the committee had something with the same effect upon the American Theatre as a whole.

A blacklisted actor felt the destructive effects of the committee's activities on the American theater were too numerous to tabulate. He believed there was an elimination of valuable talent by economic and "often literal death." As examples of the latter, he cited Mady Christian, J. Edward Bromberg, and John Garfield.

A writer claimed that "implicit censorship and explicit threats to theatrical personnel to toe the Committee line inevitably reduced the freedom of expression in the theatre." He stated that a writer

> shyed [sic] away from too piercing an examination of any controversial subjects since non-production was a virtual certainty, and if by some odd chance, the controversial work did show promise of being staged, economic pressure sufficed to kill it early on.

Another writer believed that a careful study could document the committee's role in the final dissolution of the Group Theatre and that its activities also had an effect on the writing of Clifford Odets, Arthur Miller, and many others.

Still another writer felt the destructive effect was "atmospheric." He believed there was

> a general sense of fear, fear to attack the status quo, fear to assert revolutionary solutions to social ills. (Or indeed to assert that social ills were a proper subject for dramatic treatment.) It's difficult, unfortunately, to be specific. It was something one felt in discussions with fellow writers; a tendency toward self-censorship.

Another writer concurred in the belief that dramatists exercised self-censorship, pointing out that "there was no point in writing plays that couldn't attract investors or Broadway producers."

A director with a background in both theater and films stated that theater is worth attending "only when it stands high above film and T.V. It can do so only when ideas are rampant."

And another writer described the destructive effects he believed the committee's activities had on Clifford Odets and Elia Kazan:

> By terrorizing sensitive and creative people, such as the late Clifford Odets, who subsequently testified as a friendly witness, and denounced many of the people who had been closest to him, and the very substance on which his talent had fed, the theatre lost a beautiful and lyrical voice. This was also true of men like Elia Kazan who realized, I believe, with great bitterness that they had sold off their most valuable possession.

Another director with a background in theater and films believed that the unstructured character of the American theater minimized the kind of organized blacklisting that was operative in other media. He concluded:

> In a broader sense, however, the impact of HUAC—and the subsequent rise of McCarthy for which it paved the way—can not be discounted. The protestant spirit that vitalized all the arts in America during the 30's and the early 40's wilted and virtually disappeared.

An actress noted that within a year after the hearings (she did not say which one) the Actors' Lab ceased to function as a school or production unit for "live" actors. Another actor agreed that the Actors' Lab died as a result of the California State Un-American Activities Committee hearing on its purported subversiveness and concluded that "that same hearing brought up the sordid information that the Actors' Lab specialized in subversive plays by Shaw, O'Casey and Chekov."

Question C under "probable effects" asked for an opinion on results of the committee's activities that can not yet be evaluated.

A director said he could not be specific but he believed "that a whole generation of critical creativity [was] discredited." He further attested that much of the "inarticulate, abstract, introverted theatre" which followed (some of it of considerable value) came because of an instinctive avoidance by the new and rising talents of turning toward confrontations of issues which, because of the committee's activities, had been made to seem un-American and dangerous. He concluded that

> there were really no noteworthy plays about such enormous events as the Korean War, the developing nuclear threat, the tragic deterioration of white-black relationships in the decade which followed the committee. The fear which the committee inspired on the various campuses left incalculable damage, which cannot yet be evaluated—as it did in all areas which need free and open inquiry.

A producer and director said he was not sure that the blacklist is over today. When he was recently engaged to direct a segment of a particularly successful New York-based television show he learned that the actors had to be cleared with an office downstairs at CBS before he could hire them for the program. He asked, "Is it over?"

A writer believed that "there are effects which we will never know, like what plays weren't written, which might have been or what writers were in effect killed—literally and figuratively—who might have written meaningful plays."

A First Amendment witness speculated on the harm the committee's activities did to the careers and lives of thousands of people. He stated: "Only by specifically interrogating every individual who did not cooperate with the Committee and asking what specifically happened to their career and life as a result of the position they took, could these effects be evaluated."

A director observed:

> Although the gradual recovery of our culture from the debilitating effects of that era have been substantial, there is the danger that Americans, once having submitted to that kind of suppression, may have developed a tolerance and susceptibility to its possible recurrence.

A writer noted "the fact that a blacklist could have been effected gives credence to the fear that it may well happen again." He said, "A fear that a controversial play—using an anti-establishment theme can be used in the future to stigmatize an artist who participates in such a project would stop him from writing or acting in it."

An actor-director said:

> If it were possible to find out the total of blasted careers, and lives of a few prominent people and literally hundreds of little people, totally innocent people, actors, writers, directors who suffered by this monstrous hoax of the American people it would make a story for which every effort would be made to bury for all time.

An unfriendly witness believed that we are rather "astigmatic" in evaluating the period of the early fifties in America. He said, "it caused a fear to 'think-feel-and-experience concern' in our *entire* population. I do not believe we have yet recovered. It is possible that we lost a generation."

Another writer believed that Arthur Miller in his play *After the Fall* gave certain hints of the committee's effect on the playwright. He speculated further that the period of McCarthy and the committee's activities undoubtedly put certain limitations on Miller's dramatic themes, imagination, and his choice of material. And another writer mentioned that self-censorship "is a difficult habit to break, persons who might today be contributing to the theatre . . . have long since given up."

Finally, under "possible effects," questions D and E asked about a blacklist on Broadway. Though one writer stated that he had in his possession "the literal blacklist in circulation among all studios and covering the entire entertainment field," no specific evidence was available concerning a blacklist in the New York theater.

General observations were made along the lines that some friends of the persons responding to the questionnaire may have lost work in the theater, but this was impossible to pin down. One writer mentioned the rumor that Larry Parks could not get work on Broadway. And, finally, an unfriendly witness indicated that a director named Mervin Williams was fired at the Pasadena Playhouse after doing two impressive productions, for what he implied were political reasons. The actor further stated that members of the cast of a play left when they heard he had been hired and that he was expelled from the staff of a Los Angeles-based theatrical venture for his political position, which was described as "too risky."

The third category concerned the actual effects of the committee's activities on the American theater. Questions 1 and 2 under A, concerning the Federal Theatre, asked if the person was working in the Federal Theatre at the time it was closed and to name other theaters closed as a result of the committee's activities.

The Actors' Lab was once again cited as a theater that was closed indirectly by the committee in the sense that many unfriendly witnesses were members of the Lab. The group was also investigated by the California Un-American Activities Committee. Hence, economic attrition followed the unfavorable publicity given the witnesses and the theater closed.

One writer speculated that the Group Theatre came to an early end as a result of the climate of the times, which included the committee's activities. Another writer observed that the University of Washington Theatre Workshop (he believed it was called by that name) under Florence Bean James "was virtually destroyed by the activities of a State Committee whose methods were identical with the Federally appointed House Committee."* There was no other evidence that any additional theaters were closed as a result of the committee's activities.

Question B under "actual effects" asked how the committee hearings affected lives in four areas: income, career change, theater activity, and personal relationships. The blacklisted writers followed the familiar pattern of going underground and writing for the black market—and for salaries considerably less than they commanded previous to their blacklisting.

After his appearance before the committee as an unfriendly witness, an actor related that his income came to a complete halt and he did not earn another cent at his profession for

---

* The theater's name was the Seattle Repertory Playhouse and the state committee's chairman was Albert Canwell.

twelve years. He stated, "There were personal relationships that were hinged to professional activities and this ultimately effected [*sic*] quality and frequency of contacts." And the actor concluded, "By and large—the meaningful relationships were not at all altered—at least no more so than they are in the course of living a life blacklisted or not. . . ."

Another actor indicated that his salary went from $40,000 a year to nothing as a result of the blacklist and that for three years he worked in a variety of businesses outside of the theater before he gradually began his return to show business.

A blacklisted writer was unable to find work for three years and thereafter started working under a pseudonym and was forced to accept any job at any price and received no credit for the work. He commented:

> . . . one was driven to move in a tight circle of people who were in a similar plight. Some former "friends" were fearful of association—others were unappealing after sessions on witness stand during which they named all their dearest chums.

Another blacklisted writer was forced to move to England to continue his career and observed that

> unfriendly witnesses were shunned socially; it was bad business to be friendly with an unfriendly. And the friendly witnesses named their friend—who else? So relations were severed.

Another blacklisted writer who was forced into exile in England claimed to have endured considerable financial hardship after comparable affluence in Hollywood. He also stated that he lost some very frightened "liberal" friends and he believed that the breakup of his marriage also was helped by the blacklist; he noted further that "dozens of Hollywood and theatre marriages foundered on this same political rock."

A Fifth Amendment unfriendly witness had his contract terminated by a major Hollywood studio when he refused to cooperate with the committee.

Another blacklisted writer indicated he had no income for several years as a result of his being an uncooperative witness and was forced to work as a maître d' and a salesman until he was able to start writing again and then under another name. He further stated that as a result of his political position his wife was forced to go to work also, which left much less time for them to be with their children. He said that "they [the children] had no idea why their lives were so uprooted."

Another writer living abroad reported that his wife's passport was withdrawn by the local American embassy concurrent with his being identified as a Communist by a friendly witness. The writer remained abroad after being blacklisted and found it

> difficult to write for my own theatre, aside from the enormous disadvantages of blacklisting. Theatre must come from deeply indigenous experience; I did not feel I knew enough about the new world I was suddenly experiencing, and I felt myself alienated from my own.

He went on to say that during the period of McCarthy, people with whom he had previously been closely associated "sedulously avoided" him and his family.

A blacklisted television director stated he remained friendly with Elia Kazan because he thought he was an artist and believed he was going through "hell" with his own conscience. The director referring again to Kazan said:

> I don't know why he gave names. He didn't have to. Perhaps he was fearful of losing his career in Hollywood. But he could have been distinguished in the theatre. I never discussed it with him since it's his personal problem. I think he knows I took a different stance, and we enjoy mutual respect. I felt the same way about Robert Rossen, who informed on people, after holding out for a long time. I guess it may have killed Bob finally. But I thought he was a man of talent and I was not going to be his judge, so when we met I was friendly.

Another First Amendment witness and writer declared he was blacklisted in Hollywood for twenty years and suffered a disastrous decline in his income as a result of the committee's activities. He believed that "many playwrights who showed 'promise' in the 30's ceased writing for production as a result of the committee's activities." He concluded by saying that his friendships have never been restricted to people who shared his "radical views."

A blacklisted writer indicated he could not get a passport from the United States State Department and therefore had no way of seeking work in the film industries of Europe.

A blacklisted actress noted that her career came to a complete halt and that she was turned down by the PTA when her son was in elementary school for what she believed to be her political posture.

A blacklisted actor commenting on personal relationships stated that the committee's activities "increased the number of former friends."

After returning from prison, a blacklisted writer was forced to work as a waiter and cook in a restaurant and a stock clerk in a warehouse because he could not get work in his field. The writer had been earning $30,000 a year and his income dropped to nothing. He became a carpenter but claimed that he could not consider himself a martyr because he enjoyed the work thoroughly. He noted that his former wife was a cooperative witness, which created a difficult situation for the children for a while. The problem has since been resolved.

An unfriendly witness declared:

> In 1951 or early '52 I wrote a long one-act play which was based upon some security hearings which had occurred at the Brooklyn Navy Yard around the year 1949. I had secured a copy of the transcripts from the lawyer who defended three men in what I can only describe as a Kafka-esque hearing. When I finished the play, I found that there was no group in the United States able to produce it. By this I don't mean a professional theatre since it was not a full length play but an over-length one-act play. However, in the 1930's I had written a number of one-act plays which had found production in quite a few left wing amateur groups in different states in the United States. All of these groups had ceased to exist in the '50's. It is my belief that the activities of the committee were considerably involved in this changed picture.

A writer indicated he was no longer interested in maintaining a relationship with a former friend of his who had become a friendly witness after having been uncooperative in his first appearance before the committee.

Question C under "actual effects of the committee's activities" asked how the publicity surrounding the hearings affected those involved.

A writer indicated that the primary reason for taking his

children out of the Beverly Hills schools and going to Europe to live for eleven years was the publicity surrounding the hearings. He added that he found those years the most rewarding of his life and that there was no doubt in his mind that he did owe the House Committee on Un-American Activities a "thank you" note.

A producer-director whom Martin Berkeley identified as being a Communist declared that Berkeley was in error. A lawyer for the producer-director had felt that if Berkeley were challenged it would invite an appearance before the committee and thus become a "circus." The lawyer had believed the committee would back up and protect Berkeley if he were challenged for lying, and then there would be a subsequent contest over perjury and Berkeley would be in the patriot's role. Hence, the lawyer's advice had been to forget the whole thing.

Another writer who was involved with a popular television show at the time his name was publicly mentioned by a friendly witness was dropped "within minutes" from the show. He was subsequently dropped as a client by the agency that represented him. And another writer believed that because of the fact that he was named frequently by friendly witnesses this gave a different attitude toward his writing work. He said, "What I thought was mildly satiric comedy was judged as though having some subversive goal."

A director felt it was prudent to turn down a script that was thematically "daring" out of concern for the fact the past publicity attendant to him might impair the script's chances for public acceptance.

A blacklisted actor felt that it spoke well for the American community that in spite of the unfairness of the blacklist, one was able to live and function anyway and that he personally was not denied his GI education because of his political beliefs.

Another writer felt that the publicity surrounding the hearings strengthened certain personal ties by cutting off all business possibilities and "even agents were inaccessible" as a result of the publicity. A blacklisted writer believed that his elder child was disturbed by the publicity and his wife to a somewhat lesser degree was emotionally distressed well beyond the economic difficulties resulting from the writer's loss of employment.

Another blacklisted writer said a cross was set on fire with lighter fuel on his front lawn and his wife lost her job in an entirely different field; friends who wished to hire him had to request that he get a "clearance" by "cooperating" or they could not give him a job.

A First Amendment witness felt that his career as a writer was adversely affected by the many articles and newspaper magazines attacking him because of the stand he took before the committee. Additionally, he declared his life was threatened several times by anonymous telephone calls, which had a further unsettling effect on him. He stated he received a considerable number of hate letters which were not enjoyable reading. He felt that the publicity surrounding his decision to test the constitutionality of the committee's activities adversely affected his teen-age son in his school work. A subsequent move out of the country did not alleviate the pressures for the son, and the writer declared the whole thing was a very "painful" process for the son. He concluded by saying he believes his decision to leave the country was partially, not wholly, motivated by a desire to try to free both of his children from public pressures they felt in their own peer group as a result of the hearings.

A writer stated that "the evening of the day I appeared a neighbor whom I scarcely knew brought me a bunch of roses from his garden." An actor blacklisted in films returned to acting in the theater, where he had been active for twenty years, and found no evidence of blacklisting there.

Question D under "actual effects" asked how the committee hearings generally affected lives.

A blacklisted writer assessed the effect of the committee hearings on his life: "loss of income from work—economic disaster—social status destroyed—life work broken." A writer who was forced to work in a restaurant because of the blacklist had that job exposed in a Hollywood gossip column and the resultant publicity helped him move out of the restaurant business.

An actor stated the blacklist changed the course of his life for twelve years. He named John Houseman, Theatre Guild and

Playwright's Company, Lawrence Langer, and others who were kind enough to use him in the theater as early as 1955. He returned to film work in the sixties. A blacklisted actress who had done well in pictures and television had no work after the committee hearings.

A writer commented:

> . . . it is admittedly not easy to be denied the practice of a profession to which you have devoted all of your adult years. (It must be infinitely more shattering to an actor—a writer can at least sit down and write something.) Self-doubt can become a problem. But it can be worked through.

An actor stated that the hearings broke up his marriage and changed his life entirely. A blacklisted writer believed that books he had authored were removed from American and foreign libraries as a result of his name and its relationship to the committee hearings. He felt he could not prove this charge but was certain it was true. Another blacklisted writer felt that it was a valuable experience because he found he "could survive without assured security such as a place in the 'show biz' establishment," and the blacklist made it possible for him to take greater positive chances with his career with what he described as "very positive results." Two writers agreed that the blacklist had taken them out of active political participation because of the subjective feeling that their names lent to a cause might do it harm rather than good.

Finally, a blacklisted writer who, previous to being identified as a Communist, had worked alternately in the theater and for the screen found that after being blacklisted he felt it was impossible to write for the theater under a pseudonym. He turned more and more to film work and finally moved to Europe, where he writes exclusively for the cinema.

The final question under "actual effects" asks for information regarding vigilante-type organizations and their effect on individuals. The Motion Picture Alliance for the Preservation of American Ideals and the American Legion were cited as organizations devoted to protecting the country from internal Communist subversion.

A blacklisted writer concluded that he did not know of any such organization, but "it was common knowledge however, that every studio and TV organization had its 'clearance' fellow whose job it was to keep 'tainted' folk from being employed."

Evaluation of the Data

The committee's stated purposes were generally viewed by those cooperating in this study as unbelievable—if not unconstitutional. Words such as "subversion" and "un-American" were meaningless unless clearly defined by those who chose to apply their use. Since these terms were never clarified by the committee, the charges leveled at the witnesses were directed from a group of men who had, at best, a vague interpretation of who was a good American and, at worst, an undefined interpretation.

The committee's unstated purposes were quite clear, however, and it was in this area that the investigators were most successful. They managed to stir up a lot of publicity by constantly charging persons in the entertainment field with subversion and they managed to suppress dissent by creating an atmosphere of fear. The persons silenced, however, were not only Communists but, unfortunately, liberals as well.

The committee's great search for subversives appeared at least debatable on constitutional grounds and highly suspect on grounds of national security. Their investigators' activities clearly overlapped the efforts of the always efficacious Federal Bureau of Investigation. The bureau was interested in keeping tabs on American Communists, whereas the committee was apparently more interested in the task of trying to prove a relationship between a foreign-dominated Red conspiracy and American organizations and individuals. The investigators were as unsuccessful in this task as they were in producing any significant legislation meaningful to the security of the United States. Therefore, the probable effects of the committee's activities had little to do with the results the tribunal purported to achieve in its public statements of resolve.

The persons who responded to the questionnaire and who consented to be interviewed for this book were in complete agreement on the fact that they would stand by their past public positions on answering the committee's questions. The rules of the game were clear to the witnesses and the purchase of immunity from the blacklist was made at the price of informing on their friends. The committee functioned in this sense as a punisher of people rather than as a legislative body intent upon making laws to protect the country from domestic Red subversion.

Since the time of their public declaration of attitude toward the committee's right to question them, several witnesses considered variations on the black or white choice of informing or going to jail and/or being blacklisted. None of the witnesses, however, was certain what alternatives are available and legal should he be in a like situation today or tomorrow.

Had the committee been honest about its alleged goal of seeking information about Communist subversion in the entertainment field, it could have avoided putting the witness into an either-or position when answering questions. It is clear that many Fifth Amendement witnesses did not object to talking about themselves and their prior political activities but became uncooperative only when they were asked to name names.

The committee had a stated public responsibility to deliver data concerning the Red menace in show business, and rather than do so, they closed off any potential information by forcing the suspect witnesses into taking constitutional refuge prematurely.

It is entirely possible that the term "Fifth Amendment Communist" might never have come into being if the Supreme Court of 1950 had been of the same political balance as the 1947 court. Had the Hollywood Ten's use of the First Amendment been justified by the high court, undoubtedly all the subpoenaed witnesses of the fifties would have used that ruling as their legal reason for declining to answer questions. The unexpected deaths of the two justices changed the course of hundreds of lives in the entertainment world and probably affected thousands more.

Other than inspiring a few plays, the committee's activities had no constructive influence on the American theater. Arthur

Miller's *A View from the Bridge, The Crucible,* and *After the Fall* all dealt loosely with the subject of informing, and Conrad Bromberg's *Dream of a Blacklisted Actor* was a personal chronicle of his father's experiences resulting from the committee's work. To this extent, the theater offered material to the audience that might not have been written or produced were it not for the invidious nature of the times.

The destructive results of the committee's probes on the American theater and the influence of that body's work that cannot yet be evaluated are indeed actual and are assessed as such in this study.

These actual effects were two in number. First, the 1938 Dies committee investigation of the Federal Theatre contributed heavily to the already controversial atmosphere surrounding the project. The negative publicity generated by those hearings helped make it possible for Congress to cut off funds for the WPA theater with only a minimal challenge from the Roosevelt New Dealers. In short, the committee's activities regarding the Federal Theatre clinched the termination of that institution and with it the hope of a national theater for America.

Second, the committee's postwar investigations created economic chaos, career change, and personal unhappiness and tragedy for hundreds of artists in all areas of the entertainment field—with the theater being actually, if only somewhat indirectly, affected. One indirect result of the federal committee's work was the creation of similar committees on the state level which, through their investigations, helped close theaters in California and Washington.

Another indirect but apparently actual result of the committee's work is less easily proved. The atmosphere of fear created by the investigations undoubtedly produced self-censorship in the field of writing, if not outright avoidance of controversial themes. One can only speculate on what subjects were not tackled because of the committee's activities, but it is safe to assume, based on the new data, that such a situation did exist.

All the blacklisted artists suffered a grave loss of income, but the actors were the hardest hit. The writers could go underground and continue working on the black market under pseudonyms. This process was demeaning as well as financially unrewarding when compared to their preblacklisting salaries. But they could get by.

The majority of the actors who earned most of their income from films and television were forced into alien occupations for nearly a decade. The living theater, particularly in New York, was able to sustain only a few of them. When there was acting work on Broadway, the blacklist did not deter artists from securing employment there. But the general paucity of employment in the living theater, in addition to the far smaller salaries offered by stage work, made life for the blacklisted actors far less endurable than for the writers who faced the same problem.

The personal relationships that were modified by the committee's activities seemed to have no consistent pattern. Some blacklistees continued their friendships with cooperative witnesses. Others avoided such contacts, sometimes out of revulsion and sometimes out of compassion. The writers in the black market generally kept in contact with each other for economic purposes. The actors had no such need and their personal relationships that were not tied to professional activities varied only slightly. As one actor stated, the "meaningful relationships" were not harmed.

In at least one instance, a blacklisted writer enjoyed his temporary career change and another felt the committee's investigations helped the quality of his writing because the blacklist protected him from Hollywood commercialism.

Finally, isolated instances of passport problems, marital troubles, and family alienation completed the personal troubles faced by the blacklistees.

Publicity created exile for some artists and a diffusion of concentration on their work for others. Fear of further adverse publicity deterred at least one artist from challenging the person who identified him as a Communist. On the other hand, one writer appreciated the negative publicity because it forced him to move to Europe—a move he enjoyed and believed he would not have made were it not for the committee. The publicity problem of guilt by association extended past personal relationships and in several instances made objective nonpolitical examination of the writing work of the blacklistees impossible.

Overt physical violence resulting from publicity was not a problem, but the threat of it was. Generally, the new data indicated that it was difficult to distinguish whether publicity was the cause or result of being blacklisted. The deaths of certain persons because of the committee's investigations are speculative and therefore impossible to document.

The general effects of the committee hearings on the lives of the blacklistees have already been discussed. In addition to economic attrition, personal sadness, and career destruction, the investigations definitely suspended further active participation in politics for all unfriendly witnesses. Fear of contaminating the "cause" was the reason for their self-imposed moratorium on political involvement.

Fear of reprisal for unpopular political positions has no place in a democracy. In this sense, the committee created the very situation they were supposedly endeavoring to stamp out—a totalitarian climate that had no room for politically intolerable ideas.

Chapter VIII

Conclusions and Implications

Conclusions

The Special House Committee on Un-American Activities was formed in 1938 after nearly a decade of extreme economic and social unrest in the United States. Its alleged purposes were outlined in extraordinarily general terms in a resolution authorizing the formation of the committee. Words such as "un-American" and "subversive" and phrases such as propaganda that "attacks the principles of the form of government as guaranteed by the Constitution" were used by the committee to label and describe those persons or organizations with whom they disagreed.

Because the committee was generally chaired, composed, and staffed by Congressmen and persons with a conservative political viewpoint, the overwhelming majority of their investigations centered on liberals—whom the investigators rightly and wrongly labeled Communists.

The chief, but not the only, function of an investigatory committee of Congress is to investigate for the purpose of creating legislation. The committee's show business hearings created no significant laws vital to the security of the nation in the twenty-year period examined. The hearings were punitive rather than legislative in their effect and were used to harass, punish, and economically boycott those individuals whose ideas, in the opinion of the committee, were judged dangerous to the safety of the United States. Since the First Amendment clearly states that Congress cannot legislate against ideas, it is clear that the committee, for either its alleged or actual purposes, should not have been allowed to investigate ideas.

The committee learned almost from its inception that the area that could generate the most publicity for its activities, members, and chairmen was the field of entertainment. The committee's first chairman, Martin Dies, undertook to examine Communism and Communists in the government-sponsored Federal Theatre. The 1938 Dies investigation and the extravagant publicity attendant on it contributed heavily to the decision made by Congress on June 1, 1939, to eliminate the theater from the Roosevelt New Deal.

The liberal Democratic administration, already under fire from myriad conservative and Republican sources, made no effort to save the Federal Theatre. Thus, America lost its first and only subsidized theatrical venture—a venture that, had it been allowed to continue, might have produced a national theater for America and international recognition comparable to the National Theatre of Great Britain.

The Federal Theatre hearings were the first major publicity triumph for the committee and they knew the reason—show business draws attention. In killing the Federal Theatre, the committee and Congress not only put more than 8,000 persons back on relief rolls but also ended truly controversial theater of a political and social nature and, most importantly, America's unique contribution to the drama—the "living newspaper."

Because of America's tactical alignment with the Soviet Union during World War II, the committee's chief nemesis, Communism, was temporarily avoided as a subject for investigation. Immediately after the war, Communism was again the enemy and the committee, with its new chairman, J. Parnell Thomas, turned its publicity-seeking attention to Communists of the Hollywood variety. They were not disappointed. Hollywood's elite paraded before the cameras and chose sides on the issue of whether the committee had the right to ask a man

about his political beliefs. Eventually, when it appeared the
Hollywood Ten were not going to turn out to be the heroes
their enthusiasts believed them to be, those same enthusiasts,
particularly a group named the Committee of 100, retreated
from publicity as hastily as they had sought it.

Again, as a result of the media's awareness of the public's
interest in show business, the committee had its second major
publicity triumph. In 1947, the Hollywood Ten refused to
answer the committee's questions about their private political
beliefs, basing their reticence on the First Amendment. Their
declination resulted in contempt charges, and when the Supreme Court refused to reverse the citations, the ten went to jail
for their beliefs.

In 1951 and 1952, concomitant with the rise of Senator
Joseph McCarthy as the foremost cold war hunter of Reds, the
committee under Chairman John Wood made its most extensive
and thorough probe of Communist infiltration of show business. During these hearings, the uncooperative witnesses, not
wishing to go to jail, took the Fifth Amendment instead of the
First. The Fifth Amendment kept the unfriendly witnesses out
of jail—and out of work. The unfriendly witnesses who did not
subsequently appear as friendly witnesses and persons identified
by cooperative witnesses as Communists made up the show
business blacklist.

The persons named on that list were unemployable in motion
pictures and television and radio for nearly a decade. The
majority of these persons were writers. They were able to
continue working at considerably reduced salaries and without
credit on the black market that grew up as a result of the
committee's work. The actors were less fortunate, and many
were driven into other occupations until the anti-Communist
public passions began to cool in the early 1960's.

The one area that was not intimidated by the committee or
the blacklist was the living theater. When jobs were available in
the theater, ability was the test, not political beliefs. Actors'
Equity Association and the League of New York Theatres drew up an antiblacklist agreement and the resolution
was scrupulously implemented by both organizations. With rare

and not properly documented exceptions, the New York theater and the American theater in general had no organized
blacklist.

According to the new data, the damage done to the living
theater was in another area not easily documented—words that
were not written. What subjects of a controversial nature were
avoided is impossible to ascertain, but the fear of not getting
such subjects produced—or the fear that there might be harsh
punitive reprisals in the future for views or positions held in the
past—were unquestionably valid fears that did exist. And their
existence is directly traceable to the committee, whose methods
and procedures silenced perhaps a generation of writers, writers
who might have contributed bounteously to a healthy theater in
a democratic society.

By the end of 1952 the committee was running out of
publicity-attracting names, and with the election of Dwight
Eisenhower to the Presidency and the return, after two decades,
of Republicanism to Washington, D.C., the House business of
sleuthing for show business Reds was ebbing.

Shortly after the time of Senator McCarthy's censure by his
peers and his subsequent decline in national prominence, the
committee made a brief 1955 investigation of Communism in
the New York theater. No important publicly known persons
were involved and all but one of the twenty-three witnesses
subpoenaed refused to be intimidated by the committee's
former awesome public image.

The entertainment field, always previously capable of ensur-
ing headlines for the investigators, had run out of big names and
therefore important public relations value for the always
publicity-conscious committee.

In 1956 the committee investigated the right of two prominent show business persons to retain their United States
passports. One, Paul Robeson, was admittedly sympathetic to
Communism and the other, Arthur Miller, a well-credentialed
liberal-intellectual. The committee, deporting itself in a vastly
different manner with each man, had one last brief respite from
publicity oblivion when it engaged in a yelling confrontation
with Robeson.

In June, 1958, the committee closed down its twenty-year investigation of Communism in the entertainment world with an uneventful and hardly publicized examination of a dozen suspect, but unknown by the public, Reds from the New York theater. Names, time, and publicity had run their course for the committee's entertainment investigations and hundreds, perhaps thousands, of careers and lives were changed, wrecked, or destroyed in their wake.

Though little specific evidence was available, I felt that any assessment of the general, probable, and possible effects of the committee's work on the American theater should include the following observations.

With few exceptions, the overwhelming majority of the unfriendly witnesses came ill-advised and ill-prepared for their appearance before the committee. Commencing with Hallie Flanagan in 1938—whose inept testimony can be excused by the fact that she was the first theater notable to be interrogated—through Arthur Miller's 1956 testament, the uncooperative witnesses made no apparent effort to assess the biases and prejudices of their interrogators.

The fact that Lillian Hellman, among a few others, was able not to name names and still avoid taking constitutional refuge clearly indicates that such avenues of testimony were possible. It is also entirely possible that these avenues were not used by the unfriendly witnesses because most of them did not have the financial resources to pursue and prepare the extensive legal advice necessary for such a maneuver.

If one is inclined to believe in a Kremlin- and/or Peking-directed international Communist conspiracy—a conspiracy that was and is fomenting a near domestic violent revolution in twentieth-century America—then it is fair to say that the investigators possibly frightened off this conspiracy. In this context, the above intimidation could then be judged to be a constructive result of the committee's work. However, it is more probable that the major part of the fear produced by the committee's work occurred in liberal rather than Communist circles.

The possibility of opportunism should not be overlooked

when assessing the reasoning behind many artists' decisions to affiliate in one way or another with the CP. From a way to meet girls to being identified with humanitarian causes are only a few of the many possible reasons why a naïve person might have been romanced into Red-oriented or -dominated groups.

With the possible exceptions of John Howard Lawson, Paul Robeson and Roy Huggins, virtually no unfriendly witnesses evidenced any public record of Marxist acumen. Nor did any of the investigators indicate any particular keenness of insight into Communist dogma. Further, the Congressmen certainly made little or no effort to plenish that vacuum when they almost incessantly asked the $64 question concerning CP membership at the outset of the interrogation.

The committee had enough hard evidence to make laws affecting Communists and Communism in the United States, if that was indeed its real intention. However, it is far more probable that the investigators' real interest was, as stated earlier, publicity rather than legislation. Their failure to question carefully the alleged Communists for purposes of eliciting new information about CP activities in the United States is patent throughout the public record of the tribunal.

It is also certain that the committee's activities not only contributed substantially to the demise of the Federal Theatre but probably blunted all theater of the left, a theater that had demonstrated enormous vitality and scope throughout much of the post-World War I period. The drastic change in the social and political nature of the drama before and after World War II is therefore a definite probable result of the committee's efforts.

Finally, this author concludes that the committee, as constituted and procedurally operated since its inception, served so little benefit to the nation compared with its enormous injustices to individuals that it should be abolished from the House investigatory bodies.

Implications

Though I favor the abrogation of the House Committee on

Un-American Activities (currently titled the House Internal Security Committee), I do not hold with that legion of militant thought that believes no assessment of Communist activities in America is necessary.

A new type of bipartisan committee, with a mandate from Congress to examine honestly the historical time factor in the Communist movement in America, could well prove to be an important contribution to the political education of the American public. An education that clearly distinguishes between the real and the imagined internal Communist threat to the nation would be a valuable service to a populace sadly steeped in the Red mythos created by political panderers.

This new type of committee should conduct its hearings in a manner that would evoke the maximum amount of information about domestic Communism with a minimum amount of personal damage to the witnesses. Counsel should have the right at all times to function for their clients as they normally would in a civil court of law. And, most significantly, at no time should the witnesses be placed in the position of incriminating former or present acquaintances for the purpose of soliciting the benevolence of said new committee.

APPENDIX I

The Friendly Witnesses and the Persons They Identified as Communists

This section contains an extensive list of the friendly witnesses and the persons they named as Communists. The list is necessarily incomplete because some testimony given in executive session has never been released.

The information was compiled from the transcripts of the committee's hearings, cumulative indexes and supplements, and its annual reports.

The names of the cooperative witnesses are in alphabetical order with the exception of Martin Berkeley, who appears first for reasons of his role as the number-one friendly witness who provided the committee with the most names, names that were later authenticated by the investigative panel and other witnesses. In addition, Berkeley's documentation was the most thorough of any of the Hollywood attestants.

MARTIN BERKELEY, writer

Appeared September 19, 1951

Appeared in executive, or secret, session in 1953. Testimony not made public.

Sam Albert, musician
Robert Ames, craftworker, movie industry
Louis (Lou) Amster, writer
Mrs. Adelaide Klein Annenberg, actress*
Spencer Austrian, attorney for CP fraction of which Berkeley was a member
Sonora Babb, writer
Ben Barzman, writer (collaborated with Bess Taffel on scripts)
George Bassman, musician-composer
Kay (Mrs. George) Bassman
Leon Becker, musician
Albert Bein, writer
Nicholas (Nick) Bela, writer
Edward Biberman, artist and one of the organizers of the Artists' Union of the WPA Art Project
Sonja Dahl (Mrs. Edward Biberman), actress, secretary of Hollywood

Anti-Nazi League
Herbert J. Biberman, writer-director-producer
Gale Sondergaard (Mrs. Herbert J. Biberman), actress
Leo Bigelman, MD, Los Angeles physician
Henry Blankfort, writer
Laurie (Lorry) Blankfort, writer
Allen Boretz, writer
John Bright, writer
Josephine (Mrs. John) Bright, CP organizer, Los Angeles Mexican-American community
J. Edward (Joe) Bromberg, actor
Goldie (Mrs. J. Edward) Bromberg
Harold Buchman, writer (brother of Sidney Buchman)
Sidney Buchman, writer
Beatrice (Bea) Buchman (Mrs. Sidney Buchman) Beatrice Buchman was active in the Hollywood Anti-Nazi League
Miss Jessie Burns, motion picture studio reader
Hugo Butler, writer
Alan Campbell, writer
Dorothy Parker, writer (Mrs. Alan Campbell)
Harry Carlisle, CP functionary; said to be

*C.f., 1957-58 New York Entertainment Hearings, p. 2536. The committee's staff director, Richard Arens, indicated that Berkeley told the committee Mrs. Annenberg had been a member of the CP.

a former writer and native of Australia

Edward (Ed) Chodorov, writer-producer

Jerome Chodorov, writer

Maurice Clark, writer

Paul Cline, CP functionary, Los Angeles-Hollywood area

Lester Cole, writer

Richard (Dick) Collins, writer

Norvel Crutcher, organizer, Technicians Local, IATSE

Miss Leona D'Ambarey, motion picture studio secretary

Robert (Bob) D'Ambarey, brother of Leona D'Ambarey

Danny Dare, producer-director

Howard da Silva, actor

Howard Dimsdale, writer

Carl Dreher, motion picture studio engineer and technician

Arnaud d'Usseau, writer

Susan Wells (Mrs. Arnaud d'Usseau), head of Communist bookshop

Edward Eliscu, writer

Cyril Endfield, writer-director

Guy Endore, writer

Eve Ettinger, motion picture studio story editor

Francis Faragoh, writer

Mary Virginia Farmer, actress

Carl Foreman, writer-director

Ed Gilbert, motion picture studio set designer

Kelly Gleichman (former husband of Viola Brothers Shore), organizational secretary, Hollywood area CP

Harold Goldman, writer

Kathleen (Mrs. Harold) Goldman

Donald Gordon, motion picture studio reader, assistant story editor

Michael Gordon, director

Jay Gorney, musician-song writer

James (Jimmy) Gow, writer (collaborated with Arnaud d'Usseau on stories)

Morton Grant, writer

Dashiell (Dash) Hammett, writer

Louis (Lou) Harris, publicity writer, later a producer, according to Berkeley's testimony

Vera (Mrs. Lou) Harris

Lillian Hellman, playwright

Irving Paul Hentschel, craftworker member IATSE

Edward (Eddie or Ed) Huebsch, writer

Ian McLellan Hunter, writer

Alice Goldberg (Mrs. Ian Hunter), secretary

Daniel (Dan) Lewis James, writer

Lilith James (Mrs. Daniel L. James), writer

Paul Jarrico, writer

Gordon Kahn, writer

Charles Katz, attorney for CP fraction of which Berkeley was a member

Roland William Kibbee, writer

Jeff Kibre, CP functionary, later an official in the Fishermen's Union

Michael (Mike) Killian, actor

Victor Killian, actor (father of Michael Killian)

Herbert Klein (or Kline), editor of *New Theatre*, later produced documentary films. Not to be confused with Herbert Arthur Klein, former wire-service correspondent, later a teacher, and active in Los Angeles-Hollywood area CP

Lester Koenig, writer-producer

Hyman (Hy) Solomon Kraft, writer

Ring W. Lardner, Jr., writer

Marc Lawrence, actor

Stanley Lawrence, CP functionary, organizer of motion picture studio professionals, former Los Angeles taxicab driver

John (Jack) Howard Lawson, writer

Robert (Bob) Lees, writer

Isobel Lennart, motion picture studio reader, later a screenwriter

Charles Leonard, writer

Alfred Lewis Levitt, writer

Helen Slote (Mrs. Alfred Lewis Levitt), secretary of CP fraction in Actors' Laboratory and also former secretary to actor John Garfield

Melvin (Mel) Levy, writer

Albert Maltz, writer

Arnold Manoff, writer

Allen Matthews, actor

John "Skins" Miller, actor*

Patricia (Mrs. John) Miller

Josef Mischel, writer

Maurice Murphy, actor, CP functionary

Mortimer Offner, writer

Samuel (Sam) Ornitz, writer

Sadie (Mrs. Samuel) Ornitz

Charles Page, writer and former executive secretary, Screen Writers Guild

Matt Pellman (also known as Mike Pell, Max Appelman, Max Appelbaum), CP organizer

Mortimer William (Bill) Pomerance, former business agent, Screen Cartoonists Guild, Local 852, AFL, Painters International; later executive

*"Skins" Miller was formerly a partner in the vaudeville team of Miller and Mack.

secretary, Screen Writers Guild

Gertrude Purcell, writer

Maurice Rapf, writer

Robert (Bob) Reed, member of CP actors' fraction, Federal Theatre Project, New York City

Ann Roth Morgan Richards (Mrs. Robert L. Richards), former assistant executive secretary, Screen Writers' Guild

Frederick (Fred) Rinaldo, writer (collaborated with Robert Lees on scripts)

W. L. River, writer

Marguerite Roberts, writer (Mrs. John Sanford)

Robert B. (Bob) Roberts, producer

Catherine O'Neal (Mrs. Robert B. Roberts)

Wayne Ronka, musician

Robert Rossen, writer-director-producer

Madelaine Ruthven, ex-writer, CP tunctionary, organizational secretary for Hollywood section CP

Lee Sabinson, motion picture studio reader, later a Broadway producer

Frances Sage, actress

Waldo Salt, writer

John Sanford, writer

Budd Wilson Schulberg, writer

Mrs. Virginia Schulberg (former wife of Budd W. Schulberg; later Mrs. Peter Viertel)

Eva Shafran, CP educational director, Los Angeles-Hollywood

Victor (Vic) Shapiro, publicist

Viola Brothers Shore, writer

Wilma Shore, writer (daughter of Viola Brothers Shore and wife of Louis [Lou] Solomon)

George Sklar, writer

Lionel Stander, actor

Alice Twitchell (the former Mrs. Lionel Stander)

Donald Ogden Stewart, writer

Arthur Strawn, writer

Elliott (Ely) Sullivan, actor

Bess Taffel, writer

Shepard Traube, theatrical director-producer

Paul Trivers, writer

Dalton Trumbo, writer

Frank Wright Tuttle, director

Tania (Mrs. Frank W.) Tuttle (Berkeley referred to her as "Sonia" in his testimony.)

Herta Uerkvitz, motion picture studio architectural researcher

Michael H. (Mickey) Uris, writer

Dorothy Tree, actress (Mrs. Michael H. Uris)

Bernard Vorhaus, director

John Weber, agent

Richard Weil, writer

John Wexley, writer

Irving J. White, radio writer-director

George Willner, writers' agent

Tiba (Mrs. George) Willner

CHARLOTTE DARLING ADAMS, former secretary, Screen Cartoonists' Guild, Local 852, AFL, Painters' International

Appeared March 26 and June 2, 1953

Cecil Beard, cartoonist

Edward Biberman, artist

Sam Cloner, studio laborer

Norval Crutcher, organizer, Technicians' Local, IATSE

Frank Drdlik, set designer

Eugene Strong Fleury, artist and art instructor

Bernyce Polifka Fleury, artist and teacher (Mrs. Eugene Fleury)

Ed Gilbert, set designer

Donald Gordon, motion picture studio reader, assistant story editor

David Hilberman, cartoonist

Libby (Mrs. David) Hilberman

Maurice Howard, succeeded M. William Pomerance as business agent, Screen Cartoonists Guild.

Evelyn (Mrs. Maurice) Howard

John Hubley, cartoonist

Jeff Kibre, CP organizer, motion picture studios

Phil Klein, cartoonist

Joe Kromberger, studio electrician

Kate Lawson (Mrs. John Howard Lawson)

Hank Morley, laboratory technician

Mary Nolan (Mrs. Frank Nolan)

Paul Robert Perlin, motion picture studio worker

Henry Peterson, motion picture studio carpenter, son of:

Hjalmar Peterson, also a motion picture studio carpenter

Mortimer William (Bill) Pomerance, former business agent, Screen Cartoonists Guild, Local 852, AFL Painters International, later executive secretary, Screen Writers Guild

Edwina (Mrs. M. William) Pomerance

Naomi Robeson, ex-actress, CP functionary

Zachary Schwartz, cartoonist, later an artist and designer of TV advertising

MORRIS L. APPELMAN, CP functionary

Appeared January 10, 1952

John Howard Lawson, writer

Charles Page
Polly (Mrs. Charles) Page
HAROLD J. ASHE, magazine writer, CP functionary

Appeared September 17, 1951

Mildred Ashe, his former wife
John Broman, CP name for Jack Wilson
Charles Daggett, newspaperman
Will Geer, actor
Louis (Lou) Harris, publicity writer
Vera (Mrs. Lou) Harris
Jeff Kibre, Fishermen's Union, San Pedro
Virginia (Mrs. Jeff) Kibre
Herbert (Herb) Arthur Klein, former wire-service correspondent in Germany (not to be confused with the editor of *New Theatre*)
Minna (Mrs. Herbert A.) Klein
Stanley Lawrence, CP functionary, organizer of motion picture studio professionals, ex-Los Angeles taxicab driver
John Howard Lawson, writer
John Leech, writer, CP functionary
Ralph Smith, set designer
Lionel Stander, actor (CP name, J. or Jay Stander)
Lucy Stander (formerly Mrs. Lionel Stander)
Tania (Mrs. Frank W.) Tuttle. Ashe indicated that the wife of the director was also a CP functionary.
Rena Vale, WPA Writers' Project

MILDRED ASHE, CP functionary, former wife of Harold J. Ashe

Appeared September 17, 1951

Harold J. Ashe, ex-husband
John Bright, writer
John Broman (real name John "Jack" Wilson), newspaperman
Charles Daggett, newspaperman
Carl Dreher, motion picture studio engineer and technician
Mary Virginia Farmer, actress, held high position in Federal Theatre Project
Louis (Lou) Harris, publicist
Vera (Mrs. Lou) Harris
Jeff Kibre, CP functionary
Virginia (Mrs. Jeff) Kibre
Herbert (Herb) Arthur Klein, former wire-service correspondent, later a teacher
Minna (Mrs. Herbert A.) Klein
John Leech, writer, CP functionary
Arnold Manoff, writer
Walter McElroy, writer
Lionel Stander, actor

Lucy Stander, former wife of Lionel Stander

LEOPOLD LAWRENCE ATLAS, writer

Appeared March 12, 1953

Lewis Allen, playwright
Ben Barzman, writer
Ben Bengal, writer
Leonardo Bercovici, writer
Alvah Bessie, writer
Mrs. Alvah Bessie
Herbert J. Biberman, writer-director-producer
Tom Chapman, motion picture studio reader
Clarice (Mrs. Tom) Chapman
Johnny Cole
Lester Cole, writer
Guy Endore, writer
Ann Froelich, writer
Lester Fuller, director-writer
Gertrude (Mrs. Lester) Fuller
Morton Grant, writer
Elizabeth (Betty, Mrs. Morton) Grant
Anne Green, writer (Mrs. Howard Koch)
Gordon Kahn, writer
John Howard Lawson, writer
Alfred Lewis Levitt, writer
Melvin (Mel) Levy, writer
Albert Maltz, writer
Arnold Manoff, writer
Abraham Lincoln (Abe) Polonsky, writer-director
Ann Roth Morgan Richards, former assistant executive secretary Screen Writers Guild (Mrs. Robert L. Richards)
Marguerite (Maggie) Roberts, writer (Mrs. John Sanford)
Naomi Robeson, ex-actress, CP functionary
John Sanford, writer
Victor (Vic) Shapiro, publicist
Phillip (Phil) Edward Stevenson, writer
Arthur Strawn, writer
Bess Taffel, writer
Dalton Trumbo, writer
Mrs. John Weber
George Willner, writers' agent
Elizabeth (Betty) Wilson, writer (Betty Anderson; Mrs. Richard Wilson)

GEORGE BASSMAN, musician-composer

Appeared January 28, 1952

Sonora Babb, writer
Martin Berkeley, writer
Victor (Vic) Shapiro, publicist

GEORGE BECK, writer

Appeared September 25, 1951

Lester Cole, writer
Richard Collins, writer
Ann Froelich, writer
Morton Grant, writer
Elizabeth (Mrs. Morton) Grant
Louis (Lou) Harris, publicist
John Howard Lawson, writer
Albert Maltz, writer
Arnold Manoff, writer
Mortimer Offner, writer
Madelaine Ruthven, CP functionary, ex-writer
John Sanford, writer
Leo Townsend, writer
Dalton Trumbo, writer
Frank Wright Tuttle, director
John Wexley, writer
George Willner, writers' agent
Mrs. Elizabeth (Betty) Wilson, writer (Mrs. Richard Wilson)

NICHOLAS (NICK) BELA, actor-writer-director

Appeared December 14, 1954

Dorothy Babb
Sonora Babb, writer
Ben Barzman, writer
Martin Berkeley, writer
Edward Biberman, artist
Sonja Dahl, actress (Mrs. Edward Biberman)
Herbert J. Biberman, writer-director-producer
Thomas (Tom) Brandon, CP organizer and operator of Brandon Films, New York City
J. (Joe) Edward Bromberg
Miss Jessie Burns, motion picture studio reader
Lester Cole, writer
Richard Collins, writer
Dorothy Comingore, actress (Mrs. Michael H. Uris)
Carl Dreher, motion picture studio engineer and technician
Rose (Mrs. Carl) Dreher
Arnaud d'Usseau, writer
Edward (Ed) Eliscu, writer
Stella (Mrs. Edward) Eliscu
Guy Endore, writer
Mary Virginia Farmer, actress
James (Jimmy) Gow, writer (collaborated on scripts with Arnaud d'Usseau)
Edward (Ed) Huebsch, writer
Paul Jarrico, writer
Gordon Kahn, writer
Marc Lawrence, actor

John Howard Lawson, writer
Robert Lees, writer
Isobel Lennart, writer
Albert Maltz, writer
Margaret (Mrs. Albert) Maltz
Mortimer Offner, writer-director
Samuel (Sam) Ornitz, writer
Gertrude Purcell, writer
Maurice Rapf, writer
Frederick (Fred) Rinaldo, writer
Mrs. Meta Reis Rosenberg, former head of literary department, motion picture talent agency, Hollywood
Robert Rossen, writer-director-producer
Lee Sabinson, Broadway producer
Waldo Salt, writer
Budd W. Schulberg, writer
Martha Solomon, poet
Elliott (Ely) Sullivan, actor
Herta Uerkvitz, motion picture studio reader
George Willner, writers' agent

MAX NATHAN BENOFF, writer

Appeared March 24, 1953

Richard Collins, writer
Paul Jarrico, writer
Gordon Kahn, writer
Ring W. Lardner, Jr., writer
John Howard Lawson, writer
Albert Maltz, writer
Robert Rossen, writer-director-producer
Dalton Trumbo, writer

MILDREN (MRS. MAX N.) BENOFF

Appeared February 17, 1953

Elena (Mrs. George) Beck
Marie (Mrs. Frederick) Rinaldo
Mrs. Pauline S. Townsend, writer (Mrs. Leo Townsend)
Tania (Mrs. Frank W.) Tuttle

WILLIAM FRANK BLOWITZ, publicist

Appeared September 20, 1951

Alvah Bessie, writer
Lester Cole, writer
Mrs. Lester Cole
Elizabeth Leech Glenn, CP functionary
Morton Grant, writer
John Howard Lawson, writer
Mrs. John Howard Lawson

LLOYD BRIDGES, actor

Appeared October 22, 1951

Self (The actor furnished the committee with "an executive sworn statement, testifying fully as to his former Communist Party membership. It has not been made public.")*

LOUIS F. BUDENZ, editor-writer

Appeared January 15, 1952

Michael Seymour Blankfort, writer ("appeared before committee January 28, 1952 and denied Communist Party membership; still under investigation."**)
Mike Gold, author

MRS. CARIN KINZEL BURROWS† (MRS. ABE BURROWS), actress-writer-director

Appeared May 5, 1953

Harmon (Hy) Alexander, radio writer
Georgia Backus, actress (Mrs. Hy Alexander)
Henry Blankfort, writer
Angela Clarke
Mrs. Pauline Lauber Finn, executive secretary, Hollywood Writers Mobilization
Charles Glenn, writer, CP functionary
Elaine Gonda, in charge of radio transcription company (Mrs. Charles Glenn)
Annette Harper, radio actress
Dwight Hauser, radio writer-director
Pauline Hopkins, radio writer (Mrs. Owen Vinson)
Nina (or Anna) Klowden, radio actress
Mitchell Lindeman, radio director, associate producer
Leon Meadows
Sam Moore, radio writer
Silvia Richards, writer
Reuben Ship, radio and screen writer
Robin Short, CP radio group, Hollywood
Eugene R. Stone, radio writer
Lynn Whitney, actress

LEE J. COBB, actor

Appeared June 2, 1953

Phoebe Brand, actress (Mrs. Morris Carnovsky)
Lloyd Bridges, actor

*U.S. Congress, House Committee on Un-American Activities, *Annual Report for the Year 1952*, Eighty-second Congress, Second Session, p. 40.

**1952 *Annual Report, op. cit.*, p. 68.
†It is interesting to note that the committee did not query Mrs. Burrows about her husband's relationship with the CP; neither did Mrs. Burrows vouchsafe any comments, according to the transcript of her testimony.

Morris Carnovsky, actor
Jeff Corey, actor
Ludwig Donath, actor
Rose Hobart, actress
Victor Killian, actor
Marc Lawrence, actor
John Howard Lawson, writer
Peter (Pete) Lyons, radio writer
Arnold Manoff, writer
Larry Parks, actor
Robert (Bob) Reed, actor
Anne Revere, actress
Shimen Ruskin, actor
Gerry Schlein, actress (Mrs. Charles Schlein)
Gale Sondergaard, actress (Mrs. Herbert J. Biberman)
Elliott (Ely) Sullivan, actor
Dorothy Tree, actress (Mrs. Michael H. Uris)
George Tyne, actor

RICHARD J. (DICK) COLLINS, writer

Appeared April 12, 1951

Leonardo Bercovici, writer
Martin Berkeley, writer
Herbert Blaché
Mrs. Herbert Blaché
John Bright, writer
Lester Cole, writer
Mrs. Pauline Lauber Finn, executive secretary, Hollywood Writers Mobilization
Charles Glenn, writer, CP functionary
Elizabeth Leech Glenn, CP functionary (Mrs. Charles Glenn)
Nora (Mrs. George) Hallgren, CP functionary
Paul Jarrico, writer
Gordon Kahn, writer
Ring W. Lardner, Jr., writer
John Howard Lawson, writer
Albert Maltz, writer
Samuel (Sam) Ornitz, writer
Abraham Lincoln (Abe) Polonsky, writer-director
Robert Rossen, writer-director-producer
Madelaine Ruthven, CP functionary
Waldo Salt, writer
Ambur Dana, secretary (Mrs. Waldo Salt)
Budd Wilson Schulberg, writer
Frank Wright Tuttle, director

CHARLES DAGGETT,* newspaperman

Appeared January 21, 1952

Harold J. Asche, magazine writer, CP functionary
Ben Barzman, writer
William Frank Blowitz, publicist

*Daggett named a number of newspapermen, several attorneys, and others as members of the CP in the Los Angeles-Hollywood area, but they were not in the show-business fractions of the CP.

John (Jack) Broman (also known as John [Jack] Wilson), newspaperman
Morris Carnovsky, actor
Miss Urcel Daniel, newspaperwoman
George Glass, motion picture publicist
Jay Gorney, musician-song writer
Sondra (Mrs. Jay) Gorney
Paul Jarrico, writer
Gordon Kahn, writer
Herbert Arthur (Herb) Klein, former wire-service correspondent, teacher
Minna (Mrs. Herbert A.) Klein
Ring W. Lardner, Jr., writer
Henry Meyers, writer
Karen Morley, actress (Mrs. Lloyd Gough)
Larry Parks, actor
Abraham Lincoln (Abe) Polonsky, writer-director
Lucy (Mrs. Lionel) Stander
George Thomas, Jr., publicist
Leo Townsend, writer
Dalton Trumbo, writer
Robert Wachsman, publicist

MISS URCEL DANIEL,* newspaperwoman

Appeared July 8, 1952

Lou Amster, writer
Charles N. Judson, newspaperman
Herbert Arthur (Herb) Klein, former newspaperman, teacher
Minna (Mrs. Herbert) Klein

DANNY DARE, producer-director

Appeared March 23, 1953

Herbert J. Biberman, writer-director-producer
Jessie Burns, motion picture studio reader
Mrs. Pauline Lauber Finn, executive secretary, Hollywood Writers Mobilization
John Howard Lawson, writer
Ray E. Spencer, writer
Tanya (Mrs. Frank W.) Tuttle
Irving J. White, radio writer, director

THOMAS F. DELANEY, organizer, Local 155, UE (United Electrical Workers)

Appeared October 13, 1952

Howard Fast, author and writer, New York City

EDWARD DMYTRYK, director

Appeared October 29, 1947, and refused to answer questions concerning Communist Party membership.

*Miss Daniel named a number of newspapermen and other persons as members of the CP, but they were not in the show-business sector of the CP.

Appeared again April 25, 1951, and testified freely about former party membership

Leonardo Bercovici, writer
John (Jack) Berry, director
Alvah Bessie, writer
Herbert J. Biberman, writer-director-producer
Henry Blankfort, writer
Maurice Clark, writer
Lester Cole, writer
Richard Collins, writer
George Corey, writer
Mrs. George Corey, department store advertising executive
Jules Dassin, director
Francis Faragoh, writer
Elizabeth (Mrs. Francis) Faragoh
Michael Gordon, director
Gordon Kahn, writer
John Howard Lawson, writer
Albert Maltz, writer
Arnold Manoff, writer
Sam Moore, radio writer
George Pepper, executive secretary, Hollywood Council of Arts, Sciences, and Professions
Adrian Scott, writer-producer
Paul Trivers, writer
Frank Wright Tuttle, director
Michael H. Uris, writer
Bernard Vorhaus, director
John Wexley, writer

ROY ERWIN, writer

Appeared March 13, 1953

Harmon (Hy) Alexander, radio writer
Georgia Backus, actress (Mrs. Hy Alexander)
Harry Carlisle, writer, CP functionary
Bert Cooper, radio
Dwight Hauser, radio writer-director
Pauline Hopkins, radio writer (Mrs. Owen Vinson)
Nina Klowden, radio actress (also known as Anna)
Paul McVey, radio actor
Sam Moore, radio writer
Karen Morley, actress (Mrs. Lloyd Gough)
Ben Pollin, photographer for radio network
John Rapf, radio
Jack Robinson, radio writer
Mary Robinson, radio writer (Mrs. Jack Robinson)
Owen Vinson, radio director
Herman Waldreen, radio actor (also known as Herman Waldman and David Wolfe)
Lynn Whitney, actress

EVE ETTINGER, motion picture studio story editor

Appeared September 10, 1951

Nicholas (Nick) Bela, actor-writer-director
Martin Berkeley, writer
Lester Fuller, writer-director
Lee Sabinson, Broadway producer

MISS RUTH FISCHER, sister of Hans and Gerhart Eisler

Gerhart Eisler
Hans Eisler, composer-musician

MRS. BERNYCE POLIFKA FLEURY, artist (Mrs. Eugene Fleury)

Appeared September 24, 1951

Edward (Ed) Biberman, artist
Eugene Strong Fleury, her husband
David Hilberman, cartoonist
Mortimer William Pomerance, former business agent, Screen Cartoonists Guild, Local 852, AFL Painters International, later executive secretary, Screen Writers Guild

EUGENE STRONG FLEURY, artist-art instructor

Appeared September 10, 1951

Bernyce P. Fleury, his wife
David Hilberman, cartoonist
Libby (Mrs. David) Hilberman
John McGrew, animator
Mortimer William Pomerance, former business agent, Screen Cartoonists Guild, Local 852, AFL Painters International, later executive secretary, Screen Writers Guild

ANNE RAY FRANK, writer (Mrs. Melvin Frank) (sister of Virginia Schulberg Viertel)
Appeared September 10, 1951

Harold Buchman, writer
Richard (Dick) Collins, writer
Paul Jarrico, writer
Gordon Kahn, writer
Ring W. Lardner, Jr., writer
John Howard Lawson, writer
Albert Maltz, writer
Mrs. Meta Reis Rosenberg, head of literary department Hollywood motion picture talent agency
Robert Rossen, writer-director-producer
Dalton Trumbo, writer

CHARLES H. GARRIGUES, newspaperman

Appeared March 27, 1953

Lou Amster, writer
Libby Burke, dancer
Miss Urcel Daniel, newspaperwoman
Minna (Mrs. Herbert A.) Klein (Garrigues identified her as a writer)

Tom O'Connor, newspaperman
William E. (Bill) Oliver, newspaperman, drama critic
Ed Robbins, newspaperman

GEORGE GLASS, motion picture publicist and producer

Appeared January 21, 1952

Ben Barzman, writer
Charles Daggett, newspaperman
Jay Gorney, musician-song writer
Gordon Kahn, writer
Ring W. Lardner, Jr., writer
Henry Meyers, writer
Abraham Lincoln (Abe) Polonsky, writer-director
Janet Stevenson, writer (Mrs. Philip Edward Stevenson)
Leo Townsend, writer

JULIAN GORDON, former motion picture technician; later worked for independent motion picture producer making stock and accessories

Appeared March 24, 1953

Self; as former Communist and president and one of the founders of the Communist Club of Hollywood. Did not name any other members of the CP

GEORGE HALL, actor

Appeared August 17, 1955

Sarah Cunningham, actress (Mrs. John Randolph)
Irma Jurist, composer
David Kanter, assistant stage manager
George Keane, actor
Betty Winkler, actress (Mrs. George Keane)
Alan Manson, actor
John Randolph, actor
Joshua Shelley, actor

DWIGHT HAUSER, radio writer-director

Appeared March 30, 1953

Harmon (Hy) Alexander, radio writer
Georgia Backus, actress (Mrs. Hy Alexander)
Henry Blankfort, writer
Abram (Abe) Burrows, writer
Carin Kinzel Burrows, actress-writer-director (Mrs. Abe Burrows)
Roy Erwin, writer
Annette Harper, radio actress
Nina (or Anna) Klowden, radio actress

Paul Marion, actor
Paul McVey, radio actor
Sam Moore, radio writer
Naomi Robeson, ex-actress, CP functionary
Owen Vinson, director of radio programs
Murray Wagner, radio actor and announcer (also spelled "Murry")
Lynn Whitney, actress

STERLING HAYDEN, actor

Appeared April 10, 1951

Robert Lees, writer
Karen Morley, actress (Mrs. Lloyd Gough)
Maurice Murphy, actor
Abraham Lincoln (Abe) Polonsky, writer-director
Bernadette (Bea) Winters, secretary at Hollywood talent and literary agency, later secretary to a producer

HAROLD ADOLPH HECHT, producer

Appeared March 23, 1953

Martin Berkeley, writer
Edward Biberman, artist
Herbert J. Biberman, writer-director-producer
Gale Sondergaard, actress (Mrs. Herbert J. Biberman)
John Bright, writer
Gordon Kahn, writer
Roland William Kibbee, writer
John Howard Lawson, writer
Melvin (Mel) Levy, writer
Albert Maltz, writer
Gertrude Purcell, writer
Mrs. Meta Reis Rosenberg, head of literature department of Hollywood motion picture talent agency
Madelaine Ruthven, CP functionary, ex-writer
Budd Wilson Schulberg, writer
Frank Wright Tuttle, director
Elizabeth Wilson, writer (Mrs. Richard Wilson; Betty Anderson)

Hecht named the following as having held membership in the CP and described them as "aspiring actors and actresses" in the Federal Theatre Project:

Georgia Burns
Rose Pearson
Trudy Peck
Robert Sloan

LEROY TRAVERS HERNDON, JR.,

teacher; assigned by CP to Hollywood Professional Section CP

Appeared March 27, 1953

Anne Kinney (CP name Jane Howe), CP member-at-large

ROY HUGGINS, writer-producer

Appeared September 29, 1952

Ellenore (Mrs. Murray) Abowitz*
Murray Abowitz, MD*
Ben Barzman, writer
Norma Barzman, writer (Mrs. Ben Barzman)
Val Burton, writer
Harry Carlisle, CP functionary
Howard Davis, optometrist
Leslie (Les) Edgley, writer
Guy Endore, writer
Elliott Grennard, writer
Lilith James, writer
Robert Lees, writer
Albert Maltz, writer
Robert L. Richards, writer
Ann Roth Morgan (Mrs. Robert L.) Richards, former assistant executive secretary, Screen Writers Guild
Wilma Shore, writer
George Sklar, writer
Janet Stevenson, writer (Mrs. Philip E. Stevenson)
Philip Edward Stevenson, writer

LEON JANNEY, actor

Appeared February 13, 1952

Self

("Janney appeared in executive session and testified fully as to his former membership in the Communist Party. It has not been made public." **

MANNING JOHNSON, former FBI agent

Paul Robeson, singer-actor

CHARLES W. JUDSON,[†] newspaperman

*Testimony of a number of witnesses revealed that Dr. and Mrs. Abowitz were active in CP show-business activities in Hollywood, as were many other business and professional men and women from the Greater Los Angeles area.

**1952 Annual Report, op. cit., p. 41.

† Judson, a former member of the CP, named a number of other newspapermen and CP functionaries who were not in the show-business sector of CP activities.

Appeared January 26, 1952

 Charles Daggett, newspaperman
 Miss Urcel Daniel, newspaperwoman
 Charles H. Garrigues, newspaperman
 Herbert Arthur (Herb) Klein, former
   wire-service correspondent, teacher
 Minna (Mrs. Herbert A.) Klein

ELIA KAZAN, director

Appeared April 10, 1952

 Sid Benson (also known as Ted Well-
   man), CP functionary
 Phoebe Brand, actress (Mrs. Morris Car-
   novsky)
 J. Edward Bromberg, actor
 Morris Carnovsky, actor
 Anne Howe, executive secretary Con-
   temporary Theatre and former of-
   ficial in the League of Workers' Thea-
   tres
 Tony Kraber, actor
 Lewis Leverett, actor
 Paula Miller, actress (the former Mrs. Lee
   Straskey)
 Clifford Odets, writer
 Robert (Bob) Reed, actor
 Art Smith, actor

FRED KEATING, actor

Appeared July 19, 1951

 Self

("Keating appeared in executive session and
testified fully as to his former membership
in the Communist Party. It has not been
made public."*)

ROLAND WILLIAM KIBBEE, writer

Appeared June 2, 1953

 George Bassman, musician-composer
 Herbert J. Biberman, writer-director-
   producer
 John Bright, writer
 Harold Buchman, writer
 Richard Collins, writer
 Arnaud d'Usseau, writer
 James (Jimmy) Gow, writer
 Louis (Lou) Harris, publicity writer
 Jeff Kibre, CP organizer, motion picture
   studios
 Ring W. Lardner, Jr., writer
 John Howard Lawson, writer
 Maurice Murphy, actor
 Samuel (Sam) Ornitz, writer

* *1952 Annual Report, op. cit.,* p. 41.

 Maurice Rapf, writer
 Waldo Salt, writer
 Paul Trivers, writer
 Elizabeth Wilson, writer (Mrs. Richard
   Wilson; Betty Anderson)

MISS ANNE KINNEY (CP name Jane
Howe), CP member-at-large

Appeared December 22, 1952

 Ellenore Abowitz (Mrs. Murray Abo-
   witz)
 Harold J. Ashe, magazine writer, CP
   functionary
 Mildred Ashe, CP functionary, (the
   former Mrs. Harold J. Ashe)
 John Bevins, motion picture studio
   worker
 Howland Chamberlin, actor
 Leona McGinty (Mrs. Howland Cham-
   berlin)
 Bea Burke, writer
 Miss Urcel Daniel, newspaperwoman
 Charles A. (Brick) Garrigues, newspaper-
   man
 Julian Gordon, former motion picture
   technician
 Carl Grant
 Ann Howe, executive secretary of Con-
   temporary Theatre
 Barta Humouna, teacher, active in Con-
   temporary Theatre
 Libby Jacobson
 Herbert Arthur (Herb) Klein, ex-
   correspondent
 Minna (Mrs. Herbert A.) Klein
 John Leech, CP functionary, writer
 Elizabeth Leech, CP functionary
 Bella Lewitsky, dancer (Mrs. Newell
   Reynolds)
 Jay Moss
 Ed Robbins, newspaperman
 Jack Wetherwax
 Jane Wilson (also known as Jane Wal-
   lace), CP functionary (Mrs. John
   [Jack] Wilson)
 Dolph Winebrenner, newspaperman

BABBETTE LANG (Mrs. David A. Lang),
secretary

Appeared June 2, 1953

 David A. Lang, her husband, writer
 Russell William Burnstein, motion pic-
   ture studio engineer
 Clare (Mrs. Russell W.) Burnstein
 Guy Endore
 Henriette (Mrs. Guy) Endore
 Carl Foreman, writer-director
 Estelle (Mrs. Carl) Foreman

Catherine Larkin (sister of Margaret Maltz)
Jean (Mrs. Robert) Lees
Charles Leonard, writer
Helen (Mrs. Charles) Leonard
Albert Maltz, writer
Margaret (Mrs. Albert) Maltz
Eunice Mindlin, motion picture studio secretary
Ann Roth Morgan (Mrs. Stephen Morgan, later Ann Roth Morgan Richards), former assistant executive secretary, Screen Writers Guild
Stephen (Steve) Morgan, CP contact man, Hollywood (deceased)
Samuel (Sam) Ornitz, writer
Sadie (Mrs. Samuel) Ornitz
Estelle (Mrs. Oscar) Saul
Viola Brothers Shore, writer
Esther Jerry Wagner, radio announcer
George Willner, writers' agent
Tiba (Mrs. George) Willner
Michael Wilson, writer, CP functionary

DAVID A. LANG, writer

Appeared March 24, 1953

Sol Barzman, writer
George Bassman, musician-composer
Nicholas (Nick) Bela, writer
Max Nathan Benoff, writer
Connie Lee Bennett, writer
Seymour Bennett, writer
Alvah Bessie, writer
Edward Biberman, artist
Arthur Birnkrant, writer
Henry Blankfort, writer
Laurie (Lorry) Blankfort
William Frank Blowitz, publicist
Allen Boretz, writer
John Bright, writer
Harold Buchman, writer
Val Burton, writer
Hugo Butler, writer
Maurice Clark, writer
Lester Cole, writer
Richard Collins, writer
Dorothy Comingore, actress
Paul Curtiss
Howard Dimsdale, writer
Arnaud d'Usseau, writer
Edward Eliscu, writer
Cyril Endfield, director
Guy Endore, writer
Carl Foreman, writer
Estelle (Mrs. Carl) Foreman
Morton Grant, writer
Elliott Grennard, writer
Edward (Ed) Huebsch, writer

Daniel Lewis (Dan) James, writer
Paul Jarrico, writer
Gordon Kahn, writer
Lester Koenig, writer-producer
Pauline Lagerfin, writer
Millard Lampell, writer
Ring W. Lardner, Jr., writer
John Howard Lawson, writer
Isobel Lennart, writer
Charles Leonard, writer
Helen (Mrs. Charles) Leonard
Alfred Lewis Levitt, writer
Arnold Manoff, writer
Henriette (Henrietta) Martin, writer
Henry Meyers, writer
Eunice Mindlin, studio secretary
Stephen (Steve) Morgan, CP contact man, Hollywood
Mortimer Offner, writer
Samuel (Sam) Ornitz, writer
Maurice Rapf, writer
W. L. River, writer
Marguerite Roberts, writer
Robert B. (Bob) Roberts, producer
Robert Rossen, writer-director-producer
Louise Rousseau, writer
Madelaine Ruthven, CP functionary, ex-writer
Waldo Salt, writer
Adrian Scott, writer-producer
Victor Shapiro, publicist
Wilma Shore, writer
George Sklar, writer
Joseph (Joe) Solomon, writer
Louis (Lou) Solomon, writer
John Stanford, writer
Bess Taffel, writer
Frank Tarloff, writer
Paul Trabusis, writer
Paul Trivers, writer
Dalton Trumbo, writer
Michael H. Uris, writer
John Wexley, writer
Michael Wilson, writer, CP functionary
Julian Zimet, writer

MARC LAWRENCE, actor

Appeared April 24, 1951

J. Edward Bromberg, actor
Morris Carnovsky, actor
Lester Cole, writer
Richard (Dick) Collins, writer
Jeff Corey, actor
Howard da Silva, actor
Lloyd Gough, actor
Karen Morley, (Mrs. Lloyd Gough)
Sterling Hayden, actor
Gordon Kahn, writer

Larry Parks, actor
Anne Revere, actress
Robert Rossen, writer-director-producer
Lionel Stander, actor

ISOBEL LENNART, writer

Appeared May 20, 1952

Martin Berkeley, writer
Alvah Bessie, writer
Herbert J. Biberman, writer-director-producer
Henry Blankfort, writer
J. (Joe) Edward Bromberg, actor
Miss Jessie Burns, motion picture studio reader
Lester Cole, writer
Elizabeth Leech Glenn, CP functionary
George Hallgren, studio employee
Nora (Mrs. George) Hallgren, CP functionary
Paul Jarrico, writer
Gordon Kahn, writer
Roland William Kibbee, writer
John Howard Lawson, writer
Albert Maltz, writer
Maurice Murphy, actor
Madelaine Ruthven, CP functionary, ex-writer
George Sklar, writer
George Willner, agent
Tiba (Mrs. George) Willner
Elizabeth (Betty) Wilson, writer (Mrs. Richard Wilson; Betty Anderson)

MELVIN (MEL) LEVY. writer

Appeared January 28, 1952

Martin Berkeley, writer
William Frank Blowitz, publicist
Lester Cole, writer
Carl Foreman, writer-director
Edward Huebsch, writer
Alfred Lewis Levitt, writer
Mortimer Offner, writer
George Willner, writers' agent
Elizabeth (Betty) Wilson, writer (Mrs. Richard Wilson)

BART LYTTON, writer, later head of a savings and loan company bearing his name

Appeared March 25 and 26, 1953

George Beck, writer
Maurice Clark, writer
Elizabeth Leech Glenn, CP functionary, writer
Jay Gorney, musician-song writer
Daniel Lewis (Dan) James, writer
Lilith James, writer (Mrs. Dan James)
John Howard Lawson, writer

Stanley Prager, actor-writer
Ann Roth Morgan Richards, former assistant executive secretary, Screen Writers Guild
John Wexley, writer

EDITH MACIA, undercover agent, FBI, Los Angeles area

Appeared March 28, 1953

Harold Demsdale, writer
Charles Ellis (name changed to Charles Stone), radio actor-writer
Shirley Ellis (Mrs. Charles Ellis)

PAUL MARION, actor

Appeared October 2, 1952

Harmon (Hy) Alexander, radio writer
Georgia Backus, actress (Mrs. Hy Alexander)
Jeff Corey, actor
Ellen Davidson, ex-actress
Charles Glenn, writer, CP functionary
Lloyd Gough, actor
Karen Morley, actress (Mrs. Lloyd Gough)
Margaret Gruen, writer
Alvin Hammer, actor
Annette Harper, radio actress
Pauline Hopkins, radio writer (Mrs. Owen Vinson)
Paul Jarrico, writer
Nina (or Anna) Klowden, radio actress
Marc Lawrence, actor
Mitchell Lindeman, radio director, associate producer
Edwin Miller Max, actor
Sam Moore, radio writer
Benjamin (Ben) Polin, photographer for radio network
Jack Robinson, radio writer
Mary Robinson, radio writer (Mrs. Jack Robinson)
Arthur (Art) Shapiro, radio writer or publicist
Reuben Ship, radio and screen writer
Eugene R. Stone, radio writer
Owen Vinson, radio director
Herman Waldreen, (also known as Herman Waldman and David Wolfe) radio actor
Stanley Waxman, actor and radio announcer
Irving J. White, radio writer-director; playwright; screen writer
Lynn Whitney, actress
William (Billy) Wolff, radio writer

HARVEY NARCISENFELD

Appeared November 12, 1952,

> Jody Gilbert, actress

CLIFFORD ODETS (deceased), writer-director

Appeared May 19 and 20, 1952

> Sid Benson (also known as Ted Wellman), CP functionary
> Phoebe Brand, actress (Mrs. Morris Carnovsky)
> J. Edward Bromberg, actor*
> Elia Kazan, director
> Tony Kraber, actor
> Lewis Leverett, actor

LARRY PARKS, actor

Appeared March 21, 1951. Additional executive testimony released in 1953

> Roman Bohnan, actor
> J. Edward Bromberg, actor
> Morris Carnovsky, actor
> Lee J. Cobb, actor
> Lloyd Gough, actor
> Victor Killian, actor
> John Howard Lawson, writer
> Karen Morley, actress
> Anne Revere, actress   /
> Sam Rosen
> Gale Sondergaard, actress (Mrs. Herbert J. Biberman)
> Dorothy Tree, actress (Mrs. Michael H. Uris)

GERTRUDE PURCELL, writer

Appeared April 8, 1953

> Herbert J. Biberman, writer-director-producer

PAUL BENEDICT RADIN,** radio-TV agent

Appeared March 12, 1953

> Lester Cole, writer
> Richard Collins, writer
> Jay Gorney, musician-song writer
> Sondra (Mrs. Jay) Gorney
> Joseph Losey, director †

Mrs. Joseph Losey
Mrs. Meta Reis Rosenberg, head of literary department, Hollywood motion picture talent agency
Waldo Salt, writer
Leo Townsend, writer
Pauline Swanson Townsend, writer (Mrs. Leo Townsend)
John Weber, agent
John Wexley, writer

DAVID RAKSIN, composer

Appeared September 20, 1951

> Mischa Altman, musician
> Herbert J. Biberman, writer-director-producer
> Leo Bigelman, MD
> Richard Collins, writer
> Bernice Fraser
> Paul Jarrico, writer
> John Howard Lawson, writer
> Madelaine Ruthven, ex-writer, CP functionary
> Waldo Salt, writer
> Budd Wilson Schulberg, writer
> Frank Wright Tuttle, director

SILVIA RICHARDS, writer

Appeared March 25, 1953

> Harmon (Hy) Alexander, writer, radio
> Georgia Backus, actress (Mrs. Hy Alexander)
> Lewis Allen, playwright
> Mrs. Lewis Allen
> Carin Kinzel Burrows, actress-writer-director (Mrs. Abe Burrows)
> Edward Chodorov, writer
> Howard Dimsdale, writer
> Charles Glenn, writer, CP functionary
> Lee Gold, writer
> Pauline Hopkins, radio writer
> Tamara Hovey, writer
> Millard Lampell, writer
> Mrs. Millard Lampell
> Arnold Manoff, writer
> Sam Moore, radio writer
> Ed Rolfe, writer
> Lynn Whitney, actress
> George Willner, agent
> Tiba (Mrs. George) Willner

JEROME ROBBINS, choreographer

Appeared May 5, 1953

> Edward (Ed) Chodorov, writer-producer
> Jerome Chodorov, writer
> Lloyd Gough, actor

---

*Odets testified on May 19, 1952, that Bromberg recruited him into the CP.

**Radin swore that he was not a member of the CP, that dues were collected at CP meetings, but not from him

†Radin testified that Losey tried to recruit him into the CP.

Madelaine Lee, CP functionary and actress (Mrs. Jack Gilford)
Edna Ocko
Elliott (Ely) Sullivan, actor

STANLEY ROBERTS, writer

Appeared May 20, 1952

Ben Barzman, writer
John (Jack) Berry, director
Herbert J. Biberman, writer-director-producer
Edward Biberman, artist
Sonja Dahl, actress (Mrs. Edward Biberman)
Hugo Butler, writer
Jean Butler (Rouverol), writer (Mrs. Hugo Butler)
Richard (Dick) Collins, writer
Arnaud d'Usseau, writer
Susan Wells, (Mrs. Arnaud d'Usseau), head of Communist book shop
Carl Foreman, writer
Lloyd Gough, actor
Karen Morley, actress (Mrs. Lloyd Gough)
Alex Greenberg, CP organization secretary for the group to which Roberts belonged
Edward Huebsch, writer
Mrs. Edward Huebsch
Gordon Kahn, writer
John Howard Lawson, writer
Robert Lees, writer
Irwin Lieberman, TV writer
Mrs. George Pepper, official Hollywood Council, Arts, Sciences, and Professions
Abraham (Abe) Polonsky, writer-director
Bernard C. Schoenfeld, writer
Paul Trivers, writer
Jane (Mrs. Paul) Trivers
Dalton Trumbo, writer
Dorothy Tree, actress (Mrs. Michael H. Uris)
Michael H. Uris, writer
Bernard Vorhaus, director

MRS. META REIS ROSENBERG, former head of literary department, motion picture agency, former motion picture story editor

Appeared April 13, 1951

Edward Biberman, artist
Herbert J. Biberman, writer-director-producer
Lester Cole, writer
Richard Collins, writer
Francis Faragoh, writer

Paul Jarrico, writer
Gordon Kahn, writer
John Howard Lawson, writer
Albert Maltz, writer
Carleton Moss, writer
Samuel (Sam) Ornitz, writer
Abraham (Abe) Polonsky, writer, director
Robert Rossen, writer-director-producer
Madelaine Ruthven, CP functionary
Waldo Salt, writer
Dorothy Tree, actress (Mrs. Michael H. Uris)
Frank Wright Tuttle, director
Tania (Mrs. Frank W.) Tuttle
Michael H. Uris, writer
George Willner, writers' agent

ROBERT ROSSEN, writer-director-producer

Appeared June 25, 1951, denied former Communist Party membership

Appeared again May 7, 1953, and answered all questions regarding former membership in the party

Georgia Backus, actress (Mrs. Hy Alexander)
Ben Barzman, writer
Alvah Bessie, writer
Henry Blankfort, writer
William Frank Blowitz, publicist
John Bright, writer
Harold Buchman, writer
Sidney Buchman, writer
Hugo Butler, writer
Maurice Clark, writer
Lester Cole, writer
Richard Collins, writer
Edward Dmytryk, director
Guy Endore, writer
Francis Faragoh, writer
Pauline Lauber Finn, executive secretary, Hollywood Writers Mobilization
Lester Fuller, director
Morton Grant, writer
Louis (Lou) Harris, publicity writer
Ian McLellan Hunter, writer
Daniel (Dan) Lewis James, writer
Lilith James, writer (Mrs. Dan James)
Paul Jarrico, writer
Hyman (Hy) Solomon Kraft, writer
Ring W. Lardner, Jr., writer
John Howard Lawson, writer
Isobel Lennart, writer
Melvin (Mel) Levy, writer
Albert Maltz, writer
Henry Meyers, writer
Josef Mischel, writer

Sam Moore, radio writer
Mortimer William (Bill) Pomerance, former business agent, Screen Cartoonists Guild, Local 852, AFL Painters International, later executive secretary, Screen Writers Guild
Gertrude Purcell, writer
Maurice Rapf, writer
Ann Roth Morgan Richards, assistant secretary Screen Writers Guild (Mrs. Robert L. Richards)
Fred Rinaldo, writer
Marguerite Roberts, writer
Stanley Roberts, writer
Mrs. Meta Reis Rosenberg, literary agent, talent agency
Madelaine Ruthven, CP functionary, ex-writer
Waldo Salt, writer
Adrian Scott, writer-producer
Budd Wilson Schulberg, writer
Victor Shapiro, publicist
Louis Solomon, writer
Glenda Sullivan
Leo Townsend, writer
Paul Trivers, writer
Dalton Trumbo, writer
Frank Wright Tuttle, director
Michael H. Uris, writer
Bernard Vorhaus, director
John Wexley, writer

BERNARD C. SCHOENFELD, writer

Appeared August 19, 1952

John (Jack) Berry, director
Herbert J. Biberman, writer-director-producer
Gale Sondergaard, actress (Mrs. Herbert J. Biberman)
Hugo Butler, writer
Richard (Dick) Collins, writer
Edward (Ed or Eddie) Huebsch, writer
John Howard Lawson, writer
Albert Maltz, writer
Henry Meyers, writer
Stanley Roberts, writer
Mrs. Meta Reis Rosenberg, former head of literary department of Hollywood motion picture talent agency
Dorothy Tree, actress (Mrs. Michael H. Uris)
Paul Trivers, writer
Jane (Mrs. Paul) Trivers
Dalton Trumbo, writer
Frank Wright Tuttle, director
Tanya (Mrs. Frank W.) Tuttle
Michael H. Uris, writer
Bernard Vorhaus, director

Hetty (Mrs. Bernard) Vorhaus
Michael Wilson, writer, CP functionary

BUD WILSON SCHULBERG, writer

Appeared May 23, 1951

Herbert J. Biberman, writer-director-producer
John Bright, writer
Harry Carlisle, writer, CP functionary
Lester Cole, writer
Richard Collins, writer
Paul Jarrico, writer
Gordon Kahn, writer
Ring W. Lardner, Jr., writer
Stanley Lawrence, CP functionary
John Howard Lawson, writer
Tillie Lerner, writer
Mrs. Meta Reis Rosenberg
Waldo Salt, writer
Robert Tasker, writer
Tania (Mrs. Frank W.) Tuttle

ZACHARY SCHWARTZ, cartoonist; later artist and designer of TV advertising

Appeared May 7, 1953

Edward Biberman, artist
Mrs. Bernyce Polifka Fleury, artist
Edward Nolan

SOL SHOR, writer

Appeared March 12, 1953

Leopold Lawrence Atlas
George Beck, writer
Nicholas Bela, writer
Mrs. Nicholas Bela
Herbert Biberman, writer-director-producer
Miss Jessie Burns, motion picture studio reader
Hugo Butler, writer
Tom Chapman, reader
Clarice (Mrs. Tom) Chapman
Maurice Clark, writer
Lester Cole, writer
Richard Collins, writer
Dorothy Comingire, actress
Edward Eliscu, writer
Carl Foreman, writer
Ann Froelich, writer
Morton Grant, writer
George Hallgren, credit manager, Twentieth Century-Fox
Nora (Mrs. George) Hallgren
Harold A. Hecht
Lester Koenig, writer
Ring W. Lardner, Jr., writer
John Howard Lawson, writer
Alfred Lewis Levitt, writer

Melvin Levy, writer
Arnold Manoff, writer
Henry Meyers, writer
Josef Mischel, writer
Mortimer Offner
Maurice Rapf, writer
W. L. (Les) Rivers, writer
David Robeson, motion picture studio
  reader or writer
Madelaine Ruthven, ex-writer, CP func-
  tionary
Harold Salemson, publicity
Waldo Salt, writer
John Sanford, writer
Bernard Skadron, business manager for
  motion picture celebrities
Lillian (Mrs. Bernard) Skadron
Ray E. Spencer, writer
Paul Trivers, writer
Frank Wright Tuttle, director
Michael H. Uris, writer
Bernard Vorhaus, director
Ruth (Mrs. John) Weber
Irving J. White, radio writer, director
Elizabeth (Betty) Wilson, CP function-
  ary, writer, (Mrs. Richard Wilson)
Michael Wilson, writer

MAX SILVER, former organizational secretary, CP Los Angeles

Appeared January 23, 1952

Dorothy Comingore, actress
Paul Robert Perlin, studio worker

ALLAN E. SLOANE, radio-TV-screen-
writer

Appeared January 13, 1954

Lan Adomian, composer
Millard Lampell, writer
Peter Lyon, radio writer

LEO TOWNSEND, writer

Appeared September 18, 1951

Ben Barzman, writer
Norma (Mrs. Ben) Barzman, writer
Nicholas (Nick) Bela, writer
Ben Bengal, writer
Sidney Benson, CP functionary
Alvah Bessie, writer
Phoebe Brand, actress (Mrs. Morris Car-
  novsky)
Harold Buchman, writer
Morris Carnovsky, actor
Elizabeth Leech Glenn, ex-writer, CP
  functionary
Charles Glenn, writer, CP functionary
Jay Gorney, musician, song writer

Sondra (Mrs. Jay) Gorney
Edward Huebsch, writer
Daniel (Dan) James, writer
Paul Jarrico, writer
Sylvia (Mrs. Paul) Jarrico
John Howard Lawson, writer
Robert Lees, writer
Joseph Losey, director
Louise (Mrs. Joseph) Losey
Arnold Manoff, writer
Marjorie (Mrs. Arnold) Manoff, (also
  known as Marjorie Potts and Marjorie
  MacGregor)
Henry Meyers, writer
Karen Morley, actress (Mrs. Lloyd
  Gough)
Mortimer Offner, writer
Larry Parks, actor
Joy Pepper, CP functionary
Abraham Lincoln (Abe) Polonsky,
  writer-director
Sylvia (Mrs. Abraham) Polonsky
Maurice Rapf, writer
Frederick (Fred) Rinaldo, writer
Robert Rossen, writer-director-producer
Waldo Salt, writer
Bess Taffel, writer
John Weber, agent
John Wexley, writer

PAULINE SWANSON TOWNSEND, writer
(Mrs. Leo Townsend)

Appeared March 12, 1953

Lewis Allen (Louis Allan), playwright
Dorothy (Mrs. Leopold) Atlas
Ben Barzman
Norma Barzman, writer
Sol Barzman, writer
Elena Beck
Catherine Becker
Nicholas Bela, writer
Ben Bengal, writer
Max Benoff
Mickey (Mrs. Max) Benoff
Mildred Benoff
Arthur Birnkrant, writer
Mrs. Goldie Bromberg
Harold Buchman, writer
Mrs. Harold Buchman
Ruth Burrows
Harry Carlyle
Beatrice Lubitz Cole
Richard Collins
Ernest Dawson
Andreas Dinam
Susan Wells d'Usseau
Leslie Edgley, writer
Mrs. Leslie Edgley
Cyril Endfield, director, writer

Elizabeth Faragoh
Howard Fast, writer
Pauline Lauber Finn
Mrs. Elizabeth Leech Glenn
Jay Gorney
Sandra (Mrs. Jay) Gorney
Alice Hunter, head, Hollywood Democratic Committee, or its successor, the Hollywood Independent Citizens' Committee of the Arts, Sciences, and Professions
Dan James, writer
Lilith James, writer
Louise Janis
Shirley Kanter
Ring Lardner, Jr., writer
John Howard Lawson, writer
Helen (Mrs. Charles) Leonard
Peter Lyon, radio writer
Bart Lytton
Marjorie MacGregor
Ben Maddow, writer
Henrietta Martin, writer
Patricia (Patsy) Moore
Louise Moss (Mrs. Joseph Losey)
Richard O'Boyer
Edwina (Mrs. William) Pomerance
William (Bill) Pomerance, producer, writer
Stanley Prager, actor-writer
Paul Radin
Maurice Rapf, writer
Mrs. Maurice Rapf
Robert L. Richards, writer
Ann Roth Morgan Richards (Mrs. Robert L. Richards)
Fred Rinaldo, writer
Marguerite Roberts, writer (Mrs. John Sanford)
Meta Reis Rosenberg, attorney for Music Corporation of America
Paul Rosenfeld
Robert Rossen
Mrs. Sue (Robert) Rossen
Madelaine Ruthven
Waldo Salt, writer
John Sanford, writer
Artie Shaw, orchestra leader
Mrs. Robert (Mary) Shaw
Robert Shaw, writer
Reuben Ship, radio and screen writer
Louis Solomon, writer
Janet Stevenson, writer
Phillip (Phil) Stevenson, writer
Janet (Mrs. Phillip) Stevenson
Frank Tarloff, writer
Tania (Mrs. Frank W.) Tuttle
Clara (Mrs. Mischa) Walden
John Weber, agent

Everett Weill
John Wexley, writer
Cookie (Mrs. John) Wexley
Angus Wooley
Barbara (Mrs. Angus) Wooley (Barbara Roberts)
Julian Zimet, writer

FRANK WRIGHT TUTTLE, director

Appeared May 24, 1951

John (Jack) Berry, director
Alvah Bessie, writer
Edward Biberman, artist
Sonia Dahl (Mrs. Edward Biberman)
Herbert J. Biberman, writer-director-producer
John Bright, writer
J. Edward Bromberg, actor
Goldie (Mrs. J. Edward) Bromberg
Hugo Butler, writer
Maurice Clark, writer
Lester Cole, writer
Richard Collins, writer
Jules Dassin, director
Edward Dmytryk, director
Charles Glenn, writer, CP functionary
Michael Gordon, director
Nora Hellgren, CP functionary
Edward Huebsch, writer
Ring W. Lardner, Jr., writer
Stanley Lawrence, CP functionary
Elizabeth Leech (Mrs. Charles) Glenn, CP functionary
John Howard Lawson, writer
Robert Lees, writer
Albert Maltz, writer
Fred Rinaldo, writer
Mrs. Meta Reis Rosenberg, agent
Madelaine Ruthven, ex-writer, CP functionary (assisted John Howard Lawson in CP hierarchy in Hollywood)
Waldo Salt, writer
Eva Shafron, CP functionary (deceased)
Robert Tasker, writer (deceased at that time)
Dorothy Tree, actress (Mrs. Michael H. Uris)
Clark Trivers, writer
Paul Trivers, writer
Dalton Trumbo, writer
Michael H. Uris, writer
Bernard Vorhaus, director

OWEN VINSON, director of radio programs

Appeared October 2, 1952

Harmon (Hy) Alexander, radio writer
Georgia Backus, actress (Mrs. Hy Alexander)
Lee Barrie, singer

Abram (Abe) Burrows, writer
David (Dave) Ellis, radio actor-writer
Charles Glenn, radio writer
Elaine Gonda (wife of Charles Glenn named in this testimony), in charge of radio transcription company
Annette Harper, radio actress
Nina Klowden, radio actress (also known as Anna Klowden)
Mitchell Lindeman, radio director, associate producer
Paul Marion, radio actor
Edwin Miller Max, actor
Sam Moore, radio writer
Ken Pettus, radio writer
Naomi Robeson, ex-actress, CP functionary
Jack Robinson, radio writer
Mary Robinson, radio writer
Louis Scofield, radio writer-actor
Janette (Mrs. Louis) Scofield
Reuben Ship, radio and screen writer
Eugene R. Stone, radio writer
Louis Terkel, radio actor-writer
Ida (Mrs. Louis) Terkel
Herman Waldreen (also known as Herman Waldman and David Wolfe), radio actor
Stanley Waxman, actor
Lynn Whitney, actress
William (Billy) Wolff, radio writer

ELIZABETH WILSON, writer (Mrs. Richard Wilson) nee Elizabeth (Billy) Anderson

Appeared September 21, 1951

George Beck
Herbert J. Biberman, writer-director-producer
Leo Bigelman, MD
John Bright, writer
Harold Buchman, writer
Beatrice (Bea) Buchman (Mrs. Sidney Buchman), "very active" in Hollywood Anti-Nazi League

Jessie Burns, reader at studio
Harry Carlisle
Thomas (Tom) Chapman, studio reader
Lester Cole, writer
Richard (Dick) Collins, writer
Sonja Dahl (Mrs. Edward Biberman)
Ambur Dana (Mrs. Waldo Salt)
Richard (Dick) Fiske, studio worker
Elizabeth Leech Glenn (Mrs. Charles Glenn), CP functionary
Morton Grant, writer
Betty (Mrs. Morton) Grant
Margaret (Peggy) Gruen, writer
Lou Harris, publicity writer
Vera (Mrs. Lou) Harris
Paul Jarrico, writer
Sylvia (Mrs. Paul) Jarrico
Ring W. Lardner, Jr., writer
John (Jack) Howard Lawson, writer
Sue (Mrs. John H.) Lawson
Robert (Bob) Lees, writer
Melvin (Mel) Levy, writer
Arnold Manoff, writer
Marjorie (Marge) (Mrs. Arnold) Manoff (also known as Marjorie Potts and Marjorie MacGregor)
Allen Matthews, actor
Maurice Murphy, actor
Mortimer (Mortie) Offner, writer
Samuel (Sam) Ornitz, writer
Sadie (Mrs. Sam) Ornitz
Maurice Rapf, writer
Fred Rinaldo, writer
Madelaine Ruthven, CP functionary
John Sanford, writer
Budd Wilson Schulberg, writer
Virginia Schulberg (then Mrs. Budd Schulberg)
Louise Seidel
Gale Sondergaard, actress (Mrs. Herbert J. Biberman)
Robert Tasker, writer
John Staff, CP functionary
Herta Uerkvitz, studio researcher

APPENDIX II

The Committee's Evidence of Communist Party Membership of Two of the Unfriendly Ten

The committee's chief investigator, Louis J. Russell, and his aides read into the record the list of Communist affiliations of the Unfriendly Ten immediately following their uncooperative appearance before the committee during the October, 1947, hearings.

Investigation by the committee and its staff revealed that all of the ten had been issued numbered Communist Party registration cards in Los Angeles County. Eight of the CP membership cards were reproduced in the exhibits introduced into evidence at the hearings.* The cards for Edward Dmytryk and Adrian Scott do not appear in the exhibits, but they were read into the record by Russell.**

Information from the Files of the Committee on Un-American Activities, United States House of Representatives, on the Communist Affiliations of John Howard Lawson:

John Howard Lawson is a screen writer and one of the most active Communists in the Hollywood movie industry. He has written the following scripts: Dynamite (M-G-M); The Sea Bat (M-G-M); Blushing Brides (M-G-M); Ship From Shanghai (M-G-M); Bachelor Apartment (Radio Films); Success at Any Price (RKO-Radio), 1934; Goodbye Love (RKO-Radio), 1934; Treasure Island (M-G-M), 1934; Party Wire (Columbia), 1935; Blockade (United Artists-Wanger), 1938; Algiers (United Artists-Wanger), 1938; They Shall Have Music (United Artists-Goldwyn), 1939; Four Sons (20th Century-Fox), 1940; Earthbound (20th Century-Fox), 1940; Sahara (Columbia), 1943; Counterattack (Columbia), 1945.

The files of the House Committee on Un-American Activities show that—

1. Rena M. Vale, a former member of the Communist Party and a screen writer, testified before the Special Committee on Un-American Activities on July 22, 1940, that Mr. Lawson had been identified to her as a Communist Party member when she met him at a Communist Party fraction meeting. She further testified that Mr. Lawson during the meeting gave advice on inserting the Communist Party line into drama. The State

---

* U.S. Congress, House Committee on Un-American Activities, *Communist Infiltration of Hollywood Motion-Picture Industry,* Hearings, 1947; Appendix, pp. 538-49.

** *Ibid.,* Dmytryk record, pp. 462-66; Scott record, pp. 468-69.

legislative committee investigating un-American activities in California has cited Mr. Lawson as "one of the most important Marxist strategists in southern California," in its 1945 report, page 118. The California report notes on the same page that Rena M. Vale also testified before the State legislative committee and that the witness identified Lawson as a member of the Communist Party fraction of the Screen Writers Guild who had given advice on the Communist Party program in the writing of the play, Sun Rises in the West. The State legislative committee states further, in its 1947 report, page 260, that Mr. Lawson directed a Communist bloc of about 65 members in local 47, the Hollywood local of the American Federation of Musicians, AFL, between the years 1937 and 1940.

2. The Communist Party has been publicly defended by John Howard Lawson. The Daily Worker, in an article on April 16, 1947, page 2, and reprinted in the Sunday edition of April 20, 1947, page 8, announced that Mr. Lawson was one of the signers of a statement opposing any legislative attempts to restrict the activities of the Communist Party. The organization sponsoring the statement was the Civil Rights Congress, which the House Committee on Un-American Activities, in a report published September 2, 1947, declared to be "dedicated not to the broader issues of civil liberties, but specifically to the defense of individual Communists and the Communist Party." The Civil Rights Congress is now defending such persons as Gerhart Eisler, an agent of the Communist International convicted of passport fraud, and Eugene Dennis, Communist Party general secretary, convicted of contempt of Congress. The Civil Rights Congress is the successor to the International Labor Defense, former legal arm of the Communist Party, according to former Attorney General Francis Biddle. John Howard Lawson also came to the support of the Communist Party on another occasion, according to the Daily Worker for March 18, 1945, page 2. Mr. Lawson was listed in this issue as one of the signers of a statement hailing a War Department order allowing military commissions for Communists. Sponsor of the statement was the National Federation for Constitutional Liberties, which was cited as a Communist front organization by former Attorney General Biddle. Biddle pointed out the organization's defense of such prominent Communist leaders as Sam Darcy and Robert Wood, party secretaries for Pennsylvania and Oklahoma, respectively. The organization was also cited as a Communist front by the Special Committee on Un-American Activities on June 25, 1942, and March 29, 1944.

3. John Howard Lawson has given his support to a number of individual Communists. The People's World, official west coast Communist organ, reported on October 22, 1942, page 2, that Mr. Lawson was backing Mrs. La Rue McCormick, a candidate for the California State Senate on the Communist Party ticket. Mr. Lawson was one of the signers of a statement in defense of the Comintern agent Gerhart Eisler, according to the Daily

Worker for February 28, 1947, page 2. The organization sponsoring this statement in behalf of Eisler was the Civil Rights Congress.

Mr. Lawson was a sponsor of the Schappes Defense Committee, according to an undated letterhead of the organization. This committee worked for the release of Morris U. Schappes, an avowed Communist teacher convicted of perjury in New York City, and the organization was cited as a Communist front by the Special Committee on Un-American Activities on March 29, 1944. Mr. Lawson was also a signer of an open letter which the Schappes Defense Committee sent to New York Gov. Thomas Dewey in an effort to have Schappes pardoned. This fact was reported in the New York Sun, September 27, 1944. Mr. Lawson was a member and sponsor of the Citizens Committee for Harry Bridges, according to an organization letterhead dated September 11, 1941. Bridges, who led the disastrous San Francisco general strike of 1934, was identified as a Communist Party member by the Daily Worker itself. The Daily Worker of February 13, 1937, page 2, announced Mr. Lawson as a signer of a cable sent to the Brazilian Chamber of Deputies on behalf of Luis Carlos Prestes, former member of the Communist International Executive Committee and a Brazilian Communist leader, and on behalf of Arthur Ewert, another Comintern representative and a former Communist deputy of the German Reichstag, both of whom were imprisoned by the Brazilian Government in connection with an attempted revolt. The cable was sent under the auspices of the Joint Committee for the Defense of Brazilian People, which was organized specifically for the defense of Communists Prestes and Ewert.

4. John Howard Lawson has long been affiliated with the Communist Party's official organ, the Daily Worker. On May 18, 1934, page 1, the Daily Worker headlined the arrest of its "correspondent" John Howard Lawson for "being present" at a trial of strike leaders in Birmingham, Alabama, printed a long story by Lawson on the trial. Lawson's story eulogized one of the strike leaders, whom he identified as a Communist Party organizer. He reported that the organizer at one point in the trial told the court in ringing tones that "The Communist Party is actively participating in strike struggles and building a powerful trade-union movement * * * in order to establish a Soviet America as part of the world struggle of the toiling masses for communism." This article was the basis of a libel suit against Lawson, according to the Daily Worker which appeared later (June 7, 1934, p. 1). This later issue of the Daily Worker also claimed that the arrest of Lawson in Birmingham had been aimed at driving the Daily Worker from the South. The Daily Worker officially listed Mr. Lawson as one of its contributors in the issue of December 21, 1935, page 3. Mr. Lawson has contributed articles to the publication as recently as June 1, 1947, page 7. Mr. Lawson's support of the publication has also included appeals for financial aid. In the issue of September 6,

1935, he wrote that he wished "to add my voice to the appeal of the Daily Worker for a $60,000 sustaining fund." The same article, appearing on page 5, refers to the Soviet Union as "the great toiler for peace."

5. Other Communist publications have also received support from John Howard Lawson. New Masses is an official Communist weekly magazine. Mr. Lawson has been listed as a contributing editor in New Masses issue for October 1927, page 3; December 15, 1936, page 35; January 5, 1937, page 23; February 18, 1941, page 30; January 27, 1942, page 24; and April 30, 1946, page 2. The People's World is an official west-coast Communist paper. According to the Daily Worker for April 15, 1946, page 11, Mr. Lawson served as chairman of a meeting held on April 9, 1946, in Los Angeles under the auspices of the People's World. The Worker reported that in his speech at the meeting, Mr. Lawson called for an end to fear of the word "Marx." A prowar press conference held in behalf of the People's World on August 4, 1943, in Los Angeles was endorsed by Mr. Lawson, according to the issue of the People's World for July 9, 1943. On June 24, 1944, the People's World reported that Mr. Lawson had praised the paper. Mainstream is a literary magazine which has been promoted by the Communist press and which advertises itself in the Daily Worker as a "Marxist literary quarterly" (Daily Worker, June 11, 1947, p. 4). Mr. Lawson is listed as a member of the editorial board of Mainstream, according to the issue of Political Affairs for November 1946. The 1947 winter issue of Mainstream carries an article by Mr. Lawson on page 23. On June 11, 1947, Mr. Lawson, together with Hanns Eisler, composer of the Comintern, addressed a meeting sponsored by Mainstream in New York City, according to a leaflet put out by the publication.

6. John Howard Lawson has been affiliated with numerous organizations whose principal purpose was the defense of Communists. He served as treasurer of both the National Committee for the Defense of Political Prisoners and the National Committee for People's Rights, according to letterheads of these organizations. Attorney General Francis Biddle (in the Congressional Record, September 24, 1942, p. 7686) stated that the "National Committee for the Defense of Political Prisoners is substantially equivalent to International Labor Defense, legal arm of the Communist Party" and pointed out that the organization had defended such Communists as Earl Browder and Angelo Herndon. "In January 1938," the Attorney General went on to say, "its (National Committee for the Defense of Political Prisoners) name was changed to the National Committee for People's Rights." The Special Committee on Un-American Activities cited the National Committee for Defense of Political Prisoners as a Communist front on June 25, 1942, and March 29, 1944, and cited the National Committee for People's Rights as a Communist front on the same dates.

7. The International Labor Defense, in addition to being identified as the legal arm of the Communist Party by Attorney General Biddle, has

been cited for its Communist character by the Special Committee on Un-American Activities, Prof. John Dewey's Committee for Cultural Freedom, Massachusetts House Committee on Un-American Activities and the California Committee on Un-American Activities. The official publication of the organization which defends Communists is called the Labor Defender. John Howard Lawson was a contributing editor to the Labor Defender, according to an issue of the publication for October 1936, page 3. John Howard Lawson also served as a sponsor of the Sleepy Lagoon Defense Committee, which was supported by the International Labor Defense, according to a letterhead of August 9, 1944. In addition, the California State Legislative Committee on Un-American Activities has noted that Mr. Lawson was a sponsor of the Citizens Committee for the Defense of Mexican-American Youth (1945 report, p. 195). The latter committee was the predecessor of the Sleepy Lagoon Defense Committee and was avowedly organized by La Rue McCormick, one-time Communist candidate for California State senator.

8. John Howard Lawson endorsed legislation sponsored by the American Committee for Protection of the Foreign Born, according to the Daily Worker for April 11, 1938, page 5. The committee, which specializes in defending foreign-born Communists like Gerhart Eisler and Harry Bridges, was cited as a Communist front by the Special Committee on Un-American Activities on June 25, 1942, and March 29, 1944, and by Prof. John Dewey's Committee for Cultural Freedom in April 1940. Mr. Lawson was also a member of the American Committee for Anti-Nazi German Seamen, according to a committee letterhead dated January 8, 1939. The organization was engaged in defending German seamen active in distributing Communist literature in Germany. New Masses for December 6, 1938, page 20, reports that Mr. Lawson was one of the signers of a telegram sent to Peru pleading for the release of Communist political prisoners in that country.

9. John Howard Lawson has shown an active interest in the Soviet Union. The Daily Worker of April 28, 1938, page 4, shows that Mr. Lawson was a signer of a statement by the American Progressives Defending the Moscow Trials, which was the usual name affixed to a series of trials then being held in the Soviet Union for numerous opponents of dictator Stalin. It has been established that these trials had for their aim the purging of all political enemies of Josef Stalin and his political cohorts, although the Communist press portrayed the subjects of these trials as being counter-revolutionists and collaborators with Great Britain in an attempt to overthrow the Soviet regime by furnishing military information to alleged British espionage agents.

10. The National Council of American-Soviet Friendship was cited as a Communist front by the Special Committee on Un-American Activities on March 29, 1944. Mr. Lawson acted as a sponsor of a reception for Mikhail Kalatzov, Soviet film representative, which was held in Hollywood on

August 22, 1943, under the auspices of the National Council of American-Soviet Friendship. According to the Daily Worker for July 5, 1943, page 4, Mr. Lawson also signed a statement defending the film, Mission to Moscow, which had been charged by a number of authorities on the Soviet Union with being distorted and unreliable. The statement was promoted by the National Council of American-Soviet Friendship.

11. Soviet Russia Today was the official monthly publication of the Friends of Soviet Union, the predecessor of the National Council of American-Soviet Friendship. The magazine was cited as a Communist front by the Special Committee on Un-American Activities on June 25, 1942, and March 29, 1944. John Howard Lawson contributed to Soviet Russia Today, according to the issue of the publication for March 1935, page 9. The same publication of September 1939, page 25, listed Mr. Lawson as one of the signers of an Open Letter for Closer Cooperation with the Soviet Union. The publication for November 1937, page 79, records the name of Mr. Lawson as one of the signers of a Golden Book of American Soviet Friendship.

12. The American Council on Soviet Relations has been cited by Attorney General Francis Biddle as a Communist front (Congressional Record, September 24, 1942, p. 7688) and has received the same citation from the Special Committee on Un-American Activities on March 29, 1942. Prof. John Dewey's Special Committee for Cultural Freedom in April 1940 characterized the organization as under Communist control, influence, or in collaboration with the Communist Party. One of the signers of an open letter sent to the president of the American Council on Soviet Relations was John Howard Lawson, according to an official folder of the council.

13. Many Communist-front organizations which supported Soviet foreign policy were backed by John Howard Lawson. The American League Against War and Fascism was active in support of Soviet foreign policy against the democracies between 1932 and 1937. It has been cited by Attorney General Biddle as an organization seeking "to create public sentiment on behalf of a foreign policy adapted to the interests of the Soviet Union" (Congressional Record, September 24, 1942). The Special Committee on Un-American Activities has cited this organization as subversive on January 3, 1940, and March 29, 1944. The Daily Worker for June 27, 1934, page 1, reveals that Mr. Lawson was a speaker at a were backed by John Howard Lawson [sic]. The American League Against War and Fascism [sic]. Mr. Lawson was a sponsor of the New York City Conference Against War and Fascism, which was organized by the American League Against War and Fascism, according to the Daily Worker for January 11, 1937, page 2. Mr. Lawson has also contributed to Fight, the official publication of the American League Against War and Fascism, according to an issue of Fight for October 1934, page 3. The league was dedicated to an openly treasonable program.

14. When the Communist line changed in favor of a united front of the democracies against the Fascist aggressors, the Communists in America formed a successor to the American League Against War and Fascism in 1937, known as the American League for Peace and Democracy. The theatrical subsidiary of the American League for Peace and Democracy was the Theatre Arts Committee, which was cited as a Communist front by Prof. John Dewey's Committee for Cultural Freedom in April 1940. The Theatre Arts Committee was also affiliated with the League of Workers Theatres, a section of the International Union of the Revolutionary Theatre with headquarters in Moscow. John Howard Lawson was a member of the advisory council of the Theatre Arts Committee, according to an undated letterhead of the organization.

15. After the Stalin-Hitler Pact was signed in 1939, the Communists established the American Peace Mobilization, which opposed lend-lease, aid to Britain, the defense program, and picketed the White House. It also supported a number of strikes in defense industries. The organization has been cited as a Communist front by the Attorney General Francis Biddle, by the Special Committee on Un-American Activities, and the California Committee on Un-American Activities. An official program listed John Howard Lawson as a sponsor of a meeting held by the American Peace Mobilization in New York City on April 5 and 6, 1941.

16. Among the new Communist fronts that sprang up when the Soviet Union and the United States were allies in a war against fascism was the Artists' Front to Win the War, which made its debut at a mass meeting at Carnegie Hall in New York City on October 16, 1942. The organization was cited as a Communist front by the Special Committee on Un-American Activities on March 29, 1944. The official program for the mass meeting at Carnegie Hall listed John Howard Lawson as one of the sponsors. Thus, Mr. Lawson has publicly avowed his allegiance to the line of the Communist Party during four distinctly divergent periods.

17. At the Seventh World Congress of the Communist International, held in Moscow in 1935, George Dimitroff, general secretary, called upon all affiliated Communist parties to make the greatest efforts in behalf of the campaign of the Spanish Communists during Spain's civil war. A number of projects were organized by American Communists in response to this request. Among them were the Medical Bureau and North American Committee to Aid Spanish Democracy, cited as subversive by the Special Committee on Un-American Activities on April 21, 1943, and March 29, 1944, and the American Society for Technical Aid to Spanish Democracy, cited as a Communist front by the Special Committee on Un-American Activities on March 29, 1944. John Howard Lawson served as secretary and as a member of the board of directors of the American Society for Technical Aid to Spanish Democracy, according to the issues of New Masses for February 16, 1937, page 28, January 19, 1937, page 25, January 26, 1937, page 32, and an organizational letterhead dated

February 19, 1937. Mr. Lawson was one of the patrons of a benefit performance and dance sponsored by the Manhattan chapter of the Medical Bureau to Aid Spanish Democracy, according to an undated announcement of the dance, held May 22, 1937. On a letterhead dated April 29, 1939, the Medical Bureau and North American Committee to Aid Spanish Democracy announced that Mr. Lawson was a member of its theater-arts committee.

18. The American Committee to Save Refugees was part of the Communist campaign for Spanish Communists and was cited as a Communist front by the Special Committee on Un-American Activities on March 29, 1944. The organization provided transportation and support for international Communist agents such as Gerhart Eisler. John Howard Lawson was the signer of a statement sponsored by the American Committee to Save Refugees, according to an undated leaflet of the organization entitled "For the Rescue of Refugees."

19. The Joint Anti-Fascist Refugee Committee likewise is engaged in providing transportation and support for international Communist agents like Gerhart Eisler. It was cited as a Communist front by the Special Committee on Un-American Activities on March 29, 1944. It was cited for contempt of Congress on April 16, 1946, and its leaders were convicted in a Federal court on June 27, 1947. John Howard Lawson was one of the sponsors of a dinner held by the Joint Anti-Fascist Refugee Committee in New York on October 27, 1943, according to a dinner program.

20. The League of American Writers was an affiliate of the International Union of Revolutionary Writers, with headquarters in Moscow, and the league was pledged to the defense of the Soviet Union and the use of "art as an instrument of the class struggle." This organization was cited as a Communist front by the Special Committee on Un-American Activities on January 3, 1940, June 25, 1942, and March 29, 1944. Attorney General Francis Biddle said that "The overt activities of the League of American Writers in the last 2 years leaves little doubt of its Communist control" (Congressional Record, September 24, 1942, p. 7686). The league was founded at a Congress of American Revolutionary Writers held April 26 through 28, 1935 in New York City. The Daily Worker for January 18, 1935, page 5, reveals that John Howard Lawson was one of the signers of the call for this Congress of American Revolutionary Writers. The Daily Worker for April 29, 1935, pages 1 and 2, further revealed that Mr. Lawson presented a reading of Technique in the Drama at this writers' congress. Mr. Lawson was listed as a member of the executive committee of the League of American Writers in the Daily Worker for April 30, 1935, and as vice president of the League of American Writers in New Masses for June 17, 1941, page 10, and the Daily Worker for September 14, 1942, page 7. A statement sponsored by the league in behalf of a second front was signed by Mr. Lawson according to the Daily Worker for September 14, 1942, page 7. A statement signed by John Howard Lawson appears on

page 67 of a league pamphlet entitled "We Hold These Truths." Mr. Lawson was a signer of the call to the second biennial meeting of the League of American Writers, according to New Masses for May 4, 1937, page 25. Mr. Lawson signed the call for the third congress also, according to the magazine, Direction, for May-June 1939, page 1. Mr. Lawson signed the call for and also attended the fourth congress of the league which was held in New York June 6 through June 8, 1941, according to New Masses for June 17, 1941, pages 9-10, and for April 22, 1941, page 25.

21. The League of American Writers operated a writers' school at 1717 North Vine Street in Hollywood. The People's World for February 11, 1943, page 5, listed Mr. Lawson as a lecturer at the writers' school.

22. At this same time, the Communists were operating a Los Angeles workers' school. Eva Shafran, a Communist organizer, was the director, and La Rue McCormick, who was a candidate for California State senator on the Communist Party ticket, served on the board of directors. According to official literature of the school, John Howard Lawson taught at the Los Angeles workers' school in 1943, 1944, and 1945.

23. The People's Educational Center in Los Angeles also was Communist-directed. It was started in the fall of 1943 with a loan of $1,000 from the writers' school of the League of American Writers and it received a rather complete Communist library from the Los Angeles workers' school. The People's Educational Center has been cited as a Communist-front organization by the joint fact-finding committee on un-American activities of the California Legislature and records show that numerous members of the faculty and staff of the People's Educational Center were card-holding members of the Communist Party, among them Carl Winters, Eva Shafran, Mildren Raskin, and Bruce Minton. A booklet announcing the curriculum of the center for the winter of 1947 lists John Howard Lawson as a member of the board of directors of the People's Educational Center. Also leaflet America's 10th Man lists John Howard Lawson as a lecturer for a series starting September 26, 1944.

24. The Hollywood Writers Mobilization was the name given to the Hollywood League of American Writers after the League of American Writers could no longer conceal its Communist domination. The original pledge of the League of American Writers to defend the Soviet Union and to use "art as an instrument of the class struggle" is now the basis upon which the policies of the Hollywood Writers Mobilization are founded. John Howard Lawson is a member of the editorial board of the Hollywood Quarterly, a publication sponsored by the Hollywood Writers Mobilization, according to the 1947 report of the California legislative committee investigating un-American activities (p. 107). The Hollywood Citizen News for January 13, 1947, lists John Howard Lawson as the proposer of a plan adopted by the Hollywood Writers Mobilization to set up a committee to investigate any investigators of Communist influence in the movie industry. Mr. Lawson presented the plan at a meeting of the mobilization on

January 12, 1947, in the El Patio Theater in Hollywood, the newspaper reported. Mr. Lawson also served on the general committee in charge of a writers' congress held by the Hollywood Writers Mobilization at the University of California at Los Angeles October 1 through 3, 1943, according to an official program of the congress.

25. Book Union, Inc., is a Communist book-of-the-month club, which was launched at the initiative of International Publishers, a Communist publishing house. The Book Union was closely associated with the League of American Writers and was cited for Communist character by the Special Committee on Un-American Activities on March 29, 1944, and by Prof. John Dewey's Committee for Cultural Freedom in April 1940. John Howard Lawson is listed as a member of the advisory council of the Book Union in an undated letterhead of the organization. The letter offered members the book, Soviet Communism: A New Civilization?

26. The American Youth for Democracy is the official successor of the Young Communist League. It has been the subject of a report by the House Committee on Un-American Activities which described its character in detail. Its "sinister purposes" have been denounced by the director of the Federal Bureau of Investigation (Congressional Record, March 24, 1947, p. A1298). John Howard Lawson is listed as a national sponsor of the American Youth for Democracy in the organization's publication, the Spotlight, for April 1944, page 19.

27. The New Theatre was the official monthly magazine of the League of Workers Theatres, a section of the International Union of Revolutionary Theatre, with headquarters in Moscow. The league was used to present Communist propaganda plays and to raise funds for Communist purposes. The magazine was cited as a Communist front by the Special Committee on Un-American Activities on March 29, 1944. John Howard Lawson contributed to the New Theatre of June 1935, page 10, and he is listed as a contributing editor in the issues for February 1934, page 3, and November 1934, page 11.

28. The New Theatre League was a successor of the League of Workers Theatres. It was formed in January 1935 and was cited for its Communist character by the Special Committee on Un-American Activities on March 29, 1944, and by Prof. John Dewey's Committee for Cultural Freedom in April 1940. It also presented Communist propaganda plays and raised funds for Communist purposes. The New Theatre League published the Theatre Workshop on which John Howard Lawson served as a contributing editor, according to an issue of the publication for January 1937. The Daily Worker for April 23, 1936, page 5, reported that Mr. Lawson sent greetings to the biennial national conference of the New Theatre League in Philadelphia.

29. The Theatre Union was one of the affiliates of the League of Workers Theatres, which in turn was tied to the Moscow-directed International Union of the Revolutionary Theatre. Theatre Union reflected the

current line of the Communist Party in its propaganda and was used to raise funds for Communist purposes. It produced plays by such writers for New Masses as George Sklar and Albert Maltz. A leaflet of the Theatre Union announced that John Howard Lawson was a member of its advisory board.

30. Frontier Films were producers and distributors of pro-Communist films, including a film on the Communist-led strike at the Allis-Chalmers plant in Milwaukee. The organization was headed by the following contributors to the Communist press: Albert Maltz, Kyle Crichton, Irving Lerner, Clifford Odets, Edwin Rolfe, and George Seldes. It was cited for a Communist character by the Special Committee on Un-American Activities on March 29, 1944, and by Professor John Dewey's Committee for Cultural Freedom in April 1940. The Daily Worker for April 6, 1937, page 9, shows that John Howard Lawson was a member of the staff of Frontier Films.

31. The Hollywood Democratic Committee was the successor of the Hollywood Anti-Nazi League, which was organized by Isaac Romaine, alias V. J. Jerome, a member of the central committee of the Communist Party. An official ballot of July 26, 1944, lists John Howard Lawson as a candidate for the executive board of the Hollywood Democratic Committee. The People's World for August 3, 1943, reported that Mr. Lawson enunciated a program of action for the Hollywood Democratic Committee at a meeting of the committee in 1943.

32. The Independent Citizens Committee of the Arts, Sciences, and Professions has been charged with being Communist-dominated by Harold Ickes and other liberals, who previously had supported it. It was cited as a Communist front by the House Committee on Un-American Activities on September 2, 1947. John Howard Lawson was a member of the board of directors of the Hollywood branch, according to the 1947 report of the California Committee on Un-American Activities, page 297.

33. The Progressive Citizens of America was founded as a frankly pro-Communist group as a result of the split in the Independent Citizens Committee of the Arts, Sciences, and Professions after Harold Ickes and other liberals had condemned the Independent Citizens Committee as Communist-dominated. The Progressive Citizens of America was cited as a Communist front by the House Committee on Un-American Activities in a report of June 12, 1947. An official ballot of February 11, 1947, listed John Howard Lawson as a candidate for membership on the executive board of the southern California chapter of the Progressive Citizens of America. An official pamphlet of the organization also listed Mr. Lawson as a sponsor of the second State-wide legislative conference of the Progressive Citizens of America, held on February 15, 1947, in the California Junior High School, Sacramento, California.

34. John Howard Lawson has won favor in official Communist circles on a number of occasions. The Communist Party's official organ in this

country, the Daily Worker, on October 18, 1935, page 5, lauded Mr. Lawson as one of the persons who have forced the attention of "bourgeois critics" on a left cultural movement which has "established the revolutionary theater in the top flight of dramatic art." The Daily Worker identified the revolutionary theater as one that "claims * * * that the theater is a weapon in the class struggle." On June 8, 1947, page 11, the Daily Worker carried a sympathetic interview of Mr. Lawson by the Daily Worker's film critic, David Platt. Two of Mr. Lawson's plays, Marching Song and Saga Center, were heralded in International Literature, No. 6, 1935, page 104. International Literature is the official organ of the International Union of Revolutionary Writers, which has its headquarters in Moscow.

35. The writings of John Howard Lawson himself have indicated his closeness to the Communist Party. In an article in New Theater magazine, November 1934, page 12, Mr. Lawson bluntly asserts that "as for myself, I do not hesitate to say that it is my aim to present the Communist position, and to do so in the most specific manner." "This is what I believe to be a correct approach," he writes. His article was concerned with the technique and approach of playwrights.

Mr. Lawson stresses the influence on playwriting by Marx and Engels, the founders of the Communist philosophy, in his book Theory and Technique of Playwriting, published in New York in 1936. On pages 45 through 48 he describes the theories of Marx and Engels as they affect playwriting and challenges criticism which has been leveled against the theories. "The success of the Russian Revolution, and the rapid economic and cultural growth of the Soviet Union, have centered the world's attention on the theories of Marx," Mr. Lawson also points out.

The rise of the revolutionary theater is hailed by Mr. Lawson in an article which appeared in the New Theater magazine for June 1, 1934, pages 6. and 7. Mr. Lawson criticizes Broadway theater productions, saying that "Broadway is sick because it represents a sick bourgeoisie * * *" and predicting that "the reactionary theater will continue to show signs of decay * * *." He states that the "revolutionary theater is on the threshold of its vital growth" and asserts that "creative work draws its whole inspiration and meaning from the vital forces of its periods; in our day, the vital forces at work are the growing strength of the revolution, the upsurge of a new class * * *." Mr. Lawson concludes at another point that "there is only one direction in which the drama can move forward: it must join the march of the advancing working class; it must keep pace with the quickening momentum of the revolution."

The Communist Party line was also advanced in the screen play which Mr. Lawson wrote for the movie, Blockade, according to the California Committee on Un-American Activities in its 1945 report, page 118.

The files, records, and publications of the Committee on Un-American Activities contain the following information concerning the Communist-front affiliations of Dalton Trumbo:

1. According to the Hollywood Reporter, August 22, 1946, well-known trade publication of the motion-picture industry, Dalton Trumbo was asked if he was the holder of Communist Party Book No. 36802. The committee knows of no denial by Mr. Trumbo of this fact. He has, however, openly endorsed Communist candidates, Communist legal defendants, and has openly cooperated with the Communist Party and its instruments. According to the Los Angeles Times of November 2, 1942, Mr. Trumbo endorsed Mrs. La Rue McCormick, Communist candidate for State senator. In a speech quoted in the Worker of June 22, 1947, page 11 (magazine), Mr. Trumbo is quoted as follows:

And the defense of the rights of the Communist Party, and of all real or alleged Communists, is the duty not only of liberals and progressives, but all men and women who have love for their country and respect for its Constitution.

At an official meeting of the Communist Party featuring as its chief speaker, William Z. Foster, party chairman, the poem, Confessional, by Dalton Trumbo, was presented, according to the People's World of September 10, 1947, page 4.

2. In April 1940, during the period of the Stalin-Hitler pact when the Communist Party was actively denouncing President Roosevelt as a warmonger, and agitating against lend-lease and the defense program, the Daily Worker published in serial form Dalton Trumbo's antiwar story entitled "Johnny Got His Gun." This book was widely sold at all Communist Party book shops and also extensively circulated at meetings of the American Peace Mobilization. A synopsis of this story appeared in the People's World of May 22, 1940. Both of these papers are official Communist Party organizations. Mr. Trumbo has been a contributor to the New Masses, official Communist Party weekly magazine, according to its issues of April 15, 1941, page 13, and September 26, 1944, page 28. The New Masses has been cited as a Communist periodical by Attorney General Biddle, according to the Congressional Record of September 24, 1942. It has been cited as a Communist magazine by the Special Committee on Un-American Activities on June 24, 1942, and March 29, 1944. According to the People's World of July 16, 1943, Mr. Trumbo was a member of a committee to sell paintings at an auction for the benefit of the New Masses, which was held in Hollywood. Mainstream is a Communist quarterly magazine specializing in the literary field. It is being actively promoted by the official Communist press at the present time. Mr. Trumbo is listed in the winter 1947 issue of Mainstream as a member of its editorial board. It should be noted in this connection that it has been a long-standing practice for Communist publications to utilize only Communists as staff members and frequent contributors.

3. Mr. Trumbo has made it a practice to appear in defense of Communist cases. He defended Harry Bridges, according to the Los Angeles Examiner of May 25, 1941. Bridges was cited as a member of the Communist Party by the Daily Worker, the official Communist organ. Mr.

Trumbo was at a testimonial dinner in behalf of Harry Bridges at Park Manor Hotel, Los Angeles, on April 12, 1941, according to the San Diego Labor Union Weekly of April 18, 1941. Jesus Hernandez Tomas, a leading Spanish Communist, was barred from entry to this country by the State Department. Dalton Trumbo enlisted in his defense, according to the People's World of November 30, 1943. Mr. Trumbo was also the author of a pamphlet entitled "Harry Bridges," which was written for defense purposes. According to the New York Times of December 22, 1943, page 40, Mr. Trumbo was a signer of a declaration issued by the so-called Reichstag Fire Trial Anniversary Committee honoring George Dimitrov, former general secretary of the Communist International.

4. The American Peace Crusade was organized by the American Peace Mobilization. Attorney General Biddle has stated that: "The most conspicuous activity of the American Peace Mobilization was the picketing of the White House, which began in April 1941, in protest against lend-lease and the entire national defense program. * * * On the afternoon of June 21, 1941, he (Frederick V. Field, national secretary) suddenly called·off the picket line around the White House" (Congressional Record, September 24, 1942). Mr. Trumbo was a speaker at a mass meeting held under the auspices of the American Peace Crusade on April 6, 1940, according to the New Masses of August 6, 1940, page 22. He was a speaker at a peace rally at the Los Angeles Olympic Auditorium on April 6, 1940. He was also a speaker for the American Peace Mobilization at the Shrine Auditorium in Los Angeles on February 24, 1941. Mr. Trumbo was the author of a skit which was presented at a meeting of the American Peace Mobilization in Los Angeles on February 24, 1941.

5. The International Workers Order has been cited by Attorney General Biddle as "one of the strongest Communist organizations" (Congressional Record, September 24, 1942). This organization has consistently supported Communist candidates, the Communist press and Communist campaigns. It was cited as a Communist front by the Special Committee on Un-American Activities on January 3, 1940, and June 25, 1942. According to the People's World of May 28, 1943, page 3, Mr. Trumbo was a speaker for the International Workers Order.

6. The American Youth for Democracy, according to the official statements of its leaders, was formerly the Young Communist League. On April 17, 1947, the Committee on Un-American Activities issued a report on the American Youth for Democracy in which it called upon the governors or legislatures of the various States and the administrative heads of the colleges and universities "to thoroughly expose the Communist connections of the American Youth for Democracy as well as the inimical objectives of the Communist Party in America." The Congressional Record of March 24, 1947, page A-1298, contains a statement made by the Honorable J. Edgar Hoover, Director of the Federal Bureau of Investigation, in which he spoke of the American Youth for Democracy as the

organization "which conceals the evils and the corruption of American communism. This name is but a new one for the former Young Communist League. It reflects all the sinister purposes of the Communist Party of the United States. It employs the same techniques and has the same objectives, namely the conversion of our haven of liberty and freedom to worship as we choose to a godless, totalitarian state where the adversaries of democracy can do as they please." The American Youth for Democracy was also cited as a Communist front by the Special Committee on Un-American Activities in the report of March 29, 1944. According to the letterhead of the American Youth for Democracy for December 1, 1944, Dalton Trumbo was a sponsor.

7. The Joint Anti-Fascist Refugee Committee is engaged in providing transportation and support for international Communist agents such as Gerhart Eisler. The Joint Anti-Fascist Refugee Committee was cited for contempt of Congress on April 16, 1946, and its members were convicted in a Federal court on June 27, 1947. According to a letterhead dated February 26, 1946, issued by the Spanish Refugee Appeal of the Joint Anti-Fascist Refugee Committee, Mr. Trumbo was a national sponsor. Mr. Trumbo is also listed as a sponsor of a dinner held by the Joint Anti-Fascist Refugee Committee at the Hotel Astor in New York City on October 27, 1943, according to its printed invitation.

8. The National Federation for Constitutional Liberties has been cited by Attorney General Biddle as part of the "Communist solar system" and he stated that "The defense of Communist leaders such as Sam Darcy and Robert Wood, party secretaries for Pennsylvania and Oklahoma, have been major efforts of the federation" (Congressional Record, September 24, 1942). This organization has been cited as a Communist front by the Special Committee on Un-American Activities on June 25, 1944, and March 29, 1944. Mr. Trumbo signed an open letter published by the National Federation for Constitutional Liberties under the title of "600 Prominent Americans."

9. The Sleepy Lagoon Defense Committee was an auxiliary of the International Labor Defense, properly termed by Attorney General Biddle as the "legal arm of the Communist Party." According to a letterhead of this Defense Committee, dated August 9, 1944, Mr. Trumbo was a sponsor.

10. The League of American Writers was the American affiliate of the International Union of Revolutionary Writers, with headquarters in Moscow. It has been cited as a Communist front by the Special Committee on Un-American Activities on January 3, 1940, June 25, 1942, and March 29, 1944. It has also been cited as under Communist auspices by Attorney General Biddle in the Congressional Record of September 24, 1942. The organization has been pledged to the defense of the Soviet Union and "use of art as an instrument of the class struggle." The Daily Worker on September 5, 1940, page 7, lists Mr. Trumbo as a member of the League of

American Writers. The League of American Writers held a conference in Hollywood on June 20-21, 1942. According to the People's World of June 10, 1942, June 17, 1942, Mr. Trumbo was head of one of its speakers panels. According to People's World of March 31, 1943, page 5, Mr. Trumbo lectured at a conference sponsored by the West Coast Chapter of the League of American Writers, during the summer of 1942 in Hollywood. He was also a contributor to a magazine called Clipper published by the League of American Writers.

11. The Writers Congress held on October 1, 2, 3, 1943, was sponsored by the Hollywood Writers Mobilization, successor to the Hollywood Branch of the League of American Writers, which has been cited as a Communist front by the Special Committee on Un-American Activities and by Attorney General Biddle and the Committee for Cultural Freedom, headed by Prof. John Dewey. Mr. Trumbo was an active participant in one of the panels of the Writers Congress according to the People's World of October 13, 1943, page 5.

12. The Hollywood Writers Mobilization, previously known as the Hollywood Chapter of the League of American Writers, arranged a series of forums at the El Patio Theater in Hollywood, beginning December 2, 1946. Mr. Trumbo was a speaker at these forums.

13. The Hollywood Forum was held under the auspices of the Daily People's World, official west coast organ of the Communist Party, according to the Daily Worker of April 15, 1946, page 11. Mr. Trumbo was a speaker at a forum meeting held on April 9, 1946.

14. The Hollywood Democratic Committee was the successor to the Hollywood Anti-Nazi League which was organized by Isaac Romaine, alias V. J. Jerome, member of the Central Committee of the Communist Party. The Hollywood Anti-Nazi League dissolved during the time of the Stalin-Hitler pact. According to the People's World of August 3, 1943, page 38, Mr. Trumbo made a collection speech in behalf of the Hollywood Democratic Committee.

15. The Motion Picture Democratic Committee was cited as a Communist front by the California Joint Fact-Finding Committee on Un-American Activities in the 1943 report, and by the House Committee on Un-American Activities on September 2, 1947. Melvin Douglas and Philip Dunne resigned from the executive board on the Motion Picture Democratic Committee because of its Communist control. According to the bulletin of the Motion Picture Democratic Committee dated March 26, 1940, Mr. Trumbo was a speaker at its meeting held on April 6, 1940. His subject was "America Declares Peace." This meeting was held during the period of the Stalin-Hitler pact.

16. According to the Daily Worker of October 7, 1942, page 7, Mr. Trumbo was a sponsor of the Artists' Front to Win the War. The Artists' Front to Win the War was an organization which supported the then current Communist demand for a second front. Many of its sponsors were

writers for the Communist press who had opposed the war during the Stalin-Hitler pact, such as Alvah Bessie, Angelo Herndon, Alfred Kreymborg, Albert Maltz, and Ruth McKenney. On September 14, 1942, a meeting was held by the so-called Citizens for Victory Committee at the Philharmonic Auditorium in Los Angeles. Mr. Trumbo was the author of a six-page article entitled "An Open Letter to American People," which was distributed at this meeting, urging the readers to petition and wire the President for the opening of a second front.

17. Another Communist promoted enterprise was the so-called Council for Civic Unity. The People's World, official west coast Communist organ for April 28, 1944, mentioned that Dalton Trumbo made a collection speech for this organization which netted $3,000. A similar group, known as the Academic and Civil Rights Council, mentions Dalton Trumbo as a speaker in the People's World of January 2, 1941. Affiliated with the Council for Civic Unity were the following Communist groups: American Youth for Democracy, formerly known as the Young Communist League; Morning Freiheit Association, supporting the Morning Freiheit, Yiddish organ of the Communist Party; the International Workers Order and other organizations.

18. Paul Robeson, who has a long record of Communist affiliations, was the moving spirit in what was known as American Crusade to End Lynching which organized a pilgrimage to Washington, D.C., for September 23, 1946. This venture was actively supported by the Communist press. Mr. Trumbo was a signer of the call for this pilgrimage, which was another example of Communist efforts to organize mass marches and mass demonstrations on capital cities.

19. According to the People's World of January 15, 1941, page 5, Mr. Trumbo was listed as a speaker at a banquet sponsored by the North California Civil Rights Council held at the Whitcomb Hotel in San Francisco on January 18, 1941. This meeting was primarily concerned with efforts to defend the Communist Party and Communist cases. Mr. Trumbo also took part in a series of meetings held about May 10, 1942, for the purpose of launching a committee to free Earl Browder.

20. According to the program of a members meeting of the Hollywood Arts, Sciences, and Professional Council of September 17, 1947, Mr. Trumbo was listed as a speaker. The Hollywood Arts, Sciences, and Professional Council is a branch of the Progressive Citizens of America which was formed by the left wing group of the ICCASP after the latter organization was dissolved when its Communist denominations could no longer be concealed.

21. The Daily People's World, official Communist Party publication on the west coast, dated May 2, 1947, listed Dalton Trumbo as one of the sponsors of the Los Angeles Chapter of the Civil Rights Congress.

22. The Worker, official publication of the Communist Party dated September 22, 1946, published a picture of the editor and editorial board

of a new magazine entitled "Mainstream," which was referred to as a "Marxist literary magazine." Dalton Trumbo, whose picture appeared with this article, was stated to be a member of the board of directors.

23. A circular announcing a "People's Rally for Peace" meeting at the Shrine Auditorium in Los Angeles on April 24, 1941, under the auspices of the American Peace Mobilization listed Dalton Trumbo as one of the speakers. The purpose of this meeting, according to the circular, was to urge the defeat of the House of Representatives bill for lease-lend.

The Daily People's World, a Communist newspaper for the west coast, dated July 15, 1941, states that Trumbo was in attendance at a meeting of the American Peace Mobilization held at the Hollywood Town Forum, Hollywood, California, on May 17, 1941.

24. The Daily Worker, dated June 20, 1941, listed Trumbo as a speaker at a Free Speech Rally sponsored by the Southern California Branch of the National Federation for Constitutional Liberties held at the Embassy Auditorium in Los Angeles, June 18, 1941.

25. The Clipper, official magazine of the League of American Writers, described above, for the month of August 1941, stated that Dalton Trumbo had been a contributor for the past 12 issues of this magazine.

A circular avertising [sic] the School for Writers sponsored by the Hollywood Chapter of the League of American Writers for the 1941-42 term mentioned Dalton Trumbo as a lecturer.

The Daily People's World, dated March 31, 1943, in an article entitled "Young Writers Develop Technique in Workshop," stated that Dalton Trumbo participated in the writers conference held during December 1942, under the slogan "The Pen Is a Sword," in which beginners, veteran screen writers, novelists, poets, and writers in every medium discussed just how each writer could make his pen a weapon for democracy. The article further stated that the conference was called by the Writers Workshop, which was sponsored by the League of American Writers.

The Screen Writer, the official publication of the Screen Writers Guild, for the month of June 1946, published an edited transcript of an informal discussion held under the auspices of the Hollywood Writers Mobilization between the noted Russian writer Konstantin Simonov and members of the Screen Writers Guild. The forum was presided over by Dalton Trumbo.

26. The California Eagle, dated March 7, 1946, listed Dalton Trumbo as one of the sponsors of the American Youth for Democracy, formerly the Young Communist League, dance held in Los Angeles on March 4, 1946, for the benefit of the United Electrical Workers who were on strike. This is a Communist-controlled union.

A pamphlet advertising the "Salute to Young America" program under the auspices of the American Youth for Democracy to be held at the Hotel Hollywood, Hollywood, California, on December 1, 1944, listed Dalton Trumbo as a member of the sponsoring committee and Mrs. Trumbo as secretary of the committee.

The Daily People's World for December 5, 1944, stated that Trumbo was a speaker at the above meeting.

A pamphlet advertising the "Youth Conference" under sponsorship of the American Youth for Democracy, scheduled for October 21, 1945, at the Los Angeles City College, listed Dalton Trumbo as a sponsor.

A printed advertisement announcing a "Welcome Home, Joe" dinner sponsored by the Los Angeles County American Youth for Democracy, scheduled to be held December 16, 1945, listed Dalton Trumbo as one of the dinner committee members. This meeting was avertised [sic] to be held at the Ambassador Hotel in Los Angeles, California.

27. The Daily Worker, dated October 19, 1942, listed Dalton Trumbo as a sponsor of a dinner under the auspices of the Joint Anti-Fascist Refugee Committee to be held at the Astor Hotel, New York City, on October 27, 1942. This organization has been described above.

A pamphlet issued by the Joint Anti-Fascist Refugee Committee, dated October 21, 1944, listed Dalton Trumbo as one of the national sponsors of this organization. Letterheads of the Joint Anti-Fascist Refugee Committee, 192 Lexington Avenue, New York City, obtained for the years 1945 and 1946, also listed Dalton Trumbo as a national sponsor of this organization.

28. The Daily Worker, dated September 16, 1944, in an article entitled "Film Front," lists Dalton Trumbo as being affiliated with the Hollywood Democratic Committee. This organization has been described above.

29. The Daily Worker, dated November 22, 1944, stated that Dalton Trumbo was elected to the board of directors of the Screen Writers Guild.

The Screen Writer, official publication of the Screen Writers Guild, in the 1946 issues reflected that Dalton Trumbo was the editor of the Screen Writer.

A proposal appeared in the Screen Writer, edited by Dalton Trumbo, July issue, 1946, for an American Authors Authority. According to this report, the authority is to be a marketing monopoly which will copyright and lease to users all writings by American authors. It is to begin with scripts for screen and radio and articles for magazines. By controlling this lucrative field, the authority will be the exclusive agent for America's most successful writers.

30. A letterhead for the People's Educational Center, dated January 11, 1945, announced the second annual meeting of the People's Educational Center, a Communist school at the Shoreham Hotel, Los Angeles, California, on January 21, 1945. The announcement listed Dalton Trumbo as a speaker during the evening session on the subject, Role of the Motion Picture in Shaping the Future.

Page 33 of the report of the California State Legislature's Joint Fact-Finding Committee on Un-American Activities, dated 1947, classifies the People's Educational Center as a Communist front.

31. The Daily People's World, dated July 22, 1946, published a

photograph of Dalton Trumbo along with an article stating that Trumbo would be "an inaugural guest speaker Saturday evening, August 10, 1946, at the California Labor School Term for White Collar and Professional Workers on the Monterey Peninsula." The article further stated that reservations would be accepted at the California Labor School, 216 Market Street, San Francisco, California.

Page 101 of the report of the California State Legislature's Joint Fact-Finding Committee on Un-American Activities, dated 1947, lists the California Labor School as a Communist school.

32. The Daily Variety, a Hollywood trade magazine, for the month of June 1945, listed Dalton Trumbo as a member of the executive council of the Hollywood Independent Citizens Committee of the Arts, Sciences, and Professions. This organization has been described above.

33. The Daily People's World, official Communist Party publication on the west coast, dated May 2, 1947, listed Dalton Trumbo as one of the sponsors of the Los Angeles chapter of the Civil Rights Congress.

The Civil Rights Congress has been engaged in defending Gerhart Eisler, Comintern agent, and Eugene Dennis, executive secretary of the Communist Party.

34. The Daily People's World, dated March 20, 1946, stated that Dalton Trumbo was a speaker at a meeting held at the Shrine Auditorium in Los Angeles, California, under the auspices of the Mobilization for Democracy.

The Daily People's World, dated April 5, 1946, in an article entitled "We Are With—Trumbo Pledges Every Effort on Fight of Native Fascists," comments on a speech by Dalton Trumbo delivered at a meeting of the Mobilization for Democracy held previously in Los Angeles in which Trumbo is reported to have outlined several undertakings by the United States Government, such as Expedition Muskox, Bikini, and the policies of MacArthur in Japan, all of which Trumbo interpreted as an indication of United States imperialism and the work of Fascist reaction in the United States.

35. The California Sentinel, dated May 8, 1947, published a list purported to be the official list of the officers and board of directors of the Southern California Progressive Citizens of America. Dalton Trumbo was listed as a member of the board of directors.

Page 236 of the report of the California State Legislature's Joint Fact-Finding Committee on Un-American Activities, dated 1947, refers to the Los Angeles Chapter of the Progressive Citizens of America as a consolidation of the National Political Action Committee and the Hollywood Independent Citizens Committee of the Arts, Sciences, and Professions, which are referred to as Communist fronts.

36. The Daily People's World, dated October 19, 1942, listed Dalton Trumbo as one of 400 prominent people who signed an open letter to President Roosevelt urging the United States to sever diplomatic relations with Spain. This letter was made public, according to the article, by the

Council for Pan-American Democracy, which has attacked alleged American imperialism.

37. The Daily People's World, dated November 6, 1945, carried an advertisement under the heading, "Break relations with Spain," advising that a meeting was scheduled for the Shrine Auditorium in Los Angeles, California, for November 16, 1945, at which Dalton Trumbo would serve as chairman. The meeting was said to be under the auspices of the American Committee for Spanish Freedom. This was part of the Communist campaign in behalf of Loyalist Spain initiated at the seventh Congress of the Communist International—the summer of 1935.

38. The Daily Worker, dated May 24, 1947, listed Dalton Trumbo as one of the speakers at the Artists Fight Back meeting sponsored by Mainstream, to be held at Manhattan Center, New York City, on June 11, 1947. The article stated that the rally would give the answer of the writers and artists to the "Un-American Committee's" attacks on democratic culture in America.

The New York World Telegram, dated June 11, 1947, listed Dalton Trumbo as one of the speakers at the Artists Fight Back rally held at Manhattan Center, New York City, on June 11, 1947.

The Worker, dated March 23, 1947, published a write-up on the magazine Mainstream showing the table of contents for the winter edition, 1946, listing Dalton Trumbo as a contributor with a poem entitled "Confessional." This magazine has been described above.

39. The Daily People's World, dated October 24, 1942, listed Dalton Trumbo as one of the persons who endorsed LaRue McCormick as Communist Party candidate for State senator of Los Angeles County.

The Daily People's World, dated July 6, 1944, announced that Dalton Trumbo would be one of the judges of a short-story contest sponsored by the Daily People's World to run from August 1, 1944, to February 1, 1945.

The Daily People's World, dated March 26, 1946, listed Dalton Trumbo as a speaker at a forum held at the Embassy Auditorium on April 8, 1946, under the auspices of the Daily People's World entitled "Art—Weapon of the People." A photostatic copy of this publicity is attached.

APPENDIX III

The Briefs of the Hollywood Ten

This section contains the opening statements of the Hollywood Ten as published in Gordon Kahn's book *Hollywood on Trial.*

Statement of John Howard Lawson

For a week, this Committee has conducted an illegal and indecent trial of American citizens, whom the Committee has selected to be publicly pilloried and smeared. I am not here to defend myself, or to answer the agglomeration of falsehoods that has been heaped upon me. I believe lawyers describe this material, rather mildly, as "hearsay evidence." To the American public, it has a shorter name: dirt. Rational people don't argue with dirt. I feel like a man who has had truck-loads of filth heaped upon him; I am now asked to struggle to my feet and talk while more truck-loads pour more filth around my head.

No, you don't argue with dirt. But you try to find out where it comes from. And to stop the evil deluge before it buries you—and others. The immediate source is obvious. The so-called "evidence" comes from a parade of stool-pigeons, neurotics, publicity-seeking clowns, Gestapo agents, paid informers, and a few ignorant and frightened Hollywood artists. I am not going to discuss this perjured testimony. Let these people live with their consciences, with the knowledge that they have violated their country's most sacred principles.

These individuals are not important. As an individual, I am not important. The obvious fact that the Committee is trying to destroy me personally and professionally, to deprive me of my livelihood and what is far dearer to me—my honor as an American—gains significance only because it opens the way to similar destruction of any citizen whom the Committee selects for annihilation.

I am not going to touch on the gross violation of the Constitution of the United States, and especially of its First and Fifth Amendments, that is taking place here. The proof is so overwhelming that it needs no elaboration. The Un-American Activities Committee stands convicted in the court of public opinion.

I want to speak here as a writer and a citizen.

It is not surprising that writers and artists are selected for this indecent smear. Writers, artists, scientists, educators, are always the first victims of attack by those who hate democracy. The writer has a special responsibility to serve democracy, to further the free exchange of ideas. I am proud to be singled out for attack by men who are obviously—by their own admission on the record—out to stifle ideas and censor communication.

I want to speak of a writer's integrity—the integrity and professional ethics that have been so irresponsibly impugned at these hearings. In its illegal attempt to establish a political dictatorship over the motion picture industry, the Committee has tried to justify its probing into the thought and conscience of individuals on the ground that these individuals insert allegedly "subversive" lines or scenes in motion pictures. From the viewpoint of the motion picture producer, this charge is a fantasy out of the Arabian Nights. But it is also a sweeping indictment of the writer's integrity and professional conduct. When I am employed to write a motion picture, my whole purpose is to make it a vital, entertaining, creative portrayal of the segment of life with which it deals. Many problems arise in writing a picture. Like all honest writers, I never write a line or develop a situation, without fully discussing its implications, its meaning, its tendency, with the men in charge of production. Where a line or a situation might relate to controversial issues, I am particularly insistent on full discussion, because such issues affect studio policy, critical response and popularity of the picture.

My political and social views are well known. My deep faith in the motion picture as a popular art is also well known. I don't "sneak ideas" into pictures. I never make a contract to write a picture unless I am convinced that it serves democracy and the interests of the American people. I will never permit what I write and think to be subject to the orders of self-appointed dictators, ambitious politicians, thought-control gestapos, or any other form of censorship this Un-American Committee may attempt to devise. My freedom to speak and write is not for sale in return for a card signed by J. Parnell Thomas saying "O.K. for employment until further notice."

Pictures written by me have been seen and approved by millions of Americans. A subpoena for all those who have enjoyed these pictures and recognized them as an honest portrayal of our American life.

Thus, my integrity as a writer is obviously an integral part of my integrity as a citizen. As a citizen I am not alone here. I am not only one of nineteen men who have been subpoenaed. I am forced to appear here as a representative of one hundred and thirty million Americans because the illegal conduct of this Committee has linked me with every citizen. If I can be destroyed no American is safe. You can subpoena a farmer in a field, a lumberjack in the woods, a worker at a machine, a doctor in his office—you can deprive them of a livelihood, deprive them of their honor as Americans.

Let no one think that this is an idle or thoughtless statement. This is the course that the Un-American Activities Committee has charted. Millions of Americans who may as yet be unconscious of what may be in store for them will find that the warning I speak today is literally fulfilled. No American will be safe if the Committee is not stopped in its illegal enterprise.

I am like most Americans in resenting interference with my conscience and belief. I am like most Americans in insisting on my right to serve my country in the way that seems to me most helpful and effective. I am like most Americans in feeling that loyalty to the United States and pride in its traditions is the guiding principle of my life. I am like most Americans in believing that divided loyalty—which is another word for treason—is the most despicable crime of which any man or woman can be accused.

It is my profound conviction that it is precisely because I hold these beliefs that I have been hailed before this illegal court. These are the beliefs that the so-called Un-American Activities Committee is seeking to root out in order to subvert orderly government and establish an autocratic dictatorship.

I am not suggesting that J. Parnell Thomas aspires to be the man on horseback. He is a petty politician, serving more powerful forces. Those forces are trying to introduce fascism in this country. They know that the only way to trick the American people into abandoning their rights and liberties is to manufacture an imaginary danger, to frighten the people into accepting repressive laws which are supposedly for their protection.

To anyone familiar with history the pattern for the seizure of dictatorial power is well known. Manufactured charges against "reds," "communists," "enemies of law and order" have been made repeatedly over the centuries. In every case, from the Star Chamber in Stuart England to the burning of the Reichstag in Nazi Germany, the charges have included everyone with democratic sympathies; in every case the charges have been proven false; in every case, the charges have been used to cover an arbitrary seizure of power.

In the terrible wave of repression that swept England at the end of the eighteenth century, Charles James Fox asked a simple question: "We have seen and heard of revolutions in other states. Were they owing to the freedom of popular opinions? Were they owing to the facility of popular meetings? No, sir, they were owing to the reverse of these." The writers and thinkers who were jailed and silenced at that time were all cleared a few years later. The great scientist, Priestley, whose home was burned, was forced to flee to America where he was honored as an apostle of liberty. The persecutions under the Alien and Sedition Acts in our own country in 1798 were all proved to be the irresponsible means by which a reactionary political party sought to maintain itself in power. Congress officially repaid all the fines collected under the Sedition Act. The cry of sedition was again raised through the land in 1919 in order to build up the illusion of a non-existent national emergency and thus justify wholesale violations of the Bill of Rights, designed solely to crush labor, prevent American participation in the League of Nations, and keep reaction in power.

Today, we face a serious crisis in the determination of national policy. The only way to solve that crisis is by free discussion. Americans must know the facts. The only plot against American safety is the plot to conceal facts. I am plastered with mud because I happen to be an American who expresses opinions that the House Un-American Activities Committee does not like. But my opinions are not an issue in this case. The issue is my right to have opinions. The Committee's logic is obviously: Lawson's opinions are properly subject to censorship; he writes for the motion picture industry, so the industry makes pictures for the American people, so the minds of the people must be censored and controlled.

Why? What are J. Parnell Thomas and the Un-American interests he serves, afraid of? They're afraid of the American people. They don't want to muzzle me. They want to muzzle public opinion. They want to muzzle the great Voice of democracy. Because they're conspiring against the American way of life. They want to cut living standards, introduce an economy of poverty, wipe out labor's rights, attack Negroes, Jews, and other minorities, drive us into a disastrous and unnecessary war.

The struggle between thought-control and freedom of expression is the struggle between the people and a greedy unpatriotic minority which hates and fears the people. I wish to present as an integral part of this statement, a paper which I read at a Conference on Thought Control in the United States held in Hollywood on July 9th to 13th. The paper presents the historical background of the threatening situation that we face today, and shows that the attack on freedom of communication is, and has always been, an attack on the American people.

The American people will know how to answer that attack. They will rally, as they have always rallied, to protect their birthright.

Statement of Dalton Trumbo

Mr. Chairman:

As indicated by news dispatches from foreign countries during the past week, the eyes of the world are focused today upon the House Committee on Un-American Activities. In every capital city these hearings will be reported. From what happens during the proceedings, the peoples of the earth will learn by precept and example precisely what America means when her strong voice calls out to the community of nations for freedom of the press, freedom of expression, freedom of conscience, the civil rights of men standing accused before government agencies, the vitality and strength of private enterprise, the inviolable right of every American to think as he wishes, to organize and assemble as he pleases, to vote in secret as he chooses.

The quality of our devotion to these principles will be weighed most thoughtfully by all who have been urged to emulate the American way of life. Whether we wish it or not, the Committee and its witnesses appear here before the world as a living test of American democracy in action. By reason of this we have all been committed to a very heavy responsibility.

I shall therefore pass quickly over the hearsay and slander of witnesses classified as friendly to this Committee, as well as over other evidence already established as perjury. I call your attention only briefly to political coincidence that nearly all friendly witnesses summoned by the Committee have violently opposed the ideals of Wendell Willkie and Franklin Roosevelt, while without exception the unfriendly witnesses have supported such ideals. I shall make no comment at all on the petty professional jealousies, the private feuds, the intra-studio conflicts which here have been elevated to the dignity of the record. And only with reluctance and shame do I find it necessary to recall how fulsomely this Committee has complimented witnesses who have proposed that all who disagree with them be deprived of citizenship and handed over to the mercy of mobs.

There are three principal points which I wish to stress in my statement to this Committee:

First: In the course of these hearings your Committee has launched a direct attack upon the constitutional rights of property and of management and of that system which we call private enterprise. You have attempted to compel management to hire and fire at your own dictation, without any regard for rights and agreements already established between management and labor within the motion picture industry. But even beyond this, you have attempted to dictate to industry what kind of product it shall make and what kind it shall not make.

Let every business man in America clearly understand that if this Committee can usurp the rights of management in one industry, it has established the precedent by which it can usurp the rights of management in all industries. Modern history reveals many instances abroad where workers in private industry have resolutely defended the rights of management against the encroachments of a corporate state. I am certain they will make such a defense in this country against the attempt with which this Committee is presently engaged.

Second: The Committee in its hearings has consistently attacked the constitutional guarantees of a free press, which encompass the guarantee of a free screen. The American film, as a medium of communication, as a purveyor of ideas, is completely beyond the investigatory powers of this Committee. No committee of the Congress can dictate to the motion picture industry what ideas it shall and shall not incorporate into films, nor can it dictate to the American people what ideas they may and may not see upon the screens of their neighborhood theaters.

But you have not exclusively attacked the principle of a free screen. In the past, you have sought to intimidate workers in the radio industry. And during these hearings you have thanked witnesses who have testified against the theater, the publishing business, and the press itself. This constant attempt to interfere with the rights of every medium of free expression provides the consistent brown thread which binds together all testimony thus far presented by friendly witnesses. It clearly reveals your intention to establish a slave screen, subservient to the cultural standards of J. Parnell Thomas and the humanitarian precepts of John E. Rankin.

Third: The Committee throughout its hearing has approved even the grossest attacks upon the right of the artist to express his ideas freely and honestly in his work. Similarly, you have sought testimony attacking his right to function in craft organizations and trade unions for the advancement of his interests. You are now attacking his right to think, and seeking by public inquisition to ferret out his innermost ideas and his most private and personal convictions. No institution on earth possesses this power over American citizens. You violate the most elementary principles of constitutional guarantees when you require anyone to parade for your approval his opinions upon race, religion, politics, or any other matter.

We must furthermore remember always that the defense of constitutional rights is not simply a convenience to be invoked in time of need, but a clear and continuous obligation imposed equally upon all of us at all times. We are, as citizens, literally commanded by its implications to defend the Constitution against even the slightest encroachment upon the protective barrier it interposes between the private citizen on one hand and the inquisitors of government on the other.

Already the gentlemen of this Committee and others of like disposition have produced in this capital city a political atmosphere which is acrid with fear and repression; a community in which anti-Semitism finds safe refuge behind secret tests of loyalty; a city in which no union leader can trust his telephone; a city in which old friends hesitate to recognize one another in public places; a city in which men and women who dissent even slightly from the orthodoxy you seek to impose, speak with confidence only in moving cars and in the open air. You have produced a capital city on the eve of its Reichstag fire. For those who remember German history in the autumn of 1932 there is the smell of smoke in this very room.

Statement of Albert Maltz

I am an American and I believe there is no more proud word in the vocabulary of man. I am a novelist and a screen writer and I have produced a certain body of work in the past fifteen years. As with any other writer, what I have written has come from the total fabric of my life—my birth in this land, our schools and games, our atmosphere of freedom, our tradition of inquiry, criticism, discussion, tolerance. Whatever I am, America has made me. And I, in turn, possess no loyalty as great as the one I have to this land, to the economic and social welfare of its people, to the perpetuation and development of its democratic way of life.

Now at the age of 39, I am commanded to appear before the House Committee on Un-American Activities. For a full week this Committee has encouraged an assortment of well-rehearsed witnesses to testify that I and others are subversive and un-American. It has refused us the opportunity that any pickpocket receives in a magistrate's court—the right to cross-examine these witnesses, to refute their testimony, to reveal their motives, their history, and who, exactly, they are. Furthermore it grants these witnesses congressional immunity so that we may not sue them for libel for their slanders.

I maintain that this is an evil and vicious procedure; that it is legally unjust and morally indecent—and that it places in danger every other American, since if the rights of any one citizen can be invaded, then the constitutional guaranties of every other American have been subverted and no one is any longer protected from official tyranny.

What is it about me that this Committee wishes to destroy? My writings? Very well, let us refer to them.

My novel, The Cross and the Arrow, was issued in special edition of 140,000 copies by a war-time Government agency, the Armed Services Edition, for American servicemen abroad.

My short stories have been reprinted in over 30 anthologies by as many publishers—all subversive, no doubt.

My film, The Pride of the Marines, was premiered in 28 cities at Guadalcanal Day banquets under the auspices of the United States Marine Corps.

Another film, Destination Tokyo, was premiered aboard a United States submarine and was adopted by the Navy as an official training film.

My short film, The House I Live In, was given a special award by the Academy of Motion Picture Arts and Sciences for its contribution to racial tolerance.

My short story, The Happiest Man on Earth, won the 1938 O. Henry Memorial Award for the best American short story.

This, then, is the body of work for which this Committee urges I be blacklisted in the film industry—and tomorrow, if it has its way, in the publishing and magazine fields also.

By cold censorship, if not legislation, I must not be allowed to write. Will this censorship stop with me? Or with the others now singled out for attack? If it requires acceptance of the brand of un-Americanism, then who is ultimately safe from this Committee except members of the Ku Klux Klan?

Why else does this Committee now seek to destroy me and others? Because of our ideas, unquestionably. In 1801, when he was President of the United States, Thomas Jefferson wrote:

Opinion, and the just maintenance of it, shall never be a crime in my view; nor bring injury to the individual.

But a few years ago, in the course of one of the hearings of this Committee, Congressman J. Parnell Thomas said, and I quote from the official transcript:

I just want to say this now, that it seems that the New Deal is working along hand in glove with the Communist Party. The New Deal is either for the Communist Party or it is playing into the hands of the Communist Party.

Very well, then, here is the other reason why I and others have been commanded to appear before this Committee—our ideas. In common with many Americans, I supported the New Deal. In common with many Americans I supported, against Mr. Thomas and Mr. Rankin, the anti-lynching bill. I opposed them in my support of OPA controls and emergency veteran housing and a fair employment practices law. I signed petitions for these measures, joined organizations that advocated them, contributed money, sometimes spoke from public platforms, and I will continue to do so. I will take my philosophy from Thomas Paine, Thomas Jefferson, Abraham Lincoln, and I will not be dictated to or intimidated by men to whom the Ku Klux Klan, as a matter of Committee record, is an acceptable American institution.

I state further that on many questions of public interest my opinions as a citizen have not always been in accord with the opinions of this majority. They are not now nor have my opinions ever been fixed and unchanging, nor are they now fixed and unchangeable; but, right or wrong, I claim and I insist upon my right to think freely and to speak freely; to join the Republican Party or the Communist Party, the Democratic or the Prohibition Party; to publish whatever I please; to fix my mind or change my mind, without dictation from anyone; to offer any criticism I think fitting of any public official or policy; to join whatever organizations I please, no matter what certain legislators may think of them. Above all, I challenge the right of this Committee to inquire into my political or religious beliefs, in any manner or degree, and I assert that not only the conduct of this Committee but its very existence are a subversion of the Bill of Rights.

If I were a spokesman for General Franco, I would not be here today. I would rather be here. I would rather die than be a shabby American, groveling before men whose names are Thomas and Rankin, but who now carry out activities in America like those carried out in Germany by Goebbels and Himmler.

The American people are going to have to choose between the Bill of Rights and the Thomas Committee. They cannot have both. One or the other must be abolished in the immediate future.

Statement of Alvah Bessie

It is my understanding of the First Amendment to our Constitution that it expressly forbids Congress to pass any law which shall abridge freedom of speech or of opinion. And it is my understanding of the function of Congressional Committees, that they are set up by the

Congress for the express purpose of inquiring into matter that may lead to the initiation of legislation in the Congress.

Now either the Constitution and its Bill of Rights mean what they say or they do not mean what they say. Either the First Amendment is binding upon Congress and all legislative bodies of our Government, or it means nothing at all. I cannot agree with this so-called Committee in its implied belief that the Bill of Rights means whatever this body chooses it to mean, or is applicable only to those with whose opinions this Committee is in agreement.

I am not in agreement with the opinions, activities, or objectives of this Committee or any Committee remotely resembling it. And since the only legislation this Committee could possibly initiate would automatically abridge freedom of speech and opinion, and would therefore be automatically unconstitutional, I have come to the conclusion, that will eventually be borne out by events, that this body is totally unconstitutional and without power to inquire into anything I think, believe, uphold, and cherish, or anything I have ever written or said, or any organization I have ever joined or failed to join.

As a one-time newspaperman I have been deeply interested in the mounting reaction of disapproval by the press of the nation of the activities of this Committee. When the conservative New York Herald Tribune can say ". . . the beliefs of men and women who write for the screen are, like the beliefs of any ordinary men or women, everybody's business but their own, as the Bill of Rights mentions. Neither Mr. Thomas nor the Congress in which he sits is empowered to dictate what Americans shall think . . ."; and when the Chicago Times can say, "Of course, the real object of Chairman Thomas and the reactionary Republican majority of the House Un-American Activities Committee is not primarily to uncover subversive influences in Hollywood. It is to smear New Dealers and whatever their progressive successors may be called. . ." —then it is not difficult to any intelligent person to realize that if this investigation is permitted to achieve its immediate objective it will not hesitate to move on from the motion-picture industry it has emasculated, to the throttling of the press, the radio, the theater, and the book publishers of America. We saw this pattern at work before, in Hitler's Germany, and we understand it thoroughly. The true purpose of this Committee on Un-American Activities is to provide the atmosphere and to act as the spearhead for the really un-American forces preparing a Fascist America.

In calling me from my home this body hopes also to rake over the smoldering embers of the war that was fought in Spain from 1938 to 1939. This body, in all its previous manifestations, is on record as believing that support of the Spanish Republic was and is subversive, un-American, and Communist-inspired. That lie was originally spawned by Hitler and Franco, and the majority of the American people—in fact, the majority of the people of the world—never believed it. And I want it on the record at this point that I not only supported the Spanish Republic but that it was my high privilege and the greatest honor I have ever enjoyed to have been a volunteer soldier in the ranks of its International Brigades throughout 1938. And I shall continue to support the Spanish Republic until the Spanish people in their majesty and power remove Francisco Franco and all his supporters and reestablish the legal government Franco and his Nazi and Italian Fascist soldiers overthrew.

The understanding that led me to fight in Spain for that Republic, and my experience in that war, teach me that this Committee is engaged in precisely the identical activities engaged in by un-Spanish Committees, un-German Committees, and un-Italian Committees which preceded it in every country which eventually succumbed to fascism. I will never aid or abet such a Committee in its patent attempt to foster the sort of intimidation and terror that is the inevitable precursor of a Fascist regime. And I therefore restate my conviction that this body has no legal authority to pry into the mind or activities of any American who believes, as I do, in the Constitution, and who is willing at any time to fight to preserve it—as I fought to preserve it in Spain.

Statement of Samuel Ornitz

I wish to address this Committee as a Jew, because one of its leading members is the outstanding anti-Semite in the Congress and revels in that fact. I refer to John E. Rankin. I refer to this evil because it has been responsible for the systematic and ruthless slaughter of six million of my people. Nor were they alone to die. Thirty million others died, including American boys. It may be redundant to repeat that anti-Semitism and anti-Communism were the number one poison weapon used by Hitler—but still terribly relevant, lest we forget.

In speaking as a Jew, I speak in a deeper sense as an American, as the one who has to take the first blow for my fellow-Americans. For when Constitutional guarantees are overridden, the Jew is the first one to suffer . . . but only the first one. As soon as the Jew is crushed, the others get it. Or haven't we been through this . . . the most horrible of wars to date!

Nor did this evil die with Hitler. He and his emulators like Rankin propagated it well. The current Fortune Magazine poll shows that thirty-six percent of the adult American people have become anti-Semitic and twelve percent anti-Catholic. It reveals a more devastating fact, namely, that this anti-Semitic and anti-Catholic feeling tends to run highest where Jews and Catholics are the fewest, in remote American communities . . . how sad, to be able to hate someone you haven't even seen!

I am struck forcibly by the fact that this Committee has subpoenaed the three men who made Crossfire, a powerful attack on anti-Semitism . . .

and appalled by the fact that you characterized them as "unfriendly" witnesses before they were heard and thus prejudiced opinion against them.

Is it mere coincidence that you chose to subpoena and characterize as "unfriendly" the men who produced, wrote, directed or acted in the following feature length pictures and short subjects, which attacked anti-Semitism. or treated Jews and Negroes sympathetically . . . Pride of the Marines, The House I Live In, Don't Be a Sucker, None Shall Escape, Of Mice and Men, The Brotherhood of Man, The Commington Story, Freedom Road, Body and Soul, New Orleans, The Master Race, and The Jolson Story.

On the front page of the Washington papers today we find reported that our Attorney General Tom C. Clark feels "humiliated" because the American Negro people have had to appeal to the United Nations for redress against lynching and discrimination, and as a result, Mr. Clark is going to enlarge the civil rights section of the United States Department of Justice.

The eyes of the world are on this Committee. Let them not see that the civil rights have become a mockery in America in a Congressional caucus room, of all places!

Your Committee and its so-called "friendly" witnesses have been unable to name a single line . . . let alone a picture, that is un-American or subversive by any stretch of the imagination.

Therefore, I ask as a Jew, based on the record, is bigotry this Committee's yardstick of Americanism and its definition of subversive? Indeed—another member of Congress, Senator Glenn H. Taylor, has described the conduct of your Committee as—"Fascist-minded . . . parallel to those pre-war leaders in Germany, Italy, and Japan." I declare that the record bears him out.

Therefore, I feel that I stand here in the first line of the defense of our Constitution and Freedom. I must not fail—nor for one moment falter before the threat of contempt, which word sounds like the short way of saying concentration camp.

I am now ready for your questions. I shall answer them conscientiously.

Statement of Herbert Biberman

I have listened to, watched and read the so-called "testimony," at the so-called "hearings," of the so-called "Committee on Un-American Activities," which the English cartoonist Low has characterized as "a 10 cent version of the American Way of Life," for a week.

I do not consider this Committee to be stupid. On the contrary, I consider it to be evil. It is not Communism the House Committee on Un-American Activities fears, but the human mind, reason itself. It is not force and violence this Committee is investigating, but earnest, unceasing citizenship. This Committee is in the course of overthrowing, not Karl Marx, but the constitutional way of American life.

Intimidation and political bullying is and always has been a great evil. Against it, in America, there is and has been, one and only one protection—the fundamental law, the conscience, the mind and the heart of America, embodied in the Constitution of the United States of America and its progressive ten amendments, the Bill of Rights.

Had this Committee on Un-American Activities been born a century and three-quarters ago, there is little doubt it would have voted against the Bill of Rights, and gone down the drain of history with the Tories of that time. But finding the Constitution in existence, and an obstacle in its path, this Committee seeks to undo it, by bullying the American people into surrendering their respect for, and their faith in, this charter of individual freedom.

This Committee, disregarding the individual American's right to choose his thoughts, at least as freely as he chooses his brand of cigarettes—by bullying and intimidation, diverts attention from the Bill of Rights, so that it may erect in its place "rule by accusation." It must divert attention from the Bill of Rights because it knows it can never erect "rule by accusation" in a country of free, unrestrained, outspoken citizens. It therefore coddles Mr. Adolphe Menjou into this bit of fashionably treacherous advice, "He won't last long if he is labeled a Communist" and thanks him for his assistance in subverting the American concept of the free individual.

The Bill of Rights was not conceived primarily to protect the status-quo. Those who won national independence for the American people understood very well that the status-quo, by virtue of its inherent strength, is always in the very most protected position, well able to attend to its own security. The Bill of Rights was conceived for those who needed it most; those with wider visions than the status-quo ever represents in respect to man's potential. To those who saw farther horizons for America's development, who felt compelled to push beyond its very real accomplishments, who believed in the perfectability of man and his brotherhood—to them was guaranteed by the Bill of Rights, the calm, the security of mind and person, the dignity necessary to expand the American dream by advocating it and pressing for its fullest realization. Against this right to vision and the right to advocate this vision, the Constitution and the Bill of Rights yielded to no other right, the right of way.

But this Committee is now engaged in an attempt to crush this unyieldable right and to put an end to the calm, the security, and the dignity upon which it feeds. This has been attempted often in our country's history, by other groups of officialdom. Such attempts have had their moments, their hours, even their years, but they have never had a single uninterrupted decade in the long life of our Republic and they never will. America will change, but not into its opposite. America will change out of its own growing nature—the self-confidence, the neighborliness, and the non-intimidability of the American people.

As an American I am proud of a fairly long record of discussion and advocacy of social and economic change under the law. Americans have developed a sense of easy access to public forums, of whatever size, and this has accustomed us very naturally to take our feelings, our opinions, and our desires to our fellow citizens constantly and passionately.

I have never been a stand patter. This has always seemed to me a very dull, uncreative and unrewarding frame of mind. My advocacy of this or that issue has often failed of popular acceptance. In the light of developing history, I have sometimes been proven in error, whether of degree or kind, but I have never felt the necessity of apologizing for error, or boasting of success, because I have felt myself bound to my fellow citizens with a single common tie—the hard, slow and patient work necessary if one is to contribute to the correction of social and economic short-comings, and the development of solutions under law.

If I were guilty of acts of force and violence I would never have been called before this Committee. I would be in the courts. And if I were guilty of such acts against this, my country, and this, my people—I should be in the courts, and convicted and condemned.

It is because I have committed no acts against my country and my people that I am here. It is because I have been an active citizen that I am here. No slothful, lazy, self-satisfied or cynical citizen is brought here—except those who are in the service of, or in the same bed with, the members of this Committee. I am here because I love, believe in, respect, and have unlimited faith in my fellow citizens. I have been brought here because I believe they will constantly achieve a richer social and economic life under the Constitution, which will eliminate prejudice and inequality in spite of the efforts of this Committee to prevent it. I have been brought here because I believe the American people will not give up the holy struggle for a peaceful world, will not be bullied into an hysterical war. I have been brought here not because I have dreamed these dreams but because I committed the sin of devoting ten years to energetic advocacy of my faith in the American people under our Bill of Rights. For this I have earned the hatred of this Committee, and of this hatred I am especially proud.

Because my professional life and my life as a free man have been so uncensorable by decent ·standards, this Committee for Un-American Activities, in order to attempt to embarrass and intimidate me, has, without power or authority under the Constitution, been forced to set up a series of categories such as "Foreign Agent," "Subversive," in order to attempt, by use of these scare phrases, to poison the public mind against me, and against the many, many other Americans who with slow, hard and patient persistence have tried to be the most effective citizens their powers permit.

Between this Committee and the nineteen "unfriendly" witnesses there is an impassable gulf. We are the ends opposite of American life. Either this Committee will be abolished or it will abolish the Bill of Rights and the American way of life along with it. This question will not be decided by the Committee or by us but by the American people. And this decision will be a decision of, by, and for the continuance of popular constitutional government in our country.

In this hearing I will not merely rely upon the Constitution—I will fight for it and defend it against all possible intimidation.

Here as well, I am a free man—accustomed to slow, hard, patient and passionate defense of what I believe to be American.

There is a hymn we sing, and teach our children to sing, which scans as follows:

> My country 'tis of thee
> Sweet land of liberty
> Of thee I sing
> Land where our fathers died
> Land of the Pilgrim's pride
> From every mountain side
> Let Freedom ring!

Statement of Adrian Scott

I do not believe it is necessary for me to raise my voice against the open war now being waged on civil liberties and on a free screen by the Committee on Un-American Activities. Voices more eloquent than mine have spoken.

I wish to speak about another way. I would like to speak about the "cold war" now being waged by the Committee of Un-American Activities against the Jewish and Negro people.

The evidence is clear and incontrovertible.

Edward Dmytryk, who directed Crossfire, and I, who served Crossfire as producer, have extended invitations to the Committee to view this picture. Our invitations were ignored or refused.

We who made this picture are proud of it. We are proud to lend our voices, however small, in the enormous fight now being waged—and yet to be waged—to destroy the un-American practice of anti-Semitism. We detest anti-Semitism. We detest anti-Catholicism. We detest anti-Protestantism. We detest any practice which degrades any minority or any religion or any people.

We expected the Committee to refuse our invitation to see and to discuss Crossfire. We expected them to refuse to discuss measures by which the practice of anti-Semitism could be abolished. To do this would be incompatible with the Committee's bigoted record and bigoted support.

Individually a member of this Committee may protest that he is not anti-Semitic. He may say that some of his best friends are Jews—or even that some of his best constituents are Jews. Or he may say, in protest, that he loves the Negro people; and the Negro people love him—that, in his poll tax district, the colored man knows that he loves him, providing the colored man keeps his place. But despite his protestations of individual innocence, the evidence of the Committee's collective guilt is cynically clear.

Let the committeeman say he is not anti-Semitic. But the rabble rousing anti-Semitic Gerald L. K. Smith publicly approves and supports him.

Let the committeeman say he is not against the colored people. But the anti-Negro Ku Klux Klan and all hate groups love and work for him.

Let the committeeman whisper in the cloak room that he disapproves of the hatemonger, John Rankin of Mississippi. But has he disavowed him publicly? Has he repudiated his racist doctrine? Has he, more important, recommended legislation which would destroy John Rankin's racist doctrines?

Let the committeeman say he is opposed to inhuman treatment of minorities—and bad housing and unsanitary ghettos. But what measures has the committeeman personally recommended to change all this? Where has his hand been evident in assisting minorities to take their rightful place among their fellow men? What has he done to make fair employment practices a reality?

Let the committeeman say he is not anti-Semitic. But let the record show he does the work of anti-Semites.

Let the committeeman say he is not anti-Negro. But let the record show that he does the work of the Ku Klux Klan.

Today this Committee is engaged in an attempt to destroy nineteen subpoenaed witnesses. The record of these men is clear. They have always stood for issues which are beneficial to the great mass of the American people.

Many times in their films they have presented the Jew and the Negro (and other minorities as well) in unstereotyped terms. They have made it an uncompromising rule in motion pictures to treat all minorities with dignity.

These men oppose and actively work against Gerald L. K. Smith and the Ku Klux Klan and the Black Legion and the Columbians and all kinds and varieties of hate groups.

They not only say they are against minority oppression, they do something about it.

The Committee is now attempting to deprive these nineteen men of jobs, to establish a blacklist. By slander, by vilification, this Committee is attempting to frighten and intimidate these men and their employers; to silence those voices which have spoken out for the Jewish and the Negro people and other people.

The Committee wants these eloquent voices stilled.

This is the cold war now being waged by the Committee on Un-American Activities against minorities. The next phase—total war against minorities—needs no elaboration. History has recorded what has happened in Nazi Germany.

For myself and my colleagues, we will not be intimidated. We will not be frightened. We will not permit our voices to be put into moulds or into concentration camps. We will continue to lend our voices so that fundamental justice will obtain for Jews, Negroes, and for all citizens.

Here is the partial motion picture record of these men in behalf of minorities:

Robert Rossen wrote the anti-lynch picture They Won't Forget. His latest picture is Body and Soul which treats Negro and Jew with dignity and justice as free men.

Howard Koch wrote Casablanca and In This Our Life. The Negro is treated honestly as a free man.

Albert Maltz wrote Pride of the Marines and The House I Live In which was sung by Frank Sinatra. Both pictures exposed anti-Semitism and religious and racial intolerance.

Waldo Salt wrote the Commington Story for the OWI. An attack on anti-Semitism.

Ring Lardner, Jr., wrote the Brotherhood of Man calling for more understanding among races and religions.

Herbert Biberman produced New Orleans, hailed by the Negro press as intelligent treatment of Negroes.

Lewis Milestone directed Of Mice and Men in which the Negro was handled with dignity. And, lest we forget, Nazi Storm Troopers stopped the showing of his anti-war film All Quiet on the Western Front, in 1931, in Germany.

Lester Cole wrote None Shall Escape which exposed Nazi brutality to the Jews.

Richard Collins wrote Don't Be a Sucker for the armed services. Subsequently, it was released to the public. It exposed anti-Semitism and kindred hatreds.

Irving Pichel directed A Medal for Benny, which treated a Mexican minority with dignity.

Will the American people allow this bigoted Committee to sit in judgment of these men and their records?

Statement of Edward Dmytryk

It is my firm belief that democracy lives and thrives only on freedom. This country has always fulfilled its destiny most completely when its people, through their representatives, have allowed themselves the greatest exercise of freedom with the law. The dark periods in our history have been those in which our freedoms have been suppressed, to however small a degree. Some of that darkness exists into the present day in the continued suppression of certain minorities. In my last few years in Hollywood, I have devoted myself, through pictures such as Crossfire, to a fight against these racial suppressions and prejudices. My work speaks for itself. I believe that it speaks clearly enough so that the people of the country and this Committee, which has no right to inquire into my politics or my thinking, can still judge my thoughts and my beliefs by my work, and by my work alone.

The freedom which is so necessary for the fullest development of a democratic nation is also indispensable for the fullest development of any institution within that nation which deals with ideas and ideals. For without the free expression of ideas, both favorable and critical, no nation can long hope to remain free. This principle has been stated many times before, in far better words than mine. It is a shame that it should have to be repeated here before this Committee.

But the intent is clear. This Committee has demanded that the producers "clean their own house," under the supervision of the Committee's members. They will name the names and the producers must make out the blacklist. But where will it end? History is all too clear on procedures of this kind. There is no end. Is a Committee member anti-Semitic? He will force the producers to blacklist men who deplore anti-Semitism. Is a Committee member anti-labor? He will force the producer to blacklist men who are pro-labor. Is a Committee member against low-cost housing? He will force the producer to blacklist men who advocate low-cost housing. And thus, even without special legislation, he will succeed in throttling, both artistically and financially, one of the greatest industries in the United States. For he will have succeeded, through threats and intimidation, in effectively censoring a screen which has just within the last few years begun to emerge from a never-never land into a dim realization of its responsibilities to the people of this nation and of the world. As an added touch of grim humor, this attempt at censorship is being made just at the time when, as has been remarked by every responsible critic in the country, foreign motion pictures are successfully challenging ours largely because of their free, open and honest approach to the problems that beset modern man.

The men who have here been attacked, and countless others in Hollywood who have stood up in their behalf, have behind them a body of work, completely open to inspection, which expresses their point of view. They have always begged for understanding and enlightment. They have also preached the elimination of certain institutions, yes! They have preached the elimination of the institution of poverty, of slums, of disease, of racial intolerance, and of all that bigotry which prevents men from living in peace and understanding, one with another.

If the Committee succeeds in forcing the producers to blacklist these men it can only result in the destruction of the industry in which they are now employed. For the loss of these men will inevitably lead to the squelching of the ideas they represent, and which they have freely exhibited to the people in such pictures as The Best Years of Our Lives, Pride of the Marines, Crossfire, The Farmer's Daughter, yes, and even Margie! The resulting deterioration in the quality of American pictures cannot fail to result in the eventual extinction of our industry, both as an artistic expression and, just as important, as a successful business enterprise.

I cannot join in this wholesale liquidation of the principle of free expression but, in company with my fellow-workers, must stand against it in the interest of the entire industry.

Statement of Ring Lardner, Jr.

I wish to speak briefly on two matters which seem to me very pertinent to these proceedings. The first is my own record as it has been impugned by the testimony of some of your witnesses.

My father was a writer in the best tradition of American literature. That tradition is very closely allied to the democratic ideal in American life. Not only I but my three brothers have also been writers. Two of these brothers were killed in separate chapters of the same great struggle to preserve that democratic ideal, one as a member of the Abraham Lincoln Brigade in Spain in 1938, the other as a war correspondent in Germany in 1944. I make no claim to the genius of my father or the courage of my brothers, but I do maintain that everything I have done or written has been in keeping with the spirit that governed their work, their lives, and their deaths.

My principal occupation is that of screen writer, I have contributed to more than a dozen motion pictures, among them Woman of the Year, for which I received an Academy Award. The Cross of Lorraine, about the anti-fascist movement in France during the war, the screen version of the play Tomorrow the World, about the effects of Nazi education, Cloak and Dagger, about the heroic work of our Office of Strategic Services, and an animated cartoon called The Brotherhood of Man, based on the pamphlet, The Races of Mankind, and exposing the myth that any inherent differences exist among people of different skin color and geographical origin. It doesn't matter to me what kind of preposterous documents your investigators produce from unnamed sources describing my affiliations under some such heavily cloaked pseudonym as "Ring L." My record includes no anti-democratic word or act, no spoken or written expression of anti-Semitism, anti-Negro feeling or opposition to American democratic principles as I understand them.

Secondly, about un-American activities in Hollywood. The atmosphere there, where I have lived for the last ten years, is considerably different than that of the small segment of Washington to which I have been exposed in the last ten days. There are a few frightened people there—men like Adolphe Menjou and John C. Moffitt throw so many furtive glances over their shoulders that they run a serious risk of dislocation. And we have a certain amount of un-American activity there; anti-Semitism, white supremacy nonsense and other efforts to subvert the democratic idea. Every note exchanged between the Motion Picture Alliance for the Preservation of American Ideals and this Committee contributes to an anti-American purpose. I wish there were a committee qualified and competent to investigate these matters. But compared to what I have seen and heard in this room, Hollywood is a citadel of freedom. Here anti-American sentiments are freely expressed and their spokesmen heartily congratulated. Here there is such fear of the effects of free speech that men are forbidden to read statements and are cut off in mid-sentence lest they expose too much of what is going on here to the public.

What I am most concerned about is the ultimate result that might come from a successful fulfillment of your purpose. On Tuesday, the Chairman said that there was subversive material in motion pictures and proposed that it be prevented in the future by an industry blacklist. The motion picture producers have not indicated that they are gullible enough to fall for such a ruse, but if they ever did, the fact that I might be prevented from working at my profession would be of little account. The really important effect would be that the producers themselves would lose control over their pictures, and that the same shackling of education, labor, radio and newspapers would follow. We are already subject in Hollywood to a censorship that makes most pictures empty and childish. Under the kind of censorship which this inquisition threatens, a leading man wouldn't even be able to blurt out the words "I love you" unless he had first secured a notarized affidavit proving she was a pure white, Protestant gentile of old Confederate stock.

Statement of Lester Cole

I want to say at the outset that I am a loyal American, who upholds the Constitution of my country, who does not advocate force and violence, and who is not an agent of a foreign power.

This Committee has announced many times its interest in facts pertinent to this inquiry. I believe many such facts are embodied in this statement.

I have been a working screen-writer in the Motion Picture Industry since 1932. To date, I have written thirty-six screen plays, the titles of which and companies which produced them are attached.

I was working in Hollywood in 1933 when screen writers, faced with an arbitrary fifty percent cut in salaries, formed the Screen Writers' Guild for the purpose of collective bargaining.

From the very start there were attempts to create strife within the industry by groups who used the same technique employed by this Committee.

After years of failure by James Kevin McGuinness, Rupert Hughes and other of your friendly witnesses to disrupt the Screen Writers' Guild, and with it the industry, a desperate appeal was made to Martin Dies, former Chairman of this Committee. Or maybe Martin Dies made the appeal; at any rate the investigation began.

When the Dies investigation proved unsuccessful because of the united resistance of the men and women of the industry, a new tactic was employed. Willie Bioff and George S. Browne were called into the fray.

These two men, Browne and Bioff who ran the IATSE, the union which was represented here the other day by Mr. Roy Brewer, took on the job of creating chaos in the industry. They bought full page advertisements in the Hollywood trade papers, the Reporter and the Daily Variety, announcing their intentions of taking over all independent Hollywood Guilds and Unions, but only, of course, for one purpose; the eradication of Communism. You will recall that Al Capone, just before going to jail, called upon the American people to "eradicate" all subversive un-American influences in American life, including Communism. By a strange coincidence, the warning of Browne and Bioff also was issued but a short time before they too went to jail for the extortion of huge sums of money; a shakedown of the motion picture industry.

For fifteen years these men have engaged in slander, malicious gossip, near libel; in fact, in every method known to man but one—traditional American democratic procedure.

As in years gone by they accommodated Martin Dies, and later extortionists Browne and Bioff, today McGuinness, Incorporated is playing footsie with the House Committee on Un-American Activities. They think the Committee is stooging for the Motion Picture Alliance; the reverse is true.

From what I have seen and heard at this hearing, the House Committee on Un-American Activities is out to accomplish one thing, and one thing only, as far as the American Motion Picture Industry is concerned; they are going either to rule it, or ruin it.

This Committee is determined to sow fear of blacklists; to intimidate management, to destroy democratic guilds and unions by interference in their internal affairs, and through their destruction bring chaos and strife to an industry which seeks only democratic methods with which to solve its own problems. This Committee is waging a cold war on democracy.

I know the people in the motion picture industry will not let them get away with it.

APPENDIX IV

Cover Letter and Questionnaire Used in Securing New Primary Data

One hundred requests for new information were sent to seventy unfriendly witnesses, twenty friendly witnesses, and ten nonwitnesses. Appendix IV contains a copy of the cover letter and questionnaire used by this researcher in seeking the new primary data.

ROBERT VAUGHN

January 15, 1970

Mr. Elia Kazan
c/o Directors Guild of America, Inc.
7950 Sunset Boulevard
Hollywood, California 90046

Dear Mr. Kazan:

I would like to introduce myself. I am Robert Vaughn, known to most of the people in the entertainment field as a Television or Cinema actor. However, there is another side to my life and that is the reason for this correspondence. I am currently completing my doctoral dissertation at the University of Southern California with a major in Communication. My area of study is: A HISTORICAL STUDY OF THE INFLUENCE OF THE HOUSE COMMITTEE ON UN-AMERICAN ACTIVITIES ON THE AMERICAN THEATER, 1938-1958.

I need your assistance to complete this work. I am sending the enclosed questionnaire to a relatively small group in the entertainment field who may have been affected by the activities of the Committee. Since I am contacting only a small number of people, the importance of each individual's response is magnified. The success of this study depends on virtually 100 percent cooperation and your response is valuable.

The University of Southern California is extremely conscious of the individual's dignity and right to privacy. All responses will be kept confidential and well within the bounds of good taste and discretion.

I want to thank you in advance for your cooperation. Upon completion of this study, I will share with you the results of my findings. I hope to hear from you soon. Until then, I remain,

Sincerely,

Robert Vaughn

Encls.

SURVEY OF THE INFLUENCE OF THE HOUSE COMMITTEE ON UN-AMERICAN ACTIVITIES ON THE AMERICAN THEATER 1938-1958

Last Name   First Name   Date

This study is primarily concerned with the Committee's influence on the American *theater* as distinguished from cinema, television, radio and allied entertainment fields. As one whose name was directly involved in the Committee's hearings or printed records, please give your candid recollections of the probable, possible, and actual effects of the Committee's activities on your own professional career and on the American Theater.

(PLEASE USE REVERSE SIDES OF ANY PAGES WHERE MORE ROOM IS NEEDED)

I. PROBABLE EFFECTS:

A. On May 26, 1938, the United States House of Representatives authorized the formation of the Special House Committee on Un-American Activities. The purposes of this committee were stated as follows:

"Resolved, that the Speaker of the House of Representatives be, and he is hereby, authorized to appoint a special committee to be composed of seven members for the purpose of conducting an investigation of 1) the extent, character, and object of un-American propaganda activities in the United States, 2) the diffusion within the United States of subversive and un-American propaganda that is instigated from foreign countries or of a domestic origin and attacks the principle of the form of government as guaranteed by the constitution, and 3) all other questions in relations thereto that would aid Congress in any necessary remedial legislation."

Please describe how, in your opinion, the Committee did or did not achieve its purposes as stated above:

B. The possibility to either answer the committee's questions or to refuse to do so was an alternative faced by all of the witnesses subpoenaed. If you were a witness and therefore were confronted by this alternative, please describe your resolution. If you were not a witness, yet were aware you might be, how were you prepared to resolve this choice?

WITNESS: NON-WITNESS:

II. POSSIBLE EFFECTS:

A. Describe any constructive effects you feel the Committee's activities may have had on the American *theater*. Please be specific.

B. Describe any destructive effects you feel the Committee's activities may have had on the American *theater*. Please be specific.

C. In your opinion are there any effects of the Committee's activities that cannot yet be evaluated?

Yes: No:

If yes, please specify:

D. There has been much debate on the issue of a "blacklist" on Broadway.

1. Do you know whether there was a "blacklist" on Broadway against *alleged* Communists?

Yes: No:

If yes, please state the nature of your knowledge:

2. Do you know whether there was a "blacklist" on Broadway against *witnesses* who gave the names of alleged Communists?

Yes: No:

If yes, please state the nature of your knowledge:

III. ACTUAL EFFECTS:

A. As a result of the Committee's activities, the Federal Theatre was closed on June 30, 1939.

    1. Were you working in the Federal Theatre on June 30, 1939?

       Yes: No:

       Too young to be working:

    2. Can you recall any other theaters or productions that were closed because of the committee's activities?

       Yes: No:

       If yes, please fill out the following to the best of your recollection:

B. Specifically, did the Committee Hearings affect your life in the following areas since 1947:

    1. Income loss or gain: Yes: No:

       If yes, please describe in what manner:

    2. Career change: Yes: No:

       If yes, please describe in what manner:

    3. *Theater* activity: Yes: No:

       If yes, please describe in what manner:

    4. Personal relationships: Yes: No:

       If yes, please describe in what manner:

C. Did the publicity surrounding the hearings affect you?

       Yes: No:

       If yes, in what manner:

D. Generally, would you please briefly state in what way the Committee Hearings affected your life, if at all: (Please add any effects not covered by B and C.)

E. "Vigilante" type organizations and publications such as *Counter-attack*, *Red Channels*, AWARE, Inc., and persons like Laurence Johnson sprung up during and after the hearings in 1947.

   1. Please list other groups, publications and persons you were aware of as well as the date, location and nature of their activities.

      Group, Organization or Person   Date
      (Circle One)

      Location:

      Nature of their activities:

      Group, Organization or Person   Date
      (Circle One)

      Location:

      Nature of their activities:

      Group, Organization or Person   Date
      (Circle One)

      Location:

      Nature of their activities:

   2. Did any of the above directly affect you?

      Yes: No:

      If yes, please describe the circumstances:

BIBLIOGRAPHY
Books and Plays

Andrews, Bert, *Washington Witch Hunt.* New York, Random House, 1948.

Barck, Oscar Y., Jr., *A History of the United States Since 1945.* New York, Dell Publishing Company, Inc., 1965.

Barrett, Edward L., Jr., *The Tenney Committee; Legislative Investigation of Subversive Activities in California.* Ithaca, N. Y., Cornell University Press, 1951.

Baxandall, Lee, *Marxism and Aesthetics, a Selective Annotated Bibliography.* New York, Humanities Press, Inc., 1968.

Beck, Carl, *Contempt of Congress; a Study of the Prosecutions Initiated by the Committee on Un-American Activities, 1945-1957.* New Orleans, La., The Hauser Press, 1959.

Bentley, Elizabeth, *Out of Bondage.* New York, Conservative Book Club, n.d. [1966?].

Bessie, Alvah, *Inquisition in Eden.* New York, The Macmillan Company, 1965.

——, *The Un-Americans.* New York, Cameron Associates, Inc., 1957.

Biberman, Herbert [Joseph], *Salt of the Earth; the Story of a Film.* Boston, Beacon Press, 1965.

Bird, Caroline, *The Invisible Scar.* New York, Pocket Book Division, Simon & Schuster, Inc., 1967.

Block, Anita, *The Changing World in Plays and Theatre.* Boston, Little, Brown and Company, 1939.

Bottomore, T. B., *Critics of Society; Radical Thought in North America.* New York, Pantheon Books Division of Random House, Inc., 1968.

Bromberg, Conrad, *Dream of a Blacklisted Actor.* New York, Flora Roberts, Inc., 1969.

Browder, Earl, *Communism in the United States.* New York, International Publishers, 1935.

——, *The People's Front.* New York, International Publishers, 1938.

——, *What Is Communism?* New York, Workers Library Publishers, 1936.

Brown, Ben W., *Theatre at the Left.* Providence, R. I., The Bear Press, 1938.

Buckley, William F., Jr., ed., *The Committee and Its Critics.* Chicago, Henry Regnery Company, 1962.

——, and Bozell, L. Brent, *McCarthy and His Enemies: the Record and Its Meaning.* Chicago, Henry Regnery Company, 1954.

Budenz, Louis F., *Men without Faces; the Communist Conspiracy in the U.S.A.* New York, Harper & Brothers, 1950.

Burnham, James, *The Web of Subversion; Underground Networks in the U.S. Government.* New York, The John Day Company, 1954.

Carr, Robert K., *The House Committee on Un-American Activities, 1945-1950.* Ithaca, N. Y., Cornell University Press, 1952.

Chambers, Whittaker, *Witness.* New York, Random House, 1952.

Cogley, John, *Report on Blacklisting,* Vol. I. *Movies*; Vol. II, *Radio—Television.* New York, The Fund for the Republic, Inc., 1956.

Cohn-Bendt, Gabriel and Daniel, *Obsolete Communism: The Left-Wing Alternative,* trans. by Arnold Pomerans. New York, McGraw-Hill Book Company, 1968.

Cooke, Alistair, *A Generation on Trial: U.S.A. vs. Alger Hiss*. New York, Alfred A. Knopf, Inc., 1950.

De Antonio, Emile, and Talbot, Daniel, producers, *Point of Order! A Documentary of the Army-McCarthy Hearings*. New York, W. W. Norton & Co., Inc., 1964.

De Toledano, Ralph A., *Seeds of Treason: The True Story of the Chambers-Hiss Tragedy*. Belmont, Mass., Western Islands, 1965.

Dies, Martin, *The Trojan Horse in America*. New York, Dodd, Mead & Company, 1940.

Dilling, Elizabeth, *The Red Network*. Kenilworth and Chicago, Ill., by the author, 1934.

Dissertation Abstracts, 1950-1969. Ann Arbor, Mich., University Microfilms, n. d.

Donner, Frank J., *The Un-Americans*. New York, Ballantine Books, Inc., 1961.

Draper, Theodore, *Abuse of Power*. New York, The Viking Press, 1967.

——, *American Communism and Soviet Russia; the Formative Period*. New York, The Viking Press, Inc., 1963.

——, *The Roots of American Communism*. New York, The Viking Press, Inc., 1963.

Fagan, Myron C., *Red Treason in Hollywood*. Hollywood, Calif., Cinema Educational Guild, Inc., 1949.

Faulk, John Henry, *Fear on Trial*. New York, Simon & Schuster, Inc., 1964.

Faulkner, Harold Underwood, *American Political and Social History*. New York, Appleton-Century-Crofts, Inc., 1957.

Feis, Herbert, *1933: Characters in Crisis*. Boston, Little, Brown & Company, 1966.

Flanagan, Hallie, *Arena; the History of the Federal Theatre*. New York, Benjamin Blom, Inc., 1965.

——, *Dynamo*. New York, Duell, Sloan and Pearce, 1943.

——, *Shifting Scenes of the Modern European Theatre*. New York, Coward-McCann, Inc., 1928.

Foster, William Z., *History of the Communist Party of the United States*. New York, International Publishers Company, Inc., 1952.

The Fund for the Republic, Inc., *Bibliography on the Communist Problem in the United States*. New York, The Fund for the Republic, Inc., 1955.

——, *Digest of the Public Record of Communism in the United States*. New York, The Fund for the Republic, Inc., 1955.

Gagey, Edmond M., *Revolution in American Drama*. New York, Columbia University Press, 1947.

Gellermann, William, *Martin Dies*. New York, The John Day Company, 1944.

Gitlow, Benjamin, *I Confess; the Truth about American Communism*. New York, E. P. Dutton & Co., Inc., 1940.

——, *The Whole of Their Lives; Communism in America; a Personal History and Intimate Portrayal of Its Leaders*. New York, Charles Scribner's Sons, 1948.

Glazer, Nathan, *The Social Basis of American Communism*. New York, Harcourt, Brace & World, Inc., 1961.

Gold, Michael, *The Hollow Men*. New York, International Publishers Co., Inc., 1941.

Goldman, Eric F., *The Crucial Decade—and After; America, 1945-1960*. New York, Alfred A. Knopf, Inc., 1960.

Goldwater, Walter, *Radical Periodicals in America, 1890-1950; a Bibliography with Brief Notes*. New Haven, Conn., Yale University Library, 1966.

Goodman, Walter, *The Committee; the Extraordinary Career of the House*

Committee on Un-American Activities. New York, Farrar, Straus & Giroux, 1968.

Harrington, Michael, *The Other America; Poverty in the United States.* New York, The Macmillan Company, 1962.

Hart, Henry, ed., *American Writers' Congress.* New York, International Publishers, 1935.

Hayden, Sterling, *Wanderer.* New York, Alfred A. Knopf, Inc., 1963.

Hellman, Lillian, *An Unfinished Woman; a Memoir.* Boston, Little, Brown and Co., 1969.

Hicks, Granville, *et al.*, eds., *Proletarian Literature in the United States; an Anthology.* New York, International Publishers Company, Inc., 1935.

Himelstein, Morgan Y., *Drama Was a Weapon.* New Brunswick, N. J., Rutgers University Press, 1963.

Hofstadter, Richard, *Anti-Intellectualism in American Life.* New York, Vintage Books Division of Random House, Inc., 1962.

——, *The Paranoid Style in American Politics and Other Essays.* New York, Alfred A. Knopf, Inc., 1965.

Howe, Irving, and Coser, Lewis, *The American Communist Party, 1919-1957.* New York, Frederick A. Praeger, Inc., 1962.

Hughes, Glenn, *A History of the American Theatre, 1700-1950.* New York, Samuel French, 1951.

Iversen, Robert W., *The Communists and the Schools.* New York, Harcourt, Brace and Co., 1959.

Kahn, Gordon, *Hollywood on Trial.* New York, Boni and Gaer, Inc., 1948.

Kazin, Alfred, *On Native Grounds; an Interpretation of Modern American Prose Literature.* Garden City, N. Y., Doubleday & Company, Inc., 1956.

Kempton, Murray, *Part of Our Time; Some Monuments and Ruins of the Thirties.* New York, Dell Publishing Company, 1967.

Kendrick, Alexander, *Prime Time; the Life of Edward R. Murrow.* Boston, Little, Brown and Company, 1969.

Kipphardt, Heinar, *In the Matter of J. Robert Oppenheimer,* trans. by Ruth Speirs. New York, Hill & Wang, 1968.

Krutch, Joseph Wood, *The American Drama Since 1918,* rev. ed. New York, George Braziller, Inc., 1967.

Lasch, Christopher, *The New Radicalism in America 1889-1963; the Intellectual as a Social Type.* New York, Alfred A. Knopf, Inc., 1965.

Latham, Earl, *The Communist Controversy in Washington, from the New Deal to McCarthy.* Cambridge, Mass., Harvard University Press, 1966.

Lawson, John Howard, *Film in the Battle of Ideas.* New York, Masses and Mainstream, 1953.

——, *The Hidden Heritage.* New York, The Citadel Press, 1950.

——, *Theory and Technique of Playwriting.* New York, Hill & Wang, 1960.

Leighton, Isabel, ed., *The Aspirin Age, 1919-1941.* New York, Simon & Schuster, 1949.

Levy, Leonard W., *Origins of the Fifth Amendment.* New York, Oxford University Press, 1968.

Liebling, A. J., *Mink and Red Herring: The Wayward Pressman's Casebook.* Garden City, N. Y., Doubleday & Co., Inc., 1949.

Luthin, Reinhard H., *American Demagogues, Twentieth Century.* Gloucester, Mass., Peter Smith, 1959.

Mandelbaum, Seymour J., *The Social Setting of Intolerance: The Know-Nothings, the Red Scare, and McCarthyism*. Glenview, Ill., Scott, Foresman and Co., 1964.

Mathews, Jane DeHart, *The Federal Theatre, 1935-1939, Plays, Relief, and Politics*. Princeton, N. J., Princeton University Press, 1967.

Matusow, Harvey, *False Witness*. New York, Cameron & Kahn, 1955.

McCarthy, Joseph, *The Fight for America*. New York, The Devin-Adair Company, 1952.

Meyer, Frank S., *The Moulding of Communists; the Training of the Communist Cadre*. New York, Harcourt, Brace & World, Inc., 1961.

Miller, Arthur, *The Crucible*. New York, The Viking Press, 1964.

———, *A View from the Bridge*. New York, Dramatists Play Service, Inc., 1957.

Miller, Merle, *The Judges and the Judged*. Garden City, N. Y., Doubleday & Company, Inc., 1952.

Moley, Raymond, with the assistance of Elliot A. Rosen, *The First New Deal*. New York, Harcourt, Brace & World, Inc., 1966.

Morros, Boris, as told to Charles Samuels, *My Ten Years as a Counterspy*. New York, The Viking Press, 1959.

Murrow, Edward R., *In Search of Light; the Broadcasts of Edward R. Murrow, 1938-1961*, Edward Bliss, Jr., ed. New York, Alfred A. Knopf, Inc., 1967.

National Americanism Commission of the American Legion, *Isms; a Review of Alien Isms, Revolutionary Communism and Their Active Sympathizers in the United States*, 2d ed. rev. Indianapolis, n. p., 1937.

Nevins, Allan, and Commager, Henry Steele, *A Short History of the United States*, 5th ed., rev. and enl. New York, Alfred A. Knopf, Inc., 1966.

Nixon, Richard M., *Six Crises*. New York, Pyramid Books, 1968.

Nizer, Louis, *The Jury Returns*. New York, Simon & Schuster, Inc., Pocket Book Edition, 1968.

Ogden, August Raymond, *The Dies Committee*, 2d ed. rev. Washington, D.C., The Catholic University of America Press, Inc., 1945.

Philbrick, Herbert A., *I Led Three Lives: Citizen, "Communist," Counterspy*. New York, Grosset & Dunlap, 1952.

Potter, Charles E., *Days of Shame*. New York, Coward-McCann, Inc., 1965.

Rabkin, Gerald, *Drama and Commitment*. Bloomington, Ind., Indiana University Press, 1964.

Red Channels; the Report of Communist Influence in Radio and Television. New York, American Business Consultants, Inc., 1950.

Reeves, Thomas C., *Freedom and the Foundation; The Fund for the Republic in the Era of McCarthyism*. New York, Alfred A. Knopf, 1969.

Rollins, Alfred B., Jr., ed., *Franklin D. Roosevelt and the Age of Action*. New York, Dell Publishing Company, Inc., 1960.

Rossiter, Clinton, *Marxism: The View from America*. New York, Harcourt, Brace & World, Inc., 1960.

Rovere, Richard H., *Senator Joe McCarthy*. New York, Harcourt, Brace & Company, 1959.

Schlesinger, Arthur M., Jr., *The Age of Roosevelt*, Vol. I, *The Crisis of the Old Order, 1919-1933*; Vol. II, *The Coming of the New Deal*; Vol. III, *The Politics of Upheaval*. Boston, Houghton Mifflin Company, 1957-60.

Schumach, Murray, *The Face on the Cutting Room Floor; the Story of Movie and Television Censorship*. New York, William Morrow and Company, 1964.

Seldes, George, *Witch Hunt: The Technique and Profits of Redbaiting.* New York, Modern Age Books, 1940.

Stillman, Edmund, and Pfaff, William, *The Politics of Hysteria; Twentieth-Century Conflict.* New York, Harper & Row, Inc., 1964.

Stouffer, Samuel A., *Communism, Conformity, and Civil Liberties: A Cross-Section of the Nation Speaks Its Mind.* New York, John Wiley & Sons, Inc., 1966.

Taylor, Telford, *Grand Inquest; the Story of Congressional Investigations.* New York, Ballantine Books, 1961.

Tenney, Jack B., *Red Fascism; Boring from within by the Subversive Forces of Communism.* Los Angeles, Calif., Federal Printing Company, 1947.

Tynan, Kenneth, "Theatre and Living," in Tom Maschler, ed., *Declaration.* New York, E. P. Dutton & Company, Inc., 1958.

Warren, Frank A. III, *Liberals and Communism; the "Red Decade" Revisited.* Bloomington, Ind., Indiana University Press, 1966.

Whitman, Willson, *Bread and Circuses; a Study of Federal Theatre.* New York, Oxford University Press, 1937.

Zeligs, Meyer A., *Friendship and Fratricide; an Analysis of Whittaker Chambers and Alger Hiss.* New York, The Viking Press, Inc., 1967.

Articles and Periodicals

"The Dance: The New Dance Group; An Analysis." *New Theatre* (March, 1934).

English, Richard, "What Makes a Hollywood Communist?" *The Saturday Evening Post* (May 19, 1951).

Flanagan, Hallie, "Scenery or No Scenery? A Symposium." *Theatre Workshop*, Vol. II, No. 1 (April-June, 1938).

Freeman, Ezra, "What to Dance About." *New Theatre* (March, 1934).

Gessner, Robert, "Massacre in Hollywood." *New Theatre* (March, 1934).

Hollywood Citizen-News (1947).

Jennings, C. Robert, "The Hollywood Ten, Plus Twenty." Los Angeles *Times, West Magazine* (September 3, 1967).

Lardner, Ring, Jr., "My Life on the Blacklist." *The Saturday Evening Post* (October 14, 1961).

Lavery, Emmet, "Who Killed Federal Theatre?" *The Commonweal* (August 4, 1939).

Los Angeles *Daily News* (1947).

Los Angeles *Examiner* (1947).

Los Angeles *Herald-Express* (1947).

Los Angeles *Times* (1947).

New Theatre, Social Theatre Publications, Inc. (1934-36).

New Theatre and Film, Vol. IV, Nos. 1 and 2 (March and April, 1937).

New York *Times* (1930-69).

Pudovkin, V. I., "Sound and the Future of the Cinema." *New Theatre* (March, 1934).

"The Senator and the Economist." *The Commonweal* (April 1, 1955).

Shapiro, Jack, "Theatre Collective." *New Theatre* (October, 1934).

TAC, Issued by Theatre Arts Committee, Vol. I, No. 1 (July, 1938) to Vol. II, No. 4 (December, 1939).

Watts, Richard, Jr., "Hollywood Sees Pink." *New Theatre* (November, 1934).

Wilson, Edmund, "Appeal to Progressives." *New Republic*, LXV (January 14, 1931).

Worker's Theatre, Vol. I, No. 4 (July, 1931), No. 11 (February, 1932), No. 12 (March, 1932).

Public Documents

California Legislature, *Fifth Report of the Senate Fact-Finding Committee on Un-American Activities.* Sacramento, Calif., 1949.

———, *Fourth Report of the Senate Fact-Finding Committee on Un-American Activities: Communist-Front Organizations.* Sacramento, Calif., 1948.

———, *Report of the Joint Fact-Finding Committee on Un-American Activities in California.* Sacramento, Calif., 1943.

———, *Third Report of the Joint Fact-Finding Committee on Un-American Activities.* Sacramento, Calif., 1947.

U.S. Congress, House Committee on Un-American Activities, *Annual Report,* 1950, Eighty-first Congress, Second Session.

———, *Annual Report,* 1951, Eighty-second Congress, Second Session.

———, *Annual Report,* 1952, Eighty-second Congress, Second Session.

———, *Annual Report,* 1953, Eighty-third Congress, First Session.

———, *Annual Report,* 1955, Eighty-fourth Congress, Second Session.

———, *Annual Report,* 1956, Eighty-fifth Congress, First Session.

———, *Annual Report,* 1957, Eighty-fifth Congress, Second Session.

———, *Annual Report,* 1958, Eighty-sixth Congress, First Session.

———, *Communism in the New York City Area (Entertainment),* Hearings, Eighty-fifth Congress, Second Session, 1957-1958.

———, *Communist Infiltration of Hollywood Motion-Picture Industry,* Hearings, Eighty-second Congress, First Session, 1951, Parts I-VI; Eighty-second Congress, Second Session, 1952, Parts VII-X.

———, *Communist Methods of Infiltration (Entertainment),* Hearings, Eighty-third Congress, Second Session, Parts I and II.

———, *Cumulative Index to Publications of the Committee on Un-American Activities, 1938-1954.*

———, *Guide to Subversive Organizations and Publications (and Appendixes).* Eighty-seventh Congress, Second Session, House Document No. 398. Rev. and published December 1, 1961, to supersede *Guide* published on January 2, 1957.

———, *Hearings Regarding the Communist Infiltration of the Motion Picture Industry,* Eightieth Congress, First Session, 1947.

———, *Investigation of Communist Activities in the Los Angeles Area,* Hearings, Eighty-third Congress, First Session, 1953, Parts VI and VII.

———, *Investigation of Communist Activities in the New York City Area,* Hearings, Eighty-third Congress, First Session, 1953, Parts I-IV.

———, *Investigation of Communist Activities, New York Area (Entertainment),* Hearings, Eighty-fourth Congress, First Session, Parts VI-VIII.

———, *Investigation of So-Called "Blacklisting" in Entertainment Industry*—Report of the Fund for the Republic, Inc., Hearings, Eighty-fourth Congress, Second Session, 1956.

———, *Investigation of the Unauthorized Use of United States Passports,* Hearings, Eighty-fourth Congress, Second Session, 1956.

———, *Report,* Eightieth Congress, Second Session, December 31, 1948.

———, *Supplement to Cumulative Index to Publications of the Committee on Un-American Activities, 1955 through 1960, Inclusive.*

U.S. Congress, House Special Committee on Un-American Activities, *House Report No. 1476* (Annual Report for 1939), Seventy-sixth Congress, Third Session, January 3, 1940.

——, *Investigation of Un-American Activities and Propaganda, House Report No. 2* (Annual Report for 1938), Seventy-sixth Congress, First Session, January 3, 1939.

——, *Investigation of Un-American Propaganda Activities in the U.S.*, Hearings, Seventy-fifth Congress, Third Session, Vol. I.

——, *Investigation of Un-American Propaganda Activities in the U.S.*, Hearings, Seventy-fifth Congress, Third Session, Vol. IV.

——, *Investigation of Un-American Propaganda Activities in the U.S., Report No. 1476*, Seventy-sixth Congress, Third Session, January 3, 1940.

Pamphlets

Antonius (pseud.), *The Hollywood "Trial,"* introduction by Arthur Calder-Marshall. London, Notable Press, Ltd., n. d.

Blake, Ben, *The Awakening of the American Theatre*. New York, Tomorrow Publishers, 1935.

Braden, Anne, *House Un-American Activities Committee: Bulwark of Segregation*. Los Angeles, Calif., National Committee to Abolish the House Un-American Activities Committee [1964].

Budenz, Louis G., *May Day, 1940*. New York, Workers Library Publishers, [1939 or 1946?].

Censored! (Also contains Richard Pack, *The Censors See Red!* and Mark Marvin, *For a Free Stage*.) New York, National Committee Against Censorship of the Theatre Arts, 1935.

Chambers, Whittaker, *Can You Hear Their Voices?* New York, International Pamphlets, 1932.

Citizens Committee to Preserve American Freedoms, *Courage Is Contagious; the Bill of Rights versus the Un-American Activities Committee*. Huntington Park, Calif., n. p., 1953.

Communist Party, U.S.A., *The McCarran Conspiracy against the Bill of Rights; the Communist Party's Answer to the Charges of the Attorney-General under the McCarran Act*. New York, n. p., 1951.

Dunne, Father George H., *Hollywood Labor Dispute: A Study in Immorality*. Los Angeles, Calif., Conference Publishing Company, [1949?].

Eisenstein, S., *The Soviet Screen*. Moscow, Foreign Languages Publishing House, 1939.

Eisler, Gerhart, *My Side of the Story; the Statement the Newspapers Refused to Print*. New York, Civil Rights Congress, 1947.

Emerson, Thomas I., and McNamara, Francis J., *Dialogue on the Constitutionality of the Committee of the House of Representatives, 89th Congress*. Los Angeles, Calif., National Committee to Abolish the House Un-American Activities Committee, [1965?].

Fagan, Myron C., *Hollywood's Reds Are "on the Run."* Dublin, The Catholic Cinema and Theatre Patrons' Association, 1950.

"Fellow Citizens: Our Husbands Are in Prison! . . ." (Eight wives make appeal for members of "Unfriendly Ten.") Privately printed, n. d.

"For Justice and Peace." (Wives of some members of "Unfriendly Ten" appeal to U.S. Supreme Court with this "brief, amicus curiae" for grant of rehearing for Lawson and Trumbo.) Hollywood, Calif., Committee for the Hollywood Ten, n. d.

Jerome, V.J., *Culture in a Changing World*. New York, New Century Publishers, Inc., 1947.

——, *Social-Democracy and the War.* New York, Workers Library Publishers, Inc., 1940.

Maltz, Albert, *The Citizen Writer.* Hollywood, Calif., West Coast Chapter, League of American Writers, 1943.

——, *The Citizen Writer: Essays in Defense of American Culture.* New York, International Publishers Company, Inc., 1950.

Marshall, Herbert, *Soviet Cinema.* London, The Russia Today Society, 1945.

Meiklejohn, Alexander, *et al., Brief Submitted by Cultural Workers in Motion Pictures and other Arts, and of Members of the Professions, as Amici Curiae, to U.S. Supreme Court, October Term, 1949.* Los Angeles, Calif., Parker & Company, Law Printers, 1949.

New York State Committee, Communist Party. *No Career in No Man's Land: A Message to the Artists Who Make Up America's Great Amusement Industry.* New York, n. d. [1940?].

Reuben, William A., *The Honorable Mr. Nixon and the Alger Hiss Case.* New York, Action Books, 1956.

A Salute to John Howard Lawson. (Prepared for testimonial dinner honoring Lawson's sixty-first birthday.) Los Angeles, Calif., Privately printed, November 12, 1955.

Sondergaard, Gale, and Maltz, Albert, *On the Eve of Prison: Two Addresses.* Hollywood, Calif., The Arts, Sciences and Professions Council, 1950.

Trumbo, Dalton, *The Devil in the Book.* Los Angeles, Calif., California Emergency Defense Committee, 1956.

——, *The Time of the Toad.* Hollywood, Calif., The Hollywood Ten [1949?].

Encyclopedias

The Biographical Encyclopaedia and Who's Who of the American Theatre, 1966.

Theater Programs

Golden, I. J., *Precedent.* Chicago, The Workers' Theatre, April 8 and 9, 1933.

Unpublished Materials

"Communism in the Motion Picture Industry." [Hollywood?], April, 1960. (Mimeographed.)

Suber, Howard, *The Anti-Communist Blacklist in the Hollywood Motion Picture Industry.* Unpublished PhD dissertation, University of California at Los Angeles, 1968.

——, *The 1947 Hearings of the House Committee on Un-American Activities into Communism in the Hollywood Motion Picture Industry.* Unpublished master's thesis, University of California at Los Angeles, 1966.

Other Sources

Armed Forces Security Questionnaire, June 1, 1959. (Includes "Organizations designated by the Attorney General, pursuant to Executive Order 10450 . . .") Washington, D.C., Government Printing Office, 1968.

Bromberg, Conrad, Correspondence with the author, November 6, 1969.

Friebus, Florida, Taped interview with the author, November 11, 1969.

"Organizations Designated under Executive Order No. 10450." (Compiled from memoranda of the Attorney General dated April 29, July 15, and September 28, 1953; January 22, 1954; April 4, September 21, and October 20, 1955. Consolidated List, November 1, 1955.) Form No. DJ-90 (Ed. 1-22-59).

Sloane, Allan, Correspondence with the author, March 5, 1970.

U.S. Congress, House Committee on Un-American Activities, *100 Things You Should Know about Communism in the U.S.A.* 1948.

U.S. Works Progress Administration, *Federal Theatre.* Bulletin of the Federal Theatre Project, Vol. II, No. 1 [1937?].

Index

Abel, Walter, 66
Abowitz, Ellenore (Mrs. Murray), 159
Abraham Lincoln Brigade, 87
Academy of Motion Picture Arts and Sciences, 97
Actors' Equity Association, 55, 160, 208, 269
Actors' Laboratory, The, 121, 125, 130, 137, 144, 159, 233, 252, 255
Adler, Stella, 39
After the Fall (drama), 221, 254, 264
Age of Anxiety (ballet), 183
Agitprop play, 44
Aldrich Family, The (TV show), 192
Alexander, Leon, 44
All God's Chillun Got Wings (drama), 217
All My Sons (drama), 221
All-Nations Hospital (Los Angeles), 87
America Firsters, 187
American Business Consultants, 193
American Commission to Investigate Labor and Social Conditions in Cuba, 161
American Legion, 77, 175, 202, 204, 208, 209, 261
American National Theatre Academy, 154
American Peace Mobilization, 139
American Shakespeare Festival, 229
Americans for Democratic Action, 221
Anderson, Maxwell, 39
Annenberg, Adelaide Klein, 231, 241
Anthony Adverse (drama), 123
Anti-Communist films, 107
Anti-Defamation League, 204
Anti-Fascist plays, 53
Anti-New Deal press, 68
Anti-Semitism, 102, 103, 183, 187, 195, 222
Arbuckle, Fatty, 171
Arens, Richard, 203, 204, 206, 210, 218, 219, 220, 222, 225, 226-28, 229, 231, 233, 234
Ashe, Harold J., 158
Ashe, Mildred, 159
Asphalt Jungle (film), 156
Associated Actors and Artistes of America, 66
Atkinson, Brooks, 55, 62
AWARE, Inc., 197, 202, 206, 208
Awful Truth, The (film), 83

Backus, Georgia (Mrs. Hy Alexander), 159, 241
Ball, Lucille, 193
Barrymore, John, 66
Barzman, Ben, 241
Bassman, George, 166
Bay, Howard, 195
Beck, George, 158
Behrman, S. N., 38
Bela, Nicholas, 196
Belfrage, Cedric Henning, 188
Bellamy, Ralph, 66, 241
Bells of St. Marys (film), 83
Bercovici, Leonardo, 134, 140, 145
Berg-Allenberg (film agency), 135
Berkeley, Martin, 134, 155, 202, 231, 259
Berry, Jack, 145
Bessie, Alvah, 77, 93, 100, 101, 110, 145

Biberman, Edward, 136
Biberman, Herbert Joseph, 93, 101-2, 110, 123, 145, 241
Biggest Thief in Town, The (film), 153, 187
Bilbo, Theodore, 90
Bill of Rights, 94, 95, 98, 99, 114, 121, 122, 139, 156, 198, 231, 245
Black, Ivan, 200
Black Boy (drama), 217
Black Panthers, 32, 220
Blacklisting, 109-110, 113, 128-29, 146, 155, 156, 170-73, 176, 185, 186, 192-93, 197, 199, 202-6, 208, 232, 244, 249-65 *passim*, 269
Blankfort, Henry, 145, 158
Blankfort, Michael S., 166, 241
Blondell, Joan, 66
Bloomgarden, Kermit, 231
Bloor. *See* Mother Bloor
Blowitz, William Frank, 158, 159
Body and Soul (film), 141
Boehm, Sydney, 81
Boudin, Leonard B., 227
Brand, Phoebe, 65
Brecht, Bertolt, 104, 107, 108
Brewer, Roy M., 92, 136, 137, 140, 145-46, 205
Bright, John, 134
Bromberg, Conrad, 154, 205, 264
Bromberg, J. Edward, 154, 171, 205, 207, 251
Brough, Spangler Arlington. *See* Taylor, Robert
Browder, Earl, 52, 58
Buchman, Harold, 136
Buchman, Sidney, 157, 241
Bund, 187, 190
Burman, Robert, 87
Burrows, Abram S. "Abe," 166, 167-70, 171, 172, 190, 222
Burrows, Carin Kinzel, 190-91

Cacchione, Peter C., 189
Cage, The (ballet), 183
Cagney, James, 66
California State Un-American Activities Committee, 252, 255
Call Me Madam (musical), 183
Can You Hear Their Voices? (drama), 51
Canwell, Albert, 240n.
Capitalist press, 56, 58
Carbone, Eddie, 217
Carlson, Oliver, 92
Carmichael, Stokely, 221
Carnovsky, Morris, 133, 138-40, 171, 172-73
Carpenter, Clifford, 234
Carr, Robert K., 111, 114
Carrington, John W., 120
CBS, 253
Censorship, 198, 243; implicit, 251. *See also* Self-censorship
Chamberlin, Howland, 158-59
Chambers, Whittaker, 51
Chaplin, Charles, 141
Character assassination, 146
Charney, George, 231

Chekov, Anton, 252
Christian, Mady, 251
Civil rights, 67, 244-45
Civil Rights Congress, 121, 130, 139
Clamage, Edward, 209-10
Clardy, Kit, 181, 188, 190
Clark, Jim, 32
Clark, Maurice, 145
Class consciousness, 48
Class struggle, 42, 62
Cleaver, Eldridge, 220
Clurman, Harold, 39
Cobb, Lee J., 158, 192, 206
Cogley, John, 202-6, 210, 211
Cohn, Harry, 134
Cole, Lester, 78, 81, 93, 104, 110, 134,
    145, 241
Collins, Richard J., 93, 125, 134, 135, 140,
    143, 145, 152
Columbia Pictures, 134
Columbia Studios, 131
Comintern, 82
Committee for the First Amendment, 141
Committee of One Hundred, 269
Commonweal (publication), 202, 203
Communism, 31, 50, 68, 78, 84, 85, 86, 87,
    91, 105, 107, 110-12, 118, 166
Communist code words, 193-94
Communist Party, foreign, 90, 230
Communist Party, U.S.A., 34, 35, 37, 43,
    44, 45, 49, 50, 58, 70, 71, 82, 83, 85,
    86, 87, 98, 106, 108, 120, 124, 129,
    144; membership, 93, 95, 96, 101, 102,
    103, 104, 105, 108, 114, 124, 130,
    131-32, 134, 137, 150, 153, 157, 160,
    168, 185, 193, 218, 226-27, 229, 231,
    272
Communist Political Association, 129, 137,
    166, 183
Communist press, 44, 56, 72. See also Daily
    Worker; People's World
Communist propaganda, 82, 84, 86, 88,
    108, 110, 166, 184
Conference of Studio Unions, 145
Connor, Bull, 32
Cooper, Gary, 76, 88, 90
Constitutional rights, 99. See also Bill of
    Rights; Eighth Amendment; Fifth
    Amendment; First Amendment; Fourth
    Amendment
Copton, Judith, 144
Contempt charges, 103, 104, 110, 114, 120,
    157, 197, 201, 221, 226, 233, 246, 247
Corey, George, 145, 241
Corey, Jeff, 143, 155-57, 171, 173
Council of the Arts, Sciences, and Profes-
    sions, 139
Counter-Attack (film), 188
Counterattack (publication), 193, 197, 202,
    206
Crabbe, Buster, 90
Crawford, Cheryl, 39
Cromwell, John, 82
Crosby, John, 242
Cross and the Arrow, The (novel), 97
Crossfire (film), 102, 103
Crucible, The (drama), 221, 226, 235, 249,
    264
Cunningham, Sarah, 197
Cyrano de Bergerac (drama), 147
Czar Theodor (drama), 192

Daggett, Charles, 158

Daily Worker (newspaper), 44, 55, 85, 121,
    123, 148, 151, 152-53, 161, 174, 189,
    192, 193
Darkness at Noon (drama), 164
Da Silva, Howard, 121-23, 143, 150, 171,
    172, 241
Dassin, Jules, 145, 152
Davis, Benjamin, 148, 149
Dawe, Robert Shaen. See Shayne, Robert
Dawson, Leo, 53
Democrats, liberal, 31, 67, 68, 87, 268. See
    also New Deal
Depression, 37, 38, 39, 43, 44, 46, 118
Destination Tokyo (film), 97
Diamond, Muni, 66
Diary of Anne Frank, The (drama), 231
Dickstein, Samuel, 32, 33, 34, 35, 36, 110
Dies, Martin, 48ff., 110, 233, 242, 268
Dimsdale, Howard, 241
Disney, Walter E. "Walt," 76, 82, 84
Dmytryk, Herbert, 97, 102-3, 107, 136,
    140-45
Donath, Hannah Schwartz, 158
Donath, Ludwig, 158
Doyle, Clyde, 120, 125, 126-28, 132-33,
    137, 181, 190
Dream of a Blacklisted Actor (drama), 154,
    264
Dubin, Charles S., 230
D'Usseau, Arnaud, 190
D'Usseau, Susan, 199

Eastland, James O., 219
Edwards, Paul, 70
Eighth Amendment, 200
Eisenhower, Dwight D., 76, 100-1, 211, 270
Eisler, Hans, 106, 107
Emperor Jones, The (drama), 217
Endore, Guy, 77
Epstein, Julius, 77
Epstein, Philip, 77
Erickson, Leif, 66
Erwin, Roy, 180
Esslin, Martin, 105
Ettinger, Eve, 157

Facsimile (ballet), 183
Fair Deal, 31
Fancy Free (ballet), 183
Faragoh, Elizabeth, 145
Faragoh, Francis, 135-36, 145
Farmer, Francis, 65
Farmer, Mary Virginia, 159, 241
Fascism, 84, 86, 87, 118, 183, 249
Fast, Howard, 107, 231
Faulk, John Henry, 207
Faulkner, William, 172
Federal Arts Project, 65
Federal Bureau of Investigation, 207, 262
Federal Theatre, 39-40, 45, 48 ff., 197, 250,
    264, 268, 272
Federal Writers' Project, 37
Fellow-travelers, 79, 134, 194
Ferrer, Jose, 147-50, 172, 218
Fields, Jack, 241
Fifth Amendment, 120, 121, 124, 126, 127,
    128, 129, 136, 137, 138, 139, 140, 147,
    153, 156, 162-63, 180, 185, 188, 197,
    199, 200, 204, 206, 218, 219, 227, 229,
    231, 232-33, 245, 246, 248, 250, 253,
    256, 257, 260, 263, 268, 269

"Fifth Amendment Communist," 262
Finian's Rainbow (musical), 188
First Amendment, 110, 120, 125, 136, 153, 156, 184, 197, 200, 229, 231, 268. *See also* Committee for the First Amendment
Fish, Hamilton, 33, 34, 36
Flanagan, Hallie, 39, 48 ff., 271
Fleury, Bernyce Polifka, 158
Fleury, Eugene, 157, 158
Focus, 221
Fonda, Henry, 66
Ford, Henry, 90
Ford, John, 65
Foreman, Carl, 155, 157, 241
Forster, Arnold, 204
Forster, E. M., 248
Fortas, Abe, 147
Fountainhead, The (novel), 76
Fourth Amendment, 200
Foxy (musical), 110
Frank, Henry, 52
Frank, Jack, 158
Frank, Melvin, 157
Frankel, Osmund K., 189-90
Frazier, James B., 120, 181
Friebus, Florida, 208, 241
From Here to Eternity (film), 211
Fund for the Republic, Inc., 202, 210

Garfield, John, 140, 142-43, 146-47, 159, 171, 251
Geer, William, 122, 124-25, 150, 171, 172, 229
Gerson, Simon W., 189
Gersten, Bernard, 229
Gibney, Sheridan, 77
Gilford, Jack, 200, 206
Gilmore, Frank, 66
Gilmore, Margalo, 208
Glenn, Charles, 134, 151
Going My Way (film), 76, 83
Golden Boy (drama), 140-41
Goodman, Walter, 108, 135, 157, 210
Gordon, Donald, 159, 171
Gordon, Michael, 152, 155, 172, 241
Gorney, Jay, 190
Gough, Lloyd, 132, 140, 143, 241
Graff, Fred, 129
Grant, Cary, 38
Grant, Lee, 227-28
Green, Paul, 39
Green Pastures (TV), 230
Group Theatre, The, 39, 40, 44, 45, 139, 160, 251, 255
Guggenheim Foundation, 61
Guys and Dolls (musical), 167

Hagen, Uta, 209, 210
Hairy Ape (drama), 217
Hall, George, 199-200, 201
Hammer, Alvin, 140
Hammett, Dashiell, 64
Hangmen Also Die (film), 105
Harrington, Michael, 203
Hartnett, Vincent W., 205, 207
Harvard University, 62
Hayden, Sterling, 131-33, 140, 143
Hayden, Tom, 34
Hays, Lee, 199
Hearst press, 35, 57

Hellman, Lillian, 161, 162-64, 171, 172, 174, 226, 235, 271
Herbert, Hugh, 66
HICCASP. *See* Hollywood Independent Citizens' Committee
Hidden Heritage, The (film), 110
High Button Shoes (musical), 183
High Wall, The (film), 81
Hilberman, David, 85
Hill, Janet, 66
Hiss, Alger, 144
Hitler, Adolf, 35, 84, 99, 195
Hobart, Rose, 241
Hole in the Head (drama), 227
Hollywood, 40, 41, 64, 72, 107, 110, 112, 129, 130, 134, 141, 154, 170, 202, 234
Hollywood Anti-Nazi League, 65
Hollywood Independent Citizens' Committee of the Arts, Sciences, and Professions, 159, 169
Hollywood press, 111
Hollywood Reporter (periodical), 106
Hollywood Ten, 92, 108, 110, 111, 113, 120, 134, 140, 144, 170-71, 173, 184, 234, 243, 244, 247, 263, 269. *See also* Unfriendly Ten
Hollywood Unions, 144-45
Hollywood Writers Mobilization, 137
Home of the Brave (film), 188
Hopkins, Harry, 70
House Committee on Un-American Activities. *See* Special House Committee on Un-American Activities
House I Live In, The (film), 97
House Internal Security Committee, 273
Houseman, John, 260
Howard, Maurice, 85
Huffman, Hazel, 50, 51, 52, 55, 59, 61, 71
Huggins, Roy, 166-67, 272
Hughes, Rupert, 92, 106
Humphrey, William Harrison, 52
Hunt, Marsha, 241
Hunter, Ian, 110
Hutchins, Robert M., 202

IATSE. *See* International Alliance of Theatrical Stage Employees
Iceman Cometh, The (drama), 121, 230
Ickes, Harold, 70
ILGWU. *See* International Ladies' Garment Workers Union
Incident at Vichy (drama), 221
Informers, 145, 152, 172, 192, 217, 225, 236, 241, 263
Injunction Granted (drama), 50
International Alliance of Theatrical Stage Employees, 92, 145-46
International Ladies' Garment Workers Union, 45
Interplay (ballet), 183
Investigation of So-Called Blacklisting in the Entertainment Industry, 203-6
It Can't Happen Here (drama), 58

Jackson, Donald L., 133, 134, 141-43, 149-50, 156, 165, 181, 182
James, Daniel Lewis, 159
James, Florence Bean, 255
James, Lilith (Mrs. Daniel L.), 159
Jane Eyre (drama), 231
Jarrico, Paul, 125-29, 130, 134, 135, 241

Jazz Singer, The (film), 40
Jefferson, Thomas, 32, 33, 87, 98
Jenner, William E., 180
Jerome, Victor Jeremy, 120-21, 129, 151
Joe Smith, American (film), 81
John Reed Club, 51
Johnson, Manning, 219
Johnson, Nunnally, 136
Johnston, Eric Allen, 105, 113
Joint Anti-Fascist Refugee Committee, 87, 139, 141
Jolson, Al, 40, 66
Jolson Story, The (film), 130
Jones, Dorothy B., 211
Jones, Earl, 230-31
Jurist, Irma, 199

Kahn, Gordon, 75, 77, 88, 93, 102, 134, 137, 143, 145
Kanter, David, 200
Kazan, Elia, 39, 78, 112, 160, 171, 172, 225, 236, 241, 250, 252, 257
Keane, George, 200
Kearney, Bernard W., 120, 122, 147-48, 181, 224
Kenny, Robert W., 93
Kerr, Garland, 52
Kilian, Victor, Jr., 129, 241
King and I, The (musical), 183
Kingsley, Sidney, 39
Kirkpatrick, Theodore C., 193
Klein, Herbert Arthur, 159
"Knee Deep in Big Muddy" (song), 202
Koch, Howard, 77, 93
Koenig, Lester, 159
Kraber, Tony, 200
Kraft, Hyman (Hy) Solomon, 165, 241
Ku Klux Klan, 32, 97, 98
Kunzig, Robert, 189-90, 196

Labor Stage, 45
Lahr, Bert, 110
Lampell, Millard, 194, 195
Landon, Alfred M., 35
Lang, David, 241
Langer, Lawrence, 261
Lardner, Ring W., Jr., 77-78, 93, 103-4, 110, 114, 134, 241
Latham, Earl, 211
Lautner, John, 229
Lavery, Emmet G., 56, 66, 78, 105, 106, 107
Lawrence, Marc, 140, 143, 155, 171, 172
Lawrence, Peter, 185, 186, 200
Lawson, John Howard, 37, 39, 41, 78, 82, 93-95, 98, 100, 106, 109, 110, 134, 145, 159, 184, 192, 241, 272
League of American Writers, 58
League of New York Theatres, 208, 269
League of Women Shoppers, 85
League of Women Voters, 85
League of Workers Theatre, 45
Lee, Madeline, 200
Lee, Will, 231
Leeds, Phil, 197
Lees, Robert, 125, 132, 242
Leibowitz, Samuel, 67
Lenin, Nikolai, 40
Lennart, Isobel, 166, 241
Levitt, Helen Slote (Mrs. Alfred), 159
Levy, Leonard W., 121
Levy, Melvin, 166, 241

Lewis, Bobby, 39
Lewitzky, Bella, 158
Lincoln, Abraham, 32, 33, 126
Listen My Children (drama), 225
Living Newspaper, 66, 250, 268
Look Homeward Angel (drama), 231
Love Affair (film), 83
Lustig, Emil, 87

Macauley, Richard, 92
MacLeish, Archibald, 55
Maddow, Ben, 180
Mainstream (periodical), 174
Maltz, Albert, 78, 93, 99-100, 101, 110, 111, 134, 145, 191, 241
Man Who Had All the Luck, The (drama), 221
Mann, Paul, 229-30
Manoff, Arnold, 145
Manoff, Mrs. Arnold, 227
Manson, Alan, 200
Mantle, Burns, 55
Marcantonio, Vito, 66
March, Fredric, 65
Margolis, Ben, 145
Marlowe, Christopher, 48, 62, 233
Marrow, Sylvia, 140
Matusow, Harvey, 241
Mayer, Louis Burt, 75, 76, 90, 93, 134
McCarey, Thomas "Leo," 77, 82-84
McCarran Act, 127
McCarthy, Joseph, 69, 118, 119, 120, 155, 180, 212, 213, 250, 252, 254, 257, 269, 270
McCormack, John, 35, 36
McDowell, John, 77, 89-90, 91-92, 94, 100
McGuinness, James K., 92
McIntyre, O. O., 88
McNamara, Francis J., 206
McNutt, Paul, 77
Menjou, Adolphe, 76, 81-82
Metro-Goldwyn-Mayer, 75, 80, 90
Midnight Cowboy (film), 125
Milestone, Lewis, 64-65, 93, 141
Miller, Arthur, 78, 112, 217, 221-27, 234, 235-36, 251, 254, 270, 271
Million-Dollar Baby (musical), 183
Milton, Paul R., 206, 207
Minter, Mary Miles, 171
Miscegenation, 69-70
Mischel, Josef, 159
Misfits, The (film), 221
Miss Liberty (musical), 183
MMO. *See* Motion Picture Machine Operators
Moffitt, John (Jack) Charles, 92, 106, 146
Monroe, Marilyn, 221, 226, 236
Montgomery, Robert, 38, 76, 84, 87, 230
Moore, Sam, 136-37, 145
MPAA. *See* Motion Picture Association of America
Morgan, Henry, 205
Morley, Karen, 78, 132, 143, 166
Moscow Art Theatre, 192
Moscow State Conservatory of Music, 218
Moss, Carleton, 136
Mostel, Sam "Zero," 202
Mother Bloor, 122
Motion Picture Alliance for the Preservation of American Ideals, 88, 128, 261

Motion Picture Artists Committee, 64
Motion Picture Association of America, 105
Motion picture industry investigation, 75 ff.
Motion Picture Machine Operators of the U.S., 92
Moulder, Morgan M., 120, 138, 165, 233
Mr. Deeds Goes to Town (film), 38
Mr. Smith Goes to Washington (film), 38
Mrs. Miniver (film), 81
Muir, Jean, 192
Mundt, Carl, 245
Murphy, George L., 76, 85-87

National Congress of American Writers, 58
National Council of the Arts, Sciences, and Professions, 142, 231
National Lawyers Guild, 221
National security, 203, 237, 262, 267
National Theatre of Great Britain, 268
National Velvet (film), 136
Negroes, 51, 52, 69, 171, 187, 194
New Deal, 31-37 *passim*, 46, 49, 50, 53, 66-70 *passim*, 98, 127. *See also* Roosevelt administration
New Frontier, 31
New Masses (publication), 51, 57, 134, 138, 160, 168, 174
New Republic (publication), 36
New Theatre League, The, 45
New York Arts Project, 70
New York City Council, 147
New York *Herald Tribune*, 56, 104
New York *Journal-American*, 92
New York *Post*, 57, 62
New York Theatre Project, 50
New York *Times*, 56, 61, 130, 133
Niblo, Fred, Jr., 92, 146
Nichols, Dudley, 134
Niesen, Gertrude, 65
Night Must Fall (film), 84
Niles, David, 69
Nixon, Richard M., 32, 77, 88, 211
Nizer, Louis, 207
None but the Lonely Heart (film), 88, 89
Normand, Mabel, 171

O'Casey, Sean, 252
Odets, Clifford, 37, 39, 41, 78, 88, 89, 160-62, 171, 172, 250, 251, 252
Offner, Mortimer, 190
O. Henry Memorial Award, 97
O'Neil, James F., 204
O'Neill, Eugene, 120-21
On the Town (musical), 183
On the Waterfront (film), 172, 211
Opening statements, 93, 95, 96, 100, 101, 102, 103, 104, 112, 121, 123, 143, 229, 232
Ornitz, Samuel, 93, 101, 110, 112, 134
Oscar winners, 123, 136, 147
O'Shea, Michael, 65
Othello (drama), 147, 217
Ottenheimer, Albert M., 200

Page, Thad, 140
Paine, Thomas, 98, 223
Papirofsky, Joseph, 233-34
Papp, Joe. *See* Joseph Papirofsky
Parks, Larry, 93, 129-31, 132, 143, 172, 254
Pasadena Playhouse, 254
Passport problems, 216 ff., 221, 257, 265, 270
People's Radio Foundation Inc., 231
People's World (newspaper), 85, 151, 152, 158
Pepper, George, 145
Perkins, Frances, 70
Permanent Sub-Committee on Investigations of the Senate Committee on Government Operations, 119. *See also* McCarthy, Joseph
Pichel, Irving, 93
Pied Piper, The (ballet), 183
Pins and Needles (musical), 45
Playwright's Company, 261
PM (publication), 85
Polan, Lou, 197
Polonsky, Abraham, 132, 134, 140
Pomerance, William, 85
Poore, A. S., 120
Popper (attorney), 139, 140
Porgy and Bess (musical), 217
Potter, Charles E., 120, 146, 155
Pound, Ezra, 222
Powell, Dick, 66
Powell, William, 38
Power (drama), 58
Power, Tyrone, 90
Pride of the Marines, The (film), 97
Prize, The (drama), 221
Proctor, James D., 231-33
Progressive Citizens of America, 139
Prokop, Jack Prokop (Jack Frank), 158
Proletbuehne Theater, 44
Pudovkin, V. I., 40
Pulitzer Prize, 221
Purcell, Gertrude, 134

Racial equality, 67
Racial tolerance, 97
Rainer, Luise, 65
Raksin, David, 158, 159
Rand, Ayn, 76, 88, 90-92, 125
Randolph, John, 197
Rankin, John, 98, 99, 110, 111
Rauk, Joseph, Jr., 221
Ray, Anne, 157
Reagan, Ronald, 76, 87-88
Red Channels, the Report of Communist Influence in Radio and Television, 193, 202, 204, 208
Reed, John. *See* John Reed Club
Reed, Robert, 65
Reivers (film), 172
Report on Blacklisting, 202
Revere, Anne, 136, 137-38, 143, 171, 172
Revolt of the Beavers, The (drama), 59, 62, 63

Revzin, Seymour, 52
Reynolds, Mrs. Newell, 158
Rice, Elmer, 38, 52, 62
Richards, Ann Roth Morgan, 159
Richards, Robert L., 159, 241
Richards, Silvia, 241
Ridder, Victor, 50
Riesel, Victor, 202, 204, 206
Right to Live, The (living newspaper), 66
RKO, 105, 107
Robbins, Jerome, 181, 182-84, 206
Roberts, Marguerite, 159
Roberts, Stanley, 166
Robeson, Paul, 141, 204, 217-21, 234, 235,
   270, 272
Robinson, Edward G., 165-65
Rockefeller, John D., 90
Rogers, Lela, 76, 88-90, 106
Roosevelt, Franklin D., 32, 33, 35, 78
Roosevelt, Theodore, 33
Roosevelt administration, 50, 111. *See also*
   New Deal
Rosenberg, Meta Reis, 135-36, 140
Rosenthal, Lyova, 227
Rossen, Robert, 78, 93, 134, 143, 153-54,
   171, 181, 188, 257
Rosten, Norman, 225
Rothschild, House of, 90
Rousseau, Louise, 159
Rovere, Richard, 69
Rudd, Mark, 34
Ruggles of Red Gap (film), 83
Rushmore, Howard, 92
Russell, Louis J., 92, 100, 101, 102, 120
Russian theater, 43, 51, 61, 71. *See also*
   Moscow Art Theatre
Ruthven, Madelaine, 136
Ryskind, Morrie, 92, 106

Sabinson, Lee, 188-90, 206-7
Salemson, Harold J., 200
Salt, Walter, 93, 125, 134, 196
Sand Hog, The (musical), 196
Sanford, John, 159
Saroyan, William, 39
Sasuly, Richard, 234
Saunders, Sallie, 52, 53, 69
Schaeffer, Louis, 45
Schary, Dore, 105, 106, 107, 113
Scherer, Gordon H., 181, 197, 219, 220,
   222-23, 227, 232
Schlesinger, Arthur M., 35
Schmidt, Godfrey P., 206
Schoen, Max Howard, 159
Schoenfeld, Bernard C., 166
Schreiber, George, 66
Schulberg, Budd, 134, 150-52, 171, 172,
   173, 241
Scott, (Robert) Adrian, 93, 102-3, 107,
   110, 145, 241
Screen Actors Guild, 78, 84, 85, 87
Screen Directors Guild, 145
Screen Writers Guild, 93, 95, 96, 101, 102,
   103, 104, 134, 145, 155, 157, 159

Scripps-Howard papers, 57
Seale, Bobby, 220
Seeger, Peter "Pete," 200-1
Self-censorship, 251, 254
Semenov, Constantine, 141
Senate Internal Security Subcommittee, 203
1776 (musical), 172
Shakespeare, William, 48
Shaw, Artie, 65, 180-83, 206
Shaw, Bernard, 252
Shaw, Irwin, 78
Shayne, Robert (Robert Shaen Dawe), 157
Shelley, Joshua, 200
Sherman, Vincent, 241
Shifting Scenes, 51, 61
Ship, Reuben, 159
Shoemaker, James H., 43
Shore, Wilma, 241
Showboat (musical), 217
Silber, Irwin, 234
Sillen, Samuel, 134
Silver Whistle, The (drama), 147
Simon the Cyrenian (drama), 217
Situation Normal (novel), 221
Sloane, Allan E., 193-95, 207, 241
Sloane, Everett, 207
Smith, Gerald K., 247
Smith, H. A., 85, 86, 90, 92
Smith Act, 127, 222
Smothers, Dick, 202
Smothers Brothers Comedy Hour (TV
   show), 202
Socrates, 224-25
Sokolsky, George, 202, 203, 206
Solomon, Louis, 229, 241
Solotoy, Percy, 158
Sondergaard, Gale, 66, 123, 125, 171, 172
Song of Russia (film), 78, 91, 125
Sorrell, Herbert K., 82-83, 85
Special House Committee on Un-American
   Activities, 32, 40, 42, 76, 77, 92, 97,
   142, 186, 225, 230, 250, 252, 259, 267,
   272-73
   Annual Reports, 176, 236-37; effect of,
   242 ff.; and fear, 31, 198, 235, 251,
   254, 264, 271; and legislation, 119, 242,
   244, 247, 263, 267; and political expe-
   diency, 235; and publicity, 40, 69, 72,
   119, 207, 235, 242, 268, 270, 271, 272
Stage for Action, The, 231
Stalin, Joseph, 222
Stalin Peace Prize, 218
Stander, Lionel, 143, 181, 185-88, 222
Stanislavski, Konstantin, 39, 192
Stark, Wallace, 53
Starnes, Joseph, 48, 56, 57, 58, 61, 62, 68
State Un-American Activities Committees,
   264
Steel (drama), 153
Stern, Nancy, 66
Stevenson, Philip Edward, 159
Stewart, Donald Ogden, 81
Stool-pigeon activity, 131, 133, 184
Strange Fruit (drama), 230